MODERNISM AT THE BEACH

MODERNIST LATITUDES

MODERNIST LATITUDES

Jessica Berman and Paul Saint-Amour, Editors

Modernist Latitudes aims to capture the energy and ferment of modernist studies by continuing to open up the range of forms, locations, temporalities, and theoretical approaches encompassed by the field. The series celebrates the growing latitude ("scope for freedom of action or thought") that this broadening affords scholars of modernism, whether they are investigating little-known works or revisiting canonical ones. Modernist Latitudes will pay particular attention to the texts and contexts of those latitudes (Africa, Latin America, Australia, Asia, Southern Europe, and even the rural United States) that have long been misrecognized as ancillary to the canonical modernisms of the global North.

Barry McCrea, *In the Company of Strangers: Family and Narrative in Dickens, Conan Doyle, Joyce, and Proust*, 2011

Jessica Berman, *Modernist Commitments: Ethics, Politics, and Transnational Modernism*, 2011

Jennifer Scappettone, *Killing the Moonlight: Modernism in Venice*, 2014

Nico Israel, *Spirals: The Whirled Image in Twentieth-Century Literature and Art*, 2015

Carrie Noland, *Voices of Negritude in Modernist Print: Aesthetic Subjectivity, Diaspora, and the Lyric Regime*, 2015

Susan Stanford Friedman, *Planetary Modernisms: Provocations on Modernity Across Time*, 2015

Steven S. Lee, *The Ethnic Avant-Garde: Minority Cultures and World Revolution*, 2015

Thomas S. Davis, *The Extinct Scene: Late Modernism and Everyday Life*, 2016

Carrie J. Preston, *Learning to Kneel: Noh, Modernism, and Journeys in Teaching*, 2016

Gayle Rogers, *Incomparable Empires: Modernism and the Translation of Spanish and American Literature*, 2016

Donal Harris, *On Company Time: American Modernism in the Big Magazines*, 2016

Celia Marshik, *At the Mercy of Their Clothes: Modernism, the Middlebrow, and British Garment Culture*, 2016

Christopher Reed, *Bachelor Japanists: Japanese Aesthetics and Western Masculinities*, 2016

Eric Hayot and Rebecca L. Walkowitz, eds., *A New Vocabulary for Global Modernism*, 2016

Eric Bulson, *Little Magazine, World Form*, 2016

Aarthi Vadde, *Chimeras of Form: Modernist Internationalism Beyond Europe, 1914–2014*, 2016

Ben Conisbee Baer, *Indigenous Vanguards: Education, National Liberation, and the Limits of Modernism*, 2019

Claire Seiler, *Midcentury Suspension: Literature and Feeling in the Wake of World War II*, 2020

Jill Richards, *The Fury Archives: Female Citizenship, Human Rights, and the International Avant-Gardes*, 2020

Daniel Ryan Morse, *Radio Empire: The BBC's Eastern Service and the Emergence of the Global Anglophone Novel*

Modernism at the Beach

QUEER ECOLOGIES AND THE COASTAL COMMONS

Hannah Freed-Thall

Columbia University Press
New York

Columbia University Press
Publishers Since 1893
New York   Chichester, West Sussex
cup.columbia.edu
Copyright © 2023 Columbia University Press
All rights reserved

Library of Congress Cataloging-in-Publication Data
Names: Freed-Thall, Hannah, author.
Title: Modernism at the beach : queer ecologies and the coastal commons / Hannah Freed-Thall.
Description: New York : Columbia University Press, [2023] | Series: Modernist latitudes | Includes bibliographical references and index.
Identifiers: LCCN 2022023852 (print) | LCCN 2022023853 (ebook) | ISBN 9780231197083 (hardback) | ISBN 9780231197090 (trade paperback) | ISBN 9780231551977 (ebook)
Subjects: LCSH: Beaches in literature. | Seashore in literature. | Literature, Modern—20th century—History and criticism. | Modernism (Literature) | Queer theory. | Ecocriticism. | LCGFT: Literary criticism.
Classification: LCC PN56.B34 F74 2023 (print) | LCC PN56.B34 (ebook) | DDC 809/.9336—dc23/eng/20220914
LC record available at https://lccn.loc.gov/2022023852
LC ebook record available at https://lccn.loc.gov/2022023853

Cover design: Julia Kushnirsky
Cover image: Beach drag, anonymous. New York LGBT Community Center, Richard Peckinpaugh Beach Photographs, circa late 1940s.

CONTENTS

ACKNOWLEDGMENTS   vii

Introduction: The Beach Effect   1
    Constructing the Beach   7
    Off-season   16
    Littoral Choreographies   24
    Coastal Map   28

Chapter One: Proust's Leap   33
    "Gambling Fever"   35
    Beach Bodies   47
    "Nous avons regardé"   57

Chapter Two: Intertidal Woolf   65
    Waste Land   68
    Imagined Geographies   72
    Domestic Arrangements   75
    Tidal Visions   83
    "Mrs. Ramsay on the Beach"   95

CONTENTS

Chapter Three: Carson's Quiet Bower   98
    Thinking Small   99
    Postal Meter   104
    "Wee Beasts"   111

Chapter Four: McKay's Dream Port   122
    Port Effects   126
    Vagabond Picturesque   129
    Pier Effects   137

Chapter Five: Tidewrack, Beckett to Sunde   148
    Drift   149
    Fatigue   158
    "Female Solo"   163
    Waiting Room   172

NOTES   179

WORKS CITED   241

INDEX   265

ACKNOWLEDGMENTS

Life got weird during the writing of this book, and I became more grateful than ever for the support of kind and brilliant colleagues and friends.

I especially wish to thank series editors Jessica Berman and Paul Saint-Amour for their invaluable comments on the manuscript. The book was also considerably strengthened by the wise suggestions of four anonymous reviewers. And it's been a pleasure to work with editor Philip Leventhal at Columbia University Press: many thanks to him, Monique Briones, and production editor Susan Pensak for their expert guidance throughout the process.

Modernism at the Beach has been shaped by the intense and invigorating experience of living in New York City and working at NYU. For their support and encouragement, I am grateful to my excellent colleagues in the department of French Literature, Thought, and Culture. I also gained a great deal from conversations with audiences at Yale, Cornell, Duke, Columbia, Cambridge, the University of Pennsylvania, the University of Chicago, Université Sorbonne Nouvelle, Johns Hopkins, and Northwestern. So many suggestions, gleaned here and there, have made their way into the book. I'm indebted, too, to the skilled librarians who helped me navigate collections at Yale, Bates College, and New York's LGBT Center. Thanks especially to Smith College archivist and Woolf scholar Karen Kukil, who took me seriously long before I knew what I was doing. I loved writing about living artists, and am grateful to all who allowed me to reproduce their work, especially Sarah Cameron Sunde, whose beautiful *36.5/A Durational Performance with the Sea* enabled me to better conceptualize the ecological import of this book, and Shelley Seccombe, who kindly took me for a walk on the Hudson's Little Island. The highpoint of my research was getting to visit Rachel Carson's Southport cottage, where Wendy Sisson and Roger Christie graciously showed me around and patiently answered my questions.

Modernism at the Beach was supported by the Princeton Barr-Ferree Fund and an NYU Humanities Center book subvention grant. Portions of the introduction and of chapters 1 and 4 were published in the journals *Comparative Literature, Bulletin Marcel Proust,* and *Paragraph,* and parts of chapter 3 appeared in the volume *Modernism and Close Reading,* edited by David James. I wish to express my thanks to the editors of these publications for helping me to tighten my arguments and for permission to reprint.

My gratitude toward my graduate advisers has only grown with the years. Michael Lucey shaped my approach to Proust and my sense of the nonobvious pathways queer studies might take. Barbara Spackman made the fin de siècle thrillingly strange. I'll never be able to sufficiently thank Ann Smock, who helped me find my voice as a writer and whose generosity as a teacher and mentor continues to astonish me. And it's been wonderful to learn from Anne-Lise François, from whom I first heard the phrase "queer ecology" and whose reflections on literature and environmentality have lit the way for me and so many others.

My favorite aspect of academic life is the collaboration it makes possible: it's been a delight to think alongside friends who happen to be exceptionally talented scholars. Above all, from the first messy drafts through the final manuscript, this book has benefited from Sarah Ann Wells's sharp and generous critical mind. I'm so grateful for her editorial acumen and her friendship. I also extend my warmest thanks to Ellen Lockhart—my erstwhile gym buddy and Mozart duet partner—for the colloquium invitation that launched this project and for first drawing my attention to the Ballets Russes's *Le Train bleu*. I've been happy to get to work with Dora Zhang, Zakir Paul, and François Proulx, and thank them for their clear-eyed commentaries on chapters 1 and 2. I also owe a debt of gratitude to Louise Hornby for her illuminating critique of my Woolf chapter; to Marci

ACKNOWLEDGMENTS

Kwon for an encouraging conversation about the illustrations in Carson's *The Edge of the Sea*; to Michelle Clayton for a enlightening conversation about leaping; to Harris Feinsod for a helpful exchange about being "on the beach"; and to On Barak for an inspiring correspondence about beaches, energy, and heat. During the time I've been writing this book, I was fortunate to meet Annabel Kim and Morgane Cadieu, brilliant colleagues in the world of twentieth-century French literature; thanks especially to Morgane for helping me better understand the beach/port nexus and the importance of the railway to beach history. I'm lucky to know Ada Smailbegović, whose startlingly original patterns of thought first captured my imagination as we strolled through Providence's Hope Cemetery years ago, and Michael Allan, whose incisive comments on my "Beaches and Ports" article immensely improved it (and this book). And I'm grateful to Thangam Ravindranathan, dear friend and fellow traveler in French ecological thought: it was she who first mused, some years ago, that I seemed to be writing a book about the beach.

To my great surprise, I wound up composing most of these pages in my mother's sewing room. The internet may have been subpar, but the childcare was top-notch. It's not an exaggeration to say that *Modernism at the Beach* would not exist without the love and support of my amazing parents, Michael and Patricia, whose improvised preschool, "The Running Crocodile Academy," enabled me to devote 2020–2021 to writing. I also owe special thanks to the Pandemicats for donuts, cheese, and two years of workout motivation, to April for shoptalk phone dates, to Stephie for cousinly commiseration, and to Jess, Claire, Lem, and Maura for care packages and decades of friendship. My in-laws, Julie and Bob, cheered me from afar with gifts of luxury pillows and cupcakes. Aaron, Jeanette, and Mogli made Vermont the best place to hide out during a pandemic sabbatical. My emotional support puppy, Rexi, mostly caused trouble, but we adore her all the same. Finally, I am grateful beyond measure for Jillian—whose keen mind and all-around good vibe elevated this book (and all other aspects of life)—and for Leo, whose bounding appearance each afternoon ("Mama time!") fringed my working days with joy.

MODERNISM AT THE BEACH

INTRODUCTION

The Beach Effect

What is the modernist beach? A windswept, weather-beaten strip between city and sea, a stage for experimental sociabilities, a protean edge shaped by more-than-human forces. The beach is also, without question, carbon capitalism's most privileged site of leisure. In an age when nature is exploited in countless ways, the seashore has been cast as an Edenic zone of exception. Indeed, beaches have been so thoroughly marketed that it can be difficult today to see beyond the glossy stock photos and resort brochures. Yet for many authors and artists—and for the travelers, loafers, and dreamers they depict—the beach remains a strange and unsettled geography. In twentieth-century literature, especially, the shore appears as a transitional space, a terraqueous ribbon suspended between the militarized roadways of the sea, the verticality and velocity of the metropolis, and the heteronormative architecture of the home. At the beach, old habits give way to outlandish visions. Gustave von Aschenbach becomes disoriented by homoerotic hallucination on the Venetian Lido, as does, in a more euphoric mode, the shape-shifting "I" of Claude Cahun's coastally anchored prose poems. Stephen Dedalus limns the "ineluctable modality of the visible" on Sandymount Strand; Jay Gatsby sheds James Gatz on the shores of Lake Superior; Clarissa Dalloway gets lost, standing on a London curb, in memories of a morning like the "kiss of a wave"; Proust's narrator learns to see anew on the beach in Normandy, guided by a painter and a queer little band of girls; Claude McKay's vagabonding artists claim a patch of shared quiet in the margins of the industrial waterfront; Sartre's Roquentin succumbs to existential nausea while holding a damp pebble by the sea; and in Severo Sarduy's beach-set radio play, language itself undergoes a process of decomposition, and the entire coastal world seems to come undone.[1]

Taking shape at the interstice of industry and pleasure, forged by the tension between human and elemental dynamics, the beach is a vexed and contradictory setting. Commoditized, artificially engineered, heaped with debris, and eroded by rising seas, it increasingly emblematizes the ecological violence of our times. Yet the coastal edge has also flashed up throughout the last century as a figure for the promise of radical egalitarianism: one of the rallying cries during the student and worker strikes of May 1968 in France was "sous les pavés, la plage!" (beneath the paving stones, the beach!). This utopian call to arms registers a longer history of the littoral as a space of alterity and resistance: an arena for queer and creaturely encounters, a refuge for artists and other visionary types, a terrain of unremitting impermanence, and a precarious commons in which to dream up other possible futures.

In the most basic, geological sense, a beach is nothing more than sediments accumulated on a coast—available to be moved and sorted by the uprush and backwash of the waves. The littoral is intrinsically unstable because it is a marine/terrestrial interface, or ecotone—a space of transition between biomes, replete with tough and delicate life forms.[2] To cite environmentalist and marine biologist Rachel Carson, the seashore is an ecological site of extreme mutability—the most "fleeting and transitory feature of the earth."[3] Culturally speaking, however, the seashore is a fantasy. "Find your beach," the beer ad exhorts us, and the odd notion that each of us has a private shore somewhere indicates the toxic allure of "nature" as exotic diversion or as a mere exteriorization of the inner self. I aim to trouble the imperialism implicit in this familiar construction of the leisure beach. Yet this book does not eschew the pleasures of the seaside. On the contrary, it explores improvisatory riffs and variations on the modernist beach, understood in the terms that ocean studies scholar Melody Jue reserves for the sea: as an "environment for thought" and a "wild milieu for testing our most habitual concepts and categories."[4]

INTRODUCTION

Modernism has long been allied with the anonymity, speed, and crisscrossing narrative pathways of the city. What new vistas emerge when we turn our critical gaze, instead, toward the wayward intensities of the coastal zone? I propose that the beach is to modernism what mountains were to a certain strain of European Romanticism: a space not merely of anthropogenic conquest but of vital connection to the more-than-human world; a grounds on which to experiment with performances of embodiment and to devise a new grammar of sensation. Simon Bainbridge has recently explored the literary cultures of mountaineering, arguing that key Romantic-period concepts, such as transcendence, revelation, and an embodied love of movement are linked to the phenomenon of climbing.[5] My contention is that littoral practices, including tide-pooling, beachcombing, diving, and sunbathing, are similarly connected to modernist writing and aesthetic production. Both beaches and mountains offer the possibility of a vertiginous break with conventional forms of movement, perception, and sociability. But while mountains—especially in the early years of mountaineering—involve death-defying ascents and vision as the privilege of a few, the leisure beach invites a style of porous repose and fervid unthinkingness that is at once more feminized and, eventually—though tenuously—more democratized.

A beach is what anthropologist Anna Tsing calls a "weedy landscape"—a space of human ecological disturbance as well as a multispecies "gathering in the making."[6] As cultural and geological contact zones, beaches comprise a weave of materialities, including literature and visual media. Like a "plantation zone," a "flood year," or a smoggy sky, the tidelands can only be approached as a representational and geophysical overlap, a terraformed amalgamation of industrial, biological, and textual rhythms.[7] In their polyvalency, they invite a rethinking of the problem of setting, which I understand as an "enabling force" rather than a stable ground or frame.[8] In modernism, spatiotemporal environs, liberated from the obligation to reflect or frame character, take on a life of their own. Modernist setting is not a container for a person or a mere backdrop for action, but a site of encounter, a mesh of contingencies, and an atmospheric effect. Because it is such a provisional and shifting landscape—conjoining infrastructure, aesthetics, and ecology—and because it requires us to think across a variety of scales, the coastal zone epitomizes the strangeness and complexity of setting in the modernist era.

In and beyond literary representation, the question of how to apprehend the biotechnical networks, lifeworlds, and collective moods that shape and sustain us has become an urgent one. The unfurling consequences of modernity's extractivist, expansionist disruptions of earth systems make it impossible to continue to imagine "nature" as an inert decor for human action or even as an objectifiable adversary.[9] *Modernism at the Beach* therefore experiments with object and scale, moving among divergent methodological vantage points, including queer studies, ecocriticism, critical geography, aesthetic theory, and environmental history. The book explores canonical works of coastal modernism—Marcel Proust's *Within a Budding Grove* (*À l'ombre des jeunes filles en fleurs*, 1919), Virginia Woolf's *To the Lighthouse* (1927), and Claude McKay's *Banjo: A Story Without a Plot* (1929) loom large here. But I also investigate a variety of other genres and media, including seaside guidebooks, theater and performance, painting, photography, sculpture, and film. My wager is that the shoreline might be understood not just as a launching pad or limit point but as a confluence of bodies, sand, and cargo boxes, and as a matrix of literary and visual form.

One of the particularities of this book, therefore, is the variegated and shifting quality of its central concept. The beach is not one thing here. Like a figure in a dream, it transforms throughout the book, appearing from one chapter to the next as a kinesthetic springboard, a tidal pool, a Keatsean bower, a cruising grounds, an artificial hellscape, or a wasteland speckled with sea trash. Such metamorphicity is inherent in the beach, both conceptually and materially. Although I am largely concerned with the leisurification of the littoral, I also use the word *beach* to reference a less anthropocentric angle on the shore—as an ecological border zone between land and sea, a transitional environment marked by multispecies liveliness and patterned by a fierce pull between erosion and accretion. "If we pay attention," observes environmental historian Bathsheba Demuth, "the world is not what we make of it; rather, it is part of what makes us."[10] In accord with this view, I interweave a perspective that privileges human histories and social structures with one that decenters the human. The modernist beach takes form at the convergence of these realities.

Queer ecology offers a compelling critical vantage point from which to theorize this force field, in all its artifice and intractability. Guided by the writing of Roland Barthes and Eve Kosofsky Sedgwick—scholars attuned, especially in their late work, to small, offbeat textures and details and to nonheroic valances of thought—I understand queer ecology as a capacious bundling of theoretical orientations and critical moods. A once-minor strain within literary criticism and environmental discourse, increasingly synonymous with ecological thought as such, queer ecology resists the normative constructions of nature that Barthes would call "arrogant."[11] Instead, it offers a set of resources for the development of a nonessentialist, nonhomophobic relation to living beings and the spaces that hold them.[12] Sensitive to the passing and the peripheral, to shades and gradations of difference, this critical mode dovetails with close reading—not as a strict methodology but in an expanded sense: as a practice of slow, patient attentiveness to the look and feel of things and to their subtle interplay of forms. Because it emerged in the midst of the global HIV/AIDS crisis, queer studies has been particularly mindful of finitude, and, as a consequence of historical banishment from the state-sanctioned institution of the family, queers have been adept at imagining (and creating) other forms of kinship. As a style of interpretation and of affiliation, queer ecology thus indicates a loosely scripted way of traversing time and space and a capacity for living on the edge, in proximity to loss and nonbeing.

Writing about the seashore has led me to reflect in particular on two problems that I view as central to queer ecological thought: the nonmonumentalizing ethos of *transience* and the egalitarian concept of the *commons*. I'm concerned, first, with how artists engage the beach setting in order to elucidate shared conditions of vulnerability within a world of constant permutation. And, second, I'm drawn to the shoreline because it cannot be entirely owned or enclosed and thus holds out the prospect, however elusive and precarious, of devising forms of togetherness not so predicated on possession.

According to the laws of many nations, the water's edge cannot be privatized. Even when the beach itself is privately owned—as is increasingly the case in the U.S.—the intertidal zone, or at least part of it, is set aside as a public trust.[13] The idea of nature as a commons has been theorized by economists and ecologists as a matter of tragically overused and exploited resources. The premise underlying this view is that human actors will always necessarily view nature as "cheap"—which is to say, as an inert exterior reserve, the object of a selfish free-for-all scramble to stake one's claim.[14] It was with this assumption of infinite greed confronting finite resources that ecologist Garrett Hardin declared in 1968 that "freedom in a commons brings ruin to all."[15] Scholars have noted that Hardin's example—a nineteenth-century overgrazed pasture—obscures the long and rich history of indigenous and precapitalist commons.[16] Yet even if we take the temporal and affective framework of capitalist modernity as a point of departure, it is possible to conceptualize the commons differently than Hardin does—as encompassing, in an extended sense, a range of social margins or fringes in which mixing, recalibration, and queer interclass and transspecies contact might take place. As an inventive ecosocial gathering that blurs partitions and hierarchies, the beach presents one particular materialization of the late-capitalist commons.

It is true, however, that beaches have also functioned throughout the twentieth century as spectacles of exclusion, disciplinary sites in which bodies are managed and put in their place. Spaces set aside for public leisure have often been scenes of violent social domination. In this regard, the beach conjures a promise that it simultaneously retracts. As Colson Whitehead's protagonist observes in his 2009 beach-set novel *Sag Harbor*, "the Public Beach ... was open to all in Sag Harbor, i.e., the white people."[17] Ecocritic Rob Nixon describes playing as a child on the apartheid-era South African littoral as an experience that shaped his capacity, as a reader of landscapes and texts, to look for the absent elements, the figures who have been "driven off the beach."[18] "A geographical imperative lies at the heart of every struggle for social justice," contends critical geographer Ruth Wilson Gilmore, and this holds for the beach, too: the water's edge is a space not just of collective rejuvenation but of contested liberty.[19]

Without losing sight of this fact, I remain attached to the commons as a horizon of possibility, and to the aesthetic and political potential of commoning—minoritarian, nonproprietary practices of being together in the margins of the Anthropocene. As various thinkers have pointed out, the commons is less a delimited space than a relational mode.[20] Throughout this study, I ask how the styles of movement and perception that arose around the modernist seashore reflect the most visionary side of the aesthetic itself: its capacity to open a space of play that is not cordoned off to the few. This is not to deny the violent history of the leisure beach, but to look for ways in which this landscape sometimes offers what Nixon calls a "commonage restored."[21] Beaches are commons in the same way that artworks are—it's a largely unrealized promise, but one worth taking seriously all the same.

CONSTRUCTING THE BEACH

Literary critical engagements with the seaside are still relatively rare, but cultural histories of the beach abound.[22] The topic has had particular traction in France, a coastal nation that claims to have designed the bikini, and where paid vacations were a hard-fought political right.[23] Alain Corbin's *The Lure of the Sea*, for instance, offers an influential account of the "invention" of the beach in England and France. Corbin notes that in Europe, until a few centuries ago, the ocean was represented as a place of rot and decay, and the beach, as the scene of shipwreck and disaster, suitable for sailors, fishermen, and castaways, not for idle pleasure-seekers. By the eighteenth century, however, medical authorities had begun extolling the therapeutic benefits of sea bathing as a cure for melancholy and urban degeneration. In the second half of the century, "cure-takers" set off for the seashore in search of an escape from the perceived ills of city life.[24] Soon, as expanding train lines created an ever more mobile populace, the beach became a miniature civilization, a makeshift, constructed, and reconstructed encampment, increasingly commodified as an object of touristic desire. By the mid-nineteenth century, Flaubert's landlocked heroine, Emma Bovary, could declare her love of sunsets on the beach, having likely never seen one.[25]

As Jean-Didier Urbain and others have observed, this "aesthetic conquest" of the shore effectively displaced workers and native populations, as the beach increasingly became a landscape to consume.[26] The inherent transience of the seashore makes true conquest difficult, however. Northern French marine painter Eugène Louis Boudin captures the temporariness and fragility of bourgeois beach encampments in his varied depictions of the Trouville seaside. In his 1875 painting of this beach, for instance, the entire pictorial space, including its mass of stylishly dressed subjects, seems to be disintegrating into the elements.

With all of its decor, the late nineteenth-century beach became a fashion show of sorts: a variety of veils, hats, umbrellas, parasols, striped suits,

FIGURE 0.1. Eugène Boudin, *Beach at Trouville*, 1875. Courtauld Institute of Art, London.

and long ruffled gowns feature in impressionist beach paintings. Yet the beach is also a flattening, depersonalizing space, where the intensities of air, sand, and sea always threaten to reduce complex social hierarchies to a conglomeration of windswept, sensate bodies.[27] At the beach, one is at once exposed and absented. Landrin's 1873 tourist guide to French beaches, *Les Plages de France*, opens with the admission that the beach makes mental concentration impossible: "one spends hours looking at the sea without thinking about anything; its sight alone intoxicates."[28] In his 1874 fashion magazine, *La Dernière Mode*, Stéphane Mallarmé imagines his ideal "reader" as a beachgoer, a dreamer who leafs through pages, not reading at all but simply resting her eyes "in the oblivion of a vast and naked horizon."[29] As Mallarmé reminds us, even when the beach offers the spectacle of nature tamed and furnished, it resists the planned and the orderly; it is difficult to keep time at the seashore.

As a space in which industrial time is suspended and productivity set aside, the beach appealed especially to novelist Marcel Proust. *In Search of Lost Time* (*À la recherche du temps perdu*, 1913–1927) presents the seashore resort of Balbec as an improvisatory performance space—the alternative par excellence to both the aristocratic salons of Paris and the closed family nucleus of the village, Combray. Yet in Proust's earlier, unfinished novel, *Jean Santeuil* (1895–1899), the beach is not yet a stage for seeing and being seen; rather, it is an enormous bed, a queer site of intoxicating "animal life" in which one might lie beside a companion for an "indefinite" interval, book in hand but not yet reading. As Jean and Henri toss and turn among the dunes, the hero's mind is at last "empty." Jean becomes all body, simply "digesting" and gazing at sea and sky in delirious proximity to this "reservoir of all forces."[30] In *Jean Santeuil*, the seaside is a space of elemental intensity where, to cite ecocritic Ada Smailbegović, "human scale is pressed against the immensity of the sea."[31]

Linking the feeling of exposure and vitality incited by the conjunction of sea winds, sun, salt breezes, sand, and distant horizon to the general feeling of aliveness that nineteenth-century medical science termed "coenesthesis," Corbin notes that the effects of such undifferentiated sensory intensity became an obsession for a leisured class increasingly preoccupied with practices of self-observation.[32] As Boudin, Mallarmé, and Proust intimate, however, turn-of-the-century seaside repose could be disorienting, opening onto impersonal and even transspecies structures of feeling. *Modernism at the Beach* identifies a number of such coenesthetic variations, some of which blur strictures of gender and class and engage various vegetal and creaturely lifeworlds. This is the case with Proust's "zoophytic" gang of girls, Carson's ghost crabs and jellies, and Woolf's magical flounder and expanding-contracting tidal pool. Yet I also examine scenes of overexposure and collective sunstroke—more sinister remnants of coenesthetic sensory freedom. As Beckett's Winnie muses while tossing away her scorched umbrella in the scandalous beach play *Happy Days* (1961, *Oh les beaux jours*, 1963), "Shall I myself not melt perhaps in the end, or burn."[33]

Because Corbin's narrative ends in the mid-nineteenth century, before the advent of the modern tourist industry, he does not reckon with the twentieth-century transformation of the beach into real estate—a mere profitable extension of the land, another valuable (though profoundly unstable) site to be developed. Never before, observes historian John Gillis, have shores been "so rich in property values" and yet so "impoverished" as biodiverse points of contact. "Coastal" has become a mere index of a desirable lifestyle, detached from any geographical specificity.[34] In his 1884 decadent novel *Against Nature* (*À Rebours*), J. K. Huysmans already envisions this strange state of affairs. Ironizing the coastal engineering of the future, he invites readers to imagine reproducing the beach experience by means of a few well-chosen props, including saltwater, the smell of twine, a casino photograph, and a touristic guidebook.[35] Today, Huysmans's recipe has spread across the globe: beaches—or simulacra of beaches—are everywhere. Take Paris Plages, the temporary artificial beach that appears on the Georges Pompidou expressway, along the banks of the Seine, in Paris each July. Created in 2002 by a team of sociologists and theatrical set designers, Paris Plages is furnished with sand, palms, cabanas, umbrellas, deck chairs, hammocks, bocce courts, and refreshment stands—everything but the sea. As scholars have noted, to participate in Paris Plages is not to go to the beach, but to *pretend* to go to the beach, collectively, in the center of Paris.[36] Urban beaches on the model of Paris Plages have popped up around the globe, from Budapest to Tokyo. One is currently being constructed on Manhattan's Hudson River, on the very site where radical artists and queers carved out space for their renegade visions half a century ago.

In fact, such feats of dramaturgical engineering should remind us of the constructedness of even those beaches we imagine to be natural. Since 1922, when Coney Island's boardwalk was built and its beach expanded by

FIGURE 0.2. Coney Island's beach being pumped in from the sea bed. Edgar E. Rutter Photograph Collection, 1922, RUTT_0251, Brooklyn Public Library, Center for Brooklyn History.

INTRODUCTION

pumping in sand from the sea, leisure beaches have been maintained in the face of erosion and coastal flooding thanks to labor-intensive "beach nourishment" projects whereby silver sand is dredged up and transported—from underwater or from inland quarries—to the detriment of coastal ecosystems.[37] In the U.S. alone, over the past century more than 1.2 billion cubic meters of sand have been used as fill to fortify a vanishing coastline.[38]

The ubiquity of beach nourishment demonstrates a desperation to temporarily stabilize an intrinsically protean environment. Beaches are the very materialization of transience, and the effects of climate change exacerbate their instability. To hold them in place requires a manic feat of near-continuous digging and filling, an act that itself further destabilizes the beach and necessitates future replenishment. The leisure beach is thus an apt emblem of Anthropocene-era nature. Like the cruise ship and the redeveloped urban harbor, it would seem to be entirely cut off from coastal ecology and geological processes—just another "festival space" to consume.[39]

Yet there's no escaping the basic mutability of this landscape. Indeed, the early history of beach nourishment is a story of frustration. When New York City developer and parks commissioner Robert Moses built Jones Beach in the 1920s, for instance, his team pumped in forty million cubic yards of dredged-up fill—fine silver sand from the bottom of the bay that turned out to be remarkably volatile when spread across the barrier beach: "Even the lightest breeze stirred it into the air in swirls so thick that the strand looked like a desert during a violent sandstorm.... During the day, workmen would dig an excavation. At night, the sand would fill it in—so completely that the workmen couldn't even find its edges." Ultimately landscape architects had to plant beach grass by hand—a laborious process—in order to hold the dunes in place.[40] A similar problem dogged the engineers of Coney Island's renourished beach. Struggling with the unpredictability of littoral drift, "the contractor had great difficulty getting the sand to flow freely beyond the low water mark and the resulting beach profile differed considerably from that planned."[41] In the U.S., the New Jersey shore is more engineered and "nourished" than any other part of the coastline, and still the land is rapidly sinking, the water rising.[42] The beach is a canvas under continual erasure. The more urgently we refill its eroding contours, the faster it disappears.

The cultural and environmental history I have just outlined underscores both the seductiveness and the elusiveness of the beach. Another version of the story would highlight seaside revulsion rather than desire. Before and alongside its codification as a cure and a longed-for destination, the seashore has appeared as a mortuary zone, a wasteland haunted by the specter of shipwreck and decay. In 1855, Henry David Thoreau described the coast of Cape Code as "a vast morgue, where famished dogs may range in packs, and crows come daily to glean the pittance which the tide leaves them."[43] This sense of the sea as an open grave and the beach as actively repulsive is especially acute for writers grappling with the legacy of colonial violence and the trauma of the Middle Passage. Atlantic coastlines in particular are inscription sites marked by the traffic of enslavement. This is why when Saidiya Hartman arrives at the Ghanaian coast in her retracing of the Atlantic slave route, the ocean "reek[s] of things dead and rotten" and its surf is an anguished roar.[44]

In the wake of World War II, the beach became indissociable from the memory of a different kind of violence—that of mass warfare. The Normandy landings occurred only about fifty miles west of Boudin's Trouville. In France, the specter of the beach as a theater of war haunts the supposedly insouciant rituals of the postwar vacation: philosopher Paul Virilio recalls that when he first set foot on the littoral (in the summer of 1945) it had the aspect of a "deserted battlefield."[45] This effect is still perceptible in Jacques Tati's beach-set 1953 film *Monsieur Hulot's Holiday* (*Les vacances de M. Hulot*), a seaside comedy that explores the intimate relation between cultures of leisure and cultures of violence.[46] This film's location on the south coast of Brittany was chosen for its unreconstructed, bomb-damaged seafront, which left space for a cinematic set.[47] The most revealing moment in *Monsieur Hulot's Holiday* occurs toward the end, when the bumbling hero accidentally ignites a shed on the beach full of fireworks and then races around trying and failing to contain the explosions. Set to a sound track consisting of machine gun and mortar fire, this scene strongly evokes the terror of a coastal military invasion.[48] The silent message of Tati's film is not "beneath the paving stones, the beach," but "beneath the beach, the war."

Over the course of the twentieth century, vacations became big business.[49] The reinvention of the beach as a space accessible to the masses had particular resonance in France, where securing and expanding the right to paid vacations (*congés payés*) constituted organized labor's primary objective for decades. In a 1966 interview, Claude Lévi-Strauss interprets the

INTRODUCTION

FIGURE 0.3. Normandy Invasion, June 1944. Photograph by the U.S. Navy. Courtesy of Wikimedia Commons.

French preoccupation with leisure—"l'obsession passionnée de l'évasion et du délassement"—in negative terms, as the flip side of a culture of intensifying productivism. Lévi-Strauss views his contemporaries as desperate to escape the obligation to produce and become instead pure consumers—of "air," "light," "Ocean," and "nature" itself.[50] From a postcolonial perspective, one might also note that the metropolitan citizen's desire for overseas travel cannot be extricated from a dominating impulse. In interwar France, for instance, colonial tourism—justified by the discourse of the "civilizing mission"—served as an "apprenticeship" for "tourist consumer-citizens" who learned through travel to feel ownership over imperial space and superiority to its native inhabitants.[51]

This framework helps us to understand why beaches are so disgusting in some anticolonial works. The most celebrated such text in the French-language context is Aimé Césaire's 1939 *Notebook of a Return to the Native Land* (*Cahier d'un retour au pays natal*), which works to ruin the colonial beach as a metropolitan playground. In Césaire's rendering, the Martinican beach is a "blight" (*une détresse*), piled with garbage and licked by the sea's "foaming rage."[52] Similarly, Marguerite Duras refuses to aestheticize the beach in her 1950 novel *The Sea Wall* (*Un Barrage contre le Pacifique*). Set in the flooded coastal marshes of colonial Indochina, this text presents the Pacific edge as revoltingly strewn with dead rodents and birds.[53] And although Albert Camus's infamous novel, *The Stranger* (*L'Étranger*, 1942), is much more ambiguous in its ethics, it is telling that this work, too, is fixated on the beach, which it presents, in sun-bleached prose, as the stage for colonialist violence.[54]

Contemporary French novelist and playwright Marie NDiaye amplifies and reconfigures such anticolonial beach nausea in her 2001 novel *Rosie Carpe*, which is partly set in Guadeloupe. But while Césaire's beach is stained by "piles of rotting muck," "yelping" scum, and "furtive rumps relieving themselves," NDiaye's touristified Caribbean is glutted with "unwholesome," "degenerate" white flesh, which she represents in uncanny fragments, including "dry old, bandy legs . . . hastening to the beach," "enormous, vulnerable buttocks," "flabby skin," and "poorly distributed gray hairs that spiraled in little clumps."[55] In a critique of the racist logic of tourism in her native Antigua, novelist and essayist Jamaica Kincaid observes that wealthy white tourists want to sit on beaches that appear never to have been sat on before.[56] For her part, NDiaye sees the tourist industry less as a force of exclusion than as a nauseating imposition—a gross violation she allegorizes in *Rosie Carpe* when a pale old woman, crossing the street to the beach, sticks her tongue in a Black motorist's ear and then hops away, giggling, "exposed and gray in the baking sun." NDiaye's seaside is not—like Césaire's—under attack by a rabid sea; rather, it's made nasty by an excess of European pleasure, which takes the repugnant form of feverish, forced, face-distorting laughter—laughter that reveals long teeth and a red, "waggling" tongue, "little laughs" that "pierce" the stinking heat and "drown" the murmur of the surf.[57]

Yet beach sickness is not the only tone of Black and anticolonial beach writing. Anthropologist Vanessa Agard-Jones explores a different side of the Martinican seaside in her essay on sand as an unlikely queer archive. While water has played a central role in Caribbean and African diasporic studies, sand, writes Agard-Jones, is a "less embraced referent" that sticks to the body's "folds and fissures."[58] Likewise, Omise'eke Natasha Tinsley considers beaches as "intimate landscapes" in which to chart a decolonial Caribbean homoeroticism in opposition to the logic of the Northern gay tourist industry.[59] And Tiffany Lethabo King has recently theorized the shoal—an ecotonal sandbar, a shallow place in the ocean that is "difficult to map"—as a metaphor for Black aesthetics and expression.[60] Even more liminal than a beach, the shoal's key feature is that it "slows the movement and momentum of vessels." The shoal thus functions both literally and figuratively for King as an interruptor or rerouting phenomenon, a "shifty formation" from which to critique the assumptions and exclusions of Western humanist thought.[61]

Although the present study is largely anchored in the Global North, and set on the real or fictional beaches of France, England, and the U.S., I draw inspiration from these decolonial theorizations of the littoral. *Modernism at the Beach* explores the coastal zone as a visionary margin and a springboard for queer ecological imaginings. The desire for the beach—the longing to inscribe a message on the foreshore or gather treasures for one's private collection or stand astride a dune and gaze across the sea—could be understood as an attempt to master what inevitably evades mastery. Yet there's also something else at stake. This is the view of Gilles Deleuze, who notes that after the 1936 French law inaugurating paid vacations, many people could travel for the first time. Recalling his bourgeois mother's horror at having to share previously elite beaches with the working classes—a "loss of privilege and territory" more disturbing to her than the Germans occupying beaches with their tanks—Deleuze also remembers, with some wonder, having watched a girl from a landlocked region gaze in awe, for hours, at a horizon she had never seen before.[62]

Like this girl whose seaside rapture made such an impression on the young Deleuze, the authors and artists who feature in the present book are drawn to the disorienting, self-emptying effects of the edge, with its dizzying convergence of lithic, tidal, and atmospheric forces. An ecological border zone and a site of elemental intensity, the beach puts human plots and desires in perspective. As critical geographer Kathryn Yusoff puts it, "at the beach the seemingly robust reality of social construction begins to slip, denoting a littoral zone of planetary counterplay."[63] Despite its semiological and historical complexity, one of the lessons of the modernist beach is that the world is not *about* us after all.

OFF-SEASON

Presenting a stunning collision of anthropogenic and inhuman forces, the beach relativizes and decenters human emplotments. Engineered yet intractable, never fully assimilable to genealogical or economic regimes, this landscape fascinates precisely because it is such an unruly geography. In fact, the beach is not simply a desirable destination: it has been cast as the Anthropocene's most overtly eroticized image of nature, and this strange fact merits investigation.

Especially since the Second World War, the beach has been sold as a spectacle of seduction—a space in which the imposed narratives of heteronormative courtship and marriage are put under extreme pressure. Consider, for instance, the iconic 1953 adulterous beach make-out scene between Burt Lancaster and Deborah Kerr. Taking place against the backdrop of a culturally fetishized South Pacific, this kiss is probably familiar even to those who haven't seen *From Here to Eternity*.[64] By the early 1960s, Brigitte Bardot—a movie star and "beach kitten" indissociable from bikinis, creaturely sensuality, and the French Riviera—had become one of the most photographed people in the world.[65] And in a more overtly disciplinary vein, the Hollywood "Beach Party" films of this era present the littoral as a classroom in which white middle-class heterosexuality is tested and reproduced. These films present the pathway to a respectable sexuality as narrow and ringed with dangers: promiscuity or spinsterhood for young women, homosexuality for young men. Bathing-suit-clad adolescents must learn to distinguish between suitable and unsuitable forms of courtship as they defend themselves against various queer threats to heteronormativity, including biker gangs, bodybuilders, and marauding nuclear-waste zombies.[66] As these examples indicate, the leisure beach has often functioned as a cultural battleground, a place where wayward flesh is to be managed and brought back in line with the temporal orders of family and state.[67]

In the shadow of this disciplinary apparatus, however, the littoral has also offered a space for experimenting with nonnormative intimacies and styles of encounter. There is something unscripted about the beach, and this open-endedness, this lack of adherence to a set of established codes, makes it an enticing setting for queer artists in particular. According to historian George Chauncey, decades before Stonewall, drag shows were held at New York's Coney Island and Riis Beach.[68] An undated photograph, taken in the

FIGURE 0.4. Beach drag, anonymous. New York LGBT Community Center, Richard Peckinpaugh Beach Photographs, circa late 1940s.

New York area around midcentury, offers a glimpse of the beach as queer catwalk—a place for trying out alternative embodiments and expressions of desire. This image presents a striking tension between foresight and spontaneity: the transformation of towels into a hat and skirt suggests an impromptu occasion, but the shoes tell another story.

One of the arguments of this book is that to think about the beach is to think about the history of sexuality—and to explore the confluence of queer studies and ecological thought. There are few explicitly gay characters in any of the works under consideration here. Yet queerness—which I understand, following Mel Chen, as *improper affiliation* rather than in fixed, identitarian terms—is among the book's most persistent through lines.[69] Of particular interest here is the idea of the beach as a stage on which place-based, atmospheric modalities of queerness might emerge. In exploring the textured landscape of pre- and para-Stonewall queer affinities, I am guided by the pathbreaking scholarship of José Esteban Muñoz, Eva Hayward, Omise'eke Natasha Tinsley, Peter Coviello, Carolyn Dinshaw, Michael Lucey, Heather Love, and Benjamin Kahan, among others, who have shown that the binary, late twentieth-century, in-or-out Western model of sexuality simply cannot account for the rich and subtle topographies of human (and more-than-human) orientation, affection, and attachment. Throughout the book, I explore ambiguous forms of queerness that may slip under the radar—not because they are repressed or "closeted," but simply because they do not fit the prevailing paradigms of gender expression and sexual desire.

As a chronotope that hovers somewhere between the cityscape and the (constructed, fantasmatic) "wild," the beach partakes of what Jack Halberstam terms the "epistemology of the ferox." Halberstam's theory of the wild as a decolonial, "postnatural" phenomenon enables him to dispense with the fantasy of subjectivity as a secret "interior room" and highlight instead the image of a "wide-open space" across which an "unknowable self is dispersed."[70] I, too, am concerned with the problem of how to theorize the history of sexuality without recourse to the metaphor of the closet. But instead of materializing the anarchic energies of Halberstam's "untamed ontologies," the seaside appears here as a generator of offbeat temporalities and precarious modalities of coexistence.[71] The notion of "ease," so important for Claude McKay, will be a refrain in my readings, among other temporally dilated, nonappropriative ways of inhabiting space.

INTRODUCTION

The minor concept of the "off-season" encapsulates the queer untimeliness that is a recurrent motif in my study of the shore. Significant in this regard is Guy de Maupassant's 1881 short story "Tidewrack" ("Épaves"), which sketches three days on the beach in winter, narrated from the perspective of an observer who is merely passing through. The story explores the notion of the *arrière-saison*—an off-time peopled by locals and leftovers of the high season (*les épaves de l'été*), social castaways who meander, in heavy coats, past a closed casino.[72] Two decades earlier, Jules Michelet's study of the sea, *La Mer* (1861), had underscored the sublime spectacle of seaside melancholy.[73] While Michelet's Romantic coast is a graveyard for ships and a place of "sobbing" waves, Maupassant's protomodernist beach is a flat edge littered with flotsam and fishermen's nets, spotted with beached boats like "heavy dead fish" and marked by the "monotone" beat of the surf. And in contrast to the solitary contemplation that features centrally in Michelet's account of the seashore, Maupassant's winter beach is a stage speckled with artists and intellectuals, including a famous violinist who "poses" against the sea, a celebrated Swiss philosopher, two painters, and the editor of an obscure newspaper. This peculiarly antisocial social space is thus a site of potential encounter, where "off-season marriages" can be made. But the beach in December is also where unmarriageable women—the ultimate social refuse, in Maupassant's view—wash up. The sketch concludes with the narrator's observations about a couple of "disproportionately" tall, wild-haired English women—the most "tossed about" (*ballottées*) of tidewrack—contemplating the sea by moonlight. Described in weirdly electrical and creaturely terms as "telegraph poles with manes," the two women laugh and speak loudly with the voices of "serious men."[74] These off-season queer figures do not conform to any Romantic seaside type—they are neither weeping mariners' widows nor dreamy gazers—and although the narrator arrogantly insists that the women cannot understand the view they enjoy, it is he who cannot make sense of what he is witnessing.

I reference Maupassant's story (despite its aggravating misogyny) because it so aptly underscores the unruliness of the off-season as a setting. Throughout this book, I'm attentive to how the modernist seaside takes shape at the threshold of various normative temporal structures—not only the division of the year into a "high" and "low" tourist season but also the ideology of historical development and the determining framework of oedipal and heteroreproductive plotlines. Blurring the line between youth and maturity and between biological and geological time, the beach tends to suspend the telos of the novel of education, the *Künstlerroman*, and the narratives of courtship and marriage. In the littoral zone, the time of productivity and progress hits up against the lunar and gravitational pull of the surf and the tides, the slow process of lithic decomposition, and the swirl of tidewrack, drifting up languidly on the world's shores.

In Maupassant's sketch, the off-season beach is both the staging ground for the marriage plot and a refuge for its misunderstood cast-offs. This sense of the littoral as a space of alternative, nontouristic seasonality will be important throughout the chapters that follow. Proust, for instance, liked to be among the last to leave the Cabourg Grand Hôtel, and his narrator likewise lingers by the seaside into the fall, departing only when the cold becomes unbearable.[75] Woolf's *To the Lighthouse* turns what Elizabeth Freeman has termed "chrononormativity" on its head, exploring impersonal tidal and atmospheric temporalities that erode domestic and patriarchal orders. Carson loved the "different world" of the seashore by night, which she describes as "alive" with "watchful eyes and little, waiting forms."[76] McKay's *Banjo* is a "story without a plot," set in a Marseille populated by vagabonding poets and musicians who are living "on the beach" and off the clock. And in Beckett's *Happy Days,* as in a number of contemporary performance works, the beach appears as a space of intransitive waiting— simultaneously a carceral site and a zone of collective endurance.[77]

Beaches can be queer refuges in the high season as well. In their impermanence and remoteness, their dreaminess and sensual intensity, and in their relatively limited police presence (compared to the city), beaches have served throughout the twentieth century as gathering sites for those who are excluded from heteronormative spaces and institutions. This effect sometimes occurs across time and space, as, for instance, when critic Pierre Saint-Amand feels a spark of "homosexual identification" upon gazing at a photograph of a young Roland Barthes on the beach, torso in "luminous nudity," lying in a "languid pose" that bespeaks "complicitous solitude."[78] In her history of the queer enclave of Cherry Grove, Fire Island, Esther Newton writes that beachside resorts were long "the only public places where gays could socialize and assemble without constant fear of hostile straight society."[79] Fire Island in particular has served as a queer sanctuary and a space of artistic invention. Maurice Sendak composed *Where the Wild*

INTRODUCTION

Things Are in 1963 while vacationing there—a place in which one "wore less clothing and could spend uninterrupted hours sketching, writing, resting, and talking in the open air, with less inhibition."[80] As a Jew and a queer midcentury subject, Sendak felt safe on the island—safe to make art but also to experiment with embodiment and desire, even if only in imagination: in later years, he would describe the "wild rumpus" in *Where the Wild Things Are* as an orgy.[81] Queer and feminist theorist Gayle Rubin also emphasizes the important role that beaches—especially "funky," unmodernized ones, "redolent with illicit pleasures"—played in her adolescence. In these liminal zones, Rubin notes, the "usual rules of propriety were somewhat suspended."[82] This is precisely what drew many people to the unlikely beaches that emerged along New York's Hudson River in the 1970s and 1980s: during this era, the crumbling Chelsea piers became both a lively queer cruising ground and a makeshift studio for artists fascinated by the site's conjunction of architectural decay and risky outsiderness. Writing in the late 1990s, Lauren Berlant and Michael Warner underscore the improvisations at the heart of queer culture's "counterintimacies," which developed outside the rituals of matrimony and other forms of institutional support.[83] We might understand the beach, following Berlant and Warner, Sendak, Rubin, and the various queer protagonists of this study, as a space replete with improvisational possibilities.

The image of Sendak working (and playing) on Fire Island indexes another element of this setting's intrinsic untimeliness: in the tidelands, ideas and practices of queerness and childhood overlap. The beach is a zone of horizontality, both literally and figuratively. It's a space that facilitates lateral growth—outward branching into other bodily forms and sensory configurations—rather than adherence to any linear plotline. In the twentieth century, the beach resounds with what Golan Moskowitz calls "childhood's universal queerness—its wild, sensual, and irreverent oddness."[84] We see this especially in Proust and Woolf. Proust's beach-oriented *In Search of Lost Time* is, after all, a novel about a protagonist who does not grow "up" as much as he grows "sideways," to invoke critic Kathryn Bond Stockton's study of queer childhood.[85] Delighting in an embrace of "childish things," Proust mobilizes a queer strategy of surviving what Joseph Litvak calls "the ruthless cultural project of universal heterosexualization, where 'growing up' in fact means shutting down, tuning out, closing off various receptivities that make it possible to find the world *interesting*."[86]

Balbec presents the lure of a startling break from routine, teaching the adolescent narrator (and, by extension, the reader) to see with child's eyes—to practice a style of vision stripped of habitual concepts and categories. This perceptual revolution extends to the domain of sexuality as well: in the second, beachiest volume of Proust's novel, eroticism is in the air but not tethered to any plot (nor even yet individualized in any one person). Similarly, in Woolf's *To the Lighthouse,* the novel's most spotlit beach moment involves a scene in which a child, fleeing the pressures to conform to the coercive time lines of marriage and domesticity, daydreams over a tidal pool. Nancy's intertidal exploration offers a temporary reprieve from the pressures of heteroreproductivity; the moment she leaves the pool, she will run, to her horror, directly into a marriage proposal—Paul and Minta "kissing probably" behind a rock.[87]

Recourse to childhood is not the only way to dodge the pressures of universal heterosexualization. In the art of trans writer and photographer Claude Cahun and in collaborations between Cahun and their lover (and step-sister), the artist Marcel Moore, for instance, a different sort of untimeliness attends the vision of the beach. Cahun and Moore's experimental text, *Views and Visions* (*Vues et visions,* 1919), is structured on an opposition between a coastal present, set at a northern French beach resort, and scenes of reverie in Greco-Roman antiquity.[88] The beach appears here as a dreamy loophole in time and space, enabling zigzagging time travel between contrasting homophilic "visions." These temporal displacements are bookended by the insomnia of the opening fragment and the sleepiness of the concluding one—a frame that casts all the lyrical passages in between as hypnagogic dreamscapes, seaside imaginings of a half-conscious mind. Experimenting with gendered expectations, the narrator employs masculine adjective endings, describing themself, for instance, as "las" (weary) and "dépaysé" (homesick). And yet hints of Sapphic homoeroticism can also be glimpsed throughout—in images of "deux chaloupes" (two boats, gendered feminine) that brush up against one another, "seducing" the eye of the narrator, or in "deux ombres" (two shadows, gendered feminine) that move toward the unknown, "interlaced," or again, in (feminine) "white forms confused in a golden fog."[89] Moore's illustrations underscore this ambiguity, blurring masculine and feminine cues.

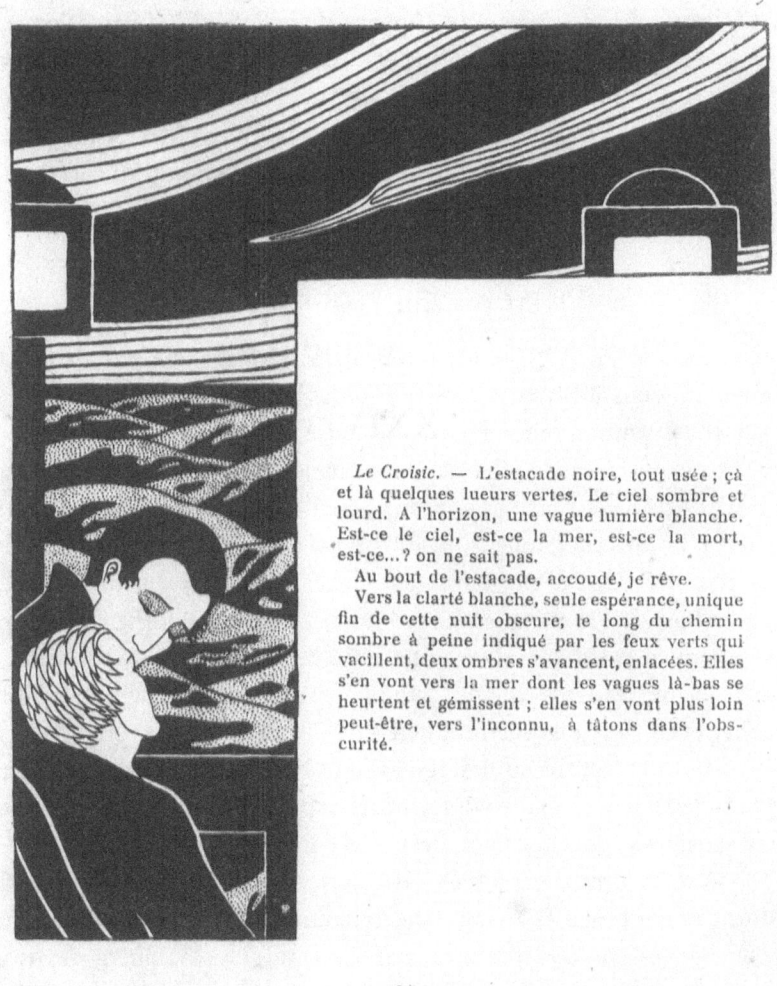

FIGURE 0.5. Page from Claude Cahun and Marcel Moore, *Vues et visions,* 1919. Courtesy of Jersey Heritage Collections.

Views and Visions explores the possibility of escaping not only the heteronormative strictures of the present but individuality altogether in favor of what Cahun curiously terms an "impartial partiality."[90] The text presents queer desire in the interstice or lag between modernity and antiquity, with the seaside as the hinge point enabling this transhistorical leap. Cahun and Moore aptly convey the modernist off-season as a minoritarian temporal mode, characterized by metrical suspensions and intermittencies of all sorts.

LITTORAL CHOREOGRAPHIES

The beach is marked by its temporal dislocations, then, but also by the heightened focus it brings to the life of the body. As Corbin intriguingly puts it, the invention of the beach as a space of leisure involved not only a new regime of the care of the self but a "major event in the history of sensibility."[91] Attuned to various human and more-than-human temporalities, the beach bodies that appear in the following chapters linger, sink, leap, doze, and drift. One of the recurring images in *Modernism at the Beach* is of a rebellious girl at the water's edge, contorted or exploding with unfeminine energies as she broods over her tide pool, plunges into the water, or soars over the head of a shocked banker, brushing his cap with her nimble feet. Yet even the most seemingly docile of littoral choreographies—the splayed-out pose of the sunbather—might be understood as a posture of active engagement with the world, an attempt to transform the entire body into a sensible surface for light, heat, and earth.

The work of filmmaker Agnès Varda has significantly shaped my understanding of the beach as an embodied phenomenon. In her 1958 documentary, *Along the Coast (Du côté de la côte)*, Varda troubles the emergent postwar touristic fantasy of the leisure beach as a space of passive, exposed flesh. At a moment when bikini-clad Brigitte Bardot had become the international emblem of beach eroticism, Varda scrambles the image of the beach bunny.[92] Although *Du côté de la côte* was commissioned by the French Tourism Office, Varda refuses to serve up glossy advertisements of the Riviera for our visual consumption. Instead, she turns her camera on bodies we don't usually see cinematically displayed, honing in on men as well as women: a close-up shot of a furry, soft, male mid-section, sunburned and adorned in a tight woolen bathing suit, is typical of her recalibrated gaze.

FIGURE 0.6. Agnès Varda, *Du côté de la côte*, 1958, dog-headed woman.

Most strikingly, she presents playfully monstrous sunbathing assemblages, surrealistically positioned such that a baby's or dog's head appears where we expect to see a woman's face. In one such tableau vivant, a prostrate sunbather lies with her face obscured by the beach's slope. A blonde toddler's head protrudes where the adult's should be—a visual gag that plays on Bardot's nickname, "B.B.," pronounced "bébé" (baby). In another shot, a perky terrier takes the place of a lolling sunbather's head. In these ludic collages, Varda riffs on what Emily Apter terms "the body-plastic," inviting us to dwell in a seaside world of unexpected hybridities and transspecies mingling.[93] Varda's seaside visions elucidate the liberatory potential of this space, indexing leisure culture's weird underside.[94]

With Varda's recast beach body in mind, could we conceptualize the brazenly passive sunbather as a feminist or queer icon? As Emma Wilson has shown, the figure of the reclining nude, so omnipresent in Western art history as an emblem of "timeless serenity," might also be seen as a "pose" and an "energy."[95] Even the sunbather's languid sprawl could be interpreted as a form of resistance. In her posture of exposure and release—her daring act of dozing in public, skin bared to the elements—the sunbather wills herself to dissolve into her environs. Becoming just another splayed-out body among so many splayed-out bodies, she absents herself from the labor of looking and being seen.

In a queer reflection on the significance of this prostrate pose, Barthes reads the late-capitalist seashore as a site of alternative, less productive and accountable temporalities and corporeal modes. In a little-known 1977 essay, Barthes describes the "beach effect" as a phenomenon of cognitive drift and sensory remapping:

> Who among us has not spent hours splayed out on the sand? I remember: sounds and bits of phrases crisscross around me. If I close my eyelids, colors persist: blue, red, yellow; if I half open them lazily, I see unknown bodies passing through my lashes. All of this forms a beach effect.

> Qui de nous n'est resté des heures étendu sur le sable? Je me souviens: des bruits, des bouts de phrases se croisent autour de moi. Si je ferme mes paupières, des couleurs persistent: bleu, rouge, jaune; si je les entrouve parasseusement, je vois passer à travers mes cils des corps dont je ne sais rien. Tout cela forme un effet de plage.[96]

In this exceptionally indolent depiction of cruising—flânerie in the horizontal mode—Barthes invites us to rethink the concept of leisure. The hypothetical tone of the passage, with its repeated "ifs" (*si*), presents the seashore as a space of unexpected pleasures and contingencies, a multisensory realm in which the haptic, visual, and acoustic cross and mingle. Barthes's eyelash-patterned beachscape involves a slowed-down, speculative scattering and reconfiguration of sound and sight—sensation queerly incarnated. As the link between sensory cause and effect is loosened, other connections become imaginable.

Sunbathing could easily signify as the ultimate posture of privilege, and yet when performed in unexpected or unsanctioned locales it becomes a transgressive act. This is the case, for instance, when sunbathers trespass onto industrial terrain, effectively reclaiming the city for the purpose of radical repose. The most striking textual example of such urban poaching occurs in McKay's *Banjo,* a novel that transforms "beach" into a verb. "To beach" in this experimental text is to dare to bask in the sun, creating space and time for the care of the self in the interstices of Marseille's urban waterfront. It is thus a practice of flagrant disregard for a hostile and racist world that codifies seaside relaxation as an exclusive practice and reduces Black bodies to the work they can do.

Prostrate or supine horizontality is only one of various corporeal stylings that the beach makes possible. For instance, practices of marine natural history (tide-pooling, beachcombing, specimen collection, or treasure hunting), which came into vogue as popular pastimes in the mid-nineteenth-century, shaped Virginia Woolf's and Rachel Carson's seaside imaginaries. Just as notable are the gravity-defying acrobatics that appear in turn-of-the-century beach-set works, indexing a new conception of the gendered body and its relation to both ground and air. Such mesmerizing exuberance is on display in Louis Lumière's early film, *Sea Bathing* (*Baignade en mer,* 1895), which presents children plunging off a pier into the sea. They fly toward the horizon at varied tempos, feet first or head over heels, before clambering ashore to jump again. The bathers have likely reached the seaside by rail—the film is shot, after all, at the coastal destination of the most famous train in cinematic history, the one featured in Lumière's own *Arrival of a Train* (*Arrivée d'un train à la Ciotat,* 1896).[97] Yet *Sea Bathing* elucidates a different scene: it explores what happens on the other end of that fabled arrival, as relentless locomotion cedes to a lighter and more improvisational modernist ethos and the passengers are released to play.

The wild leap is central to a number of other seaside representations of this era, including the windblown bodies of Charlie Chaplin's one-reel *By the Sea* (1915); the trampoline-enhanced littoral calisthenics that feature centrally in the *Ballets Russes* work, *Le Train bleu* (1924); and, especially, the airborne mobility of Proust's little band of beach girls. The Olympics had been revived in 1896, and this period was generally interested in acrobatics and athleticism—sometimes in overtly masculinist and fascistic ways.[98] But Proust's aerial turn is more akin to Mallarmé's humble practice of inscribing poems on skipping stones, which he culled in the 1890s from the beach in Normandy, and then giving them as gifts. Mallarmé's daughter later transcribed these ephemeral verses, including, for instance, the following, written for the son of the poet's host in Honfleur: "With this one, Joseph, whom I teach, / you'll play ducks and drakes upon the beach" ("Avec ceci Joseph, ô mon élève / Vous ferez des richochets sur la grève").[99]

We are accustomed to thinking of stones as weighty emblems of a vast geological temporality. As Jeffrey Cohen puts it, "a rock discovered at the shoreline opens an adventure in deep time and inhuman forces: slow sedimentation of alluvium and volcanic ash, grinding tectonic shift, crushing mass and epochal compaction, infernal heat, relentless turbidity of the sea."[100] For Cohen, stone is the foundation of narrative, and he invokes in particular the myth of Sisyphus as representative of a human-lithic "cross-taxonomic relation."[101] What if, in lieu of Sisyphus's curse, we took Mallarmé's gift—his beach-culled pebble poem—as paradigmatic for the modernist imagination? In its improbable defiance of gravity, the lyrical skipping stone encapsulates the convergence of the elemental and the aesthetic, conjuring the image of a couplet sent bouncing across the surface of the water.[102]

I invoke Mallarmé's beach-pebble poems—their sheer playfulness and gratuity, the sense they offer of art as a gesture of divestment, an act of letting go rather than holding on—as a reminder that the ever-changing, windswept expanse of the beach is an environment that multiplies possibilities for thought. The beach is many things—a stage, a fringe, a catwalk, a springboard, a dumping ground, and a space of interminable erosion and transfiguration. What it's not is a setting propitious to story, at least not any strongly teleological sense. The seaside is not a foundation or a place to put down roots. Rather, it's a threshold where narrative might drift or hang suspended for a time. Interrupting and rerouting the gendered choreography of everyday life, the beach opens new avenues for the embodied imagination.

COASTAL MAP

Each of the following chapters explores particular coastal formations, including a northern French resort town; a rocky tidal pool in Scotland (or possibly England); a sea cave on the coast of Maine; the makeshift beaches that crop up on Marseille's industrial breakwater and the derelict Hudson River piers; and a set of globally mobile artificial beaches, used as stage sets for durational performances of exposure and endurance.

INTRODUCTION

Geographically speaking, the Atlantic coast predominates in this book, though it also dips into the Mediterranean Sea and the Hudson River (an Atlantic estuary). The beaches I examine are only partly mappable places in the world. They are also sites of fantasy, and sometimes amalgamations of real and imagined coastal zones. An oneiric quality infuses even Carson's popular scientific account of the Atlantic coast: her lingering, lyrical descriptions of secret caves and translucid pools, drifting tentacles and elusive ghost crabs at times read like a love letter to the intimate friend who occupied her thoughts during the years she was writing the book. Woolf's *To the Lighthouse* is also set in a particular place, even as it is strangely dislocated from geographic specificity. Disregarding the accuracy and precision privileged by her novel's patriarchal authorities, Woolf's seaside setting flickers between her remembered childhood summer home, near Lands End, and an imagined Scottish Isle of Skye, which she had never visited. Similarly, Proust's Balbec is an invented locale that bears resemblance to Cabourg, Normandy, but was also inspired by time the author spent with his boyfriend, years before, in Brittany. And for the vagabond Black artists of McKay's *Banjo*, a beach is less a particular place than a way of being, a practice of drifting through the world with ease, against all odds. All in all, the modernists who feature here are less interested in the history of any specific coast than in the beach as a conceptual horizon and a set of embodied practices.

Chapter 1, "Proust's Leap," elucidates minor lines of flight in Proust's *In Search of Lost Time*, considering what becomes possible in the meanwhile, before (or beside) the revelation of aesthetic vocation. During the novel's improvisatory middle stretch, we linger with the narrator by the sea, admiring a little band of girls who jump and flirt on the sand. In place of the familiar emphasis on Proustian beds, cathedrals, and *petites madeleines*, the chapter explores the socioaesthetics of leaps, casinos, and champagne. Reading the *Recherche* in conjunction with works by Charlie Chaplin and the Ballets Russes, it shifts the spotlight from the village-city circuit onto a third space: the beach, springboard for new kinesthetic mobilities.

Chapter 2, "Intertidal Woolf," invites a similar shift of perspective with regard to Virginia Woolf: I approach her coastal novel, *To the Lighthouse*, with an eye to the wavering gaze of the tide pool explorer rather than the regular, governing pulse of the maritime beacon. Woolf's aesthetic imagination, I argue, pivots on a zigzagging point of view—a shifting practice of perception that affirms setting as an emergent phenomenon. *To the Lighthouse* connects this visionary style to queer types—spinster painters, opium-eating poets, and middle children who seek to escape the "horror of family life." Lingering in the margins of the domestic scene, these unmarriageable figures elucidate other, less productive and accountable ways of seeing and of being in time.

Venturing more decisively off the beaten path of modernist studies, chapter 3, "Carson's Quiet Bower," argues that Rachel Carson's 1955 seaside guidebook, *The Edge of the Sea*, is not only a work of marine biology but a performance of close reading and an experiment in queer ecology. Before she inspired the U.S. environmentalist movement with her 1962 exposé of the pesticide industry, *Silent Spring*, Carson spent years exploring intertidal ecosystems while engaged in an ardent epistolary affair with her seasonal neighbor, Dorothy Freeman. Carson had been commissioned to write a beachcomber's guidebook to the Atlantic coast, but as she moved between writing love letters and exploring the sea's edge, she stretched the limits of this codified genre. *The Edge of the Sea* is an homage to misfit intimacies: it explores small temporalities and styles of existence that conform neither to the hypermasculinist ethos of the atomic age nor to the speeded-up time-spaces of late capitalism. If Proust's beach is an enormous casino, Carson's seashore sometimes appears as a midcentury feminine interior, replete with saucers, bread crumbs, carpet, curtains, threads, and needles, and shaped by a subtle haptic eroticism. Examining the book's interplay of text and image, and comparing its sensibility to that of other coastal guidebooks of the era, I argue that transience and intermittency are what Carson most valued about the intertidal zone.

Chapter 4, "McKay's Dream Port," explores the phenomenon of the beach-as-commons—a gathering space or meeting grounds that cannot be entirely enclosed or reduced to real estate. Pushing beyond conventional depictions of the leisure beach to consider the working and ruined industrial waterfront as well, I highlight queer commoning practices—acts of erotic and/or anticapitalist reappropriation—at maritime or riverine urban edges. The first half of the chapter examines Claude McKay's novel, *Banjo: A Story Without a Plot*, which twists and morphs the noun *beach* into a verb. "To make a beach" in McKay's interwar Marseille indicates the subversive act of drifting, undocumented, at the edges of a racist world of compulsory work and identity control. Reinventing the waterfront "picturesque" not according to the logic of landscape management but as the modality of a subject who is cruising or simply passing through, McKay's international Black protagonists (or "beach boys") dare to "take it easy" in the shadow of imperialism and white supremacy. The second half of the chapter considers a later adventure in urban beaching, investigating artworks made on New York City's decaying Chelsea piers in the 1970s and 1980s. In the photography of Alvin Baltrop and Shelley Seccombe and in the "anarchitectural" building cuts of Gordon Matta-Clark, we trespass onto scenes of togetherness that echo, in a different key, the contestatory queer utopianism of McKay's diasporic littoral zone.

Further theorizing the place of the beach in a postnatural age, chapter 5, "Tidewrack, Beckett to Sunde," examines contemporary photography and sculpture made in the medium of oceanic plastic and durational performances set on artificial beaches. The Great Acceleration—the period of post-1945 environmental history marked by a sharp uptick in global consumption, carbon combustion, and waste—is also the era in which beaches have become a truly massified phenomenon. As cultural historians have shown, since the seventeenth century, beaches have functioned as key nodes in the history of hygiene. This chapter argues that they have also become emblems of capitalist exhaustion. The first part of the chapter examines the work of British sculptor Stuart Haygarth and photographer Mandy Barker, who cull their materials—sea trash—from the world's beaches. In their work, we witness impressionism's scene of beach pleasure return as an almost unthinkable quantity of debris. The second half of the chapter turns to beach-set performance art, including Beckett's *Happy Days,* a contemporary Lithuanian beach-set opera-performance titled *Sun & Sea (Marina),* and Sarah Cameron Sunde's *36.5/A Durational Performance with the Sea.* Each of these performances, I argue, presents the beach—and the act of beaching—as indexing a widespread mood of existential and climate fatigue. In each case, however, this spectacle of exhaustion gestures toward other potential futures. Works made of flotsam or set on constructed littoral zones address the sheer weirdness of our age of surfeit and slow violence, yet also underscore possibilities for collective endurance and survival under a blistering sun and against the backdrop of rising tides.

Anthropologist Marc Augé has described the beach as an "immense waiting room."[103] Michael Taussig calls it an "expensive backdrop" for the spectacle of leisure.[104] For the authors and artists who feature here, the beach is both of these things—but it's also something more. From Proust's champagne-doused stage set to the homey textures of Carson's sea caves, and from McKay's luminous industrial breakwater to Beckett's scorched dune, the beach is both an elusive boundary and a gathering place, a "weedy landscape" and a bower. With its scalar interplay and its biological, geological, and textual intensities, the littoral is compelling because it invites improvisation, reminding us that no matter how fixed an imposed order may appear, impermanence is the law of all things. At stake throughout this book is the question of what becomes visible when we consider social and ecological formations in close proximity, as a set of overlapping forces—rhythms of existence at the edge.

Chapter One

PROUST'S LEAP

The beach is a surprisingly generative site for the modernist novel. Surprising, because the city, with its dynamism and potential for interconnecting plotlines, has long been recognized as modernism's preferred narrative setting.[1] Yet even quintessential city novels are unable to resist the lure of the seaside. The urban plots and conspiracies of Andrei Bely's *Petersburg* (1913) are interrupted by a vision of "wrinkled" saltwater pools and "white-maned" waves. James Joyce's *Ulysses* (1922) twice leads us out of Dublin and onto the "seaspawn and seawrack," "razorshells" and "squeaking pebbles" of the strand—a site of philosophical and autoerotic investigations. Virginia Woolf's *Mrs. Dalloway* (1925) opens on a London morning "fresh as if issued to children on a beach."[2] And in Marcel Proust's *In Search of Lost Time* (*À la recherche du temps perdu*, 1913–1927)—a work partially drafted at a coastal resort in northern France—the seashore breaks into the novel's city-village counterpoint like an improvisation, unsettling the symmetry of time lost and regained and enabling new encounters and lines of flight.[3]

What made the beach so enticing for early twentieth-century authors like these? One possible answer—given modernism's formalist bent—lies in the perceived emptiness and isolation of this space. The seashore would appear to flatten the social and temporal heterogeneity that powers the urban novel, instead invoking what Michael Taussig calls the fantasy of a "spectacular return of the archaic within modernity."[4] Indeed, as Rosalind Krauss points out, the sea has often been perceived as a "special kind of medium for modernism." This is due, she claims, to its supposed "detachment from the social," and to the way it opens onto a "visual plenitude" that is also a "no-space of sensory deprivation." The seashore, according to this view, invites a "rapt stare" because it enables the abstraction of sheer aesthesis, offering the eye nothing but "patterns and colors and lines."[5] Krauss herself challenges this official story of modernist abstraction by exploring the unruly compulsions and disruptive forces that lurk within that entranced gaze. The present chapter also counters the mythology of the beach as an empty, asocial space, but along different interpretive lines: it examines the modernist seashore as a stage for the reconfiguration of social ritual and corporeal style. After all, the beach is only partly a matter of sand and sea. Proust in particular is fascinated by the seaside resort as a setting that facilitates intimate contact with strangers. In *In Search of Lost Time*, the quaintness of a village past is born of the contact of a *petite madeleine* with a cup of tea. Proust's beach, by contrast, appears as the end point of an intoxicated train trip. It issues not from the eucharistic meeting of pastry and herbal brew but from the head-turning encounter of beer and locomotive velocity. An extension of its casino and its vast "amphitheater" sea, Balbec is a space in which inherited scripts cede to extemporaneous performance. Site of dream and speculation, marked by "blue peaks of the sea which bear no name on any map," this is a landscape that opens not to the past but to the future.[6]

As the threshold through which the novel's key queer characters make their entrance, Balbec spotlights new corporeal mobilities and formations of the gendered body. Kindling erotic modalities that partake of the seashore's dilation and drift, Proust's beach is queer in José Esteban Muñoz's utopian sense of the term. For Muñoz, queerness indicates a "wish-landscape" and a "longed-for future;" it is bound up with the "intention to be lost."[7] Balbec might bear resemblance to the historical beach town of Cabourg, where Proust wrote some of his novel, but it's ultimately a space of imagination. This is why the narrator gets drunk for the first time on the train to Balbec, to his grandmother's chagrin: entrance to that seaside world requires an initiatory rite of intoxication, a deliberate disorientation.

PROUST'S LEAP

This chapter argues that the seaside is a crucial, critically underexamined setting in the *Recherche,* and it makes this case in three parts. I show, first, that at Balbec, expected social hierarchies and rituals of invitation and introduction give way to an atmosphere in which contingency rules. If Combray, seen from a distance, is no more than a "church summing up the town," Balbec might be "summed up" by its casino. We see evidence of what Proust called his "gambling fever" (*fièvre du jeu*) not only in his depiction of Balbec as a space of chance encounters and queer flirtation, but in his creative reshuffling of biological terminology. The second part of the chapter demonstrates that the beach in Proust enables a new conception of the body in time, emblematized by the leaping adolescent assemblage, or *petite bande* (little band, little gang) that rises one day from the seafront promenade. The rebellious airborn body becomes a leitmotif for Proust as for other early twentieth-century beach-oriented artists: I show that Proust's depiction of the seaside as a virtual "springboard" (*tremplin*) brings his novel into the orbit of cinematic and balletic works by the likes of Charlie Chaplin and Jean Cocteau. Finally, the last section of the chapter considers Proust's beach as a perceptual phenomenon, and Balbec as the novel's primary setting for aesthetic invention. Like a test kitchen or a laboratory, the Balbec chapter in *Within a Budding Grove* facilitates a variety of sensory-social investigations, including drinking, painting, and listening in the dark. This chapter is also experimental in another way: it begins and ends with curious occasions in which the narrator steps away from the command post, so to speak, and allows someone else's gaze to momentarily supplant his own. Balbec is important because it permits a reprieve from what, following Eve Kosofsky Sedgwick, we might call the "omnipotence plot" in Proust, opening the possibility of a more plural perspective on the world.[8]

"GAMBLING FEVER"

The *Recherche* has sometimes been viewed as a novel pulled between two spatial poles: the fictional village of Combray, with its surrounding countryside and ritualized family life, and the real city of Paris, with its operatic street sounds and sophisticated salon culture. William Carter notes that the opposition, and eventual convergence, of landed gentry and Parisian salons inspired Proust from the start.[9] Roger Shattuck argues that the "tidal movement of the *Search* arises . . . from a geographical and intellectual exchange between city culture and country culture."[10] And Barry McCrea organizes his compelling study of queer narrative structure around this same tension, allying the Proustian village with heteroreproductive relationality, the city with its rupture.[11]

To a certain degree, this "symbolic division" between city and countryside does structure Proust's novel. Yet these are not the only settings in the *Recherche*, which in fact evokes the fictional seaside resort town of Balbec more frequently than any other place.[12] Much of *Within a Budding Grove* (*À l'ombre des jeunes filles en fleurs*, 1919) and *Sodom and Gomorrah* (*Sodome et Gomorrhe*, 1921–22), takes place on Balbec's beach and in its hotel, casino, restaurant, and coastal environs. As a geography on the edge and a site of temporary habitation, Balbec's social rules are more open-ended than those of either Paris or Combray. Primary site of the queer gaze, Balbec offers an alternative to the city-village circuit, presenting a cut in the social order of the novel. My argument in this section of the chapter is that we cannot understand the importance of the seaside to the world of the *Recherche* without reflecting on Proust's fascination with contingency and chance as ordering and disordering forces. In his depiction of Balbec, Proust sets aside a Romantic conception of the seaside as sublime, exploring it, instead, as a place of accident and improvisation—where invitations fall by the wayside and random encounters are the norm.

The first thing to note about Proust's belle époque beach resort is that it's neither very sandy nor very wet. Balbec, consisting primarily of a relay between hotel, casino, and seafront promenade (*digue*), is a tripartite performance space connected to the world at large by crisscrossing railway lines and emergent automobile routes. In French the term for seaside resort is *station balnéaire*, a phrase that underscores the location of the place on a train line. (Turn-of-the-century posters advertise Cabourg as being a mere five hours from Paris; by 1905, an express train could make the trip in three-and-a-half.) Balbec thus stands against the sea like a steam-and-petroleum-powered mirage, a seasonal dreamworld peopled by wealthy vacationers and the vast array of workers employed to serve them.

In August 1907, Proust showed up abruptly at Cabourg's *station balnéaire*, his doctors having prescribed a coastal vacation as a remedy for his asthma. He was drawn to this resort in particular because his favorite newspaper had raved about it. On July 10, a front-page *Figaro* article praised

FIGURE 1.1. "The most beautiful beach in the world," 1892 poster, courtesy of the Bibliothèque Nationale de France. The Grand Hôtel and its adjoining casino overlook the elevated *digue*, or seafront promenade (today the Promenade Marcel Proust).

the town's newly renovated Grand Hôtel as a "veritable palace from the *Thousand and One Nights*" overlooking the "Queen of beaches."[13] Less than a month later, Proust's own name would appear in the same newspaper, in a front-page society notice about goings on at Cabourg, under the heading, "Noticed, yesterday, at tea time" ("Remarqué, hier, à l'heure du thé").[14] Indeed, during the years in which Proust was vacationing in Normandy and dreaming up his own fictional beach setting, being seen at a place like Cabourg was valuable social currency: *Le Figaro* and other belle époque newspapers regularly named the elite vacationers who had been spotted at this or that seaside attraction. On August 17, 1908, for instance, *Le Figaro* listed Proust among other notables spied on Cabourg's promenade, which the paper termed the resort's "most elegant rendez-vous." Other places for being "recognized" in the second-page *Plages* society column included the beach (where one could stroll, ride a horse, or take a dip while listening to the daily orchestra concert); the casino restaurant or ballroom; the golf course or polo field; and even the *Figaro* kiosk itself.[15]

Although he went to Cabourg on doctor's orders, the beach was not for Proust a space for horizontal repose but—especially in 1907—a social and corporeal recharging station and a hub for carbon-combusting velocity. This was not the author's first soujourn to the Cabourg area: his family had vacationed annually in Normandy. But the summer of 1907 was different—speedier, riskier, and cut free from familial connections and obligations. Proust had spent the previous year barely getting out of bed, but at Cabourg he became extremely active: strolling on the promenade, mingling with strangers in the adjoining casino, managing his asthma with vast quantities of coffee (which made him shake uncontrollably, he reported), and flying around the coast in a rented car. While Balbec is at first connected mainly by train lines and carriage routes—only on the narrator's second visit will automobility crucially come into play—Proust himself spent August and September of 1907 zipping from place to place in a red taxi driven by the nineteen-year-old chauffeur/mechanic Alfred Agostinelli, a "dare devil" and speed fanatic who would soon become the object of the author's intense crush.[16] The combination of "pure" seaside air and a "deadly dose of caffeine" enabled Proust to luxuriate in the thrill of automotive velocity, which he described as akin to being shot out of a canon.[17]

My intention here is not to romanticize the carbon-fueled mobility that so enchanted (and aroused) Proust when he vacationed on the Normandy coast. Yet it is important to acknowledge that Proust's sense of the beach is indissociable from the automobile's transfiguration of space and time. It is also bound up—as we shall see—with the gambling obsession that first took hold of this writer during his summers by the sea, where he spent hours in the hotel casino—placing bets, flirting, attending theatrical, musical, or cinematic events, and getting tips on risky (and environmentally disastrous) stock market investments, such as gold mines and petroleum companies.[18] Indeed, one might conclude that the aesthetic and erotic pleasures of the seaside function for Proust as a cover for the colonialist climate violence with which he was enthusiastically (if somewhat unwittingly) complicit. This would be one way of telling the story not only of Balbec but of modernity's beach fetish more broadly.

What interests me here, however, is that despite the importance of the seaside resort in Proust's world as a tool for signaling social domination, Balbec appears instead as a space of contingency and indeterminacy, where fixed codes of comportment cede to much chancier forms of desirous encounter. Proust may have been drawn to Cabourg because *Le Figaro* described its hotel as a fantasy "palace" overlooking an aristocratic beach, but his own fictionalization of the beach resort opens new vistas, loosening the established framework of elite sociability. In this regard, Proust's treatment of the seaside resort is similar to that of marine painter Eugène Louis Boudin, whose impressionist renderings of fashionably dressed beach-going crowds often include a variety of wind-toppled wooden chairs—signifiers of social rectitude and respectability, blown over on the sand. Balbec is a place where the usual furnishings of the bourgeois novel tilt sideways, where plots go awry and intentions are taken by the wind.

One of the primary lessons of Proust's beach is that class hierarchies are acutely unstable. "Aristocracy is a relative thing," the narrator learns during his first formative summer at Balbec.[19] Proust represents the seaside vacation at the turn of the century as an increasingly democratized activity enabling novel social configurations and human geographies. When the narrator and his grandmother dine at the Grand Hôtel restaurant for the first time, he gazes with "passionate curiosity" at the room full of strangers while she surreptitiously opens a window, "unable to endure the thought that I was losing the benefit of an hour in the open air." Her rebellious act "at once sent flying, together with the menus, the newspapers, veils and hats of all the people at the other tables."[20] This unexpected rearrangement of the room sets the mood for the adolescent acrobatics that grace this volume—a phenomenon to which I will return in part 2—and it also underscores the precariousness of social distinctions at the seaside.

The line dividing workers from the vacationers they are employed to serve is blurred at Balbec, such that the Proustian narrator performs a series of social misreadings, seeing a waiter as a bourgeois acquaintance, a hall porter as a "foreign visitor," and a (male) bathing superintendent as the fashionable Odette Swann.[21] Such confusion is widespread. A stranger strikes the hotel staff as being "of the most humble extraction," while impressing the notary's wife as "a gentleman of great distinction, of perfect breeding," and Françoise, who works for the narrator's family as a cook and domestic servant, is deemed a "lady."[22] Balbec is a place of social flexibility and inversion, where a Frenchman can claim to be king of a small island in the South Seas and declare his mistress a "queen"—although the other guests are convinced that he's a "pantomime prince" and she's a mere shopgirl. It's difficult to convince other beachgoers that you're a king when the "royal bathing hut" is available to anyone who can pay twenty francs. As one provincial guest says to another, "you can take it yourself, if you care for that sort of thing."[23] Even the most elite aristocrats have dubious value at the beach: the Marquise de Villeparisis strikes her fellow hotel guests as a "dish with a pretentious name but a suspicious appearance" deserving to be "sent away with a lofty wave of the hand and a grimace of disgust," while the Princess de Luxembourg shrinks into "a woman with yellow hair and six inches of paint on her face."[24]

Proust's beach resort is a universe in which the usual rhythms of sociability are out of sync. Parisian salons in the *Recherche* are entirely organized around the dynamics of invitation. Consider, by contrast, the refused introduction that shadows the narrator's first stay at the seashore. Earlier in the novel, the narrator's father tries—and fails—to obtain an invitation that would connect his son to a powerful family on the Normandy coast. Balbec's atmosphere of indeterminate, nonpatriarchal affiliation is made evident in this episode, which presents the resort in the guise of a quickly retracted recommendation. Legrandin, a gay engineer whose sister has married into an aristocratic family with Balbec ties, and whose lyrical effusions sound like a pastiche of Proust's own style, raves about Balbec's charming sunsets, golden beaches, rugged cliffs, and newly constructed hotel.[25] But when the narrator's father attempts to pin down a letter of introduction to the well-placed sister, Legrandin acrobatically dodges the question, vaguely intoning, when pressed, "There as everywhere, I know everyone and I know no one."[26] He evades the request out of snobbishness, of course. And yet his choice not to heed the father's interpellation could be read less as a simple refusal than as a door left open—a deferred or suspended invitation.[27] By declining to answer the question, Legrandin creates an overture of a different sort, intimating that Balbec will be a place adrift from the usual connections and back channels and untethered from any heteropatriarchal system of hospitality.

At the seaside, then, expected rituals of invitation cease to hold the social world in place. Yet it's not quite the case that Balbec is a zone of detachment and "mutual indifference," as Vincent Descombes has argued.[28] If, in Descombes's phrasing, Paris is a place in which "one receives invitations," and Combray is one in which invitations are not needed, at Balbec, invitations tend to be misplaced or blown off course: they are extended but not accepted or desired but not received. In this regard, Legrandin's refusal to grant the narrator's father the introductory letter he seeks aptly sets the scene. During his first summer by the sea, the narrator spends weeks waiting for a little group of adolescent girls to materialize on the sand and wishing he could speak to them. Yet when at last one of them directly crosses his path, their gazes simply cross like clouds in a stormy sky. At the Grand Hôtel, the narrator's grandmother and her childhood friend, the Marquise de Villeparisis, will pretend not to recognize one another until a chance meeting in a doorway forces their reacquaintance. And, in a queer variation on Legrandin's initial refusal to open a channel of introduction, when the Baron de Charlus speaks to the narrator for the first time, he extends an invitation—asking the boy to come to tea with his grandmother in Mme de Villeparisis's hotel room. But when the two arrive, they discover that their hostess is not expecting them, and Charlus himself pretends to have forgotten that he invited them.[29]

In *Sodom and Gomorrah,* the narrator's increasingly maniacal possessiveness will ultimately overshadow the luminous indeterminacy of the seaside world, as a toxic jealousy plot comes to dominate a space that was once alive with the pleasures of evanescence.[30] But in its initial scenography, at least, the Proustian seashore is a zone of ephemerality and nonfulfillment. It's a place where even a "call" from trees on a roadside remains unheeded and where, rather than provoking the apotheosis of involuntary memory, a hawthorn bush laden with potential epiphany merely engages the narrator in an absurd imaginary conversation, deferring the encounter for a later time.[31] At the seaside, encounters tend to take place by accident, and the expected pathways toward social prestige and aesthetic revelation are swept away.

A place for looking and being seen, Balbec is especially amenable to the stranger encounter. By chance, the narrator meets some of the novel's most important queer characters on the beach: Albertine and her *bande*; Saint-Loup, with his impossible elegance and his eyes the color of the sea; and Charlus, spotted in *Within a Budding Grove* as he's eyeing the narrator in front of the casino that adjoins the hotel. Each surprise appearance is an event. In each case, the emergent figure is dramatically spotlighted, as if arriving on stage. Every afternoon at Balbec, men and women come out to stroll along the promenade, observed and judged by seated "critics" in a line of chairs; it is on this virtual catwalk that Albertine and her friends first appear in the novel, silhouetted against the sea.[32] A more intimate dramaturgy structures the scene in which Saint-Loup makes his entrance: the narrator is lurking in the darkened hotel restaurant when he first spots Robert passing by through an opening in the curtains, illuminated by the sun and sporting an outfit that few men would dare to wear.[33] And when Charlus shows up, the narrator suddenly finds that he himself is on stage: he has the "sensation of being watched by someone who was not far off" and turns his head to see a man of about forty, who, "nervously slapping the leg of his trousers with a switch, was staring at me, his eyes dilated with extreme attentiveness."[34]

It is telling that this last encounter takes place in front of the hotel casino—a setting in which improvisation supplants established ritual. In the *Recherche*, the beach is not primarily a space for bathing. In fact, we never actually see the narrator enter the water, although we know that he wears a bathing suit with anchors embroidered on it, provoking Charlus's disdain.[35] We do, however, accompany him into the casino numerous times. Casinos sprang up in tandem with seaside hotels in the late nineteenth and early twentieth centuries—an association evidenced by the 1901 Normandy edition of the popular tourist guidebook *Guides Joanne,* which mentions casinos nearly as frequently as it mentions beaches.[36] Several decades later, when Walter Benjamin imagined composing a "psychological and ontological study" of gambling, he was thinking in particular about "gambling at the seaside."[37]

Yet the casino in the early twentieth century did not only enable the placing of bets. It was a dynamic social space facilitating various kinds of play: in addition to a gambling room, Cabourg's Grand Hôtel Casino comprised a theater, a private club, a dance hall, and grillroom.[38] If the casino's queerness is first indicated by the aforementioned scene in which the narrator is cruised by Charlus, this association is made explicit in *Sodom and Gomorrah,* when girls dance chest to chest in the casino dance hall, staring each other down and checking each other out with the aid of its mirrored walls. When one day the narrator spies a young woman in the casino fixing "the alternating and revolving beam of her gaze" on Albertine, he concludes that it is by these peculiar "materializations" that a dispersed Gomorrah manages an "intermittent reconstruction" of its mythical city.[39] Intermittency is the key word here: the casino is a space of flirtation where commitments can be suspended and long-term plots set aside.

At the seaside in Cabourg, during the summer months between 1907 and 1914, Proust himself moved between hotel and casino, establishing a network of intimate confidants and amateur stock market advisers and dreaming up the *Recherche.* It was also during these years that he developed what he called his "gambling fever."[40] The more he worked on his novel, the more he gambled, notes Carter. If Carter dismisses Proust's gambling as a mere escape from the pressures of writing and a distraction from poor health, I suggest that we take such play seriously.[41] Practices of risky, irrational expenditure shaped Proust's literary imagination, giving rise to a narrative that foregrounds the volatility of value and stages scene after scene of erotic, aesthetic, and epistemological misestimation and surprise. We might even say that when he financed the publication of *Swann's Way* in 1913, Proust was effectively gambling on his own fiction. This may have been the only sound investment this author ever made: during the years in which he began drafting the *Recherche,* Proust became not only an ardent gambler but an avid speculator, and by the start of the war had managed to squander about a third of his fortune on stocks.[42] The full scale of what Rubén Gallo has termed Proust's "financial masochism" is beyond the scope of the present chapter.[43] Yet Proust's love of the seaside cannot be understood without considering his affinity for the seaside casino.

Enticed by the aesthetics of risk and the modes of sociability the casino made possible, Proust spent a good deal of time in this coastal space: baccarat was his favorite game.[44] According to Thomas Kavanagh, baccarat is similar to dice—"a game of pure chance, a dialogue between the player and his luck where skill has no role to play."[45] The pleasure of baccarat lies in its offer of escape from "controlled expenditure, prudent calculation, and a careful reciprocity of services offered and expected." Baccarat's temporality is not that of continuity and accumulation; instead, it plunges the player into a "more intense yet more precarious way of being."[46] Although baccarat is only explicitly referenced once in the *Recherche*, it appears as a prop in a scene of risky queer exhibitionism: Bloch's sister and her actress girlfriend "flaunt their dangerous embraces [*leurs dangereux ébats*] before the eyes of all the world" around the baccarat table before moving on to even more scandalous acts in the casino's ballroom.[47] If Proust's attraction to this game is due in part to the thrill of relinquishing control and throwing intentions to the wind, he was equally enticed by the pleasure of vicariousness. Proust enjoyed letting others place bets for him. He doesn't just "play," but rather has play activated in his place: *il fait jouer*, as he puts it.[48] He plays or gambles via an intermediary, seduced by the experience of mediation itself. In other words, he's after the form of sympathetic collaboration or imagined proximity that sociologist Erving Goffman (another gambling aficionado) calls "vicarious fatefulness."[49] We will return at the end of the chapter to Proust's affinity for vicariousness in its diverse forms.

Contingency is the law of the casino, and the logic of what *could be otherwise* also played a key role in Proust's invention of Balbec.[50] The beach preoccupied Proust for years before he began composing his novel.[51] But if Balbec was long dreamed of, its actual existence owes much to chance. The composition of the Balbec chapters was facilitated by two unplanned occurrences: first, the 1913–1914 flight and accidental death of Proust's beloved chauffeur-secretary, Agostinelli, and, second, the outbreak of war, which closed publishing houses and granted Proust an unforeseen span of time in which to expand and reconceptualize the middle stretch of the *Recherche*—including, in particular, the Albertine story.

While some version of the *petite bande* appears in early notebooks, Albertine emerged late in Proust's writing process: she did not figure in his original plan for the novel.⁵² She could therefore be seen, as Christine Cano puts it, as something of a textual "accident."⁵³ When *Swann's Way* was published in 1913, the *Recherche* was to include only three volumes: *Swann's Way* (*Du côté de chez Swann*), *The Guermantes Way* (*Le côté de Guermantes*), and *Time Regained* (*Le temps retrouvé*). Proust most likely wrote the name "Albertine" in his manuscripts only after Agostinelli had fled his service and died during the spring of 1914 in a plane crash.⁵⁴ According to Antoine Compagnon, the appearance of an "Albertine novel" in the midst of a "novel of memory" marks an eruption in the text, disturbing the symmetry Proust had planned between the two "ways" and between time "lost" and "regained."⁵⁵ The interruption of the 1914–1918 war, and the publication hiatus it imposed, further transformed the shape of the *Recherche*, giving Proust time to expand the Balbec material and clearing space for Albertine to leap through the novel before ultimately plunging to her death. During this imposed publication hiatus, the proportions of the text began to go awry. As Suzanne Guerlac observes, the intrusion of the war into Proust's carefully planned, symmetrical form causes the narrative to "go off in new directions." With the arrival of Albertine, "something like improvisation sets in."⁵⁶

Historical contingency, then, and not a preorchestrated artistic plan, facilitated Albertine's appearance in the novel, and her sexuality is similarly protean. Despite the narrator's eventual attempts to contain her and compel her fidelity, Albertine neither accepts to play her part in a marriage plot, nor is she quite legible as a lesbian. In her ambiguous queerness, Albertine resists typification. Sedgwick underscores this point, noting that the period's predictable "inversion model" of sexuality is simply not applied to Albertine, whose practices and desires are never subjected to taxonomic scrutiny.⁵⁷ As Elisabeth Ladenson puts it, female same-sex sexuality is the "site of unpredictability" in the *Recherche* and the "exception" to the novel's stated rules.⁵⁸

Proust plays on the association of queer femininity with the contingent and the contextual in *Within a Budding Grove* when he invokes biological terminology to describe the *petite bande*. When the fluidly mobile young women materialize near the painter Elstir's villa, the group assumes a strange biological form, morphing into a vegetal-animal hybrid. The narrator is struck by the sudden apparition of "a few spores of the zoophytic band of girls" ("quelques sporades de la bande zoophytique des jeunes filles").⁵⁹ A now historical term, a *zoophyte* is a threshold phenomenon, indicating an animal with plant features, such as a sponge or a coral.⁶⁰ Drawing on a reservoir of zoophytic imagery, the Proustian narrator will later liken queer men ("inverts," in his lexicon) to jellyfish, which he imagines as the "mauve orchids of the sea."⁶¹ But it is the *petite bande*—these "young girls in flower"—that most strikingly incarnates the species-exploding possibilities of the zoophyte. Although we might typically assume that biological or zoological metaphors would function as essentializing agents, indicating congenitally immutable traits, it is just the opposite in the *Recherche*.⁶² Indeed, even the term *zoophyte* itself is stretchable and polyvalent in Proust's imagination: when the word appears for the second time in *Within a Budding Grove*, it qualifies not the girls themselves but the narrator's love for them. Oddly, *zoophyte* here means not a vegetal-animal hybrid but a deindividualized or plural form of life, rhizomatically shared out among multiple entities.⁶³ Elsewhere in the volume, Proust experiments further with the language of marine zoology in order to convey this sense of coral-reef-like assemblage or compound being. He depicts the *petite bande* as resembling "those primitive organisms in which the individual barely exists by itself, is constituted by the polypary rather than by each of the polyps that compose it."⁶⁴ Proust's beach is a stage, a casino, a network of routes; only rarely do we catch a glimpse of the more-than-human ecological world beyond the built spectacle of the resort. His zoophytic improvisations anticipate the seashore visions of Woolf and Carson—each alert in her own way to the geological and biological forces that exceed the dynamics of human leisure.

As Proust riffs in this way on biological concepts, he is working to compose a new language of desire, one that we could not easily classify in terms of a hetero-homo binary. In "Combray," the narrator is enchanted by the look and smell of hawthorn flowers, and if he also swoons over Mademoiselle Vinteuil and Gilberte Swann in turn, it is because they happen to have entered the orbit of that floral apparition. At Balbec, he expands this vegetal love to encompass marine organisms, delving into an imaginary world of polyparies and zoophytes in order to convey an exceptionally flexible and capacious form of attachment—one that resurges in variations and recapitulations, leaping from object to object. In their transient, hybrid mode of existence and their kinship with various seaside life forms, the *petite bande* is the very incarnation of the littoral zone. To fall in love with them is to fall in love with the seashore itself.

The mobile spore of adolescent girls forms the connective tissue between the expansive zoology of the seaside, with its profusion of strange life forms, and the belle époque beach resort as a dynamic and unpredictable site of encounter. In other words, Proust's fascination with female same-sex desire and gender rebellion is intimately bound not only to his affection for invented, unstable biological typologies but also to his penchant for a different kind of surprise—his "gambling fever." The queerness of Proust's casino indexes the historical alliance between nonnormative sexualities and concepts of chance and contingency, or what could be otherwise. As Valery Rohy has argued, when fin de siècle heteronormative cultures "enshrine" straightness as "the ultimate human necessity," all other forms of desire appear "radically unnecessary."[65] In describing Albertine and her friends (and their ambiguously sapphic desires) as zoophytically changeable and dynamic, Proust embraces this contingency effect.[66] Especially allied with the seaside and its casino, queer women in the *Recherche* trouble assumptions about the constancy of desire and of sexual-object choice. In this regard, the Proustian seaside gives rise to what Benjamin Kahan terms "a homosexuality not of persons, but of place—one that circulates like rumor attaching to bodies rather than one that emerges from within them."[67] The practices and affiliations of Albertine and her *bande* do not indicate a stable state but a style of existence that takes "ephemerality, mutability, transitoriness, and environmental factors" as conditions of possibility.[68] The narrator's enchantment with Albertine and her beach-born friends is ultimately an enchantment with contingency itself—and with Balbec as the site of the little gang's irrepressible and exuberant play.

BEACH BODIES

From the start, then, the beach was a fantasmatic landscape for Proust—a space of desire in which the intimate mixes with the irremediably strange. The dreamlike quality of the seashore is already evident in *Jean Santeuil*, the fragmentary novel that Proust began in 1895 (while on a seaside holiday in Beg-Meil, Brittany, with his boyfriend Reynaldo Hahn) and worked on for several years before abandoning it in 1899.⁶⁹ Many pages are devoted to the beach in this early work, which opens with a preface in which the narrator describes lingering during the off-season while vacationing in northern France. In *Jean Santeuil*, however, the beach is not yet a casino, much less a site of acrobatic social mobility. Instead, it features, tellingly, as an enormous bed. In one episode, the eponymous hero lies on the dunes with his companion for hours, reading, dozing, and digesting by day, watching the moonlight on the sea by night: "But before settling down to read during the long hours of digestion . . . the two young men would lie for long periods trying to sleep, exchanging remarks at rare intervals, smoking, turning their faces this way and that, looking at the sea or sky, keeping the sun from their faces with spread handkerchiefs."⁷⁰ This queer seaside fantasy leads to a remarkable discussion of animal life, wherein the narrator describes envying snakes, lizards, whales, seals, and owls for their ability to fully live the experience of sensory exposure and intensity that Barthes will later call "the beach effect":

> "We envy the boa constrictor whose digestion lasts a week and who can then sleep for several days on end. We envy the lizard who spends hours on a warm stone, taking in the sunshine. We envy the whale who takes lovely trips in the Pacific, the seals who play in the sunlit sea, the gulls who play in storms and let themselves be swept along by the wind."

> "Nous envions le boa pour qui digérer est l'occupation d'une semaine et qui peut alors dormir plusieurs jours de suite. Nous envions le lézard qui reste des journées sur une pierre chaude à se laisser pénétrer de soleil. Nous envions la baleine qui fait de beaux voyages dans le Pacifique, les phoques qui jouent dans la mer au soleil, les mouettes qui jouent dans les orages et se laissent porter par le vent."⁷¹

Here we see Proust exploring the seductive alterity of seaside embodiment, which he imagines in peculiarly creaturely and metabolic terms, as a "process of digestion which absorbs the whole of our being, and includes the sight of the sea and the sky and the screaming of the gulls."⁷² The experience of lying by the water's edge sparks this vision of a different rhythm of life—one in which intellect cedes to a more elemental way of being. Anticipating the transspecies improvisations of *Within a Budding Grove*, the seaside in *Jean Santeuil* is a zoomorphic interface where the human converges with its other.

When Proust wrote the beach into the *Recherche*, he no longer depicted it as a bed—although this early vision subtly shapes his account of Balbec as a dreamlike expanse on which figures appear and vanish.[73] In *Jean Santeuil*, the encounter with the unthinking intensity, or "intoxications" (*enivrements*) of seaside life occurs primarily in the horizontal mode. In the *Recherche*, it will materialize in the mobile form of a body in flight. Balbec, with its central casino, its chance meetings and unexpected mixings, is a place marked by the stylistic break, the wayward spring. On this exposed edge, which Proust describes as opening a "breach" in the middle of the world, waves "leap" one after the other like "jumpers on a springboard" ("des sauteurs sur un tremplin").[74] When a little band of adolescent girls materializes like a flock of birds and traverses time and space in a manner the narrator has never seen before, we are witness to the apparition of an entirely new corporeal style.[75] In the Paris of Proust's novel, the laws of the aristocratic salons still hold sway. At the Proustian seaside, even the laws of gravity seem to lose their hold.

How would we have to adjust our critical assumptions in order to recognize the *leap* as a quintessential Proustian posture or spatiotemporal configuration?[76] Compagnon has drawn our attention to the Proustian stumble, taking the narrator's comical performance of lurching on the uneven paving stones of the Guermantes's courtyard as evidence of Proust's penchant for disequilibrium, disproportion, and unresolved dialectic.[77] Yet readers do not readily associate this author—who famously wrote in bed—with a repertoire of mid-air poses. Indeed, the bodily posture most readers would ally with Proust is the supine position, or some variation on it. Proust, whose novel begins in the bedroom and periodically draws us back in, is a writer known to have worked long nocturnal hours in a "semi-recumbent" posture.[78] Moreover, within the diegetic universe of the novel, the bed features as a launching pad for fiction or zero degree for narrativity. As Gérard Genette has shown, the bedroom is the point of origin for narrative in the *Recherche*, functioning as the "embryonic cell" for Proustian fictionality itself. Genette demonstrates that the dynamic zigzagging from one time period to another that we see especially in the first volume is launched from a bed: an initial position of insomnia or half-sleep, a liminal space through which the narrative keeps having to pass in order to spin out each of its new scenarios.[79] It is therefore striking when, in the Balbec section of *Within a Budding Grove,* Proust instead spotlights the image of a cheeky young girl in flight, hurtling spontaneously through space. While we do learn that the narrator enjoys lying around on the dunes—"Ah, so you like basking in the sun like a lizard?" Albertine scoffs—this indolent pose scarcely features at Balbec.[80]

Art historian Linda Nochlin has observed that the invention of the leisure beach involved "the politics and policy of putting the body in its place." Anthropologist Marc Augé similarly depicts the beach as a phenomenon that draws attention to the "occupation of space and the management of the body."[81] In Proust, however, a rebellious body emerges on the sand—a collective metaphor-body that flauntingly oversteps its bounds. The narrator is waiting one day in front of the Grand Hôtel when he spots an apparition he has never seen before—a little band of adolescent girls, moving along the sea like a "stain" or "striking patch of color," a "flock of gulls," a strain of music, "a luminous comet," or "a bower of Pennsylvania roses."[82] The *petite bande* is an engine of metaphor—a shifting assemblage of features and qualities that the novel cannot stop likening to one thing or another. As if revved up to the point of flight, one of the girls suddenly breaks with the pack and takes to the air. Leaping over the head of a shocked old banker, she brushes his cap with her "nimble feet."[83] This particular episode is so important to Proust that it becomes a refrain: he will remind us of it four more times in the volume, never missing a chance to draw our attention to the image of the tall girl (Andrée, we'll later learn, though the narrator will misremember the leaper as Gisèle in *The Guermantes Way*) who jumped over the elderly gentleman—referred to, alternately, as the "old banker," the "terrified old man," the "octogenarian," and "the First President."

Here it is helpful to recall that Proust was writing—and choreographing the *petite bande*—at a cultural moment preoccupied with the expressive potential of gesture. Indeed, we might understand Andrée's leap as a turn-of-the-century "kinesthetic" or "cultural-corporeal structure of feeling."[84] Writing against the assumption that industrial capitalism "processes" bodies into "dissociated, fetishized, ultimately empty and machinable elements," Hillel Schwartz argues that modernism saw the emergence of a new kinesthetic focus on "expressive release" rather than "practiced achievement."[85] Nineteenth-century ballet was essentially a "spectacle of pirouettes, overhead lifts, set mimetic attitudes, statuesque positions and plane geometries" in which the torso remained tightly corseted and "fitted to an enduringly classical tradition."[86] By contrast, by using "the whole foot, the whole torso, the whole body," modern dance embraced "movements liberated from highly mannered codes of motion."[87] Flow was key: "dancing, one bent one's whole body to the whole music" and moved not to single beats, but to "the phrase or the center line."[88] Schwartz connects a range of early twentieth-century innovations to the "fluid, curvilinear gestures" of modern dance, including graphology, children's fingerpaints, the bicycle, the roller coaster, and even the invention of the slide fastener, or zipper. We might add the leisure beach to this list—Isadora Duncan, mother of modern dance, wrote that her "first idea of movement" came from the "rhythm of the waves." Duncan's style of dance bore some resemblance to the spectacle of the *petite bande* traversing the beach: like Duncan's, their movements include "running, hopping, jumping—sometimes, just walking."[89]

In their fluid, unscripted mobility, the *petite bande* incarnates style as difference from the norm, as swerve from good behavior, and as leap:

> They could not set eyes on an obstacle without amusing themselves by clearing it either in a running jump or with both feet together, because they were all brimming over with the exuberance that youth so urgently needs to expend that ... it can never let pass an opportunity to jump or to slide without indulging in it, interrupting and interspersing even the slowest walk—as Chopin his most melancholy phrase—with graceful deviations in which caprice is blended with virtuosity.[90]

> Elles ne pouvaient voir un obstacle sans s'amuser à le franchir en prenant leur élan ou à pieds joints, parce qu'elles étaient toutes remplies, exubérantes, de cette jeunesse qu'on a si grand besoin de dépenser ..., on ne laisse jamais passer une occasion de saut ou de glissade sans s'y livrer consciencieusement, interrompant, semant, sa marche lente—comme Chopin la phrase la plus mélancolique—de gracieux détours où le caprice se mêle à la virtuosité.[91]

The girls' impudence—"we're too badly behaved" ("nous avons trop mauvais genre"), as Albertine puts it—is an expression of their gift for "mingling all the arts:" they leap and sing "in the manner of those poets of old for whom the different genres were not yet separate."[92] Inextricable from the beach setting from which they spring, their congruous bodies traverse space like poetry in motion, ready to lift off. Examining the gesture of the leap in Homeric poetry, Alex Purves argues that "the sheer force of [the epic hero's] kinetic energy has the potential to take the narrative off track." Occasions of leaping draw the reader's attention to the possibility that the hero "might break into the now, even into the fiction of living his story as it happens, by acting spontaneously and going off-script."[93] The *petite bande*, too, draws on the plot-distorting energy of the epic leap—and yet, as "ancient" as their art may be, the *bande*'s gender-bending, collective disregard for traditional rules of genre is the mark of their modernity, and Balbec's. In the girls' improvisatory, elastic choreography, we see Proust's novel working to disrupt its own "muscle memory"—to depart from its habitual pathways and styles of movement and desire.[94]

The figure of the leap is compelling because it combines various concepts key to Proust's vision of Balbec: queer style, contingency, improvisation, and the casino as the grounds for such insouciant play. If Proust himself enjoyed gambling, his narrator invests his affections instead in the wild mobility of the *petite bande* as it bounds through the casino's halls and ballroom. The casino is in fact always associated in the *Recherche* with these girls—as a setting for their virtuosic misbehavior. The narrator accompanies them to the casino on rainy days, conspiring with their mischief and admiring them as they jump all over the place. Once again, the girls cannot seem to keep their feet on the ground:

> We would spend the day in the Casino, where on such days it would have seemed to me impossible not to go.... And I willingly joined my new friends in playing tricks on the dancing master. As a rule we had to listen to admonitions from the manager, or from some of his staff usurping directorial powers, because my friends ... could not go from the hall to the ballroom without breaking into a run, jumping over all the chairs, and sliding along the floor, their balance maintained by a graceful poise of their outstretched arms.

> Nous passions la journée dans le casino où il m'eût paru ces jours-là impossible de ne pas aller.... Et j'aidais volontiers mes amies à jouer de mauvais

tours au professeur de danse. Nous subissions généralement quelques admonestations du tenancier ou des employés usurpant un pouvoir directorial parce que mes amies... ne pouvaient pas aller au vestibule, à la salle des fêtes, sans prendre leur élan, sauter par-dessus toutes les chaises, revenir sur une glissade en gardant leur équilibre par un gracieux mouvement de bras.[95]

During his second seaside holiday, the narrator will become suspicious of Albertine's every move. But in *Within a Budding Grove* the figure of the flying leap encapsulates the ethos of Balbec—a site in which a new choreography of desire and a new modernist energy are at play.

In his turn toward the beach as a setting for kinesthetic expression, Proust brings his novel into conversation with early twentieth-century mass cultural and avant-garde art forms. One could almost imagine that his depiction of Balbec as a stage on which adolescent girls vault over bankers and kick over casino chairs was inspired by the improvisatory,

FIGURE 1.2. Windswept choreography. Screen grab from Chaplin, *By the Sea*, 1915.

gestural slapstick of Charlie Chaplin's 1915 *By the Sea*, a one-reel film shot in a single day along the Ocean Front Walk and Abbott Kinney Pier in Santa Monica.[96] (Proust probably never saw this film, but he did, in 1915, enthusiastically sport what he called a Chaplin-style moustache, according to his housekeeper, Céleste Albaret.)[97] Chaplin explores the seaside as a zone in which marital relations are suspended and other sorts of adventures and affiliations might occur: the film's first intertitle—"Wifie is Away"—invokes marriage only to set it aside. When the tramp appears, he strolls down a promenade, munching a banana, then tosses the peel and slips spectacularly on it, feet in the air—a first indication that bodies will have difficulty staying upright on Chaplin's beach. It is true that characters fall down regularly enough in Chaplin's vaudeville-inspired films, but in *By the Sea*, bodies and objects are carried by the wind, which takes on an unusual degree of agentic force. The wind features here as a wild, decorum-undermining element that represents—here as in Proust—a more general social volatility. As if the sand were but an extension of the wind that continuously knocks them off their feet, the tussling, flirting actors are whipped by the seaside breeze and thrown off balance by the beach's slippery, granular surfaces. In Chaplin's version of the Proustian hat gag, the tramp's wind-tossed bowler cap gets hopelessly mixed up with a stranger's straw boater, leading to a brawl in which the gale gets the upper hand. Chaplin's beach is thus a vaudevillean version of Balbec—a space of identity-blurring acrobatic mobility, a zone infused with *élan*, in all of its senses: energetic momentum, impulsion or thrownness; vital force; erotic rush or romantic urge.[98]

As I have noted, Proust's attention to the *petite bande*'s stylized seaside embodiment also draws him close to the early twentieth-century revolution in modern dance.[99] In fact, the seaside leap features centrally in the 1924 one-act comic ballet *Le Train bleu*, the libretto of which was written by Proust's friend (or frenemy), the poet, playwright, and filmmaker Jean Cocteau. (Cocteau believed himself to be the model for Proust's minor seaside figure of "Octave"—future playwright; virtuosic dancer, golfer, and tennis player; gambler with a preference for baccarat; "gigolo" and accessory to the *petite bande*. Octave is notable less for any personal quality than for his interruptive mode of apparition: he is always cropping up out of nowhere and just as quickly vanishing.)[100] The ballet's title is a reference to

PROUST'S LEAP

the luxury train that connected Paris to the Côte d'Azur, and according to a note in the text, the set presents an "elegant beach in 1924." This ballet, performed by the Ballets Russes that same year, was the product of a dazzling array of talents—costumes by Chanel, a curtain designed by Picasso, a score by Darius Milhaud, and choreography by Bronislava Nijinska.[101] Part avant-garde experiment, part circus act, *Le Train bleu* is a generic and tonal oddity; its cast of characters include a golf player and a tennis champion, along with a chorus of camera-waving, bathing-suit clad "gigolos" and "tarts." The ballet's light, satirical plot, like that of Chaplin's *By the Sea*, is an interplay of squabbling and flirtation; in the first scene, the curtain opens on what Cocteau calls "ridiculous gestures," involving vigorous calisthenics and postcard-like poses. The sparse, geometric set includes bathing cabins framed by a cliff and a casino. Most notably, it presents the sea in the guise of a large trampoline, so that when a bather leaps into it he bounces off and "disappears in the air into stage left."[102] The beach in *Le Train bleu* is thus not only a space of satire and pantomime but a stage on which novel

FIGURE 1.3. *Le Train bleu*, 1924. Library of Congress, Music Division.

bodily feats become possible; the ballet played especially on the gifts of a new star dancer who stood on his hands and performed "breathtaking" acrobatic stunts.[103] In a variation on both Chaplin's hat swap gag and on the first, failed kiss between the Proustian narrator and Albertine, *Le Train bleu* ends with two characters meeting at center stage for an embrace: their lips are about to touch when the young man's cap is blown into the sea. As the curtain drops, the dancers take a trampoline plunge into the waves.

Despite a shared orientation toward aerial movement, Chaplin's and Cocteau's seaside kinesthetics are clearly quite different in tone. *Le Train bleu,* set on the fashionable Riviera, epitomizes Cocteau's signature mix of avant-gardism and leisured frivolity—a phenomenon that ballet historian Lynn Garafola terms "lifestyle modernism."[104] *By the Sea*, by contrast, is set on a public beach in California where tramps, drunks, and wealthy types find themselves in close proximity—even sharing a (toppling) seaside bench in the final shot. Ultimately, though, both the ballet and the film underscore the challenge of maintaining borders and managing bodies on the beach. In his libretto, Cocteau highlights the Chaplinesque quality of interactions among characters, noting that the tennis champion and golf player should spar in a manner resembling Chaplin's cinematic fights.[105] In *By the Sea*, the problem of the unruly body is more explicit: in tandem with its wind-swept, head-over-heals choreography, the film highlights the cinematographic challenge of framing and centering bodies on the beach. Early in the film a passerby (or curious onlooker) steps into the shot at medium range and the camera pulls away. Later, an adventurous swimmer and a jauntily trotting dog cross into the background of the scene. We might interpret these intrusions of ordinary life into the cinematic frame—rare in Chaplin—as evidence of the particular porosity and commonness of the seaside as setting.[106]

The parallels between these works and the *Recherche* shed fresh light on Proust: as an aesthetic risk-taker whose experimental imagination is energized by—and in turn energizes—both mass cultural and avant-garde phenomena. Reading *In Search of Lost Time* in conjunction with cinematic slapstick and a trampoline-enhanced ballet helps us to recognize Balbec as a space of performance, with its sea like a "dazzling amphitheater" (*cirque éblouissant*), its catwalk-like promenade, and its characters who strut and leap in the spotlight. For Proust, as for Cocteau and Chaplin, the seashore is a virtual springboard on which a new kinetic grammar takes form.

"NOUS AVONS REGARDÉ"

This chapter has explored Balbec as a casino and a stage—a site of improvisation and of kinesthesis. Now it's time to go backstage, behind the scenes. Proust drafted parts of his novel in view of the beach, and Balbec, too, is sometimes revealed as a construction site rather than a finished spectacle. *Within a Budding Grove* contains some of the novel's most potently fragile points—occasions when the fabric of the text is stretched thin and the fictional illusion appears on the verge of giving way. These scenes of near-dissolution are rich with potentiality, as the spirit of contingency becomes the dominant atmospheric tone. Proust experiments in such episodes with the limits of his narrator's epistemological power and authority, allowing us to imagine what the world might look like from other points of view.

From the start of the Balbec chapter in *Within a Budding Grove*, we understand that vision and perspective will be problematic in this stretch. This breakdown of any unitary, masterful vantage point is evident during the narrator's initial trip to Balbec, when he must dash back and forth between the windows on each side of the train car in order to "reassemble" the fragments of the ever-changing morning. He tells us that he is "collecting" these bits on a "canvas" in order to "obtain a comprehensive view," but the effect is anything but comprehensive: in an inversion of the bourgeois tradition of touristic landscape aesthetics, the world is shown to be in pieces, and it will never be put back together.[107] No single perspective will suffice to encompass the whole.

Once the narrator arrives at the seaside, we encounter another hiccup in narrative focalization—an unusual instance in which the narrator relinquishes his perspectival centrality and lets another gaze supplant his own. His—and thus our—very first view of the sea is in fact mediated through his grandmother's eyes. The narrator tells us that it is she who opens his shutters early in the morning. She then relates "what time it was, what sort of day it would be, that it was not worth while my getting up and coming to the window, that there was a mist over the sea, whether the baker's shop had opened yet, what the vehicle was that I could hear passing."[108]

What should we make of this peculiar scene of shared or borrowed vision in a novel that so rarely plays with perspective in this way? The narrator downplays the occasion, describing the view his grandmother relates as the mere "introit," or opening hymn of the day's liturgical ritual—"insignificant," "trifling," a "little scrap of life." But this first vision of the sea is striking precisely in its atypicality. As Genette has shown, in Proust, generally, "it is the 'hero's point of view' that governs the narrative, with his restrictions of field. . . . Proustian descriptions are rigorously focalized: not only does their 'duration' never exceed that of real contemplation, but their content never exceeds what is actually perceived by the contemplator."[109] Of course, the Balbec window episode remains subjective and internally focalized through the hero's perceptual activity—he recounts to us what his grandmother recounted to him ("she would tell me what time it was, what sort of day it would be . . ."). Yet the scene pushes up against the boundaries of the Proustian system of focalization, exposing the limits of the narrator's mastery.[110]

This is not to suggest that *In Search of Lost Time* is otherwise static in its narrative mood. Genette notes that the *Recherche* tends to slip in "polytonal" fashion between internal and external focalization.[111] Normally, however, when the narration jumps inside the head of a character to (implausibly) expose thoughts that the narrator as embedded hero could not have known at the time, the effect is not to undermine the narrator's authority but to underscore his epistemological reach. But when the grandmother offers us our first small glimpse of the fog-covered sea, something new is happening. She substitutes for her grandson, acting as his eyes, describing a scene for him to vicariously absorb. The narrator depends on his beloved grandmother not only to assuage his night terrors but to supplement his vision by day.

As this occasion indicates, there is something ethereal and unstable about the representation of the Proustian seaside. Sometimes at Balbec, Proust underscores this effect such that it seems as if the fictional apparatus is liable to come unanchored and drift away. We catch a glimpse of the miragelike quality of the seaside when, during a carriage ride with his grandmother and the Marquise de Villeparisis, the narrator sees the entire scene begin to "dissolve" and reveal itself as a "fiction." Balbec suddenly appears as "a place to which [he] had never gone except in imagination," the Marquise as "a character in a novel," and the landscape before him as a literary fantasy—"the reality which one recaptures on raising one's eyes from the book which one has been reading and which describes an environment [*un milieu*] into which one has come to believe that one has been bodily transported."[112] In this remarkable instance of lucidity (or hallucination), it is as if the novel's very edifice—the setting and characters into which we have invested belief—begins to float. The effect is not to reduce the rich seaside world to a solipsistic projection, but to intimate that the narrator, too, might be a figure in a dream that exceeds him.

I have suggested that we interpret this volume's preoccupation with the figure of the leap as evidence of Proust's attunement to a broader cultural turn toward expressive, contextual, anticlassical gesture. Another way to think about the leap would be to connect it to other moments in the volume in which Proust plays with weightlessness or levitation. On such occasions, instead of diving down into psychic depths—as the narrator does in "Combray"'s famous scene of involuntary memory—the narrating consciousness (or the world that consciousness describes) seems to hover, unmoored. Consider, for instance, how the narrator's sense of his surroundings shifts when he experiments in this volume with drunkenness, reveling in being released from the weight of the real. Intoxication—more frequently referenced in *Within a Budding Grove* than in any other volume of the novel—induces a state of narrative irresponsibility. In this regard it offers a contrast to the productivity associated with the much more celebrated act of tea drinking, which is resonant with Christian transubstantiation and mnemonic rebirth. An entire novel can spring from a teacup in the *Recherche*, but a bottle of champagne produces nothing of substance. The seaside facilitates this turn toward surfaces and away from the rhetoric of depth.

The language of intoxication—a different kind of propulsion, airiness, or weightlessness—suffuses the scene in which the *petite bande* first appears on the beach. The narrator is certain that friendship with these girls would be "intoxicating" (*une telle ivresse*), and, immediately upon learning that one of them is named "Simonet," he transports us into an iterative dreamscape of drunken nights. Recounting evenings of drinking in the neighboring resort town of Rivebelle, he recalls occasions when the diegetic universe is transformed into airy seafoam and "everything is reduced to appearances."[113] Inebriation appears here as an experiment in narrative witness: drunk, the narrator is present only to his own immediate sensation, and the fictional world seems to float away. In his "exaltation," he exists in the pure phenomenality of the present: "all the rest, parents, work, pleasures, girls at Balbec, weighed no more than a flake of foam in a strong wind."[114] What can we make of this fantasy of the fictional world's disintegration? Here the ethos of involuntary memory is turned inside out and upside down: we are present neither to the recollection of a lost past nor to a miraculous act of aesthetic creation, but to the erosion and drift of the very foundation the fiction stands upon. Alcohol is thus introduced in this volume as a mechanism for narrative release, freeing narrator and reader alike from the weight of novelistic telos. Intoxication aligns with the logic of vicariousness in the novel, as the narrator essentially permits the drink to become his eyes. In this regard, drinking champagne recapitulates the pleasure of looking with and through his grandmother as she offers up her early morning vision of the sea.[115]

Another form of vicariousness—an alternate way of sharing out perspectival control—occurs when the painter, Elstir, enters the Balbec scene. One night while the narrator is sipping champagne in a coastal restaurant with Saint-Loup, the two spot Elstir at a neighboring table. When the narrator subsequently visits Elstir's studio, he gets a lesson in how to see. Elstir's vision decomposes type, freeing perception from category, stripping things of their names. He invites the narrator to hone his gaze away from clearly delineated, preconceived objects and focus instead on the "amphibious": on "haze" and "foam," on "dusky," "transparent," disintegrating forms—rocks that seem to have been "volatilized" by the heat and reduced to dusk, for example, or a seascape in which a "powdery haze of sunlight and crumbling waves" melds land into water, and water into land.[116] Exploring the interplay of human and more-than-human forces, Elstir's seaside is a site of elemental, nearly alchemical transfiguration.

As indicated by such fusion of touch and sight, land and sea, the modernist beach is not simply a frame for characters or a backdrop for plot. Rather, like Elstir's studio itself, it is a "laboratory" enabling "a sort of new creation of the world."[117] In particular, the painter appears to regard his surroundings with the tentacular sensibility that queer ecotheorist Eva Hayward, in an essay on starfish, calls "fingeryeyes."[118] *Within a Budding Grove* as a whole is enamored of this haptic style of visual perception: it's as if we are seeing and feeling the world through Elstir even before entering the painter's studio. So, for example, the narrator imaginatively jumbles and rearranges the visual features of the *petite bande*—"je les avais répartis et agglomérés"—as if images of rosy cheeks, green eyes, or a tiny nose were a heap of playing cards to be shuffled and dealt.[119] Likewise, the view of foamy waves, seen from the narrator's hotel room, becomes tactile, presenting the "delicacy of a feather . . . fixed in creamy enamel."[120] Even the air at Balbec is textural, sometimes made of a "transparent, dusky jelly," other times "compact" and sparkling "like a lump of rock crystal."[121]

Vicariously invested as it is in Elstir's painterly gaze, *Within a Budding Grove* is exceptionally preoccupied with light. No other volume in the *Recherche* contains as many references to *lumière* as this one does, although the sun-drenched pages of "Combray" come close. One of the things that Proust found particularly seductive about the beach is what he terms its "luminous plenitude."[122] Light is central to Proust's aesthetic imagination: the novel as a whole is speckled with luminescence. The narrator's first encounter with literature takes the form of a magic lantern show—a medieval legend flickering eerily over his childhood bedroom wall—and aesthetic epiphanies in the novel tend to feature light, such as a pinkish reflection on a pond after a rain shower, the interplay of luminous church steeples seen from a moving carriage, or a "little patch of yellow wall" in a Vermeer painting. At Balbec, such illumination is not occasional but omnipresent. The narrator arrives in Normandy expecting stormy skies and tempestuous, sea-lashed cliffs. Instead, he discovers a seaside world bathed in sunlight.

Strangely, light is not necessarily a clarifying phenomenon in this volume—it tends to be opaque rather than transparent. Riffing on Baudelaire's "sun's rays upon the sea" ("soleil rayonnant sur la mer"), Proust imagines seaside light as a kind of stretchable, mutable substance—a phenomenon of "liquid mobility."[123] His description of the seashore highlights what he calls a "diversity of lighting effects": at one moment, the "the sun spreads out" like a giant bounding down a mountainside; at the next, it "laughs" tenderly on the waves.[124] The *petite bande* is particularly allied with this radiance: their gaze plays on the narrator like "sunlight on a wall," and Albertine is described as "bathed in the light that streams from the other girls."[125] Later, Proust will gather up this figure of tactile luminosity and recast it more explicitly as the effect of queer desire, and specifically as the effect of girls desiring other girls. When the novel returns to Balbec two volumes later, the beach has become a kind of fantasmatic lesbian cruising ground. Lesbian desire is figured here as a "luminous phenomenon," desirous gazes between women leaving "a sort of phosphorescent trail going from one to the other."[126] As these examples indicate, Proust's beach is a light show and a space of vicarious, elemental desire—a desire that emerges as much from the radiant seaside itself as from any human subject.

The experimental vicariousness patterning Proust's beach is nowhere more evident than in the final scene of *Within a Budding Grove*. This last description of the beach opens a new vantage point on Balbec. In the ultimate pages of the volume, Proust places his narrator in a darkened hotel room, his heart pounding with joy as he listens to the vibrant soundscape that wafts up through his shuttered window. Here, the text asks us to imaginatively reconstruct the luminous seaside from within the shadowy room and to extrapolate a visual scene from a purely acoustic one:

> I knew that my friends were on the promenade, but I did not see them. . . . I did not see my friends, but (while there mounted to my belvedere the shout of the newsboys, the "journalists" as Françoise used to call them, the shouts of the bathers and of children at play, punctuating like the cries of sea-birds the sound of the gently breaking waves) I guessed their presence, I heard their laughter enveloped like the laughter of the Nereids in the soft surge of sound that rose to my ears. "We looked up," said Albertine in the evening, "to see if you were coming down. But your shutters were still closed when the concert began." At ten o'clock, sure enough, it broke out beneath my windows.[127]

> Je savais que mes amies étaient sur la digue mais je ne les voyais pas. . . . Je ne voyais pas mes amies, mais (tandis qu'arrivaient jusqu'à mon belvédère l'appel des marchands de journaux, "des journalistes," comme les nommait Françoise, les appels des baigneurs et des enfants qui jouaient, ponctuant à la façon des cris des oiseaux de mer le bruit du flot qui doucement se brisait), je devinais leur présence, j'entendais leur rire enveloppé comme celui des néréides dans le doux déferlement qui montait jusqu'à mes oreilles. "Nous avons regardé, me disait le soir Albertine, pour voir si vous descendriez. Mais vos volets sont restés fermés, même à l'heure du concert." A dix heures, en effet, il éclatait sous mes fenêtres.[128]

The scene is unusual because the beach has until now been described in such visual terms, as a series of lighting effects. And suddenly, Proust flicks the switch and gives us the whole thing again, this time in the dark.[129]

The narrator cannot see his friends—he insists on this point—but he can "guess their presence" in the "soft surge of sound that [rises] to [his] ears" from the beach below. The idea of a bedroom as the place in which fiction is made is not in itself unusual in Proust: both "Combray" and *The Captive* (*La Prisonnière*, 1925) open with an episode in which the narrator envisions or projects an outside world from within a closed bedroom. But the passage in which we hear the beach from inside the narrator's hotel room is different because of *where* it occurs—at the very end, rather than the opening of the volume. The reader has already spent considerable time in this seaside world, which has by now taken on a certain (virtual) weight and reality. The abrupt shift in sensory channel erodes our sense of stability, underscoring the contingency of the scene.

Yet what is most surprising about this occasion is the perspectival about-face that occurs when, without warning, the reader suddenly finds herself on the beach with Albertine and her friends, in the sun, looking up at the narrator's shuttered window. At Balbec, bodies take to the air, and this leaping effect occurs even at the level of narrative point of view. We could say that Albertine's interruption here: her line, "nous avons regardé" ("we looked up"), simply confirms the narrator's epistemological control, underscoring the correctness of his "guess." Yet this unusual moment—like the grandmother's earlier vision of the foggy sea through the window—also grants the reader a certain breathing space, permitting us to peek out of the dark projection booth and look back at it from without. At the very least, in its gentle disaggregation and remixing of sight and sound, and its sharing out of perspective, the passage flirts with the possibility of a less rigorously controlled point of view.

The narrator cannot see his friends on the promenade, and he does not rise from his bed to peek at them through the curtain. Such ocular passivity is surprising in a subject characterized by visual curiosity and given to active descriptions. His penchant for what Genette calls "acrobatic indiscretion" is frequently on display—as when he watches Mademoiselle Vinteuil and her lover through a window at Montjouvain, for instance, or spies on Charlus and Jupien through a fanlight.[130] On such occasions, the narrative focalization remains internal despite the evident insufficiency of the narrator's point of view. Compare such claustrophobic solipsism to the overlapping visual and acoustic channels evoked in the hotel room soundscape, and to the unexpected reversal of perspectives indicated by Albertine's "we looked up" ("nous avons regardé"). The eruption of the girls' point of view does not simply deflate or reroute an instance of internally focalized descriptive euphoria. Rather, it underscores the provisional quality of the narrator's perspective and, by extension, the ephemerality and precariousness of this seaside occasion. Almost at once, the moment is over and is being remembered—and remembered differently—by someone else. This is not a leap *down*—a fall from a solipsistic dream state into reality, as occurs elsewhere in the novel. It is, rather, a vicarious leap *out*— a flight toward other forms of being and perspectival possibilities. Albertine and her friends are not simply objects of the narrator's aesthetic perception here. Rather, they are active beholders; they share in the scene, which the narrator hears—or imagines hearing—but that they alone can see.

As this chapter has shown, in Proust, the beach has little to do with the logic of aesthetic redemption or time regained. Rather, it's a space of contingency, marked by the leap or luminous break. With its intoxicating, habit-disrupting social choreography, Balbec tenders a queer invitation of its own: the reader who lingers on Proust's beach is continuously reminded that things could be otherwise. At Balbec, an ethos of transgression and indetermination finds its ideal atmospheric milieu. This is a world on the edge, threshold of the unforeseen.

Chapter Two

INTERTIDAL WOOLF

Virginia Woolf's foundational childhood memory was of the beach. In "A Sketch of the Past," she recalls the feeling of "ecstasy" that overcame her as she lay "half asleep, half awake, in bed at the nursery at St. Ives . . . hearing the waves breaking, one, two, one, two, and sending a splash of water over the beach; and then breaking, one, two, one, two, behind a yellow blind." Woolf presents this seaside occasion as the "base" upon which the "bowl" of her life stands. Yet what is most striking about the scene is its unfixed and ungrounded quality—"ecstatic" means rapturous, entranced, but literally indicates a state of being spatially and temporally dislocated, out of place.[1] Indeed, Woolf describes feeling, as she heard the breaking waves and saw the light through the wind-blown blinds, "it is almost impossible that I should be here."[2] Woolf's perception of the seashore as a visual-acoustic dreamscape and a generator of rhythm, her sense of setting as both a holding environment and a zone of alterity and "ecstatic" disorientation, shaped the horizon of her thought, leaving its mark especially on that most coastal of modernist novels, *To the Lighthouse*.

Drawing on the paradoxical specificity and dislocation that animates this founding memory, the present chapter examines the queerness of Woolf's beach imaginary—understanding *queer* not in identitarian terms but as an orientation toward offbeat intimacies and "improper affiliations."[3] In the short story "Solid Objects" (1920), Woolf conceptualizes the beach as part of a constellation of urban commons and wastes—remainders of a precapitalist relation to the land. This text explores the intertidal zone's capacity to disrupt expected plotlines, transforming respectable masculine ambitions into something considerably less profitable. I argue that *To the Lighthouse* develops this vagrant line of thought, representing the beach as terrain that unsettles a Victorian epistemological and domestic inheritance. Woolf's conception of the beach in *To the Lighthouse* highlights rhythm—not only as an acoustic property but as a phenomenon of punctuated flow that shapes vision as well as sound, patterning everyday life and its contours of the expected and the imaginable. Woolf's aesthetic imagination, I argue, pivots especially in this novel on the tide-pooler's zigzagging point of view—a shifting practice of perception that affirms setting as an emergent phenomenon. *To the Lighthouse* connects this visionary style to queer types—spinster painters, opium-eating poets, and overlooked middle children who seek a different narrative path. Lingering at the edges of the domestic scene, these unmarriageable figures elucidate other, less productive and accountable ways of being in time.

Critics have long noted the importance of the sea to Woolf's literary imagination. As Laura Doyle aptly puts it: "no other English-language novelist's work is as completely flooded with waves, water, wrecks, and drowning."[4] Maritime infrastructures and sea travel—or what Nicole Rizzuto calls the "aqueous imaginary"—are important to Woolf's sense of self and nation, but I propose that it's ultimately not the ocean itself that serves as the focal point of her prose, but the shore.[5] If the sea indexes British imperial power—and the maps and routes of maritime exploration and conquest—the beach opens onto a different set of images and concepts, including tide pools, treasure hunts, and interspecies encounter. Woolf's fictions linger on this aesthetic playground, which is also a percussive, windswept edge.

Four of Woolf's major novels take place on or near a beach. *Jacob's Room* (1922) begins with the eponymous hero uncovering a sheep's jaw on the strand—archaic remainder, memento mori, and index of deathly forces that subtend and exceed this sandy rim. *Mrs. Dalloway* (1925) opens on a London day "fresh as if issued to children on a beach," and, despite its resolutely urban framing, the seashore functions as a shared chronotope connecting the novel's protagonists even as it signifies differently for each (figuring domestic "quiet" for Clarissa, existential shipwreck for Septimus, and affective "susceptibility" for Peter Walsh). *To the Lighthouse* (1927) takes place on a weirdly amalgamated Scottish/Cornish coast—more on this to follow—and represents the beach as both a parenthesis in the marriage plot and a refuge from the maritime beacon's navigational meter. *The Waves* (1931) is structured around intermittent interludes on a shore, the novel's biographical framing undercut by snapshots of a textured, more-than-human seaside temporality.

By setting her experimental fictions at the seashore, Woolf invites readers to dwell in a social and ecological margin—a transitory space in which the dominant beat or structuring metrical (and moral) order is suspended. It is true that twentieth-century beaches have often functioned as battlegrounds—sites of inequality and violent surveillance shaped by law and social custom. Beaches have frequently been segregated in one way or another. Indeed, in a 1905 diary entry, Woolf describes being told by a resident of St. Ives "how the working classes bathe, [and] where only people of good family were wont to use that privilege."[6] Yet, as the geographical interstice between land and sea, beaches also unsettle prevailing terrestrial norms. In Woolf, as in Proust, they function as cultural and aesthetic test sites—spaces for exploring alternative expressions of desire and styles of bodily movement. In *To the Lighthouse*, the beach indicates an intermediary zone beyond the home—a place where domestic gender regulations fade as the logic of social reproduction gives way to other rhythms. Woolf is especially drawn to this setting because it enables a different reckoning with time: on the beach, daily routines are relativized and conventional biographical, genealogical, and national time lines give way to the contrapuntal interplay of ephemerality and slowness. As critics have pointed out, Woolf is fascinated by scalar extremes, and her fictions often balance on the razor edge between the incandescent "moment" and the almost unimaginable expanses of "deep time."[7] Beach time is patterned by the clash of incommensurate temporal scales and by a variety of acoustic and visual, geological and biological rhythms: the insistent beat of the surf against the slower pull of the tide; the small adaptive movements of marine creatures who endure within a site of extreme exposure and mutation; and, beneath or behind it all, the ongoing dynamic of erosion and drift by which (to cite Mr. Ramsay) the sea and wind "eat away the ground we stand on."[8]

WASTE LAND

The shore for Woolf is never divorced from imperial frameworks, but it can also signify a space of imagination at the edge of patriarchal order. In a littoral variation, *A Room of One's Own* (1929) opens on the banks of a river, where the narrator is sitting, "lost in thought," fishing for ideas about women and fiction. "Thought—to call it by a prouder name than it deserved—had let its line down into the stream. It swayed, minute after minute, hither and thither among the reflections and the weeds, letting the water lift it and sink it until—you know the little tug—the sudden conglomeration of an idea at the end of one's line." The thrill of this small catch sends the fisherwoman (and her complicitous reader) "audaciously trespassing" onto turf where women are not allowed.[9] The beach in *To the Lighthouse* is similarly allied with risk and adventure and with alternatives to marriage and domesticity. Lily longs to rise at dawn to hunt for a lost jewel by the sea: she "envisag[ed] how in the dawn on the beach she would be the one to pounce on the brooch half-hidden by some stone, and thus herself be included among the sailors and adventurers."[10]

Woolf's story, "Solid Objects," presents her most explicit meditation on the beach as a space of nonpatriarchal practices and affiliations. The story examines the shifting "ambition" of John, a young man on the cusp of a successful political career. One day, John finds a piece of buried glass on the beach, and a strange new passion sets hold. Soon he is missing appointments in order to spend his time wandering London with a bag and pointed stick, gathering objects for his heteroclite collection of *objets trouvés*. "Solid Objects" is a story about the possibility of transforming one's perspective and sense of scale, and it presents the beach as the turning point or launching pad for John's new life—a site where mastery and self-possession give way to visionary vagabondage.

The story experiments with perspective from the first line: "The only thing that moved upon the vast semicircle of the beach was one small black spot. As it came nearer to the ribs and spine of the stranded pilchard boat, it became apparent from a certain tenuity in its blackness that this spot possessed four legs; and moment by moment it became more unmistakable that it was composed of the persons of two young men." "Solid Objects" initially miniaturizes the men, then fragments that "spot" into an assemblage of even smaller parts: "tiny mouths," "little round heads," "noses, chins, little moustaches, tweed caps, rough boots, shooting coats, and check stockings."[11] This scalar play then reverses. As the narration is focalized through John's point of view, the visual frame widens: John burrows his fingers down into the sand, and "remembered that, after digging for a little, the water oozes round your finger-tips; the hole then becomes a moat; a well; a spring; a secret channel to the sea."[12] It is while he is imaginatively enlarging the hole in this way that he comes upon a "large irregular lump" of glass—the "solid object" that gives the story its title. The treasure thus appears in the transitional space between scalar polarities: it materializes in the course of the slow zoom-out of John's imagination, as a small hole in the sand seems to metamorphose into an oceanic avenue.

What is most remarkable about this story is the way John's whole world gradually becomes a beach—a commons strewn with random treasures available to the perspicacious seeker.[13] Entranced by the piece of matter he digs out of the sand, John begins seeking other liminal spots in his hunt for unlikely treasures. His sense of time and space shifts: before long he is missing appointments and lingering in alleyways and other urban "waste land where the household refuse is thrown away." One day John finds a broken piece of china that resembles a starfish—a curious detail that underscores the seaside origin of his consuming hobby. Soon "he began to haunt the places which are most prolific of broken china, such as pieces of waste land between railway lines, sites of demolished houses, and commons in the neighborhood of London."[14]

Waste derives from the Latin *vastus*, meaning "unoccupied" or "uncultivated." *Waste land* indicates terrain that is not being developed or exploited for profit; historically in Britain a waste was common land for grazing and fuel gathering. Belonging to no one in particular, a waste is potentially open to all. From a profit-driven point of view, however, a waste indicates ruination, or simply an absence of culture. As Jennifer Wenzel puts it, to a developer's mindset, wastes signify the "original raw material of capitalism and colonialism awaiting transformation into arable, cultivated, revenue-producing land."[15] Thus John Locke insists that land "left wholly to nature, that hath no improvement of pasturage, tillage, or planting, is called, as indeed it is, *waste;* and we shall find the benefit of it amount to little more than nothing."[16] Raymond Williams notes that two million acres of waste land were parceled off and privatized in England in the eighteenth and nineteenth centuries by parliamentary enclosure; previously, the wastes had encompassed the "edges" and "margins," the "as yet ungrasped and undeveloped areas" of the rural class system.[17] In "Solid Objects," John is drawn to the remainders of such remainders—edge land overlooked or forgotten in the push to carve up and seize previously common terrain. His attraction to these spaces—which to him are not undeveloped voids but replete with human traces and objects of desire—is a reminder that wastes were never actually "empty frontier[s]" but places marked by shifting, unofficial, shared customs of use.[18]

In "Solid Objects," Woolf explores the tension between "waste" as unenclosed terrain and "waste" as remainder. The story revalorizes these concepts—both of which are intimately allied with the seashore—and positions them against the instrumentalist attitude of the ambitious politician. It is true that John seeks to possess and display his treasures, so perhaps we should hesitate to make too much of this story's nonpatriarchal, anti-imperialist ethos. But John's beach-born delight in gathering and arranging is also a way of holding refuse to the light, finding unexpected beauty in things "thrown away, of no use to anybody, shapeless, discarded."[19] John's attachment to these objects has no relation to profit or even to exhibition value in its usual sense; as Douglas Mao points out, the things he collects lack "cachet."[20] John is a queer figure in his over-the-top aestheticism, his capacity to cherish what appears to others as mere trash.[21]

John's last find takes place in a 120-acre plot of common land in southwest London. When he loses his election, he is unbothered because he has been that very day to Barnes Common and "there under a furze bush had found a very remarkable piece of iron."[22] Bill Brown emphasizes the way John's sense of time becomes "cosmological" when he finds this "meteorite"-like chunk of iron, setting him adrift from the "temporal dictates of modern life."[23] I would stress, rather, the way Woolf allies John's state of aesthetic absorption with spaces and patterns of commoning—vernacular customs of sharing resources outside the framework of market and state.[24]

Woolf's botanical specification is intriguing in this regard. Furze is "the popular name of Ulex europæus, a spiny evergreen shrub with yellow flowers, growing abundantly on waste lands throughout Europe."[25] Furze (also known as gorse) appears throughout Woolf's writing, often associated with coastal spaces and the struggle to find a lost object or attain a vision.[26] Furze is notable precisely because it is not special but common, in both senses of the term—ordinary or ubiquitous and linked to practices of communal use.

Characterized by spiny thorns and bright yellow flowers, furze crops up repeatedly in E. P. Thompson's account of historical commoning practices in England before the nineteenth century: in addition to this plant's usefulness for grazing cows, horses, and sheep, it was a source of fuel. Thompson cites customs stipulating that a person could take as much as he could carry on his back, with the aim of heating his own house.[27] Known for its flammability, furze was sometimes set ablaze by commoners as a form of revolt against the private seizure of shared lands—or simply as an agricultural practice meant to aid the plant's growth.[28] Woolf plays on the ambiguity of the blazing furze image in the dinner party scene in *To the Lighthouse*, when Mrs. Ramsay rails against the "iniquity of the English dairy system," provoking her family's laughter: "all round the table, beginning with Andrew in the middle, like a fire leaping from tuft to tuft of furze, her children laughed; her husband laughed; she was laughed at, fire-encircled, and forced to veil her crest." Here the flaming plant figures the conviviality of the scene, but from another point of view Mrs. Ramsay appears as the overlord and her children the commoners, burning furze in protest against her domination. In "Solid Objects," Woolf amplifies the association with commoning by referencing the site where the bush and hidden rock are found: the Barnes Common, a historic waste, or uncultivated plot of grazing land at the edge of London. "For over a thousand years, 'The Waste' has been common land traditionally used for rough grazing and by drovers as they made their way to market," according to a website dedicated to the conservation of the site.[29]

Allied with the Barnes Common and other "pieces of waste land," the beach in "Solid Objects" orients John away from the values and habits of normative British middle-class masculinity—he abandons punctuality, oratorical skills, and instrumental reason and instead devotes himself to the queer practice of lingering in edge zones and shared terrain. The beach in this text is therefore not just a hunting grounds for flotsam—it's also a place where the plot of ambition might peter out and other visions take hold. Described at the beginning of the story as "hard," "hirsute," and "virile," John is "a man standing for Parliament upon the brink of a brilliant career."[30] Before that fateful day by the sea, he had sought to represent constituents in a parliamentary system of government and thus had organized his life around the logic of exemplarity, whereby a unique individual stands in for a diverse group. As he transfers his attention away from politics and toward treasure hunting (or junk collecting, depending on your point of view), he shifts his perspective away from the abstracting logic of representation and toward sheer particularity. Brown contends that John is "propelled by a new responsiveness to form as such."[31] Yet it is not exactly "form" that draws him, but rather the inestimable singularity that each found object presents to the world. What fascinates John about the tidewrack he discovers in the sand, and about the "immense variety of shapes" he uncovers in the commons of London, is a quality of irreducible *difference*.[32] This capacity to recognize the nuances in things that, from a more rational point of view, appear identical, is a way of seeing Roland Barthes and Walter Benjamin attribute to the artist's and the child's point of view; reading for minute, subtle differences, these thinkers contend, is not necessarily a sophisticated enterprise.[33] Indeed, Woolf suggests as much by showing that John's eye for visual detail precipitates his fall from social grace: his treasure hunting disqualifies him in the eyes of others and makes him go "silent" in distinguished company.[34]

As John abandons his political career in order to devote himself to his peculiar collection, his perspective changes; he begins to see differently. When Charles visits John for the last time, he is "alarmed" by something odd in his old friend's expression.[35] Accustomed to hunting for unlikely treasures in out-of-the-way spots, John's gaze has become too "distant" for Charles's taste. This is not far-sightedness, like the questing gaze of the horizon-seeking philosopher Mr. Ramsay, but the strangely distant look of someone accustomed to "keeping his eyes upon the ground."[36] John's gaze in fact becomes blurred in focus—childish, full of wonder, all surface—during the opening scene on the beach when he discovers that first bit of tidewrack.[37] This peculiar ocular quality—neither quite near-sighted nor far-sighted, but something between and beyond these conventional categories of sight—will characterize Woolf's visionary characters in *To the Lighthouse* as well.

IMAGINED GEOGRAPHIES

To The Lighthouse depicts heteroreproductivity as a structuring meter, framework, or pulse—but it also explores a variety of other styles of intimacy and patterns of attention and attraction. In this regard, it registers the phenomenon that Barthes calls idiorrhythmy—ways of being alone-together, out of sync with the dominant beat.[38]

Key to this text's offbeat quality is its spatial dislocation. *To the Lighthouse* is both a coastal novel with a specific and intense relation to place and a meditation on imaginary geographies. Woolf's relation to setting here is blurred and deliberately imprecise: one of the text's most peculiar aspects is its disoriented cartography. From a distance, the novel appears to be set on the Isle of Skye in the Inner Hebrides, but an attentive reader will realize that the place described more closely corresponds to St. Ives Bay, Cornwall, where Virginia Stephen vacationed with her family as a child.[39] Woolf thus overlays one coast upon another, and the reader is left hovering doubtfully between the horizon of an unmappable Hebrides (which doesn't correspond to the real place) and the detailed topography of a ghostly Cornwall, never named.[40]

Proust, too, fictionalized his own favorite vacation resort, transforming the real Cabourg into the imaginary Balbec—a place-name he settled on only after trying out a variety of others, including Carquethuit, Carqueville, Querqueville, Briquebec, and Criquebec.[41] But Woolf does something odder than simply rename Cornwall; she transposes Talland House—her family's summer rental home, near Lands End, in England—to Scotland. Or rather, she partially and incompletely transposes it, the result being a curious overlay of one place upon another, with inaccuracies glaring to those who expect veracity in fiction. As John Brannigan points out, Woolf had never visited Scotland when she began *To the Lighthouse* in 1925 and did not have a clear sense of the spatial layout of the British Isles, although she does accurately reference the social and economic crises facing the region. The result is a "strange geography" that "doesn't map onto any possible location in Skye."[42]

Woolf's disregard for geographic specificity is notable throughout her work, but spatial disorientation becomes an explicit topic of conversation in *To the Lighthouse*. This novel foregrounds the problem of meteorological prediction, making its plot dependent upon the weather of the future. Questions of accuracy are raised from the first line, in which Mrs. Ramsay, protecting her son's feelings, incites her husband's fury by flaunting her preference for hopeful uncertainty over scientifically grounded predictions ("Yes, of course, if it's fine tomorrow. . . . But it may be fine—I expect it will be fine").[43] Logical Mr. Ramsay and his disciple, Charles Tansley, insist on squelching Mrs. Ramsay's irrational speculation. This opening tension between maternal and paternal viewpoints indicates the ideological weight granted to questions of exactitude in Woolf's war-shadowed novel. Meteorological forecasting, after all, has a military provenance: having arisen in naval contexts in the mid-nineteenth century, it was refined during the First and Second World Wars.[44] As Brannigan notes, "accuracy" in *To the Lighthouse* is therefore a matter of "aligning one's perspective with existing geopolitical and patriarchal knowledge."[45] Indeed, the novel's masculine authorities tend to frown upon more open-ended modalities of vision, which they dismiss as feminine. Mr. Ramsay believes that women lack a sense of direction and that "the vagueness of their minds is hopeless." As he quizzes his daughter on cardinal directions, he muses that "they could not keep anything clearly fixed in their minds." Wishing that Cam would be more "accurate," Mr. Ramsay reflects that he cannot "understand the state of mind of anyone ... who did not know the points of the compass."[46] The misogynistic Tansley incarnates this accurate relation to time and space: he holds up his bony fingers to determine with precision that the wind is "due west."[47] By contrast, painter Lily Briscoe transposes the detailed scene before her into a "purple shadow"; intoxicated poet Augustus Carmichael lies about, catlike, "catching words" on the lawn; and when nearsighted Mrs. Ramsay looks out at sea, she cannot pin down the identity of the object she sees floating there, which could equally well be a boat, a cork, a cask, or a lobster pot. Woolf builds her imprecisely located coastal novel around this conflict between punctilious geographers and uncertain, dreamy gazers.[48]

To the Lighthouse is a text pulled between the maternal pole of house (space of feminine domestic and affective labor, staged and choreographed by Mrs. Ramsay) and the paternal pole of lighthouse (space of masculine labor and object of Mr. Ramsay's long-deferred quest). Between these two poles we find the intertidal zone, where different sociabilities and gender dynamics might be tested and negotiated. This novel presents the beach as a space of play, but also as the materialization of some other—tidal, zoological, geological—span of time. Thus Mr. Ramsay looks longingly at "little sandy beaches where no one had been since the beginning of time" and Lily Briscoe and William Bankes gaze with "some sadness" on faraway dunes that seem to "outlast [the gazer] by a million years."[49] In its otherworldiness, the beach in *To the Lighthouse* appears as a space of aesthetic experiment and "brooding" affective exposure that contrasts with the oedipal imitations and rivalries shaping the family scene. As we shall see, the only chapter set entirely on and around the beach replays the story of domestic and imperial expansion that Mrs. Ramsay reads to her youngest son—the Grimm fairy tale, "The Fisherman and His Wife." The beach chapter scatters and remixes this narrative, muting its misogynistic undertones, recasting it as a moody shadow play staged by a rebellious girl.

Of all the authors and artists who feature in *Modernism at the Beach*, Woolf is uniquely attuned to the seashore as an acoustic phenomenon and a generator of rhythm—in all of that concept's social and aesthetic significance. In order to recognize the import of the intertidal zone to Woolf's queer ecological sensibility—as a force that unsettles the novel-world's predominant metrical order—we must first consider how *To the Lighthouse* establishes the temporality of the domestic sphere as its primary (but not exclusive) beat. The following section of the chapter therefore steps back from the disorienting interstice of the shoreline in order to examine *To the Lighthouse* as a textured metrical composition, paying special attention to Woolf's treatment of patriarchy and social reproduction as matters of compulsory, embodied rhythm. We will return to the beach after exploring the governing patterns of the house.

DOMESTIC ARRANGEMENTS

To the Lighthouse presents Victorian patriarchy as the ordering force of the novel's world, yet also explores the intermittent rhythms that pull away from this dominant pulse. The novel reads like a time-based performance—a work that explicitly pieces itself together in the duration of our reading. Modernist novels are generally processual, seeming to unfold in the time of our encounter with them, but this is especially true of *To the Lighthouse*, which tends to portray its characters in the act of listening to or looking at or remembering something that is actively passing by and fading away. No matter how many minds concentrate upon a scene in this novel, its momentary solidity inevitably evaporates. The characters themselves are cognizant of this. Toward the end of "The Window," Mrs. Ramsay reflects on "a scene which was vanishing even as she looked": "as she moved and took Minta's arm and left the room, it changed, it shaped itself differently; it had become, she knew, giving one last look over her shoulder, already the past."[50] This sense of the impermanence of all things is compounded in "The Lighthouse" when we follow Lily, James, and Cam as they try to recall events and images from the first section of the novel and find that those phantom images do not correspond to the reality before them. Thus James reflects that "nothing [is] simply one thing" as he conjures his childhood vision of the lighthouse as a "silvery, misty-looking tower with a yellow eye, that opened suddenly, and softly in the evening," while looking at "the tower, stark and straight . . . barred with black and white," with "washing spread on the rocks to dry."[51] *To the Lighthouse*, then, is a novel *about* ephemerality and emergence, a text that asks to be read as if it were a site-specific (but geographically unstable) "happening."[52]

Woolf's emphasis on the acoustic contributes to this effect of processual construction or time-based performance. In June 1925, she wrote in her diary: "I am making up *To the Lighthouse*—the sea is to be heard all through it."[53] The following month, she described her work in musical terms, imagining herself as "an improviser with his hands rambling over the piano."[54] Like *Mrs. Dalloway*—which makes clock-time its bass line, measuring the day's passage by the hourly chimes of Big Ben—*To the Lighthouse* is a text set to a beat. Yet the later novel's underlying metrical pattern is more variegated, consisting of a two-against-three pull (in musical terms, a hemiola). In fact, even among the novel's triple meters, we perceive difference and variation. The lighthouse beats an anapestic meter, with the emphasis on beat three, while Mrs. Ramsay's internal metronome beats an even "one, two, three, one, two, three." Like a watch ticking its "old familiar pulse," this beat urges her to keep the conversation and the social rhythm flowing, despite her fatigue.[55] Lily's painting, too, sparks a triple meter, but hers is a "dancing rhythmical movement" to which she lends her body and attention: when she returns to the picture after long absence, she begins her "pausing" and "flickering" kinesthetic pattern with a rhythmic trio of quick strokes.[56] Behind these subtly different forms of triple time, we perceive a spondaic one-two, one-two suck and crash, inhalation-exhalation of the surf—a mesmerizing elemental soundscape that both underlies and strains against the one-two-three pull of the novel's affective and industrial compositions.[57] *To the Lighthouse*'s amplification of polyrhythms sensitizes the reader to many possible ways of inhabiting a setting and eschews any monumentalizing relation to time.[58]

This novel's coastal setting is key to its transience effect—which is to say, the sense it conveys of a world unremittingly exposed to the passage of time. The seashore, after all, is the ultimate unstable ground, constituted by an ongoing phenomenon of erosion and replenishment. The beach, from this perspective, is less a place than a time-bound process: not a "setting" in any conventional, static sense, but a spatiotemporal chronotope characterized by persistent weathering, ceaseless change. We might think of the beach as a stage for the playing out of tidal cycles, which are never entirely calculable or predictable, despite our attempts to make them so.[59] In *To the Lighthouse*, this coastal dynamic of restless deformation and reformation, erasure and rescripting, informs the novel's searching mood. Moreover, in addition to exploring more-than-human geological and zoological timescales, *To the Lighthouse* investigates more-than-individual temporalities, asking how learned and practiced temporal habits bind us to certain shared modes of existence and how those patterns can be interrupted and rerouted.

The point here is not just that this novel is musical and acoustically oriented, but that it is *about* rhythm as an aesthetic and sociobiological force: rhythm as the spacing of sound or movement in time and as the means by which normative patterns are inculcated on a corporeal level. Power always "imposes a rhythm of life, of time, of thought, of speech," as Barthes has argued.[60] *To the Lighthouse* explores the multiple overlapping modes of perception that pattern social life, and it also examines how normative rhythms get imposed on bodies. Patterns of seeing and feeling, ways of inhabiting space and time, are particularly marked by gendered codes and expectations in *To the Lighthouse*—coercive scripts the novel's characters variously embrace or resist. Against power's "inflexible, implacably regular cadence," Woolf, like Barthes, elucidates alternative social and biological rhythms, asking what other shapes of feeling become possible in the intervals.[61] The beach is Woolf's privileged figure for such perceptual dislocation: her seaside is a zone of rhythmic alterity in which the known temporal and spatial coordinates fade and other relational modes come into view.

Rhythm is an exceedingly difficult concept to define, despite being, along with pitch, the "primary parameter of musical structure." While pitch concerns the disposition of notes, rhythm has to do with "durational patternings."[62] If music itself, according to philosopher Susanne Langer, is a phenomenon that "makes time audible," rhythm is the element that most directly connects to the timing of music as event.[63] It involves the "patterning of temporal flow," especially a "movement marked by the succession of strong or weak elements."[64] For linguist Emile Benveniste, rhythm is synonymous with form—but form understood as "improvised, momentary, changeable."[65]

Helpful as they are, these definitions do not get at the gripping, compulsory quality of rhythm—the way it works (to cite Susan Stewart) as "nonsemantic pull."[66] Rhythm is catchy. It involves "being-taken-hold-of," as Vincent Barletta puts it; it has the property, according to Amittai Aviram, of "inviting, urging, or seducing the listener into participation."[67] In his classic study of sound, Victor Zuckerkandl figures rhythm as a wave that "heave[s], topple[s], and break[s] against resistances."[68] Woolf, too, understands rhythm as a subsuming elemental phenomenon, or wave. In her oft-quoted 1926 letter to Vita Sackville-West, she muses that "style is a very simple matter; it is all rhythm.... A sight, an emotion, creates this wave in the mind, long before it makes words to fit it."[69] *To the Lighthouse* particularly illustrates this conception of rhythm as a "wave" that "breaks and tumbles in the mind": the novel is full of occasions in which characters get rhythmic verses stuck in their heads or find themselves murmuring a verse or phrase repetitively, as if possessed by its metric pull—"Someone had blundered"; "But I beneath a rougher sea"; "can't paint, can't write"; "Children don't forget."

In presenting gendered embodiment as a rhythm—a corporeal-affective pattern that imposes itself with coercive force—Woolf explores a concept that queer theorist Elizabeth Freeman terms "chrononormativity": "the use of time to organize individual human bodies toward maximum productivity." Akin to Bourdieusian habitus, chrononormativity indicates a "cultivated set of gestural and attitudinal dispositions," a "mode of implantation, a technique by which institutional forces come to seem like somatic facts."[70] Other theorists who focus on the forms of social life have also considered rhythm as a key vector of normative comportment. Sociologist Eviatar Zerubavel, for instance, has investigated the incorporated rhythms that comprise the "sociotemporal order," noting that a normative idea of "proper sequence" and tempo ("too fast," "too slow") regulates many aspects of life, including (heterosexual) courtship.[71] And literary critic Caroline Levine invokes this connection between power and rhythm as well, noting that "the coordination of temporal rhythms is a particularly powerful technique of social cohesion."[72]

As evidence of Woolf's preoccupation with rhythm as a coercive or liberating force, consider the eponymous lighthouse itself—the central, dominating metrical phenomenon in *To the Lighthouse*. Aligned with masculine labor, the lighthouse is an emblem of chrononormativity. Its triple pulses of light—"first two quick strokes then one long steady stroke"—organize maritime traffic, serving to regulate both commercial and military oceanic routes. This mesmerizing pattern also absorbs Mrs. Ramsay: just as she lends her sympathy and support to men, she is captivated by the lighthouse's meter, lost in the third stroke that "lift[s] up on it some little phrase or other which had been lying in her mind." This is how she finds herself unwittingly emitting the commonplace line "we are all in the hands of the Lord." Hypnotized by the mechanical regularity of the navigational pulse, she is "trapped into saying something she did not mean."[73]

To the Lighthouse reflects explicitly on how reading practices bind us to such normative rhythms. Mr. and Mrs. Ramsay are each connected with the recitation of a metrically oriented text that models gendered comportment: Mr. Ramsay recites the dactylic verses of Tennyson's "Charge of the Light Brigade" as he paces in the yard, while Mrs. Ramsay reads "The Fisherman and His Wife" aloud to James, "speaking the last words as if she had made them up herself."[74] And yet simply by weaving these texts into her novel Woolf reshapes them, indicating that the compulsory gendered performance of daily life might be interrupted and reset as well. Mrs. Ramsay oversees the rituals of domesticity, and when she abruptly cuts out, the once carefully regulated rhythms of the everyday are loosened, along with predetermined divisions of emotional and intellectual labor. The last section of the novel, "The Lighthouse," returns us to the world of "The Window," now without Mrs. Ramsay, in order to ask how things might be different if they were not anchored by the imposition of heterosexuality. In the absence of the one who manages the performance of gendered work, "a sort of disintegration set[s] in." The characters find themselves drifting, no longer certain what the chrononormative script entails. Without Mrs. Ramsay, "the link that usually bound things together" is cut and everyone "float[s]"—"down here, up there, off."[75]

To the Lighthouse is concerned with unconscious choreographies of gendered being—how we act without thinking, drawn into seemingly "natural" habits of behavior despite ourselves. It is in fact an unusually sleepy novel. States of sleep or half-sleep might connote unthinking docility and submission—or, alternatively, index an intermediary condition of potentiality from which one could at any moment awaken.[76] Mr. Ramsay is first introduced crying out like a "sleep-walker, half roused" and is later described sitting at the table "like a person in a dream"; Mrs. Ramsay reads poetry "like a person in a light sleep."[77] "Time Passes" functions like the "long night" of the novel. Described as a dark passage between two luminous points, it is punctuated at one end by Mr. Carmichael putting aside his book and blowing out his candle and, at the other, by Lily "stirring in her sleep" and then "sitting bolt upright in bed."[78] And although "The Lighthouse" opens with this startling image of awakening, the sleeping simply goes on in another key: characters and spaces alike slumber or nearly fall asleep or exist in a sleepy state of daydream. The house itself appears to be "sleeping in the early sunlight"; Cam sees the shore "wrapped in its mantle of peace . . . as if the people there had fallen asleep"; Mr. Ramsay holds up his hands "to confirm his dream"; Mr. Carmichael, reading his French novel, has fallen asleep, or is simply "lying there catching words"; Lily looks around the lawn like a traveler, "half asleep" in a train.[79] The boat "move[s] off half conscious in her sleep" before "she woke and shot through the waves"; Cam murmurs lines by Tennyson while "dreamily half asleep," and later nearly nods off as she drifts into the rhythmically swinging words and images that her mother used to recite to put her to bed.[80] Woolf explores states of somnolence in this novel because she is concerned with unconscious or semiconscious adherence to expected behavioral norms— the way we incorporate cultural expectations on the level of bodily process. But the text's sleepiness also gives the whole seaside world, with its confounding geography and its pull toward alternative, more-than-human temporalities, the allure of a waking dream.

This novel's penchant for oneiric or semiconscious states of being is one of the ways that it both adheres to and breaks from what Benjamin Bateman calls "hetero-patriarchy's well-worn script."[81] As Mary Jean Corbett points out, Woolf "situates the Victorian family as the institution that, more intimately than any other, produced and reproduced the class, racial, sexual, and gendered dynamics of late imperial English culture."[82] Yet *To The Lighthouse* is a novel about domesticity and coupledom that also asks what forms of intimacy and care are perceptible at the edges of matrimony, or in its shadow.[83] What Peter Coviello calls the "imperatives of reproductive coupledom" constitute for Woolf's characters one of the "ordering forms of the world"—but not its only form.[84] Indeed, as Melanie Micir has shown, Woolf does something queer to the temporal schema of the family saga in this novel.[85] In *To the Lighthouse,* one dominant rhythm accords with what this novel calls "custom"—implying gendered hierarchies and habitus, intellectual versus emotional labor, conventional narrative patterns of heteronormative courtship and social reproduction. But when Lily returns to her painting in "The Lighthouse" she seeks a different distribution of sensory time—she wants to "fall in with some rhythm"—a "rhythm . . . strong enough to bear her along with it on its current."[86]

Within the logic of *To the Lighthouse*'s family dynamics, Mr. Ramsay, who wears a compass on his watch, appears as the novel's most imperious timekeeper: he expects others to set their biorhythms to his beat. As Jacques Rancière points out, this Victorian patriarch is an agent of "tyrannical authority" and the primary shaper of the plot. It is he who decides that they won't go to the lighthouse in "The Window" and who insists that they do go in "The Lighthouse." He interrupts but cannot bear to be interrupted. He fumes when Mr. Carmichael holds up dinner by asking for a second bowl of soup. He storms out when the voyage to the lighthouse is delayed by a forgotten sandwich order. Yet Mrs. Ramsay, according to Rancière, is no less dominating: her "matchmaking frenzy" simply represents a "soft," more "binding" and "insidious" form of tyranny.[87] It is she who serves as conductor of the familial temporality that dominates "The Window." She is the one who keeps talk flowing at dinner; she determines the children's bedtime; and while others stand about "making jokes" she knows that "there was always something that had to be done at that precise moment."[88] Mrs. Ramsay seeks especially to placate her irascible husband, and when she succeeds it is as if the entire heteroreproductive social order has won out: "domesticity triumphed" and "custom crooned its soothing rhythm."[89] Insisting that "they must all marry" and believing that "an unmarried woman has missed the best in life," Mrs. Ramsay wants to see her family structure replicated everywhere. Her world revolves around "the sun of the love of men and women," and she cannot fathom that her daughters—or any woman—might not be drawn to that light.[90] In thrall to the marriage plot, she considers the betrothed couple, "the Rayleys," as her own legacy and imagines that her home and the values it represents "would be revived again in the lives of Paul and Minta."[91] For Mrs. Ramsay, a woman's calling is to "arrange the flowers" in a man's house.[92]

Here it is important to point out—contra Rancière—that despite her critique of Mrs. Ramsay's obsession with matrimony, Woolf takes seriously the emotional labor of the mother and wife. It is true that Mrs. Ramsay upholds the marriage plot and sympathizes not just with men but with imperialist patriarchy: "she had the whole of the other sex under her protection . . . for their chivalry and valour, for the fact that they negotiated treaties, ruled India, controlled finance."[93] She is coercive, and she knows it—"people might say she was tyrannical, domineering, masterful"—but the novel also shows how exhausting the matriarch's affective labor can be.[94] As the emotional arranger-in-chief of the household, Mrs. Ramsay finds it "natural" that she is needed all day, everyday: "They came to her, naturally, since she was a woman, all day long with this and that; one wanting this, another that."[95] But Woolf does not find this "natural." Although Andrew denigrates women as having "no control over their emotions," and Mr. Ramsay sees his wife's desire to shelter James's hope as evidence of the intrinsic "folly of women's minds," Woolf demonstrates that Mrs. Ramsay works skillfully to conduct, channel, and pacify the affective conflicts of the entire household: this is why "she often felt she was nothing but a sponge sopped full of human emotions." She gives sympathy, negotiates conflict, and absorbs and deflects the feelings of others, allowing herself to be "bespattered" by her husband's bad temper, which feels like a "pelt of jagged hail, [a] drench of dirty water."[96]

The novel thus exposes the constant effort that Mrs. Ramsay must expend on a form of quotidian work that masquerades as the innate expression of womanhood. If Mrs. Ramsay finds the labor of care fulfilling, the novel itself asks how one might evade the daily effort of arranging or being arranged and attend instead to the work of the imagination. This other kind of labor is also emotional, and it too involves a subtle practice of "arrangement." But it is not oriented toward the reproduction of a patriarchal and imperialist world order. Instead, it enables the dreaming up of other possible vantage points, other potential formations or dispositions of bodies and things. The arranging work that consumes the artist does not consist of a spongy absorption of the feelings of others, and it does not require that one cast all affections into matrimonial and reproductive patterns. Rather, it's a matter of balancing light and dark, of moving the tree to the middle of the composition, of transfiguring domestic patterns into painterly (or verbal) forms, and of zigzagging between close and distant forms of vision—looking down at a tide pool, looking out to the "wavering" line of the horizon.[97]

The question for the artists and castaways of the novel is not will we or won't we go to the lighthouse, but how is it possible to linger in what Rancière calls the space of a "deferred crossing."[98] How might one dwell—and imagine and create—in that suspended zone of "exaltation," that space of freedom in which one need not marry anyone and one is not compelled to give up one's own vision in order to arrange someone else's flowers? *To the Lighthouse* centers not only on the house and its economies, but on the adventure-laden, coastal outskirts of that orderly space.

TIDAL VISIONS

As an unmarried, childless amateur painter, Lily Briscoe is the primary agent of this divergent act of "arrangement" in *To the Lighthouse*. Although she is a house guest, and thus exists in the periphery of the Ramsay's domestic scene, Lily is arguably the novel's hero—a queer figure who resists the status quo by choosing art over social reproduction. But Lily is not the only visionary who finds herself in the margins of the marriage plot. We also see Woolf's fascination with what can be dreamed up at the edges of domestic order in the scene in which Nancy—one of the Ramsay's eight children—explores the tidal zone. Nancy is a minor character, easy to overlook. A middle child, she is largely overshadowed by her elder and younger siblings. She's also strongly associated with the parenthetical mode. Nancy's first and last appearances in the novel occur in parentheses; in both cases, she's the object of someone else's passing thought. When her name first appears, her criticism of Tansley—and of all of her father's disciples—is filtered through her mother's memory: the dog has bit Tansley "for being (as Nancy put it) the hundred-and-tenth young man to chase them all the way up to the Hebrides when it was ever so much nicer to be alone."[99] Nancy's final appearance is also parenthetical, and again she impedes her father's plot, this time nearly capsizing the narrative. Coerced into performing her mother's part in the domestic drama, she has forgotten to order sandwiches for the lighthouse trip, and her father storms out of the room in a rage. "Nancy had vanished.... Now Nancy burst in, and asked, looking round the room, in a queer half dazed, half desperate way, 'What does one send to the Lighthouse?' as if she were forcing herself to do what she despaired of ever being able to do." She then disappears again as Lily reflects on her own sense of solitude: "Sitting alone (for Nancy went out again) among the clean cups at the long table, she felt cut off from other people."[100] Nancy exits the novel as marginally as she enters it. She will not reappear, though her name will be invoked one last time—in reference to the "badly packed" parcel she sends to the lighthouse, index of her reluctant adherence to the gendered script she has inherited.[101]

It is fitting, then, that the only scene that features Nancy centrally occurs in a chapter that is parenthetical in its entirety—an unusual occurrence even in a novel riddled with this form of punctuation.[102] An entire chapter in parentheses is like free indirect style pushed to its limit: this is floating, unclaimed language, only tenuously connected to the surrounding text. The reader of a parenthetical chapter may well wonder if she is expected to invest belief in such a strangely framed segment, or if the narration has slipped into some hypothetical, speculative realm.[103] Parenthetical statements are commonly called "asides," indicating a relation of adjacency rather than subordination. Square brackets in *To the Lighthouse* function as a brutal interruption, an intrusion of the real into the ethereal fabric of the novel's memory-scape. In "Time Passes," death rips and tears with square brackets. But Woolf's parentheses are different: softer, almost unnoticeable, less an interruption than a *sotto voce* addition, a phrase uttered in a subtly modified register or issuing from a slightly different place.[104] Parentheses indicate a line that, were one reading aloud, would be voiced in an altered tone and with a slight uptick or lag in tempo. In this regard, the parenthetical marker is the linguistic analog to musical rubato, which indicates a loosening of strict tempo markers and therefore a momentary quickening or slackening of a phrase's pacing (often against a steady accompaniment). Nancy's parenthetic trip to the tidal zone thus occurs in an alternate temporality, a dreamlike other sphere. Indeed, the parenthetical enclosure is visually akin to the eyelids of a sleeper or the semitransparent yellow blind through which Woolf heard the sea in her first childhood memory—not an impossible border but a permeable one.[105] With their porous, open-closed quality, Woolf's parentheses are also suggestive of a tide pool—a miniature aqueous world formed by the intermittent ebb and flood of the sea.

Partially enclosed, ambiguously set apart, the parenthetical seashore chapter in *To the Lighthouse* suggests a suspension of the time-space of the house and a temporary reprieve from the focus on marriage and domesticity that dominates the first section of the novel.[106] This parenthetical chapter contains the scene of Minta and Paul's engagement, and in this sense it signals Mrs. Ramsay's matchmaking triumph. But it also highlights the limits of her reach as a timekeeper, since she cannot control the timing of the beach expedition, nor can she even know for certain who has gone down to the shore. The group (consisting, we learn, of Andrew, Nancy, Paul, and Minta) returns not in obedience to Mrs. Ramsay's schedule, but according to elemental realities: the tide is coming in. Further delayed by an accident (Minta's lost brooch), the beach explorers are late to dinner, unsettling Mrs. Ramsay's authority over the daily rhythms of the house.

The chapter also troubles Mrs. Ramsay's control in that it does not permit us to witness the proposal she has arranged—the speech act that will bind Minta and Paul into a socially sanctioned reproductive unit. Instead, we skirt that scene and follow Nancy as she "wades out" and "searches." Nancy's tidal play is spotlighted while the marriage proposal takes place offstage. Similarly, at the end of the novel, we will cut away from the scene of Mr. Ramsay's journey just as it reaches its triumphant conclusion—the long-deferred arrival at the lighthouse—in order to observe Lily in the act of completing her painting. *To the Lighthouse* sets up heteronormative, patriarchal plotlines only to relativize them, shedding light instead on the acts of art making, dreaming, and old-maidenly "exaltation" that occur at the periphery of dominant narrative pathways.

What can we make of the centrality of the otherwise minor character, Nancy, in this chapter? Parenthetical as she is, Nancy is notable for the speculation she induces in others. Her location is in question for much of the first section of the novel. In this regard, Nancy is the characterological equivalent of the weather in a novel that insistently asks, will it be fine or won't it? She counts less for anything she says—she speaks little, in effect—than for the puzzlement that her whereabouts produces in her mother: did she go down to the seashore with the others or not? This question, posed many times over the course of several chapters, becomes a refrain:

But possibly Nancy was with them.
Whether Nancy was there or not, she could not be certain.
Even if Nancy were with them
"Did Nancy go with them?"

(Certainly, Nancy had gone with them . . .)
"I think Nancy did go with them."
Well, then, Nancy had gone with them, Mrs. Ramsay supposed.[107]

Even when Mrs. Ramsay settles, more or less, on the idea that Nancy has gone with the others, this affirmation simply incites another speculation: she wonders "whether the fact that Nancy was with them made it less likely or more likely that anything would happen."[108] Nancy is an agent of uncertainty in the text; she creates a ripple effect of queries and doubts.

Nancy has in actuality gone down to the shore with her brother, Andrew, and the soon-to-be-engaged couple, Minta and Paul, but she's gone against her will, not wanting, as she puts it, "to be drawn into it all." Invited just as she was disappearing into her attic to "escape the horror of family life," Nancy goes, but she does not witness Paul's proposal to Minta.[109] She sidesteps that plot. Instead, she "wade[s] out to her own rocks and searche[s] her own pools and let[s] that couple look after themselves."[110]

One of the most interesting aspects of Nancy's tidal pool scene is that it inverts both Romantic and Victorian conceptions of the shore. Cognizant of her power and her powerlessness as she gazes down at a tidal pool, then up at the distant horizon, Nancy's nonappropriative, shifting gaze corresponds neither to that of the sublime-seeking Romantic wanderer nor to the collecting impulses of the Victorian tide-pooler—points to which I will return. Nor does her stance indicate the attitude of maternal care that some Romantics, according to Alain Corbin, ascribed to littoral space.[111] On the contrary, on the beach the daughter is temporarily released from the pressure to replicate her mother's pacifying domestic role. Mrs. Ramsay is her household's timekeeper and emotion-manager: she holds men (and patriarchy more broadly) under her sympathetic "protection." Playing by the sea, her adolescent daughter limns the zone where maternal care (or domination) meets aesthetic creation: she pushes sympathy to its breaking point.

The episode of Nancy's tidal pool play is the dramatic climax of the chapter, and it stands out in contrast to the tone of casual misogyny marking the trip to and from the beach. Recoiling from the way Paul claps him on the back and calls him "old fellow," Andrew casts blame on Minta and Nancy: "It was the worst of taking women on walks."[112] Later, on the way back up to the house, Andrew again generalizes about women, this time projecting on the basis of his reaction to Minta: "she had no control over her emotions, Andrew thought. Women hadn't."[113] Andrew's departicularizing dismissal of women is echoed by other men throughout the novel—particularly Mr. Ramsay and Tansley—but the text as a whole, in its sensitivity to subtle crossovers and resonances between seemingly opposed subject positions—refutes such generalizations at every turn. Nancy's perspectival experiment at the water's edge stands as a particular point of resistance to facile sexism. Andrew's reductive assessments of women stabilize and aggrandize his own subject position; similarly, Tansley repeats, "women can't write, women can't paint," not because he believes it but because "for some reason he wished it."[114] Nancy's play with scale, pattern, and vantage point indicates a world untethered from such egoic fictions.

The tidal pool scene appears aggressively anthropocentric on a first reading. Slipping away from Minta and Paul, Nancy "listened to the waves," and "crouched low down and touched the smooth rubber-like sea anemones." And then, as if she were the artist of this tidal pool,

> brooding, she changed the pool into the sea, and made the minnows into sharks and whales, and cast vast clouds over this tiny world by holding her hand against the sun, and so brought darkness and desolation, like God himself, to millions of ignorant and innocent creatures, and then took her hand away suddenly and let the sun stream down. Out on the pale criss-crossed sand, high-stepping, fringed, gauntleted, stalked some fantastic leviathan (she was still enlarging the pool), and slipped into the vast fissures of the mountain side. And then, letting her eyes slide imperceptibly above the pool and rest on that wavering line of sea and sky, on the tree trunks which the smoke of steamers made waver on the horizon, she became with all that power sweeping savagely in and inevitably withdrawing, hypnotised, and the two senses of that vastness and this tininess (the pool had diminished again) flowering within it made her feel that she was bound hand and foot and unable to move by the intensity of feelings which reduced her own body, her own life, and the lives of all the people in the world, for ever, to nothingness. So listening to the waves, crouching over the pool, she brooded.[115]

Has Nancy "no control over her emotions," as her brother would charge? She is certainly intensely aware of her feelings, and yet she is engaged here in an emotional exercise, an affective experiment. (The word *experiment* will feature a bit later in the novel, in reference to Lily's rebellious attempt to see "what happens" if she withholds her affective labor and refuses to extend soothing words to the disagreeable Tansley: "of course for the one hundred and fiftieth time Lily Briscoe had to renounce the experiment.")[116] Like Mrs. Ramsay with her lighthouse beam, Nancy allows herself to merge here with the objects of her observation. Yet there is a difference between Nancy's detached, "brooding" investigation and her mother's hypnotism. Even as Nancy gives herself over to the surf and the tides, she is playing a game. Slipping between perspectival modes, she toggles between shadow and light—between a distant, panoramic gaze and a close-up magnifying look. Gazing down on the small pool, she feels herself godlike in power, and then "let[s] her eyes slide" up to the horizon line, such that she instantly perceives her own body and life, "and the lives of all the people in the world," reduced to "nothingness." Something similar happens to John in "Solid Objects": when he finds the chunk of glass deep in the sand, his eyes change, losing their adult depth of "thought and experience."[117] For Woolf, the intertidal zone enables this alternative spatiotemporal patterning, this different mode of vision—a capacity to lose sight of conventional plots and expectations and instead become absorbed by the blurred line between the objects at hand and a distant horizon. Her fictions are energized by such perspectival and scalar play: a way of looking that is neither simply an act of close-up magnification nor a panoramic zoom-out, but a curious, vertiginous practice of moving between these perceptual extremes.

Nancy's tide pool episode in fact harkens back to a popular Victorian phenomenon. Tide pool exploration was all the rage in mid-nineteenth-century Britain, as evidenced by publications such as Philip Henry Gosse's *A Naturalist's Rambles on the Devonshire Coast* (1853); *The Aquarium: The Unveiling of the Wonders of the Deep Sea* (1854); and *A Year at the Shore* (1865); and Charles Kingsley's *Glaucus; or, The Wonders of the Shore* (1855). Mid-nineteenth-century popular science and seaside tourism were by-products of the flourishing field of academic marine biology, and, like academics, everyday Victorian naturalists were specimen collectors. They sought to decorate their sitting rooms with their seaside discoveries and outfit their home aquariums—the saltwater aquarium having come into vogue in the 1850s and 1860s.[118] Unlike John's dubious treasures in Woolf's "Solid Objects," the discoveries of Victorian beachcombers had exhibition value. As historian David Allen has shown, seaweeds became "a part of the holiday industry" during this period. Allen also notes that the era's improvement of microscope design facilitated a "surge of interest in the lower organisms," which had previously been neglected, and enabled tide-poolers to spend long hours "peering closely" through a lens at the specimens they had gathered. Victorian tide-pooling was thus a matter of collection and display, on the one hand, and of "penetrating to nature's furthermost recesses," on the other.[119]

For Victorian naturalists, the tide pool was a spectacle to be possessed, akin to an aquarium. This perception was widespread: the first public aquarium display was a tide pool replica.[120] Victorians viewed both tide pools and aquaria as parts signifying a whole or, in Amy King's phrasing, as "sites of metonymic display": the pool reflected the seashore, which in turn reflected the natural world as a whole, which reflected God's creative intelligence.[121] In Nancy's tide pool shadow play, however, the tidal microcosm overspills its bounds and scalar dilation takes on wild new proportions. Nancy's experiment with aggrandizement and shrinking is altogether different from Gosse's and Kingsley's stance of religious wonder at the perceived harmony of the visible world, and it also departs from the Victorian view of the tide pool or aquarium as a "personal water world."[122] In Woolf's vision of things, to see is not to own; humans can no longer imagine themselves as superior to the terrain in which they are enmeshed, and the ocean and its innumerable inhabitants cannot be reduced to mere ornaments or emblems of distinguished taste. Nancy is not positioned outside of or above the microcosm she observes. Rather, she feels herself to be part of the intertidal world—it grows as she does; she shrinks in tandem with it.

In this regard, British marine zoologist C. M. Yonge's *The Sea Shore* (1949) is more in tune with Woolf's ecological sensibility than are the masculinist, evangelical musings of thinkers like Gosse and Kingsley. In contrast to the Victorian preoccupation with specimen collection and religious revelation, Yonge underscores what's most unusual about the seashore as a habitat: its constant fluctuations. In the intertidal zone, he writes, it is as if seasonal shifts were occurring twice per day. The shore is "not one environment but many." Marked by exceptional variation, "the zonation of life which spreads over thousands of ascending feet on land is, on a rocky shore, telescoped within a few score yards."[123] Yonge depicts the inhabitants of the shore not as collectible objects for a display case or aquarium, but as "living things maintaining themselves in often precarious and transitory equilibrium with the manifold forces of the physical and biological environment."[124]

Woolf, too, understands the rocky shore as a site of metamorphosis. All seashores are exceptionally restless and changeable, but this is especially apparent on a rocky shore, where conditions of visibility and exposure change dramatically throughout the tidal cycle and where the beach is composed of "horizontal zones" created by tides in which "little pockets" of life can thrive.[125] Proust's beach resort is a sandy proscenium, a casino, a gallery: it's a space to see and be seen, to strut, leap, gamble, flirt, or loll in the dunes with a book or a lover. Woolf's rocky shore invites a different mode of engagement: as the human visitor scrambles and wades, she must be active and attentive, aware of the uneven and slippery footing. For Woolf, the seashore presents a space for reflecting on the conjunction of care and hostility, toughness and delicacy, and on the myriad ways in which organisms adapt themselves to this exceptionally mutable terrain. The intertidal scene in *To the Lighthouse* is marked by its temporariness: on the way to the shore, the characters remark that it would be "fatal" if the tide comes in before they get to the beach, and Nancy's reverie is cut short by her brother's shout that "the sea was coming in."[126] In the intertidal zone, as Rachel Carson puts it, the human is an "uneasy trespasser."[127]

Despite the sense of precarity and transience that infuses the episode, Nancy's gesture of shadowing the pool with her hand could be read as a violent act of domination. She is pretending, after all, to bring "darkness and desolation" to "millions" of creatures. Yet it is important to consider how Nancy's shadow play diverges not only from the practices of her Victorian predecessors but also from the habits of Woolf's other tide-pooling characters. Instead of hunting or collecting these creatures, Nancy transforms them in imagination. Andrew, whose hobby is crab dissection, and who goes to the beach armed with net and bucket, will "grumble" that she didn't call him when she saw her "leviathan," which he dismissively terms "the crayfish or whatever it was."[128] Nancy's exploration echoes, in a less violent register, an earlier tidal pool scene in Woolf: in the opening beach episode of *Jacob's Room*, Jacob, feeling childishly "heroic," climbs a rock, captures a crab, and leaves it trapped in a bucket of rainwater, out of which it will try in vain to escape, "trying again and falling back, and trying again and again."[129] Unlike Jacob and Andrew, Nancy is content to dreamily transform the "high-stepping" creature into "some fantastic leviathan," and then simply observe it as it disappears into a crack in the rock.

Moreover, Nancy assumes a posture of domination only to immediately abandon it by turning her eyes up to the horizon and feeling herself shrink in the face of it. When she gazes into the distance, she enacts her father's characteristic style of looking: in the far-sighted Mr. Ramsay's first appearance in the novel, he is described "narrow[ing] his little blue eyes upon the horizon."[130] But while Mr. Ramsay trains his gaze on a far-off point and ignores the details before him, Nancy moves between close and distant modes of sight. Her father's telescopic philosophical vision suggests the Romantic horizon-seeking *Ruckenfigur*, most famously depicted in Friedrich's *Wanderer above the Sea of Fog* (*Der Wanderer über dem Nebelmeer*, 1818): the wanderer's masterful pose above the clouds (and right in the middle of *our* view) arguably represents the ethos of the age (or at least a triumphantly masculinist version of that mood).[131] Mr. Ramsay's far-sightedness is also reminiscent of Romantic seaside ramblers who, notes Corbin, liked to "stand atop a rock as if rooted there, in a defiant attitude in the face of the elements assailing the headland."[132] Nancy, by contrast, gathers power to her and then opens her hands and releases it. She strikes a pose of mastery—and then intentionally divests herself of that force. This decidedly modernist relay between anthropocentrism and its eclipse, and between close and distant vision, suggests a microcosm of Woolf's own novelistic style.[133]

Nancy's inward-outward, expanding-shrinking rhythmic play with perspective and with light and shadow is intensely visual, and yet the reader may struggle to see the scene clearly. In Proust's *Within a Budding Grove*, the seaside is cast as the novel's painterly site par excellence: painter Elstir's chiastic vision of intertwined, reversible marine and terrestrial elements is disorienting but does not ultimately undermine the representability of the littoral itself. On the contrary, the "amphibious" quality of seaside life is revealed as the quintessence of the paintable, as it permits the artist to explore a variety of visible textures and see what happens when they meet or overlap. Nancy's parenthetical occasion of ocular experimentation is, however, difficult to envision. The "imperceptible" movement (up and out) of the girl's gaze resists display, just as her lowly, unladylike "crouch" and "brooding" gaze spoil any picturesque or framable quality of the scene. (Later in the novel, Mr. Ramsay will also "crouch"—but he assumes this bowed, crooked posture in the boat because he is "acting instantly his part—the part of a desolate man, widowed, bereft.")[134]

There is no managing or taming the strangeness of Nancy's perception—of tininess and enormity, of "leviathan"-like power and sudden reduction to "nothingness." In this regard, the episode harkens not only to the Victorian practice of tide-pooling but also to Europe's most familiar aestheticization of the sea: the Romantic sublime, with which the Scottish Hebrides were historically linked.[135] Yet Woolf turns the horizon-gazing, sublime-seeking beach pose inside out and upside down. For one thing, she has no interest in depicting the sea as wild or untouched: Paul has been quoting guide books on the walk, and when Nancy looks up at the horizon it's strewn with steamers, traces of massive anthropogenic climate change underway. This is a seaside at once industrially shaped and touristified.[136] What's more, Nancy's perception actually reverses that of Kant's sublime-stricken subject. In Kant's *Critique of Judgment*, the aesthetic judgment of the sublime initially involves a subject miniaturized and degraded by his encounter with the incalculable enormity of nature. In a second movement, however, the awestruck beholder, whose capacity for resistance has been reduced to "an insignificant trifle," affirms his distinction from and "superiority" over nature by mastering the sublime spectacle via the faculty of reason. As Kant puts it: "we gladly call these objects sublime because they elevate the strength of our soul above its usual level, and allow us to discover within ourselves a capacity for resistance of quite another kind, which gives us the courage to measure ourselves against the apparent all-powerfulness of nature."[137] Thus Kant's "Analytic of the Sublime" tells the story of nature's powers expanding and contracting in relation to a human observer who discovers his own masterful self-sufficiency—a force "against which everything in nature is small."[138] Conversely, Nancy initially perceives her *own* godlike powers in contrast to the tidal pool, which she shadows with her hand. But in a second movement, her mastery is overturned, and she feels herself and her life—and the lives of all humans—reduced to "nothingness." This is not the Romantic sublime but a modernist vision of the world without us—a world in which the human is so profoundly decentered as to be periodically knocked out of the frame.[139]

Playing at the water's edge, Nancy "broods." *Brood*—a verb repeated twice in the brief episode—is a peculiar lexical choice in a scene that otherwise offers an escape from the oedipal dynamics and gendered expectations of family life. *Brood* derives from the Germanic root, *bro-*, meaning "to warm, to heat." As a noun, it indicates offspring or young; as a verb, *to brood* means "to sit as a hen on eggs; to sit or hover with outspread cherishing wings," or, by extension, "to breed, hatch (products or projects)"; "to cherish in the mind"; "to hover over" ("said especially of night, darkness, silence, mist, storm-clouds, and the like"); or to "meditate moodily, or with strong feeling."[140] One could scarcely imagine a more feminized, maternal figure for thought than *brood*, with its henhouse associations, and yet it's an interesting verb precisely because it signifies both a cherishing stance or attitude as well as a moody or even stormy state of mind. It is a word that signifies a wide range of caretaking feelings and atmospheric conditions, ranging from protective warmth to ominous darkness.

In fact, *brood* is explicitly linked in this novel to the labor of the artist. We are not accustomed to allying artists with the seemingly passive act of laying or sitting on eggs, but Proust plays on the connection in "Combray" (1913), when his child narrator pens his first piece of writing and then squawks, joyfully, like a chicken: "as if I myself were a hen and had just laid an egg, I began to sing my head off [*à tue-tête*]."[141] Woolf's version of this hen imagery is quieter and less comic—she underscores the ongoingness of brooding rather than the eventfulness of laying. But she too presents it as the mood proper to the practice of writing. Brooding in all its modal complexity is connected in particular with Augustus Carmichael, the novel's dreamy resident poet, with his "slipper dangl[ing] from his foot" and his opium-stained beard: "And there he would lie all day long on the lawn brooding presumably over his poetry, till he reminded one of a cat watching birds, and then he clapped his paws together when he had found the word."[142] As this scene indicates, the brooding Carmichael occupies a temporality outside of the novel's domestic meter. In quiet defiance against Mrs. Ramsay's decisive punctuality, he "shuffl[es] past"; he comes "padding softly in"; he "snuffl[es] and sniff[s]"; he "lie[s] awake reading Virgil," keeping his candle burning "rather longer than the rest."[143] Carmichael is an elusive, offbeat figure who serves as a Virgilian guide for other marginal artist types in the novel—most obviously Lily, who completes her painting under his "protection" in "The Lighthouse"—but also the overlooked Nancy, shadow player, figure of speculation and uncertainty.

The final point to make about Nancy's remarkable shadow play is that, as I have noted, it explicitly scrambles and replays one of the novel's key intertexts—"The Fisherman and His Wife," the Grimm Brothers' fairy tale that Mrs. Ramsay is reading to James that very afternoon. This tale, which traces the rise and fall of a poor couple, crystallizes many of this novel's concerns. It highlights the question of human power and powerlessness with regard to the more-than-human world; it explores, like "Solid Objects," the tension between worldly ambition and alternative forms of desire and satisfaction; and it asks how rhythms bind us to or release us from compulsory form. The story's plot unfolds as follows: a fisherman encounters an enchanted flounder while fishing in the sea. Sated with what little he has, he is content to let the fish swim free. His wife, however, demands that he return to the beach to ask the magical creature to grant her wishes. Aided by the flounder, the couple trades their shack for a cottage, then the cottage for a palace; the ambitious wife then demands to be made king, then emperor, then pope, and finally to be "like God"—at which point the two find themselves cast back into their initial state of poverty. In a novel packed with intertextual references, this tale is granted particular weight—Mrs. Ramsay reads it aloud to her son over several chapters, and its echoes and allusions play out throughout the text, especially in Nancy's shadow play. Still, the tale's message remains singularly ambiguous. Centering on the tension between contentment and dissatisfaction, satiety and desire, does "The Fisherman and His Wife" amplify the novel's dominant beat, reinforcing the Ramsay's restrictive gender script? Or does it open onto other rhythms, other temporal arrangements of sound and sense? Woolf leaves this question unanswered. On one level, the tale's message is sexist: it suggests that wives should be kept in their place and their irrational wishes disregarded, lest the natural order of things be disrupted. On another level, we could also say that the story's critique of acquisitiveness and domination and its embrace of enoughness—its message of radical spiritual asceticism—resonate with the broader ethos of Woolf's novel, and particularly with Lily Briscoe's humble goal: to finish a painting that will be hung in an attic or rolled up and stashed under a sofa.

It is difficult to settle on an interpretation of "The Fisherman and His Wife," but the tale's rhythmic design is unmistakable. In accord with the wife's growing ambitions, the narrative stretches in an expanding wave pattern, with repeating lyrical refrains, until the protagonists crash back, full-circle, where they began. Nancy's tidal pool shadow play takes up the same elements: the sea and shore; God and pope (Andrew wades out to "Pope's Nose"); nothingness, darkness, desolation; power and powerlessness; enormity and tininess. Like the flounder, Nancy is possessed of seemingly magical powers as she performs an act of imaginative transformation, "enlarg[ing] the pool" and letting it "diminish" again, changing minnows into sharks and whales, and holding up her hand to bring "darkness and desolation, like God himself, to millions of ignorant and innocent creatures," before letting the sun stream down again. Yet even as Nancy plays God, changing a tiny pool into "vast fissures of the mountain side" and imagining a "fantastic leviathan" nearby, she is paralyzed by the sense of being "reduced . . . forever, to nothingness." Moreover, the reader is doubly struck by the conjunction of intensity and minorness here, since the entire occasion, as we have seen, takes place in the dubious, speculative realm of the parenthetical. The episode thus replays Mrs. Ramsay's act of reading to her son, but turns the scene of maternal care onto its shadowy otherside. In reframing and recasting the tale, Nancy's tide pool dramaturgy highlights the fundamental ambiguity inherent both in the Grimm story and in Mrs. Ramsay's performance of domestic authority. Playing all the parts, Nancy is at once the power-seeking wife, the power-granting flounder, and the state of utter destitution—or godliness?—with which the tale concludes.

"MRS. RAMSAY ON THE BEACH"

To the Lighthouse will make one last foray to the shore. In the final section of the novel, Lily recalls a windy morning on which "they had all gone down to the beach." As if it were a painting or a piece of music, Lily titles this interlude "the scene on the beach" or "Mrs. Ramsay on the beach." This second littoral sojourn presents a variation on the tidal pool scene: once again, Woolf's beach appears as a parenthetical space, offering a temporary suspension of the courtship narrative and "the love between men and women." What Lily remembers suddenly, ten years after the fact, is an occasion on which she and Tansley played ducks and drakes while Mrs. Ramsay wrote letters, losing pages to the wind and gazing up confusedly at something she could not quite see. This recovered episode of rock skipping, letter writing, and visual disorientation is "extraordinarily fertile," and its generative (but nonmaternal) intensity affects Lily "almost like a work of art."[144]

"Mrs. Ramsay on the beach" is as close as this novel gets to something like Proustian involuntary memory, whereby a chance sensation sparks a vivid recollection and a forgotten past becomes suddenly and palpably present. In the *Recherche*, such occasions engender the possibility of writing. Something similar happens to Lily as she attempts to finish her painting on the lawn outside the Ramsey's house. As she shifts her gaze between her canvas and the sea vista before her, she is abruptly transported elsewhere: she "seemed to be sitting beside Mrs. Ramsay on the beach."[145] In the "petite madeleine" episode of Proust's "Combray," involuntary memory unleashes the forgotten landscapes of childhood: an entire verdant, lively world appears to emerge from the narrator's cup of tea. Lily, by contrast, imagines burying her beach scene in the sand: sitting in memory (or fantasy) beside Mrs. Ramsay on the shore, she "ram[s] a little hole in the sand and cover[s] it up, by way of burying in it the perfection of the moment." This buried moment is metaphorized as a sort of luminous paint: a "drop of silver" into which one "dips" to light one's way through the past. At this juncture of the narrative, time becomes strange, and we cannot tell if Lily is dipping into the sand—beach-painting—in the present or the past.[146] In this regard, like the parenthetical tide pool chapter, "Mrs. Ramsay on the beach" appears to hover suspended, barely attached to the text around it. It is as if in recounting Lily's reverie—"ringed round, lit up, visible to the last detail"—the novel itself begins to dream.[147]

Notably, this episode also presents one of the text's rare scenes of writing: on the beach, Mrs. Ramsay "sat down and wrote letters by a rock. She wrote and wrote."[148] Yet the emphasis here is not on Mrs. Ramsay's authorial control, but on the way in which writing opens onto play as her pages blow into the waves. The scene also underscores the haziness of the letter-writer's vision—an imprecise, nonappropriative mode of looking that responds, in a different key, to Nancy's wavering intertidal gaze. On the beach, Mrs. Ramsay's fallibility is exposed: she can neither keep hold of her papers nor identify a floating spot in the distance, and her uncertainty become a refrain: "Is it a lobster pot? Is it an upturned boat? . . . Is it a boat? Is it a cork? . . . Is it a boat? Is it a cask?"[149] It is precisely this perceptual hesitation that stirs Lily to paint, bringing her improvisatory mood back to her. Blurry-eyed Mrs. Ramsay is no longer (to invoke Rancière) a domestic "tyrant." In the intertidal zone, we see this character in a new light. No longer occupied with governing and managing the affairs of the home, nor with closing doors and opening windows, nor with soothing children and sympathizing with ambitious men, Mrs. Ramsay instead laughs at Lily and Tansley, then sits silent, as if giving her blessing to an occasion of playful "friendship and liking" without marriageable future. "Love ha[s] a thousand shapes," Lily will reflect, and it is this pluralistic, polyrhythmic conception of intimacy and care that *To the Lighthouse*—and especially its scenes on the beach—most insistently affirms.[150]

This chapter has made a case for the Woolfian beach as a parenthesis in the plots of both marriage and ambition: an experimental aside in which to test out other temporal patterns and ways of looking. Like her beachcombing, tide-pooling, seaside-letter-writing characters, Woolf is drawn to the shore as a space for exploring perceptual grounds and horizons. On Woolf's beaches, the human observer is disoriented by perspectival and scalar shifts, mesmerized by an elemental spacing of sense and sound. In *To the Lighthouse*, the brooding tide-pooler's play with light and shadow, her "wavering" gaze, and her back and forth movement between self-aggrandizement and self-undoing suggest an alternative, nondomestic rhythm—a different arrangement of life.

Chapter Three

CARSON'S QUIET BOWER

Before Rachel Carson published her celebrated 1962 exposé of the pesticide industry, *Silent Spring,* she was a marine biologist involved in a quietly queer, long-distance love affair. The present chapter considers Carson's ecological imagination—and especially her vision of the seashore—in relation to this epistolary romance. Carson's writing about the beach, like her love letters, is patterned by the play of presence and absence, anticipation and delay. I argue that queer and ecological modes of care are particularly conjoined in *The Edge of the Sea* (1955), a book that sets aside the rhetoric of the oceanic sublime in order to examine the delicate edges and underground spaces of the shoreline. In this amply illustrated text, full of drifting tentacles and hidden sea caves, Carson explores how life forms accommodate themselves to the small worlds that both hold and expose them. Concerned with ambiguous, qualitative differences, attentive to the minute and the passing, *The Edge of the Sea* offers a queer close reading of the tidelands.

Silent Spring made Carson an international celebrity, but she had previously published several highly regarded books on marine life: *Under the Sea-Wind* (1941), *The Sea Around Us* (1951), and *The Edge of the Sea*. The latter two books were immediate best sellers, and Carson won the National Book Award for *The Sea Around Us.* It may surprise us today that books exploring marine ecology and aesthetics would have been so popular. *The Sea*

Around Us, in particular, was selected as an alternate for the Book of the Month Club, and even made it onto the *Sunday Review*'s "What Businessmen Read" column.[1] As Amanda Hagood has pointed out, Carson benefited from a postwar fascination with sea exploration.[2] In the 1950s—the beginning of the period of heightened capitalist extractivism and expansionism now known as the "Great Acceleration"—Americans wanted to own the seas, to possess them epistemologically and materially.[3] Yet if this explains to some extent the popularity of her work, Carson's treatment of sea life is at odds with such imperialistic aims. In *The Edge of the Sea*, especially, she approaches the ocean with a sense of wonder for its myriad minute and sensitive life forms. This book evades the rhetoric of polemic, its meditation on the intricacy and precarity of coastal habitats offering a subtle corrective to the attitude toward the oceans prevalent in postwar America— the assumption, that is, "that the sea was a virtually unlimited resource, as well as a readily available dumping ground, for the growth of American industries."[4] *The Edge of the Sea*, by contrast, presents the seashore as a space of vulnerability and impermanence. Although in 1955 Carson had not yet been diagnosed with the cancer that would end her life less than a decade later, this book invites us to consider how finitude gives particular force and purpose to practices of attention and interpretation.

THINKING SMALL

When an editor at Houghton Mifflin tapped Carson to write *The Edge of the Sea* in 1950, he pitched it as a highly accessible guidebook, or beachcomber's manual—"the standard book to go in every picnic basket."[5] Indeed, Carson's early titles for this work were *Guide to Seashore Life on the Atlantic Coast* and *The Beachcomber's Baedeker*. When she began her field research for the project in 1951, she conceived of it as being organized around sketches of individual marine creatures. But, realizing that she had been trying to write "the wrong kind of book," she soon turned her attention to describing the embeddedness of plants and animals in their biological and geological environments.[6] As she put it in a letter to her editor, her aspiration from the start had been to "go beyond merely finding and identifying to suggest, albeit subtly . . . what life may be like in terms of a fiddler crab's existence, or a barnacle's."[7]

The Edge of the Sea abandons the epic scale of Carson's earlier work in order to examine the interconnected animals and plants that inhabit small swaths of shore. Based on her own fieldwork and written in the first person, the book is unique in Carson's oeuvre. Forgoing the drama of plot and the pathos of character, each intricate description represents hours of patient observation, sometimes carried out in painfully cold northern waters.[8] To cite queer ecocritic Catriona Mortimer-Sandilands, we could say that Carson presents "nature" not in terms of "saved wildernesses," but rather, as a series of "unlikely refuges and impossible gardens."[9] Although the book foregrounds the tenacity of the creatures that survive in this threshold, Carson's rhetoric is not heroic. Our narrator-guide is a lingering seaside explorer who periodically appears and vanishes. When she is present, it's always in a nonobtrusive manner: one of her characteristic poses is to lie prone beside a tidal pool, examining its "pellucid depths."[10]

Carson's non-dominating mode of observation is all the more notable when one compares it to the tone of robust masculinity that characterizes the most popular and authoritative seashore guidebook of the era, Ed Ricketts and Jack Calvin's *Between Pacific Tides*, first published in 1939 and reissued in four subsequent editions. Carson borrowed the structure of this work, which was unique in grouping animals and plants not according to scientific taxonomy but ecologically—as they are actually found on the shore. Yet her tone and narrative style are quite different; as she put it, she intended her own book to be "less ambitious."[11] Here we might understand "ambition" in terms not only of scale but of mood. *Between Pacific Tides* presents the shore as a space of violent struggle—even a war zone of sorts. Ricketts and Calvin open the book with a preface describing the intertidal zone's conflictual atmosphere: "while the visitor is puzzling over his first sea anemone, a score of crabs may scurry away at his footfall or may rear up and offer battle in defense of life and liberty.... He hears scraping sounds and clicks and bubblings, perhaps sharp cracks like tiny pistol shots."[12] A 1948 preface to the second edition of *Between Pacific Tides* by Ricketts's friend and collaborator, John Steinbeck, underscores the book's virile mood. Three years earlier, Steinbeck had dedicated his novel, *Cannery Row*, to Ricketts. This insouciant hymn to automobility, intoxication, and homosocial male bonds depicts the California coast as a space of high drama, "fantastic with hurrying, fighting, feeding, breeding animals."[13] In his preface to *Between Pacific Tides*, Steinbeck builds on his fictional account of Monterey as a space of "ravening individualists," presenting the coastal explorer as a conqueror driven by the desire to "rediscover, reclassify, and redescribe."[14] Steinbeck's tone of exploratory ambition can in fact be traced back to the earliest coastal guide books, such as Charles Kingsley's mid-Victorian *Glaucus; or, The Wonders of the Shore* (1855). According to Kingsley, tide-pooling requires the "brave and enterprising" qualities of a 'knight-errant,' and is thus an activity inappropriate for "effeminate or pedantic men."[15] For Victorian thinkers like Kingsley, as Kyriaki Hadjiafxendi and John Plunkett point out, exploration of the tidelands was a "muscular," colonizing pursuit that promised to "rejuvenat[e] the male body" sapped by urban life.[16] Ricketts and Calvin push this logic even further: their tide-pooler's rugged individualism is reflected in the life forms he observes. Thus *Between Pacific Tides* casts tide pool space-sharing in negative terms, as a deprivation for those crowded creatures and plants who would presumably prefer to be alone: "the competition for attachment site is so keen that animals settle upon each other—plants grow upon animals, and animals upon plants."[17]

Carson, by contrast, emphasizes the necessity of interconnection and community even when describing antagonistic relationships. As she puts it, "the lives of many of these creatures of the low-tide rocks are bound together by interlacing ties, in the relation of predator to prey, or in the relation of species that compete for space or food."[18] Animals eat one another in *The Edge of the Sea*, but the book is not organized around the drama of predation and survival. Carson attends instead to patterns of shared existence, examining how biotic communities create conditions of refuge for one another, transforming a bleak and harsh environment into a livable one: "Here, in this mossy turf, life exists in layers, one above another; life exists on other life, or within it, or under it, or above it. Because the moss is low-growing and branches profusely and intricately, it cushions the living things within it from the blows of the surf, and holds the wetness of the sea about them."[19] Carson's seashore is not exclusively a locus of struggle and competition: it is also a space of intricate crossings and cohabitations, a "marvelous complexity of structure and function."[20] While Ricketts and Calvin present the intertidal zone as a space of visual intensity and abundance, replete with objects so "bizarre" that the casual visitor "cannot fail to notice" them, Carson highlights a subtle interplay of visibility and invisibility.[21] And while *Between Pacific Tides* underscores the human observer's dominant position in the food chain, reminding us again and again that these octopus, oysters, owl limpets, abalone, and clams are "delicious," Carson never reduces the creatures of the shore to edible market commodities.[22]

Not only are Carson's intertidal creatures not for us to eat; they are often barely available to the human sensorium. One of the primary features of *The Edge of the Sea* is the attention it pays to the small. Carson highlights the boundedness of the littoral zone, practicing a form of description that critic Joni Seager terms "radical observation."[23] It is as if Carson is trying to read smallness itself in *The Edge of the Sea*, inviting a gaze capable of recognizing the most seemingly inconsequential forms of life. The adjective *small* and its synonyms crop up everywhere in the volume, qualifying all sorts of objects, from "microscopic lights" and "miniature" tide pools to "small creature[s]" and "small beings." These entities are not simply diminutive, but range from the "nearly invisible" to the "inconceivably minute" and the "infinitely small."[24] Carson is honing in here on degrees of minutia that we are ill equipped to imagine. This is "a world so small that our human senses cannot grasp its scale, a world in which the micro-droplet of water separating one grain of sand from another is like a vast, dark sea."[25] The book investigates not only how these miniature worlds inter-exist, but how we might possibly understand their microscopic reality. Carson asks, for example, "what is the meaning of so tiny a being as the transparent wisp of protoplasm that is a sea lace, existing for some reason inscrutable to us?"[26]

Carson's account of the Atlantic coast thus invites readers to attend to forms of life and patterns of attachment that could easily pass beneath notice. Attentive to remnants, traces, and inscriptions, her aim is not just to document but to interpret these minute biotic communities. "Close reading" is not a phrase that one normally associates with marine biology. Yet Carson, sensitive to the different ways in which intertidal phenomena make themselves legible to the observer, might be considered a close reader of the shore. Indeed, she had a background in literature: growing up in landlocked central Pennsylvania, English Romantic poetry taught her to admire the ocean with a "purely vicarious love" long before she had ever laid eyes on it.[27] Later, she studied English in college until, enamored with her brilliant and charismatic professor, Mary Skinker, she switched her major to biology.[28] As a reader of rocky, sandy, and coral beaches, Carson does not simply classify objects but hones in on what we could call the language of the seaside. Her shore is a space of signs—a "riddle," often "obscure, elusive."[29] Here microplants have "written their dark inscription" and hordes of diatoms signal their message, "flashing their microscopic lights in the night sea." Tough and smooth-surfaced organisms are likened to "parchment," and even sand suggests a kind of writing: presenting a "record of other lives," it is scored with "peculiar markings.... seemingly irregular scribblings... strange insignia."[30] Its "thin net of flotsam" is an archive, a "strange composition" that weaves together "strands of dried beach grass and seaweeds," as well as "crab claws and bits of sponge, scarred and broken mollusk shells, old spars crusted with sea growths, the bones of fishes, the feathers of birds." In this drift of debris, Carson contends, one can read the imprint of "a million, million lives."[31] Such descriptions require a peculiar form of engagement on the part of the reader: we must shuttle between scalar extremes, imagining the vast temporal and spatial expanses that have been condensed into so many broken shells, bones and feathers.[32]

The tiny plants and animals that inhabit Carson's seashore exist in a state of precarity. Implicit here is the threat of rising sea temperatures on the "sensitive" life forms the book details: Carson references early on the "widespread change of climate" responsible for warming seas since at least the beginning of the twentieth century.[33] Exposed to the ebb and flow of the tides, surviving in relation to a network of other exposed beings, the creatures she details in this book are minute but tenacious, marked by their delicacy and their toughness. This dissonance is felt everywhere in *The Edge of the Sea*. For instance, small creatures like the ghost crab appear at once "delicate" and "vital," living amidst the shoreline's coarse and craggy surfaces—its "bristles," "stems and stubble," "felty roughening," and "frayed," leathery fronds. The "delicately sculptured shells of mollusks called angel wings" appear as "fragile as china," but are "able to bore into clay or rock." The large-clawed snapping shrimp provides a contrast to the "intricate passageways" in which it resides, and the rocky shore abuts "lacy cascades of foam." In a reef, one finds both "fragile, delicately branching hydroids" and a "curious shrubby form of moss animal" with "tough and gelatinous" branches. Even as Carson insists on the adaptation of such creatures to their rugged environment, she also makes us aware of their vulnerability. While listening by night to the surf "trampling" with "heavy tread," she has often wondered, she tells us, about the "baby starfish, the urchins, the brittle stars, the tube-dwelling amphipods, the nudibranches, and all the other small and delicate fauna of the moss."[34] Always conscious of the fragility of these vegetal and animal entities, Carson cultivates a gaze that is not just "close" but also light.

POSTAL METER

The "closeness" and "lightness" of Carson's reading practice in *The Edge of the Sea* cannot be extricated from the queerness of her vision. Carson's beach book departs from expected midcentury frameworks for kinship and desire in at least two ways. First, she presents the intertidal zone as a porous margin and locus of continous permutation—a world in which interconnection sometimes materializes in surprising ways. In its lively unpredictability, Carson's shoreline calls to mind the implicitly queer botanical concept of the "landscape pattern." As critic Anne-Lise François puts it, because landscape patterns involve the "*entire* interplay of floral resources and pollinators in a habitat," thus fostering "loose, diffuse, and shifting attachments," they offer a compelling alternative to heteronormative "mutualist assumptions."[35] In other words, landscape patterns are not comprised of fixed, predetermined animal-plant pairs. For François, landscape patterns, like poems, are allied with shades of difference, "context-specific variation," and the capacity to play with time. Carson's tidelands, with their tentacles and caves and their patterns of protection and predation, are similarly mutable and variegated—a point to which I will return at greater length.

Second, a certain queer sensibility can be gleaned from the book's paratexts. *The Edge of the Sea*—and especially its "Rocky Shores" chapter—constitutes a love letter of sorts to Dorothy Freeman, Carson's neighbor on the coast of Maine, where both women had summer cottages.[36] *The Edge of the Sea* was dedicated to the Freemans—a gesture Carson had planned from the start of the relationship.[37] Although they only met in 1953, Freeman was married, and their relationship was mainly epistolary, Freeman was the love of Carson's life and her most significant interlocutor during the years in which she was researching, writing, and revising *The Edge of the Sea*. As Carson put it in a letter to Freeman, whom she considered her "ideal reader": "maybe the easiest way for me to write a chapter would be to type 'Dear Dorothy' on the first page!"[38] This ardent but uncodifiable liaison was a source of both solace and inspiration for Carson. Its intermittent epistolary rhythms and its ambiguously chaste, nonexclusive intimacies shaped her aesthetic and ecological imagination, forming the backdrop and giving the tone to her investigations over the last eleven years of her life. The two women were rarely in one another's physical presence, but they exchanged hundreds of letters, taking great pleasure in deciphering each other's traces, inscriptions, and remainders.

In today's sex-positive, exposure-oriented language, we might say that the romance between Carson and Freeman was closeted. It was certainly shaped by a refusal to be read, judged, and classified according to the homophobic norms of the 1950s. But the closet, with its implications of repression, is not quite the right image. This love affair was neither unrealized nor repressed; to borrow Carson's own Keatsian language, its privileged figure was not the closet, but the "bower."[39] *The Edge of the Sea*, too, is a reflection on "bowers" or quiet refuges of various sorts. It's an examination of small temporalities and styles of existence that conform neither to the hypermasculinist ethos of the atomic age nor to the speeded up time-space of late capitalism.

Early in their relationship, in the midst of writing *The Edge of the Sea*, Carson sent Freeman some lines from book 1 of Keats's *Endymion*:

> A thing of beauty is a joy for ever:
> Its loveliness increases; it will never
> Pass into nothingness; but still will keep
> A bower quiet for us, and a sleep
> Full of sweet dreams.[40]

The *Oxford English Dictionary* defines a *bower* as a dwelling or abode, often an idealized dwelling. A bower might be an inner apartment or lady's boudoir, or, alternatively, "a place closed in or overarched with branches of trees, shrubs, or other plants; a shady recess, leafy covert, arbour." Its Keatsian associations with *shared* "beauty," "quiet," "sleep," and "dreams" differentiate the bower from the figure of the closet, which indicates a different, more fearful mode of silence. The closet implies a solitary, dark, claustrophobic space, with its shut door of homophobic repression. Conversely, as Helen Vendler observes, "in every Keatsian bower there is a rendezvous."[41] A bower is an *inside* that is also an *outside*; for Carson and Freeman, it suggests an indeterminate, anachronistic space of affection unregulated by the norms of heteroreproductivity, not necessarily organized around genital sexuality, but flush with eroticism nonetheless. As evoked by the temporally and spatially ambiguous "stillness" at the center of Carson's cited lines, the Keatsian bower might best be conceptualized less as a private or secret enclosure than as a shared realm of quiet. Thus when Freeman wrote to Carson in December 1954, anticipating a planned overnight in New York, she proposes that the two of them spend their first hour together simply sitting close together in the hotel, without speaking a word. Freeman later wrote to Carson to say that they had made their own "quiet bower" in the city.[42] The bower remained a guiding image for these women throughout their relationship: Freeman refers to it in the last letter she ever wrote to Carson, postmarked on the day of Carson's death.[43]

The relationship between Carson and Freeman was defined by its quietness and by its mediated, nonexclusive intimacy. What's notable here is that such open-handed care-at-a-distance is at the heart of Carson's ecological vision, too. Or rather, it *became* central to her ecological vision during this period. The metrical unaccountability of postal communication—with its zigs and zags and its tone of anticipation and surprise—is an analog to Carson's fascination with the unpredictability of miniature marine life-worlds. Carson and Freeman described their meeting as a "Discovery," and the realization that they loved one another as a "Revelation."[44] Similarly, Carson depicts the seashore as a space of unexpected apparition where elusive creatures emerge in their own good time. Her correspondence with Freeman also occasioned another sort of affective and temporal interplay: Carson was a professional—a trained scientist writing under a deadline—but her work was enlivened by Freeman's unschooled enthusiasm for the Maine coast and the more-than-human world. Amateurism, according to Carolyn Dinshaw, indicates a queer way of knowing: it suggests not the absence of expertise, but a different, less detached and rule-bound attachment to an object. Writing *The Edge of the Sea* with Freeman in mind, Carson calibrated her language for the passionate amateur—the "tinkerer" and "dabbler" free to "linger at moments of pleasure."[45]

Soon after she met Freeman on July 12, 1953 (a date they would treat as their anniversary), Carson's life became patterned by postal rhythms. Epistolary relations involve carnal pleasures of an indirect sort: the heart-pounding excitement of a letter's arrival, heralded by a "rattle at the mailbox," the *frisson* of unsealing the envelope, the familiar presence of the beloved's handwriting—like an extension of her body—and the tender collecting of letters, sometimes committed to memory by the force of rereading.⁴⁶ As Shira Brisman points out, belatedness and anticipation are built into the epistolary mode: a letter "uniquely combines urgency, privacy, and the awareness of its own inevitable delay."⁴⁷ Meta-epistolary commentary on the quotidian realities of anticipating, receiving, and opening letters is common in Carson and Freeman's correspondence, such phatic (channel-checking) language itself constituting a form of distanced touch.⁴⁸ Although their correspondence was voluminous—especially in the early years of their relationship—each letter's appearance was a thrill. In January 1954, Carson described to Freeman her visceral elation at the mail truck's approach: "the same leaping heart when the red, white, and blue truck came in sight, and the same sharply in-drawn breath when the envelope appeared."⁴⁹ One might imagine that Carson would have preferred full-time proximity to Freeman—the state of unbroken togetherness often assumed to be the norm or zero degree for a romantic relationship. But her letters reveal that she enjoyed the on-again, off-again rhythm of their closeness, with its anticipations, its high and low seasons, its various mediations (the post, the telephone, the automobile, the train, the airplane). Indeed, "satisfaction" is the very word Carson invokes to describe her feelings about brief intervals of physical or epistolary contact with Freeman: an exchange of letters is "deeply satisfying," an encounter in New York, "rewarding and satisfying," and a particular written response from Freeman "wonderfully satisfying."⁵⁰ Good at making do with little, adept at activating imaginative forms of proximity, Carson does not seem to need more than she has. Thus she frequently refers in letters to a sense of Freeman's "presence": "you seem very close"; "you were always with me when I wakened in the night"; "I've been mentally sending you notes all day." Both women refer to the time it takes to write a letter to the other as "[an] hour with you."⁵¹

The epistolary permits a certain temporal dilation, not unlike the lingering pace of the seaside wanderer. Carson and Freeman's insistence on the plenitude and sufficiency of indirect proximity is reminiscent of the "extravagant imagining" that Peter Coviello attributes to the experience of inhabiting an erotic self in an atmosphere of "definitional ambiguity" rather than within the frame of a publicly legible homosexuality.⁵² It also resonates with Sarah Ensor's discussion of "intransitive" contact as a queer ecological practice. Their correspondence illustrates what Ensor calls the "radical potential of touch:"; a "suspended, protracted, playful" mode of contact in which "restraint" is not incompatible with "voluptuousness" and distance and intimacy are not necessarily opposed.[53] If Carson and Freeman experienced their epistolary relationship as "satisfying," it was because they were adept at finding unexpected forms of presence within intervals of physical separation and delayed encounter. After all, as Carson puts it, a letter can be reread "so many, many times."[54] The correspondence between these women often dwells on the mundane: the frustration of a bad hairdo, the account of a social engagement, the details of an ailment. But these are also love letters—meant to be poured over and treasured, read and reread (often in bed). Thus Carson tells Freeman that she read her letter twice before turning out the light or admits that "before I went to sleep I reread (for the ninth time!) a number of your recent letters, darling," and Freeman avows that she could "practically say [Carson's] letter by heart" because she has "read it literally a thousand times."[55]

Repetition is only one of the hermeneutic modes that shape the composition of these letters. They are stylized, too, by obliqueness, circumlocution, and other techniques of evasion—forms of indirection that also feature in *The Edge of the Sea*. Describing herself as "the schemer in action," for instance, Carson proposes a cover to keep Dorothy to herself during a brief upcoming visit: "shall I be sick and have to go to bed for the duration of my visit?"[56] Later, in a typically cryptic avowal, Freeman writes: "I am shut away in the back bedroom in the corner that belongs in my heart only to you—you know where and why."[57] This is not to say that these women always sought to shut others out, however; in response to Freeman's admission that she has shared "parts of" one of Carson's letters with her husband, Carson responds, "I *want* him to know what you mean to me."[58] Each woman is highly conscious of her entourage—Carson's earliest letters to Freeman tack from "we" (including the author and her mother) to "I," and back again—and each experiments with modes of address, tinkering with the register of their closeness. Throughout their correspondence, they code their epistolary salutations differently depending on the intended addressee: those that begin with "Dearest" permitted a wider audience (Freeman's husband, Carson's mother), while envelopes marked "for you" and containing letters opening with the word "Darling" ("My Darling," "My precious darling," etc.) were for the addressee's eyes only. Certain letters, marked for the "Strong Box," were to be destroyed.[59]

Carson and Freeman improvise freely with signature lines as well. Epistolary signatures, though highly ritualized, enable a considerable degree of flexibility and artful hint. Although they boldly profess their love for one another, the women also tend to dance around such overt declarations, often signing off with suggestive short-hand phrases. These include the coy wink ("you know what"), the repurposed vow ("I do") and the neologism ("allways"). This last instance is particularly interesting as it brings the spatial concept of the "way" to bear on an invocation of temporal permanence. In "allways," the promise of constancy intersects with the more surprising image of multiply branching pathways—a provisional network of possibilities. In its homey experimentalism, "allways" is also reminiscent of the seeming incongruity, in Emily Dickinson's letters and verse, of vertiginous, otherworldly reverie expressed via humble, sing-song hymn meter and hand-stitched fascicles. Like Dickinson, Carson embraces the domestic and the everyday while refusing heteroreproductive norms. Her correspondence with Freeman echoes the desire for the spatiotemporal *otherwise* that features in Dickinson's similarly oblique love letters to Susan Gilbert. In Coviello's reading, Dickinson's syntactically disassembled epistles urgently ask the question, "*where might we love one another?*"[60] A similar query is at play in the letters that Carson and Freeman exchanged. In their inventively spelled sign-off, "allways," difference and deferral—a proliferation of routes—fracture the fantasy of immutability. The correspondence thus carves out an alternative space-time of care, a "quiet bower" not eternal but precarious and contingent.

These letters are works of imagination, attempts to find a tongue with which to speak intimate attachments beyond the heteronormative. This does not mean, however, that Carson and Freeman imagined themselves outside the world and untethered from its phenomenality—or, indeed, from the sensibilities of their era. The women's shared passion for birdsongs and flowers cannot be extricated from the popular greeting card aesthetics that mediated their correspondence. Their intimacy was shaped by the greeting card as a "quintessential emotional commodity"—yet they also played with this sentimental register according to their moods and desires.[61] One year, for instance, Carson sent Freeman multiple Valentine's Day cards, each printed with familiar preset verses ("Life has been happier, Darling / Since you and I first met"), illustrated with flowers and cats and annotated by Carson: "this one first," "this one last," and "all the valentines in all the world couldn't tell you how much I love you!"[62] By piling up such commodified expressions of devotion, Carson is appropriating popular culture to her own ends, twisting the logic of mass diffusion and mechanical reproduction to serve as signs of her own inexhaustible affection. Compounding this peculiar overlap of the unspoken and the over-the-top, Carson signs one of the cards "you know who— / and what!" Carson's tone here is at once playful and unapologetically sentimental; her quiet bower encompasses the greeting card kitten and the floral bouquet. Her sense of nature weaves together Keats, Hallmark, the tide pool teeming with life, and—as we shall see—the mysterious sea cave, in all its briny, tentacular depths.

In his valorization of the "awkwardness" of pre-Stonewall articulations of same-sex sexuality, Christopher Nealon examines the queer desire to "feel historical"—"to convert [a] harrowing privacy . . . into some more encompassing narrative of collective life."[63] In the intense affinity she developed with Freeman, Carson did not want to "feel historical." Instead, she and Freeman sought to feel more-than-human: they experienced their alliance as woven into a broader ecological and aesthetic web. Political scientist Lida Maxwell, in a recent queer reading of *Silent Spring*, argues that Carson and Freeman understood their love as a "multispecies achievement" fueled by encounters with nonhuman nature, particularly birds.[64] I would suggest that it was not only birds that served as mediating objects for these two, but all sorts of other phenomena. The objects of their shared enchantment included songbirds, freesias and white hyacinths, the full moon, Tchaikovsky's Symphony No. 6 and Mendelssohn's Violin Concerto in E minor (which they called "Our Symphony" and "Our Concerto"), their respective granddaughter and grandnephew, their cats, and the seashore—especially the tidal pools and sea caves of Maine.[65] Though decidedly middlebrow, their tastes were inflected by pagan resonance: scattered through their correspondence is the cosmic image of "stardust," a phrase they used to describe the wonder of an almost telepathic connection, when they unwittingly thought or perceived something in common though hundreds of miles apart. Despite its secretive qualities, then, their intimacy was not closed and private, but open-ended, always expanding outward.

To better understand how this vicarious mode of intimacy inflected Carson's seashore investigations in *The Edge of the Sea*, consider the case of the sea cave—a bower-like refuge that serves as the text's central image. Carson opens the book with this example—she tells us that the cave "stands apart" for its "exquisite beauty"—and then returns to it at length in the "Rocky Shores" chapter. The sea cave exemplifies the tidal zone's peculiar fusion of presence and absence, shelter and exposure, toughness and delicacy. It is a space of implicit lesbian eroticism, with its "hidden pool," "soft radiance," and baby-sea-anemone-covered walls—"little glistening mounds of soft tissue" that invite touch.[66] When Carson "explores" with her fingers among its thongs of dulse algae and Irish moss, she "begin[s] to find creatures of such extreme delicacy that [she] wonder[s] how they can exist in this cave when the brute force of storm surf is unleashed within its confined space."[67]

Given the aesthetic and epistemological centrality afforded this hidden cave, and its placement in Maine, one might assume that Freeman had been present when Carson discovered it. Yet, as Carson later explained, precisely because Freeman had not been there to see the cave, she was all the more present in the composition of the scene as its imagined addressee: "But darling—maybe you can be glad you didn't [see the cave] if you think of this—knowing you hadn't seen it, I tried to describe it *for you*, so it would become real in your mind. Maybe without that objective, the result would have been very different."[68] Later, when Carson was dying, and confined to a wheelchair, she asked Freeman to help her "try once more" to search for "a fairy cave on an August moon and a low, low tide."[69] The rocky coast of Maine was thus for Carson not just the backdrop for meeting and falling in love with Freeman: Dorothy and the coast were intertwined.

It should be clear by now that what I presented as two distinct modalities of queerness—Carson's concern for the nuances of intertidal life forms and her love for Dorothy Freeman—are in fact inseparable. Carson's vision of the tidelands, like her bond with Freeman, was marked by a nonpossessive ethos of intermittency and variation and shaped by what François calls "vanished and emergent potentialities."[70] The subtle pleasures of the marine biologist cannot be detached from the subtle pleasures of waiting for Dorothy's phone call, living by the rhythm of her letters, and being (occasionally) by her side.

"WEE BEASTS"

Drawing our attention to the fragile styles of existence that make up the landscape patterns of the shore, *The Edge of the Sea* maps out various unconventional ways of marking time. Critic Stephanie Kaza has identified four distinct temporalities that structure Carson's conception of sea and shore: tidal, seasonal, geological, and evolutionary.[71] One might add other temporal regimes to this list, as each type of shore that Carson examines (rocky, sandy, coral)—and perhaps even each creature that she describes—possesses or expresses its own particular timing. *The Edge of the Sea* does not attempt to translate the ephemeral into the monumental, but simply describes the traces and remainders left by a variety of "transient inhabitants" of the shore. Carson's style is fine-tuned to convey the variegated tempos of these tiny life forms.[72]

Fascinated by "intermediate, transitional qualit[ies]," Carson highlights the irregular rhythms that characterize life in the intertidal zone, a space that "belongs alternately to sea and land."[73] Her shore is an elusive boundary, existing in a state of restless transfiguration. Sand, for example, is a "yielding, shifting substratum of unstable nature, its particles incessantly stirred by the waves."[74] Carson employs a language of variation, not binary difference—a rhetoric marked by formulations such as "some . . . others"; "or others . . . or here . . . or again"; "here and there . . . here and there."[75] Carson's speculative tone is also notable, her prose speckled with "perhaps" and "sometimes." Underscoring this sense of possibility, her descriptions lay emphasis on the rhythmic back-and-forth of revelation and concealment. She devotes pages to discussing varieties of camouflage: she considers the particular concealment strategies of the seahorse, the "grass-green" spider crabs and small shrimp, and the baby cowfish, among others.[76] And she underscores the contrast between the mostly lifeless upper layers of sand and the unseen lifeworld beneath: "all have gone below, and in burrows, tubes, and underground chambers the hidden life of the sands is lived."[77]

Carson's observer must therefore be attentive to forms of existence that are not evident to the eye, and to all the various ways in which "life [comes] out of hiding."[78] The would-be perceiver of such apparitions learns patience as she waits for the "intervals" at which creatures show themselves, the occasions on which virtual doors to minute worlds open or close. The giant sponge, for example, conceals many life forms within it, but "there is no sign of life for the casual passer-by to read, although if he waited and watched long enough he might sometimes see the deliberate closing of some of the round openings, large enough to admit an exploring finger."[79] Here and throughout *The Edge of the Sea*, Carson is captivated by minor rhythms and unexpected interludes. This penchant for the unpredictable brings her into the orbit of modernists like Proust and Woolf, whose novels are patterned by surprise. Indeed, to invoke Walter Benjamin, we might say that the true reader of Carson's seashore, like the true reader of Proust, is "constantly jarred by small shocks."[80]

Carson's shore sometimes presents a miragelike quality, replete as it is with nearly invisible or vanishing phenomena. Consider the following passage, which depicts the peculiar temporality at play in the animation of sand by crabs:

> It is an extraordinary thing to watch the sand come to life if one happens to be wading where there is a large colony of the crabs. One moment it may seem uninhabited. Then, in that fleeting instant when the water of a receding wave flows seaward like a thin stream of liquid glass, there are suddenly hundreds of little gnome-like faces peering through the sandy floor—beady-eyed, long-whiskered faces set in bodies so nearly the color of their background that they can barely be seen.[81]

Carson's observational style here emphasizes contingency. As she examines these nearly imperceptible apparitions, she insists that the sighting is due to chance: the crabs show themselves only "if one happens to be wading." The rhetoric of this passage draws our attention to figurations of transience and intermittency; note the language of the "fleeting instant," and the episodic quality conveyed by the syntax of "one moment . . . then . . ." Above all one is struck by Carson's capacity to convey the everyday enchantment of a happening that can scarcely even be called an event: the emergence of a life form that just as quickly vanishes. "Almost immediately," she writes, "the faces fade back into invisibility."

This interplay of presence and absence structures *The Edge of the Sea* in a more material sense as well. This is the most densely illustrated of all Carson's books, and its plethora of pencil drawings transforms the text itself into a multilayered environment. It is thus an "imagetext" in W. J. T Mitchell's sense: "a composite, synthetic work" combining the visual and the verbal.[82] As one contemporary reviewer noted, the illustrations are "curiously interwoven with the text in such a way that you cannot read the one without simultaneously seeing the other."[83] Carson chose her friend and colleague Bob Hines—a self-taught wildlife artist at the Bureau of Fisheries—to illustrate the book. The pair traveled together, gathering and studying specimens along the Atlantic coast. As Carson put it, she felt that

FIGURE 3.1. Rachel Carson and Bob Hines collecting specimens of tidal life. Missouri and Ohio Keys. Florida Keys, 1955. Photo Rex Gary Schmidt. By permission of Rachel Carson Council, Inc.

by working closely with Hines it would be possible to obtain "a freshness of approach in the art as well as the writing—no repetition of the museum type of marine art."[84] In fact, author and illustrator collaborated so closely on this project that their editor at Houghton Mifflin referred to the pair simply as "Carson-Hines."[85]

The Edge of the Sea's margins are alive with illustrations. These images do not so much demand our attention as drift or burrow into view, transforming the book's pages into spaces of the underwater or the underground. A wide range of creatures and plants—from sea squirts and northern starfish to hydroids, ghost shrimp, and sea nettles—cling, float, dig, or otherwise "strew their variously hued forms" into the blocks of text, which shrink back accordingly.[86] The page takes on the qualities of a subterranean refuge or a watery surround, depending on whether a ghost shrimp is tunneling down from the top or a rockweed forest of knotted wrack is creeping up the sides.[87]

In Ricketts and Calvin's *Between Pacific Tides*, the drawings and photographs are strictly contained on separate pages and do not encroach on the text in any way. Images in this work serve the larger objective of presenting the Pacific coast in as totalizing a fashion as possible. Epitomizing this logic, each section of illustrations in the third (1952) edition of *Between Pacific Tides* opens with a full-page panoramic aerial photograph of a type of beach, courtesy of the U.S. Navy.[88] Military vision, with its ideal of total visibility and unbroken surveillance, thus structures the volume. Chapters in *The Edge of the Sea* also begin with full-page images, but these are pencil drawings, each presenting the type of beach in question not from a panoramic aerial position but from the humbler vantage point of an earthbound artist standing on the shore.

In contrast to the contained, precisely scaled diagrams and photographs of *Between Pacific Tides*, we are always aware of the handmade quality of Hines's illustrations, their pencil strokes corresponding to the individual tentacles of a jellyfish, the bristles on a sea mouse, or the ripple marks on the surface of the water. These drawings are not rendered to scale, but the effect is not deterritorializing: this is not what art historian Jennifer Roberts calls "total scalar manipulability" or ecocritic Derek Woods terms the "smooth zoom" mode of infinite scalability.[89] Rather, Hines's scalar imprecision implies a *tactile* exploration: in these drawings, the human hand and its textured objects are always in contact, each shaping and determining the other. Moreover, occasionally—as is the case with Hines's drawing of a ghost shrimp—two versions of the same creature appear side by side, at two different (unspecified, unmeasured) scales. Rather than conveying a sense of human mastery over an environment, the effect is dreamlike and disorienting. Perhaps this oneiric quality reflects the fact that Hines himself was encountering these animals for the first time. An expert illustrator of birds—especially ducks—he was a newcomer to marine zoology when he undertook this project.[90] Unfamiliar with the scientific names of the various coastal creatures he drew, he took to calling them all "wee beasts."[91]

The edge of the sea is a place of amphibious crossing and transspecies assemblage. No wonder, then, that Carson and Hines pay so much attention to tentacular species, with their luminous, supersensible appendages.

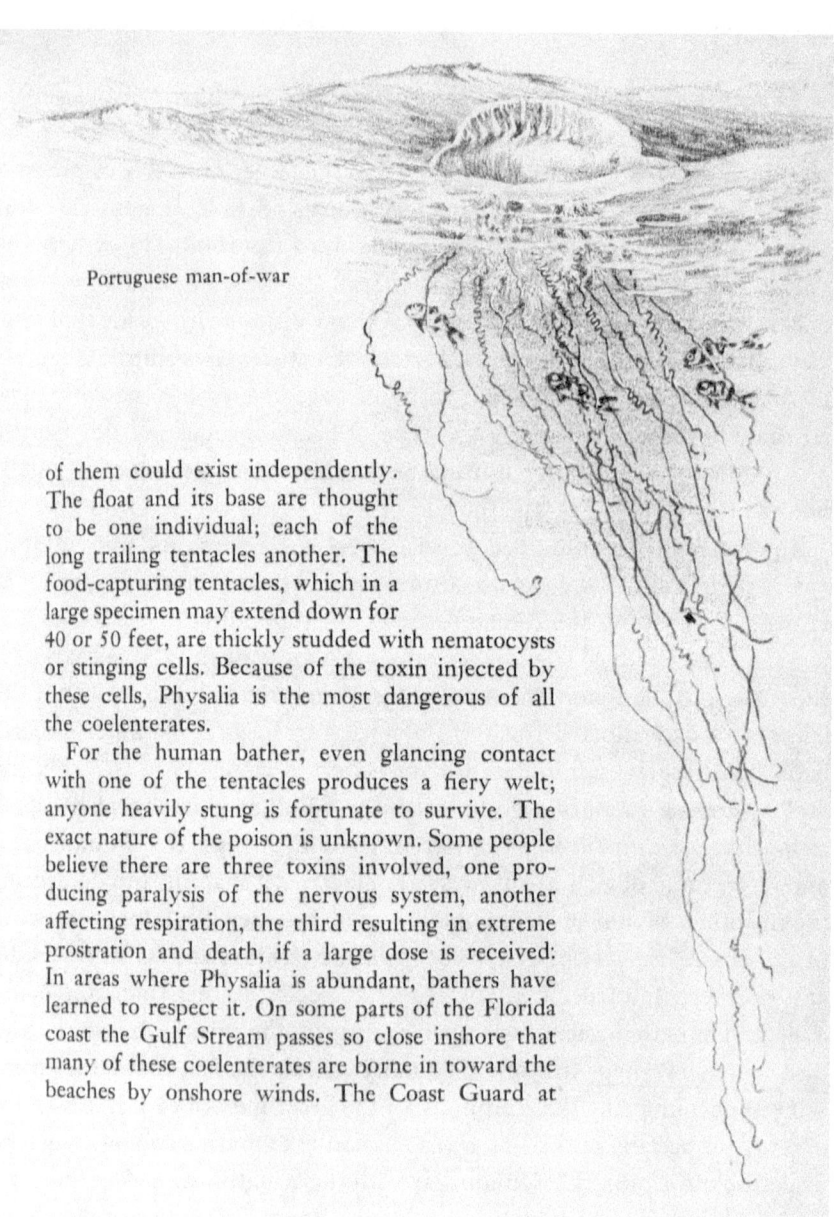

Portuguese man-of-war

of them could exist independently. The float and its base are thought to be one individual; each of the long trailing tentacles another. The food-capturing tentacles, which in a large specimen may extend down for 40 or 50 feet, are thickly studded with nematocysts or stinging cells. Because of the toxin injected by these cells, Physalia is the most dangerous of all the coelenterates.

For the human bather, even glancing contact with one of the tentacles produces a fiery welt; anyone heavily stung is fortunate to survive. The exact nature of the poison is unknown. Some people believe there are three toxins involved, one producing paralysis of the nervous system, another affecting respiration, the third resulting in extreme prostration and death, if a large dose is received: In areas where Physalia is abundant, bathers have learned to respect it. On some parts of the Florida coast the Gulf Stream passes so close inshore that many of these coelenterates are borne in toward the beaches by onshore winds. The Coast Guard at

FIGURE 3.2. Wayward man-of-war in *The Edge of the Sea*. Reprinted by permission of Houghton Mifflin Harcourt Publishing Company.

Ranging from the minute to the gigantic, these include the "petal-like" tentacles of an "exquisitely fashioned" hydroid; the tube-building worm Spirorbis's delicate and filmy "crown of tentacles"; and the immense, trailing tentacles of the Portuguese man-of-war and arctic jellyfish.[92] Hines's illustrations of the latter two emphasize the magnitude of these creatures and the difficulty of containing them within the page. Thus the curling tentacles of the man-of-war hang languorously into the text, which cuts away into a hexagon in order to make room. The arctic jellyfish's voluminous tentacles stray even more daringly from the margins: they drift into the line of print below, gently touching the words "as the tide." It is as if these tentacles—which, Carson notes, "sometimes trail for fifty feet or more"— cannot be held in place and instead float across the page, crossing the dividing line between image and text.[93] This tentacular trespass could almost be overlooked, so slight is its effect: the straying tendrils merely brush across the words in the gesture of a light caress.

In examining the drifting tentacles of Carson and Hines's arctic jellyfish, one begins to understand "tentacular thinking" as Donna Haraway does: as a figure for "non-arrogant collaboration" and an alternative to bounded individualism. Drawing on the work of anthropologist Tim Ingold, Haraway argues that to live tentacularly is to inhabit the world as a "wayfarer," enmeshed in "nets and networks," traversing "a wealth of lines" or "interlaced trails."[94] In their wayfaring mutability, these invertebrates embody transience. Like the amorphous Proustian *petite bande* of chapter 1, jellyfish seem to be "all verb instead of noun," according to theorist Eva Hayward, for whom such beings mark the intersection of transgender and animal studies.[95] Jellies are light-diffractors, Hayward notes: "living, respiring, metamorphosing diffraction patterns," they exist in "a constant state of transposing, becoming, and troping."[96] Carson also insists on the luminosity of these creatures, which she describes, variously, as "opalescent forms," "crumpled cellophane," and "white gleams."[97] Amplifying this outward-oriented diffraction effect, jellyfish offer a seemingly incongruous hub for multispecies gatherings. Carson—who, as daughter, aunt, and adoptive guardian, engaged throughout her life in many nonreproductive relations of stewardship and care—emphasizes the contrast between the apparent inhospitality of this species and the shelter it provides.[98] She writes that although the jellyfish has a powerful sting, young fish adopt it as a "nurse," resulting in a strange kind of kinship. The small fish, "traveling

sea they will bud off the tiny discs that, by some inexplicable magic of development, grow in a single season into the adult jellyfish.

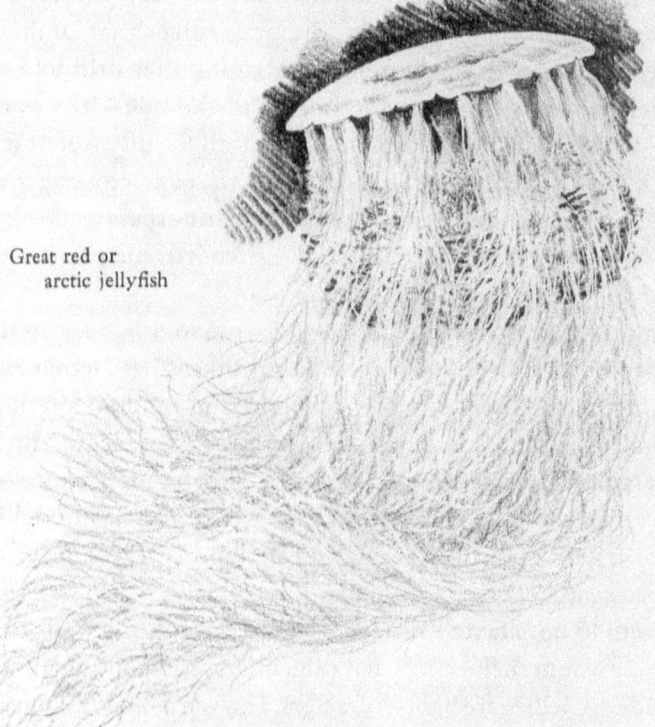

Great red or arctic jellyfish

As the tide falls below the rockweeds, the surf of the sea's edge washes over the cities of the mussels. Here, within these lower reaches of the intertidal zone, the blue-black shells form a living blanket over the rocks. The cover is so dense, so uni-

FIGURE 3.3. Tentacular trespass in *The Edge of the Sea*. Reprinted by permission of Houghton Mifflin Harcourt Publishing Company.

through the shelterless sea under the protection of this large creature" are "somehow unharmed by the nettle-like stings of its tentacles."[99]

Such mutable, "wayfarer" existence is key to Carson and Hines's vision of the tidelands. Carson's writing is as textural—and tentacular—as Hines's drawings are. *The Edge of the Sea* frequently activates the special reciprocity particular to the sense of touch.[100] "Often," Carson observes, "I find the pools of the upper third of the shore lined with a brown velvety coating. My fingers, exploring, are able to peel it off the rocks in thin smooth-surfaced sheets like parchment."[101] Sometimes a tidal pool is so transparent that the line between water and air can only be perceived, as she puts it, by "the sense of coldness on my fingertips."[102] Carson extends this haptic sensibility to her reader, inviting us, for example, to imagine handling the "leathery," "satiny," "frayed" surface of kelps—also known as "devil's aprons" and "sea tangles"—which flourish in deep pools: "if one slides his fingers down along such a stalk and grips just above the holdfast, he can pull up the plant and find a whole microcosm held within its grasp."[103] Carson sees fingers where one might not expect, tending, for instance, to measure intertidal phenomena by the handful and the finger length. She points out "handfuls of spindrift," "handfuls of grass," and a variety of life forms with finger-sized dimensions, including a flowerlike hydroid with blossom-tentacles "as large as the tip of my little finger," a limpet wearing a shell "the size of a fingernail," a browsing sea hare "about as long as my little finger," "thumbnail"-size crabs, and crab tracks that can be spanned by an index finger.[104] The objects of the explorer's curious palpation are likewise touch oriented; indeed, the "haptic-optic" perceptual modality that Hayward calls "fingeryeyes" can be felt everywhere in Carson's intertidal zone.[105] In this text, fingers are not only measuring tools but sensory appendages shared by observer and observed alike. Thus rock pools are hung with "the pink fingers of soft coral," oyster shells are coated with "fingerlike projections," and sea cucumbers explore their surroundings with soft tentacles, "which periodically they pull back and draw across their mouths, as a child would lick his fingers." The indented red fronds of dulse resemble "the shape of a hand," and when Carson references the "shaping hand" of the sea itself, even the ocean takes on haptic force.[106] Indexicality and tactility are hardly the privilege of the human observer in this text.

The textural, variegated quality of Carson's beach extends into other sensory domains as well. Like Proust and Woolf before her, Carson presents the seashore as a multisensory realm in which the haptic, visual, acoustic, and olfactory cross and mingle, producing a disorienting atmospheric effect. Thus a listener lying at the entrance to a sea cave perceives "the small sounds" of water dripping from mussels and seaweed, while a coral beach emits "sizzling and crackling," "murmurings and whisperings"—noises that suffuse the air but seem to issue from no identifiable source.[107] And beyond its visual "gleams," its acoustic "gurgles," "sighings," and "groans," Carson's rocky shores are suffused with a rich mix of odors: "the sulphur smell of sponge, the iodine smell of rockweed, and the salt smell of the rime."[108]

As indicated by the account of sea cucumbers childishly "lick[ing] their fingers," the queerness of Carson's sensibility cannot be opposed to homeyness or to the kind of ongoing care work that took up much of this writer's energy and time. Textural descriptions in particular tend to transform the seashore into an uncanny domestic space. Carson's account of the Maine sea cave floor is particularly notable in this regard, its "green crumb-of-bread sponge" forming a "thick-piled carpet built of tough little feltlike fibers laced together with glassy, double-pointed needles of silica."[109] One is struck here not only by the incongruous conjunction of images of resilience ("thick-piled," "tough,") with a language of delicacy ("little," "laced," "glassy"), but by the way domestic imagery mediates between these tonal registers: Carson's seashore is a midcentury feminine interior, replete with saucers, bread crumbs, carpet, curtains, threads, and needles. Recalling Mrs. Ramsay's maternal and domestic framing of the sea in Woolf's *To the Lighthouse* as a vision of "plates" and "pleats," Carson's Atlantic coast is strewn with creatures and plants that resemble the ordinary stuff of her own middle-class home. She describes sea laces that unfurl their crown "as one would open an umbrella," tidal pools "no larger than a teacup," and worms as delicate as a "long-stemmed goblet" or as shiny as a "Christmas tree ornament."[110]

Carson's domestic rhetoric does not simply render the seashore familiar, however. The effect of the continuous tension between delicacy and roughness is to pull the reader in close—but not too close. As Eve Kosofsky Sedgwick has argued, textural descriptions draw us away from the realm of aesthetic untouchability, instead inciting questions about the object's history ("how did it get that way?") and potential interactivity ("what could I do with it?").[111] Textural perception, in other words, invites us to engage in a more proximate and active kind of aesthetic "free play."

CARSON'S QUIET BOWER

The small creatures of Carson's intertidal zone present constellations of textural particularity, each shaped by a unique set of elemental forces and connections. We make speculative contact with the sensory-rich textures of these objects in our minds, softly running imaginary fingertips across their felty, frayed, bristled surfaces. And yet Carson's emphasis on the fragility and unfixedness of the seaside environment prevents us from caressing too insistently or holding on too tightly. The marine biologist's description of her own light touch indicates the manner in which we are asked to enter this delicate world. On "meeting" her first sea hare as it "brows[es] peacefully" among the seaweed, Carson writes: "I slipped my hand under it and gently brought it toward me, then, its identity confirmed, I returned the little creature carefully to the algae, where it resumed its grazing."[112]

As this chapter has demonstrated, *The Edge of the Sea* is a guidebook, even if not the sort of popular beachcomber's manual Carson was originally tasked with writing. Instead, it's an homage to misfit intimacies, a guide to nondominating practices of attention and to flickering, impermanent modes of presence. As a marine biologist observing the Atlantic coast, and as a midcentury queer subject, Carson found satisfaction in the ephemeral and expressed gratitude for what she knew she could never fully possess. *The Edge of the Sea* is a meditation on transience, a love letter to Dorothy Freeman, and a hymn to those imbricated life forms that endure, improbably, through rough storms and rising seas.

Chapter Four

McKAY'S DREAM PORT

What if the beach were not a fixed place, but a practice, a way of existing in the world? This chapter examines the act of "beaching" in the margins of the city. The first part considers the "life of the beach" in Claude McKay's *Banjo: A Story Without a Plot* (1929), an experimental narrative that stretches and twists the vernacular maritime expression for joblessness—being "on the beach"—until it signifies something other than a state of privation.[1] In *Banjo,* Jamaican-born Harlem Renaissance novelist and poet McKay reclaims the aesthetic category of the picturesque to describe diasporic Black waterfront collectivities in the 1920s. In so doing, he imagines an alternative kind of littoral zone—a space of collective "ease"—in the heart of Marseille's industrial port scene. The second part of the chapter turns to a different but no less capacious sort of urban beach: the rough, improvisatory, erotic and artistic underworld that flourished during the 1970s and 1980s on New York's derelict Hudson River piers. Here photographers like Alvin Baltrop and Shelley Seccombe and "anarchitecture" practitioner Gordon Matta-Clark (among many others) carved out space for their visions in dilapidated structures abandoned by the shipping industry, amidst an illicit queer scene of rest and play. Alongside Marseille's interwar traffic of break-bulk hulls and on and around New York's decaying pier platforms and forgotten storage sheds, unlikely beaches cropped up—playgrounds and harbors, precarious spaces of pleasure and repose.

Queer utopianism is a through line in *Modernism at the Beach,* though it tends to materialize obliquely—taking the shape of an exuberant seaside leap, a shadowy tide pool, or a quiet bower. The present chapter investigates utopianism's radical edge more explicitly, foregoing the spectacle of casinos, hotels, and automobile rides—and the smaller riddles of ghost crabs and brittle stars—in order to explore transgressive acts of contact, exhibition, and assembly. The industrial play zones that constitute beaches for McKay and the Hudson pier artists of the 1970s may seem a far cry from both Proust's and Woolf's moneyed seaside resorts and summer homes, as well as from Carson's intimate zoological observations. Yet my hope is that readers will recognize an improvisatory sensibility linking these divergent modernist imaginings. The shore in Proust, Woolf, and Carson indicates not—or not only—a codified holiday site but a flexible and open-ended style of perception and way of inhabiting space. McKay makes this idea explicit: his beach is not a specific locale but a collective practice and shared state of mind; it's not a place one visits, but something one "falls for."[2] His undocumented, out-of-work protagonists are not actually on holiday, but they are "always in holiday spirit."[3] Marseille, like the Hudson waterfront decades later, appears therefore to be made as much of desire as of cement and water. It's what McKay calls a "dream port"—a space of implicitly queer sociability and vagabondage, "inexhaustible interest" and "strange enticement."[4]

McKay's protagonists, like the other artist-poachers who feature in this chapter, encroach upon worlds of labor and industry, clearing space in which to gather, salvage, rest, or simply look around for a spell. In my approach to McKay's vagabond picturesque and to the trespassing practices of the Hudson pier artists, I draw inspiration from Jacques Rancière's emancipatory theory of aesthesis, according to which aesthetic comportment, broadly construed, makes thinkable different ways of sharing out of the world. For Rancière, art cannot be reduced to the logic of display or the performance of sophistication. Rather, it matters insofar as it disrupts social determinism and recalibrates the given hierarchy of bodies and ideas.[5] In this regard, Matta-Clark's avant-garde interventions into abandoned, closed-off buildings, his anarchitectural acts of decontainment—slicing through walls, letting the light in—epitomize the broader ethos of the chapter and of *Modernism at the Beach* as a whole. Yet so does, in a quieter register, Baltrop's practice of hanging suspended from a makeshift harness in old pier warehouses, camera in hand, in order to document the beauty of a clandestine scene from unexpected angles. Both are acts of aesthetic impropriety that effect what Rancière calls redistributions of the sensible. To cite one of McKay's characters, these instances of trespass are ways of "mak[ing] a new beach."[6] Like the self-taught worker-poets of Rancière's *Proletarian Nights* (*La nuit des prolétaires*) who resist an inherited social partition of time and space when they choose to spend their nights writing, this chapter's protagonists refuse to know their place.[7] Making art is for them a means of reconfiguring the divisions determining who works, who thinks, and who gets to dream.

Here, then, and throughout this book, I share Aarthi Vadde's conception of literature and art as resources for rethinking "communal forms."[8] Beaches are compelling modernist settings not only because they are so unsettled, both ecologically and sociologically, but also because they are potential commons—contact zones in which the logic of enclosure gives way to less scripted, more extemporaneous ways of being together. For McKay, Baltrop, Seccombe, and Matta-Clark, the commons is not a fixed location, let alone a natural resource to exploit, but a relational mode facilitating the expansion and remixing of social partitions and styles of vision. As Stavros Stavrides and others have shown (and as I discuss in chapter 2), a commons is not simply a place in which "anything goes," but a space open to public use in which "rules and forms of use do not depend upon and are not controlled by a prevailing authority."[9] For the protagonists of this chapter, to "make a beach" is to create new forms of "life-in-common," infusing an improvisatory ethos of care into a desocialized urbanscape.[10]

Given the way waterfronts are partitioned across the globe—commercialized, monumentalized, museified—it is easy to forget that the seashore was long seen as inappropriable. In Roman law, for instance, the seashore, the sea, the air, and running water were considered "things in common" (*res communes*).[11] Even today, shorelines tend to be legally protected from privatization. This is notably true in France and in the U.S., as well as in Mexico, Thailand, and in many other coastal nations of the Global South. An officially sanctioned public space is not equivalent to a commons—which, not being reducible to property, is neither strictly public nor private—but maritime laws protecting public access to the littoral zone at least disallow the kind of development that would definitively enclose the water's edge.[12]

Scholars have examined the history of precapitalist commoning practices, which were governed by what historian E. P. Thompson calls the "moral economy of the poor."[13] Such practices are not consigned to the past, however. Rather, we might understand commoning as a minoritarian style of being together within capitalist modernity—one that coalesces in practice and takes unpredictable forms. In philosophy, Jean-Luc Nancy's anti-universalist, anti-identitarian reflections on community as a "being singular plural" are a fertile source for this line of thought, as is Michael Hardt and Antonio Negri's theorization of the commons as an ecological and socioeconomic "altermodernity"—an "ethics of democratic political action within and against Empire."[14] These theorists help us recognize the commons that already exist— Hardt and Negri point to language and other forms of knowledge as part of a shared "common wealth"—and push beyond the impoverished, public-private, socialism-capitalism antinomies that obscure more metamorphic, non-property-based possibilities for collective life.

In a more capacious and intersectional vein, the Black radical tradition as well as queer of color critique offer crucial perspectives on the politics of commoning. From these overlapping vantage points, the commons encompasses a variety of social margins or fringes in which impromptu collectivities and scenes of resistance might take form. Saidiya Hartman, for instance, has described the early twentieth-century slum as an "urban commons where the poor assemble, improvise the forms of life, experiment with freedom, and refuse the menial existence scripted for them."[15] Hartman imagines both the ghetto alleyway and the tenement hallway (or "parlor") as rich zones of sociability, unrecognized as such by critics bent on reform. Samuel Delany invokes the erotic potential of such makeshift urban commons, mobilizing a coastal metaphor when he imagines himself as a maritime "navigator" mapping the "temporal coastline" of pregentrified midtown Manhattan, where now-demolished porn theaters, street corners, and gay bars enabled a wide range of queer interclass "contact."[16] In their study of the "undercommons" of the academy, Fred Moten and Stefano Harney valorize what they call "fugitivity" as a practice of thought and being that counters the university's reproduction of hierarchy.[17] And José Esteban Muñoz likewise underscores movement and flow in his discussion of the "brown commons" as a social ensemble that "smolder[s]" with "life and persistence."[18]

These thinkers share an understanding of the commons as a social relation rather than a fixed site. Many decades earlier, McKay explored the politics and aesthetics of commoning when he refigured *beach* as a verb: his beach is a commons that facilitates nonproprietary modes of connection. To "beach" or "make a beach" in *Banjo* is not simply to occupy a particular location but to open and expand a confining social script. As McKay makes clear, making art is sometimes akin to going on strike, and taking it easy can be a radical act.

PORT EFFECTS

How should we understand the relation between the leisure beach and the working waterfront? This question is key to the protagonists of this chapter, who explore the possibility of "beaching" at the edges of industrial ports, carving space for shared rest within a codified site of labor. As they demonstrate, if we widen our horizons and consider the beach as a mobile, relational phenomenon, a more egalitarian conception of leisure comes into view.

Beaches and ports would appear to be incommensurate spaces. While the leisure beach stages the spectacle of nonwork, the shipping port is a platform for the "concrete moving of goods."[19] Doorway between sea and land, a port is a transfer point or channel of exchange, a place for loading and unloading bodies and things. The specter of enslavement haunts the commercial port, which enabled the mass-scale, brutal commodification of human beings.[20] But ports exceed their function as sites of commerce and industry: they have also served as fundamental vectors in the history of organized labor, as a fomenting ground for strikes. As centers of diasporic community, the industrial working ports of the last century sustained a diverse, often queer social world and a "vagabond internationalism" that spilled beyond the docks.[21] In this sense, ports are zones of encounter, marketplaces for both commodified and noncommodified forms of pleasure, spaces for cruising, loitering, and carousing. It is precisely this transient collectivism—this unexpected beach effect, to invoke Roland Barthes's phrase—that makes ports such alluring milieus for artists and other visionary types.[22] As McKay and the other protagonists of this chapter demonstrate, beaches and ports are not necessarily opposites: viewed from a certain angle, each encompasses the other.

Consider, in this light, the complex history of the French word *grève* (beach).[23] Like *beach, grève* literally refers to this site's geological sediment, or sandy shingle, but the word acquired a range of other meanings over time. Today, *grève* retains its original sense but also signifies a labor strike: to be *en grève* is to strategically withhold one's labor. This semantic morphology can be traced to the Parisian Place de Grève (now known as the Place de l'Hôtel de Ville). Named for its location on the banks of the Seine, the Place de Grève served until the nineteenth century as the primary port of entry for Paris's waterborne food supply.[24] But this port was much more than just a place for unloading cargo: it was a site of pleasure and of violence, an "epicenter of rebellion" and a place of "misery and possibility."[25] The Place de Grève was infamous as the site of public executions—Balzac and Hugo reference the place in this context simply and ominously as "la Grève"—but it was also the stage for public festivals (it held the annual midsummer bonfire for the fête of Saint Jean) and for hiring fairs, especially those of migrant stonemasons.[26] Workers regularly assembled at the Place de Grève for hiring, banding together near the river when work could not be had or when the offered price was too low. As Charles Tilly observes, "to stand apart from work was therefore to *faire la grève*; strikers became *grévistes*."[27] This port was the origin of the modern labor strike, and it served more broadly as a popular gathering place during moments of political crisis or insurrection, from the 1789 Revolution to the 1871 Commune.[28] The *grève* thus invites us to hold seemingly opposed terms in our minds: festival and death, work and strike, beaches and ports.

As the multiple resonances of *grève* make clear, the beach is more than a commodified landscape: it can also function as a commons and a staging ground for collective resistance. The industrial port—or its ruins—sometimes realizes the beach's egalitarian promise, appearing not only as a site of labor and logistics but as an aesthetic and erotic experiment and a space of both contestation and delight. This is precisely how the working waterfront features in McKay's *Banjo*, which presents Marseille as a queer Black gathering place—marked by "rough rhythm" as well as by the ad hoc forms of intimacy and solidarity that make such a precarious life livable.[29]

For McKay, the signifier *beach* points in multiple directions. We happen upon the novel's eponymous protagonist—a musician and "great vagabond of lowly life"—as he is strolling along Marseille's breakwater, broke and hungry but stylishly dressed as he admires the view. Banjo has arrived in his "dream port" after making the unusual decision to get himself deported: he simply declares, despite all evidence (and to the amusement of the U.S. immigration officials) that he is not American, then signs up on the casual maritime "tramp" that eventually lands him in Marseille. Banjo has held "all the easily-picked-up-jobs," but we encounter him during a period of downtime in which he and his new friends—a group of transnational Black drifters McKay calls "beach boys"—explore the possibilities of being "on the beach."[30] Riffing on this vernacular phrase, *Banjo* explores both the pleasure and the precarity of being unemployed and off the grid, and thus part of what Brent Hayes Edwards calls a "flotsam community . . . of men without a country."[31] This is a novel that takes place in a world of work: dock work, coal work, and maritime labor are referenced throughout, in addition to service and sex work. In McKay's interwar Marseille, repose is always shadowed by toil, and aesthetic making tends to blur into other forms of hustle and trade. His beach boys slip between taking it easy and performing a variety of mostly unwaged practices, including "scavangering," panhandling, playing music, and writing, among other ruses and tricks for getting by.[32] And yet McKay spotlights what takes place in the margins of this laborious universe.[33] Joblessness in *Banjo* implies the risk and uncertainty of living on the edge, exposed to hunger and the constant threat of state violence, but it is also inseparable from the aesthetics of "quiet," the joy of collective "ease," and the insouciance of a roving, beauty-seeking eye.

McKay plays on the maritime expression *on the beach* as if it were a melody in a jazz tune, spinning out various grammatical and definitional possibilities, including: "beach boys," "beach fellows," "men on the beach," "men of the beach," "beach-combers," a "beach-known reputation," to "fall for the beach," to "land on the beach," to be "on the beach" (with or without quotation marks), to be "beaching," to "make a new beach," to "make another beach," and to lead "the life of the beach." In the most basic sense, to be on the beach is to be off the ship. In *Banjo*, it's a condition sometimes sought, sometimes accidental; lived alternately as exile, liberation, or refusal. In McKay's "beach" we should therefore hear the French word *grève*, in all of its dissonant connotations (strike, festivity, violence, repose). Only when it appears for the last time in the novel is the phrase "on the beach" enclosed in quotation marks, implying that we can interpret McKay's many unquoted invocations of the phrase in a more elastic and open-ended sense. "They were no longer 'on the beach,'" we are finally told, since Banjo has decided to return to work at sea.[34] Even here, however, McKay troubles the fixed meaning of this expression, as in fact Banjo simply goes in search of other beaches. At the novel's conclusion, he takes his advance sailor pay with the intention of going "vagabonding" once more, bringing the exiled Haitian writer Ray (the novel's other primary protagonist) with him.

As Vadde points out, in various ways *Banjo* explores "the discomfiting proximity between taking apart a stereotype and participating in its perpetuation."[35] McKay's insistent use of the phrase "beach boys" plays on this indeterminacy. The derogatory phrase indexes a violent history of infantilizing Black men, and yet McKay mobilizes it affectionately and familiarly. White vagabonds, by contrast—negatively cast in the novel and likened to dogs—are termed "beach fellows" or "beach-combers."[36] While McKay represents these "fellows" as alone in their addiction and neglected hygiene, his "beach boys" are "jolly" and possess a "wide experience and passive philosophy of life."[37] These men have found themselves off the clock in one way or another, by choice or necessity; lacking identity papers, they look out for one another and leverage their charisma and connections to scavenge food from docked ships.[38] Moving with ease in and out of the various spaces of the waterfront—breakwater and docks by day, Bum Square and Ditch by night—McKay's beach boys are "adepts at meeting, understanding, and accepting everything."[39]

VAGABOND PICTURESQUE

In *Banjo*, McKay presents a recomposed aesthetics of the maritime picturesque within a highly policed urban landscape. Given its strategic central location in a Mediterranean commercial and military network, Marseille was for several centuries a "key node" in the spatial network of French imperialism, as historian Minayo Nasiali has shown. The city was home to France's largest shipping company, the Messageries Maritimes, and it also provided a "launching point," from the eighteenth through twentieth centuries, for colonial offensives throughout the world.[40] In exploring what he terms the "picturesque" or painting-worthy quality of vagabond life within this surveilled industrial port city, McKay releases this aesthetic concept from its historical relation to estate management and landscape design. For

McKay, the picturesque names a way of seeing proper to a mobile, collective eye—not the eye of an image-collecting tourist or architect, but of one who is cruising or simply passing through.[41]

It may seem surprising that McKay invokes the picturesque in his depiction of Marseille. One does not readily ally this eighteenth-century "landscaping aesthetic" with an author committed, in Gary Holcomb's phrasing, to "permanent revolution."[42] In McKay's hands, however, the picturesque is reinvented, released from its implicitly imperialist theorization by the likes of eighteenth-century baronet Uvedale Price, for whom the concept signified the translation of human bodies into painterly figures or "ornaments to the landscape."[43] Nor does McKay's picturesque indicate a merely pleasing superficial arrangement—which is how, according to Kim Michasiw, this aesthetic has often been misconstrued by critics.[44] For McKay, the picturesque becomes instead a way of experimenting with the imbrication of setting, figure, and desire. His picturesque is an aesthetic judgment proper to a transient observer, an artist on indefinite shore leave, who gazes enchantedly at the view as he drifts by.

Historically, the picturesque is a way of seeing that translates the world into a painting.[45] William Gilpin first defined the term in his travelogue *Observations on the River Wye* (1770) as denoting a style of tasteful perception that turns nature into a series of framable tableaus or manageable pictorial "scenes."[46] Indicating an affection for landscapes that appear somewhat rough rather than polished, the picturesque's lineage nonetheless allies it with a history of power and privilege, taste and distinction. Dependent upon "distance and separation," this sensibility is linked to English gardening and landscape design; to a touristic style of vision (which reduces human inhabitants of a place to elements of the view); and, especially in the nineteenth-century U.S., to the ideology of settler colonialism, with its "wilderness-subduing, westward-moving 'I.'"[47] As Alain Corbin points out, the attitude of the picturesque tourist is proprietary: picturesque view-seekers rate landscapes and point out their flaws, traversing nature as if it were a gallery, "collect[ing]" landscapes like shells.[48] Linda Nochlin expands on this critique, noting that one of the functions of the picturesque is to "mask conflict with the appearance of tranquility." The picturesque object is always by definition positioned as "backward" and "culturally inferior" to the viewer: one's equals, Nochlin observes, cannot be viewed as picturesque.[49]

This nineteenth-century visual code is radically reconfigured in McKay's homage to Black transnational vagabondage. In *Banjo*, the concept of the picturesque is released from its inherent elitism, assimilated into a left-wing politics and a queer aesthetic sensibility. Although the picturesque had long objectified and belittled poor people by positing them as continuous with the landscape's pleasing irregularity, in McKay's prose this animate-inanimate confusion of figure and ground does not suggest the logic of colonial dehumanization. Rather, McKay's creolized picturesque is tender: he attends with affection to bodies that the dominant culture deems unworthy of regard. His Black quayside picturesque encompasses a transgressively gendered woman who "carries her excessive maternal feelings under a cloak of aggressive masculinity," a chauffeur's uniform—"old and overworked symbol of a free and reckless way of living"—and the many shades of Marseille's "bum fraternity" or "rabble."[50] Above all, Blackness itself is "picturesque" in *Banjo*, with its astonishing variety of tongues, colors, and cultures.[51] The beach boys may not be "specially created" for this scene, yet they bring to it a "rich and careless tone" that does not "spoil the picture" but rather increases its "interest."[52]

Ray, the character who most resembles McKay himself in education and livelihood, is also the novel's most adept connoisseur of picturesque codes. In his "idly-brooding moods," Ray observes Marseille aesthetically from afar: he likes to watch the ships come in on the Corniche and "speculate about making a move to some other place." Notably, however, Ray does not position himself above the "environment of the common black drifters." Rather, he loves the quayside underworld with the "poetical enthusiasm of the vagabond black that he himself was."[53] When Ray takes Banjo to see his cherished view—calling it one of the most interesting parts of the town from a "pictorial point of view"—the two of them gaze with delight, then walk the whole length of the Corniche before "leap[ing] over a wall and a murky stream, cross[ing] the race track, and com[ing] to rest and doze in the shade of a magnolia."[54] Thus the picturesque concept itself roves in McKay, indicating alternatively a state of brooding solitude or a shared ocular pleasure. Sometimes it qualifies the beheld landscape of the port—a mix of ships, factories, cement, water, light, and bodies at work or at rest—and sometimes it qualifies the beholder. Ray's anecdote about becoming sexually aroused by his own reminiscences of Harlem while posing nude for art students in Paris exemplifies the slipperiness of the picturesque gaze in this novel: the writer submits to objectification by artists who "measure" him all over to capture his lines and proportions, "not hesitating to touch [him] when they wanted to place [him] in a better light or position," but this picture-worthy object suddenly leaps out of the frame when he himself becomes a subject of desire.[55]

McKay's play on the picturesque presents an alternative to *Banjo*'s more attention-grabbing ethos of primitivism, or Black vitality, which features, as Vadde cannily puts it, as an "expression of the felt mortality of a precarious existence in a commerce-driven world."[56] When Banjo's spontaneously assembled orchestra performs in the novel's primitivist "Jellyroll" chapter, the scene derives its energy, according to Vadde, from the "friction" among intraracial and international differences. In other words, as Edwards also shows, the novel engages the "primitive" ironically— "twist[ing] it and wrench[ing] it out of shape."[57] Yet a different dynamic is at stake in moments of quiet beholding, when the text mutes its dialogic intensity. In *Banjo*, such occasions of contemplation are not fixed but mobile, as we see when Ray and Banjo delight in the harbor's "pictorial" qualities, then leap and splash their way to an afternoon nap. In this way, McKay challenges the orthodoxy of aesthetic thought, troubling the logic that posits "reflective judgment" as the province of a decorporealized judging subject, free from hunger, fatigue, and other contingencies, and capable of assessing sensory phenomena "without interest." McKay's drifting aesthetic subject, by contrast, moves with ease between contemplating a landscape, leaping over a wall, and sleeping under a tree. Neither individual nor universal, but a shared, intermittently shrinking and dilating "I," his picturesque subject is rootless and alive to the place where he happens to finds himself at any given moment.

McKay's picturesque is therefore not a postcard aesthetic but indicates an affinity for what he terms a "rough, joyous, free picture."[58] In its blurring of distinctions between bodies and setting, we might consider it a quayside "bawdy" version of the anticolonial, more-than-human ethos that Monique Allewaert has termed "Ariel's ecology."[59] But while the minoritarian ecological mode that Allewaert theorizes involves the "enmeshment" of human bodies with "bogs, fens, flats, and other natural phenomena," *Banjo*'s picturesque embeds its subjects in the "macadamized surface," bistros, and luminous breakwater of Marseille, in all of its "barbarous international romance."[60] Indeed, one of the most striking features of McKay's picturesque is its intimate connection to industrial modernity. For Gilpin, traces of industry "injure" the picturesque effect of nature.[61] As art historian T. J. Clark points out, the picturesque was constructed as the opposite of the modern; we see this, notes Clark, in nineteenth-century painting, where this aesthetic tends toward "familiar facet[s] of rural life," such as peasants returning from a fair.[62] McKay, however, orients us away from the tourist's or curator's version of a painting-worthy world and toward a queer picturesque portrayal of the working waterfront. *Banjo* limns the edges of industrial interwar Marseille, finding beauty in an urban port patterned by jarring, irreconcilable contrasts. Consider, in this regard, the following description, which merges human figures with their setting and blurs natural and industrial signifiers in a "shimmering glow":

> Along the great length of the breakwater other careless vagabonds were basking on the blocks. The day was cooling off and the sun shed down a warm shimmering glow where the light fell full on the water. Over by l'Estaque, where they were extending the port, a P.L.M. coal ship stood black upon the blue surface. The factories loomed on the long slope like a rusty-black mass of shapes strung together, and over them the bluish-gray hills were bathed in a fine, delicate mist, and further beyond an immense phalanx of gray rocks, the inexhaustible source of the cement industry, ran sharply down into the sea.[63]

Here the sunbathers' ethos of "carelessness" saturates the maritime scene, which McKay presents as a painting composed of contrasting textures and hues—black, blue, gray, bluish-gray, rusty-black—and textured by conflicting elements: light, sea, coal, factories, hills, mist, rocks, and cement. This is an industrial landscape, yet also a space in which to "bask," and the reader both observes the resting vagrants and shares their view. Despite its insistence on the "carelessness" of these lolling bodies at rest, the passage confirms the author's care for his characters and their world. McKay is attached to his beach boys' detachment, and *Banjo* presents a loving hymn to their nonchalance.

As its title intimates, this is a sonically vibrant novel: it rings with accents, dialectal particularities, songs, arguments, and laughter.[64] *Banjo*'s soundscape is complex, and yet the novel's picturesque aesthetics of beachedness also resonates with the ethos of Black "quiet" as Kevin Quashie has theorized that concept. Quiet, for Quashie, names an alternative to the public expressiveness often associated with Black culture. It also indicates an alternative to Du Bois's celebrated theory of double consciousness, which "pivots on the idea of a subject ensnared in a racialized discourse."[65] Quiet is a concept that indexes the possibility of a Blackness not bound up in the publicness of racialization, neither "faithful" nor "resistant" to the "projections of white culture."[66] It is a "capacity" akin to resistance, Quashie argues, though not synonymous with it.[67]

Here and there, *Banjo*'s joyful or combative discursive noise falls away, and a sort of hush takes over. Quiet reigns in occasions of beholding, when ordinarily verbose characters halt and simply look, moved by what McKay calls the "picturesque" beauty of the industrial waterfront. *Quiet* is a term particularly allied with Ray, who, having "drift[ed] by chance into the harbor of Marseille," first enters the text in a state of withdrawal, as "a black young man who had been sitting quietly in the back."[68] Though he is captivated by Banjo and the boisterous waterfront scene, quiet hangs around this Antillean intellectual like an aura. Quiet is for Ray both an everyday state of being—"I always prefer to listen," he says—and the special mood of aesthetic pleasure. Ray invokes this adjective to convey what he most admires about African sculpture, and when he shares his beloved view of the harbor with Banjo he is "happily moved" but says "nothing." "It's an eyeful all right," exclaims Banjo. But Ray, enchanted, simply attends quietly to the "symphony" playing on the "tendrils that linked his inner being to the world without."[69]

For Quashie, quiet is a factor of "inner life"—of "wild selffullness" and of a "stay against the social world."[70] McKay's quiet is not necessarily a marker of suspended sociality or of subjective interiority. Quiet is the quality of the writer in *Banjo*, but this word also describes how the beach boys, in their various conditions of documented identity, traverse urban space: they take the "quiet way" to reach the Ditch, or "slip quietly" out of a bistro to evade the police.[71] In this regard, McKay's aesthetics of quiet indicates a shared capacity to "take life easy" amidst the threat of violence and the din of commerce and industrial production.

As Edwards documents, Black critics of the period who were concerned with respectability and racial uplift were enraged by *Banjo*, and especially by what they saw as its characters' "disdain for labor."[72] It's true that the act of beaching constitutes a refusal to submit to the racist humiliations of the maritime industry, circa 1929, but the novel's ethos of "easiness" does not simply register resistance to work. Closely linked to quiet, McKay's conception of ease indicates a tendency to evade conflict and embrace a certain proximity to emptiness and nonhappening. Deriving from the French *aise*, which historically signified both "opportunity" and "elbow room" or "empty space beside someone" (*espace libre aux côtés de quelqu'un*), ease is McKay's version of leisure. It signifies freedom in the positive sense ("facility to act") and the negative (freedom from trouble, toil, and constraint).[73] In French, *aise* can be traced back to the Latin *adjacens*, "lying close by."[74]

This idea of a proximate, adjacent form of sociality—closely allied with the image of "empty space"—resonates with the easy mode of affiliation that McKay explores in *Banjo*. In this novel, ease indicates both a moment of lyrical release from tense dialogic sparring and a relation of proximity or besideness rather than dialectical juxtaposition. McKay's characters appear in postures of "insouciant ease" and tend to "ease away" or "ease off," quietly sidestepping scenes of confrontation. Easiness also qualifies this novel's ideal mode of erotic connection: Banjo takes Latnah (the tough, transnational, multilingual female member of their group) "as she came, easily." "Easy come, easy go" could well be Banjo's mantra; he invokes it to explain that he and Latnah are both "taking it easy."[75] Ease here indicates erotic pull but also connotes intimacy without obligation and repose in common, like that shared by the beach boys (and one woman) who dive, float, and sunbathe together by the breakwater.[76]

McKay occasionally literalizes the "beach boy" image, depicting his transient characters laying claim to the waterfront's pleasures, including treating the breakwater as their own private bathing beach: "the beach boys often bathed down the docks, making bathing-suits of their drawers. And sometimes, when they had the extreme end of the breakwater to themselves, they went in naked."[77] The experience of being "on the beach," this novel demonstrates, cannot be reduced to a simple condition of lack, nor is it always a matter of nomadic mobility. It's also a phenomenon organized around the satisfaction of suspended movement and the restfulness of "stopping here and there, staying as long as the feeling held . . . loafing after their labors."[78] McKay's beach boys are bereft of a paycheck but also free from fixed obligation; their "beach" is a zone of indigence as well as of aesthetic enjoyment and bohemian sociality. They "laugh at the logic of consulates," as Edwards puts it, but this does not mean that they live free of social bonds.[79] McKay permits us to glimpse, within such instances of drifting carelessness, a scene of collective care: the men (following Latnah's example) use the breakwater not only as a bathing beach but as a makeshift laundry, washing their shirts with a hunk of soap they have hidden behind cement blocks, and then one of them serves as lookout while the rest bathe in the nude.[80] Beaching in *Banjo* involves both "clean[ing] up" and lying "lazily in the sun," feeling "sweet in [one's] skin."[81]

This scene of repose and replenishment at the end of the breakwater is abruptly interrupted by the appearance of police officers who "throw a perfunctory glance" at the bathers, then "circle round" and ride off. The officers do not dismount from their bicycles, and yet their mere presence, and the latent threat in their glance, cut short the occasion, and the swimmers hurriedly dress.[82] The "perfunctory" glance of the state implies colonial hierarchy, temporal efficiency, and the masterful weaponization of the eye: later in the novel, Ray declares the French police to be the "rottenest in the whole world."[83] By depicting this intrusion of police surveillance upon a scene of extemporaneous beach pleasure, McKay is reminding us that such moments of easy camaraderie take shape in the shadow of imperialism and white supremacy. We should therefore understand this novel's ethos of ease in the context of the racist violence that framed and delimited practices of leisure as well as labor both in France and its overseas empire and in the United States.[84] The world of interwar Marseille is one in which different racist logics overlap, as the city is not only a Black diasporic gathering place (including many U.S. citizens, like Banjo himself), but also a central transfer point in a military and commercial imperial network.[85] McKay's reinvention of the picturesque as an aesthetics of Black ease and quiet takes place within the folds and interstices of this surveilled colonial portscape. *Banjo* spotlights a different side of this military and commercial hub, which McKay loves precisely because it is not an ornamental entryway but Europe's "best back door."[86]

McKay details similar episodes of quiet and ease in his autobiography, *A Long Way from Home*. He recounts spending the summer of 1926 in Marseille, composing stories, sometimes unloading peanuts or coconuts from ships, discussing politics with Léopold Senghor and others, and enjoying the sweet, dry heat of the Mediterranean climate. When he finished writing, he would go on "holiday" and "[take] to the water." He describes bathing at the end of the Marseille breakwater and also discovers, with an

"American friend," an even better place in l'Estaque, where, outside the polluted water of the bay "there still remains a wonderful wide sheet of splendid deep clean water." This became McKay's favorite spot: "there I went every day for the rest of the summer, floating for hours upon my back with the healing sun holding me up in his embrace."[87] This language of "holiday," this longing for a space of elemental tranquility, and the vaguely homoerotic register of McKay's description (the unnamed "friend," the masculinized sun's "embrace") play out in *Banjo* as well. When the beach boys slip, naked, into the sea beyond the breakwater, and when Banjo and Ray escape the tumult of the bistros and bars and quietly behold the "picturesque" harbor scene, the discursive action of the narrative is momentarily stilled and something else comes into view. In such occasions of collective drift, adjacent to the world of work and commerce, we glimpse the radical egalitarianism inherent in McKay's vision of the beach.

PIER EFFECTS

In *Banjo,* McKay shows that beach effects can be enfolded within the surveilled space of the working waterfront, and he explores the practice of "beaching" as a way of making do in the margins of maritime labor. Half a century later, across the Atlantic, artists and other outcasts flocked to the deserted Chelsea piers, drawn, like McKay's vagabonds, to the possibility of "making a new beach" within a seemingly inhospitable setting. Enticed by the experimental gathering places that emerged amidst industrial ruins, these artists documented illicit practices of commoning that transformed a ruined port into a lively aesthetic and erotic contact zone.

New York was long defined by its harbor. Until World War II, this port—the country's largest for over 150 years—was the dominant feature of the city's economy.[88] This changed in the mid-twentieth century, however, when containerization—and the newly accelerated and globalized phase of capitalism it facilitated—reshaped New York's waterfront. Like the steamship, the canal, and the railroad before it, the shipping container ushered in a profound shift in transportation, responding to capitalist modernity's hunger for ever more "cheap nature."[89] Eliminating break-bulk shipping's time lags and spatial pockets, shipping containers—with their accompanying "roll-on, roll-off" maritime cargo system—enabled the outsourcing and automation of labor, stretching supply chains across the globe.[90] In the case of New York, Manhattan's narrow, anachronistic wooden piers—designed to meet nineteenth-century requirements—had no hope of accommodating massive new cargo ships stacked with forty-foot containers, and so shipping traffic moved across the river, to the factory-like Elizabeth-Port Authority Marine Terminal, which opened in 1962 on a former tidal marsh just south of Port Newark. By the 1970s, many of Manhattan's neglected West Side pier platforms had begun to collapse into the water. So the city—now on the verge of bankruptcy—chained up the warehouses and left the once-bustling waterfront to its slow undoing.[91] This is when the piers' second life began.

The Chelsea piers initially became harbors for queer sex because of a homophobic crack-down in the city, an attempt to erase the signs of homosexual life in time for the 1964–65 World's Fair.[92] Soon the rotting decks and deteriorating iron structures of the piers had become a lively adult playground, literalizing a phenomenon that novelist Rose Macaulay, in another context, calls "ruin lust."[93] Recapitulating McKay's quayside picturesque in a different key, the piers staged scenes of collective repose and surreptitious encounter. Like an "extended back room after closing time," this dilapidated waterfront "presented extraordinary opportunities for experimentation and mischief."[94]

Alvin Baltrop, a queer Black photographer who attained modest fame in the art world only posthumously, was captivated by the piers. When not working as a taxi driver or self-employed mover, Baltrop took thousands of pictures documenting everyday life—amicable gatherings, erotic encounters, scenes of solitary reflection and creaturely repose—in this derelict industrial site. In his photograph of sunbathers basking on a cracked cement platform, a heterogeneous assemblage of bodies lounge in various states of dress or undress, as if on a beach. A homoerotic mural by the artist Tava appears at the photograph's bottom left, its representation of interspecies encounter echoed by the human-canine grouping on the far right.

In its explicit fragmentation of space, Baltrop's photograph of the piers subverts the tradition of the totalizing panoramic tableau, which, according to Allan Sekula, was long allied with maritime space. Unlike a panorama, which always signals "desire for a greater extension" beyond what we can see, Baltrop's picture is neither topographically complete nor "greedy" for more.[95] But what is most surprising here is the angle from which the photograph is taken. The platform appears strangely tipped, as

FIGURE 4.1. Alvin Baltrop, *The Piers (sunbathing platform with Tava mural)*. Copyright 2022 Estate of Alvin Baltrop/ Artists Rights Society (ARS), New York.

if the sunbathers were on the verge of sliding off an invisible edge—a spatial reminder that these figures, to invoke Elizabeth Freeman's account of queer temporality, are "out of sync with state-sponsored narratives of belonging and becoming."[96] This dizzying tilt might also remind us of the common etymology for *beach* in Romance languages (the Italian *spiaggia*, French *plage*, Spanish *playa*, and Portuguese *praia*). These words derive from the Latin *plaia*, which can in turn be traced to the Greek τὰ πλάγια, meaning "the sides of a mountain."[97] Like a beach, Baltrop's pier is oblique, aslant—except that instead of slanting *down* to the water's edge its cement surface inclines vertiginously *up* to the Hudson, as if it were a ship pitching in the waves. Baltrop's photograph thus merges the scenography of leisure with maritime visual cues, indicating an outcast queer world suspended between the effects of beach and port.

Baltrop shot his photographs from a range of angles—through doorways, from neighboring piers, and sometimes from above, as he hung suspended in a makeshift harness from the ceiling of pier warehouses, "watching and waiting for hours," in his words, to "preserve the frightening, mad, unbelievable, violent, and beautiful things that were going on at that time."[98] In

FIGURE 4.2. Alvin Baltrop, *Untitled*, n.d. Copyright 2022 Estate of Alvin Baltrop/ Artists Rights Society (ARS), New York.

the scenes he captured, we get a sense of the piers as a zone of attachment, a space in which tenderness and toughness are distributed in equal measure.[99] A February 11, 1987, *New York Times* article describes Manhattan as an "unhemmed dress," the westside piers as the garment's unfinished border.[100] Baltrop invites us to linger in the textures of that frayed edge. Whether he is documenting a gathering of humans on a pier or a lone kitten sunbathing perilously on the harbor rocks, his eye is sensitive to fleeting occasions of intimacy and transformation within a scene of ruin.[101]

Manhattan typically fences off its waterfront, making riverine contact difficult. But the West Side piers were different. As writer Phillip Lopate puts it, they simply ended "in air," such that one could sit at their very edge or even leap off of them.[102] As an early resident of the nearby Westbeth Artists Housing—the first subsidized apartment complex for artists—Shelley Seccombe photographed the piers year round. A music teacher who had begun experimenting with photography in the darkroom of the primary school where she worked, Seccombe, like Baltrop, was largely self-taught. She too, became fascinated by the ruined Hudson waterfront as a "suddenly available yet barely legitimate space," and her pictures capture its myriad "ragtag uses."[103]

Seccombe was especially intrigued by the piers' peculiar overlap of carnival and desolation. Witness to the "constant stream of people [who] poked around and snuck in through gaps in the fence," she documented a desire for various forms of collective intimacy as well as what she terms the "appeal" of "emptiness."[104] Underscoring the contrast of "elegant decaying structures" and "wacky activities," hers is a daytime pier world; she explores carnalities other than the erotic. In her photographs, people seek alternative forms of exposure and togetherness: they sunbathe, dance, hang out, read, play music, practice yoga or karate. After Pier 48 was damaged by fire, Seccombe observed the way its twisted skeleton served as an "ad-hoc jungle gym" for neighborhood kids.[105] Indeed, one is struck in Seccombe's photographs of the piers by the presence of children, including her own daughter. Women, too, often feature—sometimes just lolling with a newspaper, a cigarette, a camera.

Seccombe hones in particularly on different kinds of corporeal waterside play—from the kids who climb and frolic, nonchalant and generally unsupervised among the broken-down platforms, to a seemingly impromptu dance performance or a backward dive into the Hudson. One notes in these pictures an attentiveness to the sorts of bodily maneuvers that the piers

FIGURE 4.3. Shelley Seccombe, *Sunday Afternoon on Pier 49*, 1978.

FIGURE 4.4. Shelley Seccombe, *Three Stages of a Dive, end of Pier 49*, 1978.

made possible. In her photograph of the diver, for instance, Seccombe captures the man in midair as he somersaults into the river.

Hovering, inverted, above the water, Seccombe's diver is like a solitary, upside-down transposition of Proust's Andrée as she flies impertinently over the old banker at Balbec. Like the Balbec beach, the ruined pier works as a "spring board." And just as the jumping scene in the *Recherche* contrasts the girl's graceful leap to her "rasping voice" and rough slang utterance— "the poor ol' boy, I feel sorry for him; he looks half croaked" ("C'pauvre vieux, i m'fait d'la peine, il a l'air à moitié crevé")—Seccombe's photograph pits order against disorder, structure against decomposition.[106] The diver's messy pile of clothing echoes the chaotically warped metal of the broken-down pier behind him, while the vertical and horizontal lines of the wooden pier from which he leaps mirror the rectitude of the warehouse skeleton further in the background. Likewise, the diver's pose suspends him somewhere between form and formlessness. His choreography is controlled and yet slightly dissolute—the open triangle of his bent knees a tilted reflection of the triangular pier fragment protruding from the river behind him. He may pull off the maneuver and slide perfectly into the water or he may splash in with legs and arms akimbo. We can only guess what happens next.

As a final example of the sort of beach effect that the ruined piers made possible, consider Gordon Matta-Clark's *Day's End* (1975), which was created illicitly on Pier 52, where Gansevoort Street meets the Hudson. An artist, filmmaker, and practitioner of what he and his collaborators termed "anarchitecture," Matta-Clark is, according to Douglas Crimp, the figure "most completely identified with the spirit of downtown Manhattan as a site of artistic experimentation in the 1970s."[107] An exuberant innovator of what would later be called social practice art, Matta-Clark's work was radically inclusive and oppositional, encompassing drawing and film, graffiti, participatory street performances, and other site-specific acts of imagination. Intrigued by the city's overlooked "leftover" zones, Matta-Clark explores the metamorphic potential of urban edges and interstices, critiquing what he terms the "containerization of usable space."[108] He is best known today for his staged deconstructions of abandoned buildings, including *Splitting* (1974), in which he sliced into a house slated for demolition as if it were a loaf of bread, and *Day's End*, which transformed an industrial shed into a luminous space open to the water and air.[109] During his lifetime—he died young, at thirty-five—Matta-Clark created seven such "building cuts," some sponsored by institutions and some done on the sly. All of these works have been destroyed.

Matta-Clark's five blunt cuts in the Pier 52 shed transfigure a decaying structure not by fixing it but breaking it down further, exposing it to the surrounding elements. Here's how Matta-Clark's collaborator, Gerry Hovagimyan, described the effect of this waterfront warehouse transformation:

> 200 feet to the front, facing out over the river, loomed a large oval penetration in the corrugated facade of the structure. The steel web supports upon which the corrugated facade hangs had also been neatly removed with an acetylene torch. The brilliant August sunset coursed through a gap creating a physical presence. At the lower left corner, a 20-foot diameter quarter circle had been described and the floor planking removed. Way up in the clerestory, where the roof intersected two corner walls, a circular removal revealed the sky and at the edge of the interior "canal," a jaunty cut-out seemed to mimic the outline of an unfurled sail. Light, air, sky and water. Everything was alive with motion and light.[110]

FIGURE 4.5. Gordon Matta-Clark, *Day's End Pier 52.1*, 1975. Copyright © 2022 Estate of Gordon Matta-Clark/Artists Rights Society (ARS), New York.

Although the authorities soon bridged and fenced the gaping hole that Matta-Clark and his team had cut in the floor of the wharf building, these perforations were an act of exposure—peeling away the ground to reveal the shimmering water beneath, poking geometric apertures in the walls and roof to reveal the sky. *Day's End* was a spectacularly transgressive work: "few artists in the history of the avant-garde," observes Jonathan Weinberg, "have committed a criminal act on [its] scale."[111] Yet the result was an antimonumental homage to transience, as the moving light spots cast by the cuts transformed the old warehouse into a solar time-keeping device—a luminous alternative to the empty, homogeneous clock-time on which the city runs. In the artist's own words, the work was meant to draw attention to the "interplay of the sun's daily passage with the tidal surges of the river below."[112] In *Day's End,* a derelict warehouse becomes, briefly, a beach—a place saturated with light and open to the tides.

FIGURE 4.6. Alvin Baltrop, *Pier 52 (Gordon Matta-Clark's "Day's End")*, 1975–1986. Copyright 2022 Estate of Alvin Baltrop/Artists Rights Society (ARS), New York.

In a letter to a confidant, Matta-Clark draws on this beach fantasy, describing *Day's End*, semifacetiously, as the product of his own "working vacation by the water on the Hudson."[113] Like Baltrop and Seccombe, Matta-Clark was drawn to the conjunction of the rough and the delicate: the warehouse building appealed to him because it had "virtually basilical light and proportions while being a heavy industrial hangar," and he described the noisy work of cutting through its thick steel truss work as an act of "care and attention" that could "save" the structure from abandonment.[114] Ultimately, Matta-Clark and his collaborators were discovered, and the dockmaster chained up the building. Still, as the artist cheerfully put it, "a lot of people took it on themselves to break in and so keep the work in some sort of public domain."[115]

Baltrop was apparently such a trespasser; one of his photographs documents the interior of this warehouse after Matta-Clark's cuts had been made. In this picture, we glimpse two men as they traverse *Day's End*'s "canal" at different angles. Have they had a sexual encounter? Or simply crossed paths wordlessly? One of them is facing the brilliant patch of light at the far end of the building—the effect of Matta-Clark's cut, which the artist described alternately as a "sickle," a "rose window," and a "cat eye"—but his head is turned so that he appears to be gazing at a spot midway between that eye-shaped illumination and the other man. Perhaps Baltrop has caught him in the act of shifting his attention from the luminous spot to the stranger, or from the stranger to the light. The practice of cruising, after all, requires "delicacy, self-control and practice"—one must not simply stare overtly at an object of desire, but engage in a play of "reciprocal glancings."[116] The photograph captures a fleeting moment—an ephemeral passage through *Day's End*—even as it indicates the tenacity of desire, as irrepressible as light itself. As Matta-Clark noted, even after the authorities had "vandalized" his work on Pier 52 by sealing over holes and installing safety railings, "they [couldn't] stop the sun coming in through the sickle shape in the back."[117]

Baltrop's picture, which makes visible a moment of erotic possibility within an illicit space of art—or, inversely, illuminates an instant of aesthetic beholding within a clandestine zone of desire—is also a chance improvisation and a happenstance collaboration with Matta-Clark. It presents the overlapping, trespassing visions of the "guerilla renovator" (who had fled the scene of his crime) and of the quiet photographer who broke in to document the makeshift basilica's afterlife.[118]

Like McKay's drifting author, Ray—who shares his favorite views of the Marseille harbor with Banjo—Baltrop, Seccombe, and Matta-Clark invite us to wonder at the beauty of unexpected and officially unsanctioned beach effects. Each artist is energized by the waterfront as an ephemeral contact zone. Each is attuned to the possibilities of the commons—the way art cuts into enclosed space, letting the light in. Such gathering places were not exclusively traversed or occupied by humans: as we see, especially, in Baltrop's photograph of a kitten perched on the rocks, the Hudson piers were inhabited by a variety of life forms. Matta-Clark suggests as much in a 1976 interview in which he notes that *Day's End* had been "taken over" by pigeons. As an act of trespass, this antimonumental work of anarchitecture was never intended to last forever. The portal that Matta-Clark sliced in the wall invited not only light but also rain, wind, debris, and many birds. Here is how the artist describes *Day's End*'s exposure to the elements: "the other day I went back and there was this fantastic moment where a storm hit the west side, and the wind and rain poured in, a very visible column of air and water through the opening. And so its life goes on."[119]

As Matta-Clark, Baltrop, and Seccombe show, and as McKay demonstrated decades earlier, to contemplate the shoreline is to acknowledge the impossibility of holding fast to anything. Police surveil the waterfront, protecting the interests of market and state. Real estate speculators, urban developers, and home owners defend property values by building ever higher barriers against erosion and rising tides. Yet artists tend to embrace the impossibility of possessing or stabilizing this transient ecotone. For the visionaries who find themselves drawn to the tidelands, the coastal edge is a precarious commons and a space of "picturesque," improvised ease. It's a site of refuge and exposure, of work and strike—grounds for an elusive encounter, luminous passage at the end of the world.

Chapter Five

TIDEWRACK, BECKETT TO SUNDE

Beaches are everywhere in late capitalism. Laboriously and artificially maintained, branded as a suspension of toil and time, the contemporary leisure beach encapsulates the zeitgeist of an exhausted age. In an era when, as Jason Moore puts it, nature is generally "put to work," the beach is employed as an escape valve, a paradisiacal zone of exception.[1] Synonymous with cognitive drift and corporeal repose, beaches represent the potentiality—and perhaps the impossibility—of *doing nothing* in a time marked by the coercive, incessant demand to produce and consume. Anthropologist Marc Augé underscores the weirdness of seaside relaxation when he describes the leisure beach as an "immense waiting room."[2] We could conceptualize a waiting room as an ominous site of boredom and fatigue—or alternatively, as a minimally scripted social space in which fixed habits give way to more extemporaneous styles of being.

The present chapter explores late modernist and contemporary visual and performance art in which the beach appears stretched between the poles of this contradiction. It takes form, that is, as a spectacular wasteland—at once a field of debris (or treasure), available to be gathered and reassembled, and a stage for the performance of objectless waiting, under a scorching sun and against the backdrop of rising tides. The chapter first considers visual art made in the medium of sea trash, asking how such works magnify lags and dissonances within the seemingly streamlined reorganization of the globe. It then constellates several performances in which the human body itself materializes as tidewrack—half-buried in a dune, strewn on the beach, or bobbing in the waves. These experiments with fatigue and tenacity include Samuel Beckett's 1961 play *Happy Days* (*Oh les beaux jours*, 1963); a contemporary opera-performance titled *Sun & Sea (Marina)*—a collaboration by Lithuanian artists Rugile Barzdžiukaitė, Vaiva Grainytė, and Lina Lapelytė (2017); and American artist Sarah Cameron Sunde's ongoing site-specific *36.5/ A Durational Performance with the Sea* (2013–). Early twentieth-century coastal texts tend toward euphoria, depicting tidepools as visionary portals and the beach as a springboard that launches bodies into the air. In contemporary beach-set performance art, such gravity-defying exuberance gives way to the textures and rhythms of exhaustion, as the beach—no longer a refuge but a site of unremitting exposure—expands to fill the world.

DRIFT

There may appear to be something willfully perverse about underscoring temporalities of drift and decay in the context of the post-1945 period of environmental history known as the Great Acceleration.[3] If the Anthropocene is often dated to the late eighteenth-century European industrial revolution—and specifically to the invention of the steam engine—the Great Acceleration, which is characterized by massively scaled-up processes of carbon extraction and combustion, names a crisis point within that longer global history of ecological disturbance.[4] This period is defined by shifts in the structure of capitalism itself, from Fordist mass production in the immediate postwar period, to a post-Fordist system marked by the exploitative outsourcing of labor and a flexible, "just-in-time" organization of bodies and goods.[5] The term *Great Acceleration* refers to the ecological harm wrought by the frantic postwar push to transform capital into output into money into new investments and, in the process, disseminate commodities ever more rapidly across the globe.[6]

In fact, the term *Great Acceleration* is misleading in its suggestion of a simple temporal escalation. The Great Acceleration is better understood as a historical period marked by overlapping tempos of obsolescence and decay, as a hyperactive global system of extraction, production, distribution, and consumption releases a myriad of lingering toxic traces, and earth systems belatedly register the ecological violence enacted decades or even centuries ago.[7] The stuff we make, the stuff we buy, the stuff we use to fuel our high-speed lives hangs on. It persists. We fabricate and consume things in the blink of an eye, but their afterlives—what ecocritic Margaret Ronda calls their "decompositional lingering"—exceeds our fathoming.[8]

If the Great Acceleration were a piece of music, it would feature a weird overlay of extreme rapidity and extreme slowness—an eerie tension between transience and endurance. Bits of melody would emerge and appear to vanish, only to slip, ghostlike, into the bass line, where they would play on languidly, swollen to the tempo of sea level rise, coastal erosion, toxic drift, or oceanic debris swept by the tides. Artwork made in the medium of sea trash captures something of this strange music, registering the untimely feel of a postnatural age. Such works amplify lulls and glitches in a supposedly streamlined flow of goods, enabling spectators to dwell in capitalism's other temporalities—including the time of undulating, gyrating plastic, drifting haphazardly onto the world's shores.[9]

The practice of reshaping industrial flotsam into art sheds light on these forgotten choreographies. Such salvage work also invites meditation on the ocean as a vital ecohistorical force in an age that tends to reduce the sea to a set of traversable routes, a source of extractable profit, and a dumping ground.[10] Much of the plastic that washes up on shore or spins in oceanic garbage patches has fallen from a shipping container—that key emblem of the Great Acceleration.[11] Since the mid-twentieth century, the commodities that line store shelves—or the components required to assemble them—have traveled the globe in forty-foot boxes, facilitated by megaships and megaports. The containerization of late capitalism indexes the cheapening of nature, as the drop in global freight costs enables this shift toward a system that deemphasizes production and accumulation and instead places the onus on the transportation of parts and goods.[12] Today, shipping ports are no longer incorporated into the fabric of the city but have been transformed into securitized sites, while the massive ships that dock at them have become floating warehouses. The development of the containerized RORO ("roll-on roll-off") maritime cargo system means that seafarers spend less and less time on land (and often are not permitted to leave the docks at all) while huge ship-to-shore cranes are operated by remote control from half a mile away.[13] If the modern metropolis rose up around its harbor—no Manhattan without "streets [that] take you waterward," without "commerce

FIGURE 5.1. Eugène Boudin, *The Beach at Trouville*, 1863, Metropolitan Museum of Art.

[that] surrounds it with her surf"—the contemporary working port is often imperceptible to the city dweller, displaced as it is behind "layers of barbed wire and security."[14] The relative invisibility of this nerve center of contemporary capitalism is all the more striking in contrast to the hypervisibility of the leisure beach, which exposes the nonworking body for all to see.

Practices of looking and being seen have long been crucial to the beach as a social space. In late nineteenth-century paintings of Trouville, we see bourgeois subjects engaged in an act of aesthetic beholding: they contemplate the sea—at attention, in upright, wooden chairs—as if the liquid expanses before them were a staged spectacle or a framable work of art. The genius of these paintings is to expose the impossibility of such containment. On the beach, after all, it is difficult to hold anything in place. Indeed, such seaside works could be described as mixed media, as their oil paint sometimes contains traces of windblown sand.[15] In Boudin's 1863 painting of Trouville, an overturned chair in the foreground conveys a day at the beach as a windy struggle against the elements. Some cast-off garments (a red shawl, a pair of shoes) lie at the very center of Boudin's beach; the viewer's eye is drawn to these abandoned objects, which appear to belong to no one in the scene.

Today, such abandoned objects have once again taken center stage. Many contemporary artists who are pulled to the seashore work in the medium

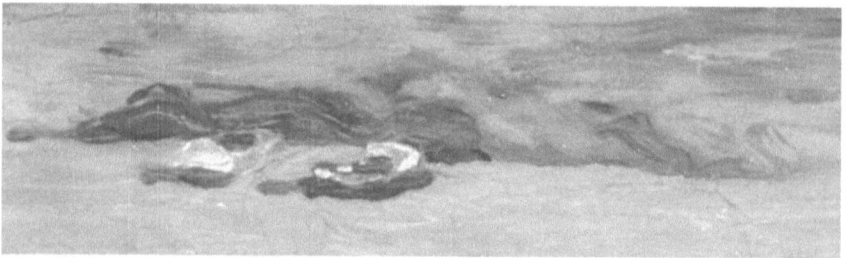

FIGURE 5.2. Eugène Boudin, *The Beach at Trouville*, 1863, detail.

of marine trash, building miniature anti-monuments to late capitalism's endless consumption. Such artwork reminds us that before and alongside their commodification as spaces of leisure, beaches have served as dumping grounds, mortuary sites, and wastelands. Thus Henry David Thoreau depicts Cape Cod as a "vast morgue," while Aimé Césaire presents the colonial Martinican beach as a ruined place where "the sea pours forth its garbage, its dead cats and croaked dogs" ("C'est là surtout que la mer déverse ses immondices, ses chats morts et ses chiens crevés").[16] Marguerite Duras similarly portrays the marshy coastal edge of colonial Indochina as repugnant—littered with the "drowned bodies of squirrels, muskrats, or young peacocks."[17] And in her investigative memoir, Saidiya Hartman describes the shock of stumbling upon a Ghanaian "toilet beach," where children play near "fetid pools" and men hunker down like "mushrooms in the sand" to defecate.[18]

Yet tidewrack can be surprisingly beautiful. This is the case in Cuban artist Severo Sarduy's experimental 1969 radio play *The Beach* (*La playa*), which casts a loving gaze on waste. In this dreamlike, contrapuntal work, set on the French Riviera, the sound of the surf mixes with a variety of scraps and leftovers: publicity photos, suntan lotion advertisements, verbal clichés, and trash deposited by the waves. Sarduy's beach is simultaneously alluring and revolting—at once "scummy," "diseased," "silvery," "haloed," and "shining." His treasure-seeking beachcombers are as likely to stumble upon a beautiful naked man asleep on the sand as upon a heap of washed-up refuse, "phosphorescent, like dead fish."[19] For Sarduy, the littoral is a permeable borderland in which differences and demarcations continuously fade. Contemporary novelist Marie Darrieussecq likewise affirms the material impurity and heterogeneity of the seaside when she describes sand as encompassing a potentially infinite variety of materials, including "crumbled cliffs, broken-down houses, baby teeth, glass, plastic, silica, spit, salt, ash, leaves, guano, book pages, and even a few molecules of Notre Dame cathedral, carried by the wind."[20]

We see another side of flotsam's allure in Stuart Haygarth's *Strand* (2012), a sculptural work composed of objects that the artist culled during a 450-mile walk along the English coast, from Graves End to Lands End. *Strand* is made entirely of oceanic debris, including tools, lids, goggles, lighters, buckets, shovels, frisbees, balls, combs, cords, sunglasses, gloves, and many varieties of shoes. Commissioned for display in the lobby of a London cancer treatment center, Haygarth's sea-trash sculpture invites reflection on both the cascading carcinogenic effects of many ordinary commodities and on the historical conception of the beach as a therapeutic space or site of cure.

Haygarth photographed many of the components of his salvaged sculptural work.[21] His picture of four mismatched rubber shoes, for instance, conjoins formal simplicity and subtle breakdown: the yellow, gray, blue, and red rubber flats appear in a state of disintegration, eaten away by saltwater and time. It is as if those abandoned shoes in Boudin's 1863 beachscape had slipped off the canvas only to resurface, across the Channel, a century and a half later.

Haygarth's rubber shoes also recall more celebrated art-historical footwear, especially Van Gogh's affectionate still lifes of wrinkled, worn peasant boots, their nails protruding and laces akimbo (*A Pair of Boots,* 1886, 1887). Rubber shoes, too—sometimes made of old tires—have been worn in peasant societies around the world.[22] Yet the seriality and randomness of Haygarth's colorful flats equally call to mind Andy Warhol's *Diamond Dust Shoes* (1980)—a silk-screened reproduction of a polaroid photograph of multihued couture pumps, piled up like leftover warehouse inventory or remainders of some disaster. Fredric Jameson has taught us to see the contrast between Van Gogh's oil painting and Warhol's silkscreen as representative of utterly distinct relations to history and labor. Drawing on Martin Heidegger's reading of the peasant boots as materializing the "accumulated tenacity" of the worker's "slow trudge" through the field, Jameson interprets

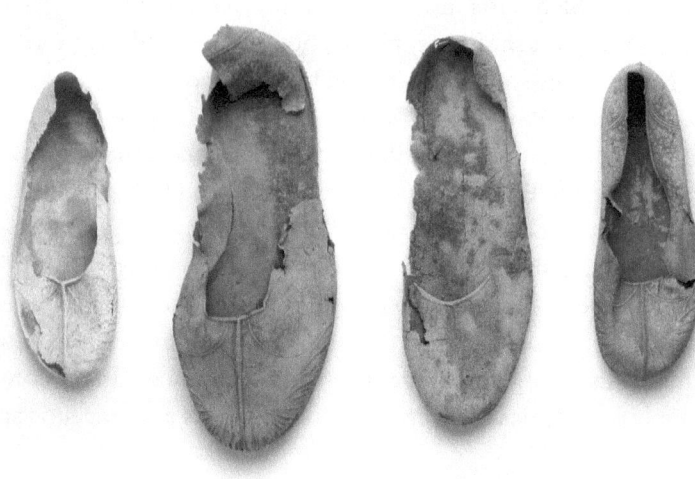

FIGURE 5.3. Stuart Haygarth, STRAND (2012)—rubber shoes. Courtesy of the artist.

these objects as icons of a lost, precapitalist relation to time.[23] The boots appear rooted in the earth, in peasant dwelling and an inimitable, singular history of use. (In fact, it is believed that Van Gogh purchased them at a flea market and purposely weathered them by wearing them in the mud.)[24] By contrast, Warhol's diamond-dusted silkscreen instantiates what Jameson famously terms the postmodern waning of historicity—the loss of our ability to "experienc[e] history in some active way": these party shoes are as glossy, unmoored, and fetishistic as an advertisement.[25] Their strewn pairlessness suggests liberation from the constraints of compulsory coupledom—and yet, post-Auschwitz, a pile of abandoned shoes inevitably hints at more sinister possibilities.

Haygarth's rubber shoes—broken down not by labor but by their own mysterious sea journey—hover somewhere between the seriousness of Van Gogh's (staged) authentic work boot and the glamorous, deathly festivity of Warhol's high-fashion pumps. The human history of Haygarth's collection cannot be reconstituted; we will never know who wore them or, indeed, if they were ever worn at all. Nor can we discern the oceanic routes that the shoes traveled before they wound up on the English shore. (We can surmise, at least, that they are unlikely to be reunited with their pairs, as oceanographers have determined that right and left shoes caught in oceanic gyres tend to drift in different directions.)[26] And yet these objects are not simply decontextualized artifacts, ahistorical *objets trouvés* posed against a white background. Rather, they conjure divergent narrative possibilities and index historical and ecological violence on multiple levels. In this regard, they represent not the waning of historicity but a conception of historical process that includes a vast array of human and more-than-human actors. Elastic, flexible, airtight, watertight, and extremely durable, rubber is an "extraordinary" substance, and its history is also extraordinarily bloody, as John Tully has shown. Whether derived from tropical plantation monoculture or made in factories—today about half the world's rubber comes from "natural" sources and half is synthetic—the production of this substance is invasive, exploitative, and wasteful.[27] Yet Haygarth's image invites us to envision other possible origins and ends for these objects. Where did they come from and where have they been? Were they discarded, or did they simply fall off a cargo ship, as so many things do?[28] In their state of partial decay, and in their imperfect, reconstituted kinship, they have taken on a life of their own.

Like Haygarth, photographer Mandy Barker specializes in flotsam. Her 2012 photographic series, *SOUP*, presents plastic sea drift gathered from the world's beaches, including a constellation of marine debris that ocean creatures tried and failed to ingest. One is as struck by the teeth marks that reshape these industrial objects as by the composition of the photograph, which makes the remnants appear to float like some strange interstellar assemblage.[29] Replete with objects we can't quite identify (only a toothpaste tube is recognizable), the picture presents the indigestible detritus of late capitalism via an aesthetics of rough edges and fray. Hovering in dark space, the constellation of rubbish brings to mind Proust's *petite bande*, traveling down the Balbec seaside like a "luminous comet." Barker is playing here, as Haygarth does, with the incommensurability between her subject matter and its dazzling arrangement. But what is most arresting in *SOUP* is how the weird temporality of plastic—in its chemical resistance to breakdown, its capacity to linger on in an eerie afterlife in flagrant disregard for its supposed disposability—contrasts starkly with the transience,

FIGURE 5.4. *SOUP: Refused* (2012). Copyright © Mandy Barker.

vulnerability, and worrisome absence of the creatures whose bite marks are on display.[30] These plastic debris are uncanny fossils, imprinted with absent life.[31]

Although the field of floating detritus spills beyond the edges of Barker's picture, the effect of *SOUP* is not one of sublime immensity, such as Timothy Morton ascribes to those industrial "hyperobjects" whose imperviousness to finitude boggles the mind.[32] Rather, one notes the smallness and delicacy of Barker's suspended objects, each with its own textural particularity. Indeed, we might consider tidewrack aesthetics in connection with earlier practices of rubbish-based art, from Emily Dickinson's envelope poems to cubist collage.[33] In its availability to continual recomposition, Barker's and Haygarth's flotsam similarly exposes the process of making and unmaking. Gathering such things into a collection is not a heroic gesture but a humble one, and in this regard the artist is akin to the creatures—unlikely collaborators—who gnaw and reshape these odds and ends.

Still, there is a grim side to Barker's gorgeous display. Expressing the "untranscendable materiality of fossil capitalism more than any other product or by-product," as Thangam Ravindranathan and Antoine Trasnel aptly put it, plastic is not an inert substance; rather, it is a "chemical sponge" that endangers not only the lives of the creatures who ingest it but the entire marine food chain.[34] Given that plastic is a toxic pollutant and that its weight in the sea is projected to exceed that of fish by 2050, the viewer is likely to regard Barker's interstellar arrangement of half-chewed colorful fragments with a mixture of aesthetic delight, bewilderment, and grief.[35] Envisioning the trajectory of this sea drift requires us to ponder multidirectional, overlapping, and incongruous concepts, including supply chains, cargo, and shipping logistics; marine zoology and oceanic currents; the unearthly petrochemical lifespan of plastic and its intangible toxins; the coastal paths and beaches that the photographer has wandered in search of such waste; and even the materialities and honed techniques of the photographic medium (not to mention the digital webs and transit routes that hold and transmit the online image).[36]

If the modernist/avant-garde rallying cry "make it new" unwittingly anticipated the rapid-fire, "just-in-time" logic of Great Acceleration commodity production and consumption, the residual quality of tidewrack art opens onto a different temporal ethos: a strange layering of evanescence and endurance. Barker's profuse constellation of inedibles and Haygarth's sculptural reconfiguration of marine rubbish are instances of what Ronda calls "remainders"—by-products or obsolescent commodities that expose the "indistinction of natural and historical phenomena amidst the processes of capital accumulation."[37] Remainders are not Romantic figures. They are neither monumental, melancholic ruins, nor isolated, exiled fragments that gesture toward a lost totality, standing as a nostalgic marker of a whole that cannot be attained. Rather, washed-up rubber shoes and nibbled toothpaste tubes entangle the natural and the historical, and artwork made of such stuff invites reflection on ecological limits and on the nearly unfathomable metamorphic lifespan of matter.[38]

For artists from Boudin to Barker, the beach is a singularly ambiguous setting. It is framed, on one end, by the disintegration of bourgeois personhood into swirling particles and abandoned objects and, on the other, by the hapless return of those fragments—in all their unsettling toxicity—as they wash up as tidewrack on the shore. In tender arrangements of such debris, we glimpse the cracks in a containerized world.

FATIGUE

As a setting for art, the beach invites our reflection on the multiple temporal regimes that are bound together in an era of climate disruption. When artists like Barker and Haygarth build tiny worlds out of beach-culled sea trash, they explore the strange perpetuity of supposedly obsolescent commodities. These works implicitly present the beach as the world's rubbish bin—which is also to say, as a waste or commons where unlikely treasures might be found. Similarly, when contemporary artists set scenes of intransitive waiting on the sand, they expose the underside of leisure, reminding us that the invention of the beach—the Anthropocene's privileged space of nonwork, its most familiar site of collective repose (or collapse)—is closely bound up with the history of capitalist fatigue.

Although it is supposed to represent pleasurable relaxation and the possibility of an invigorating recharge, the contemporary beach has instead become a figure for what Nicole Starosielski calls the "aesthetics of lag."[39] As an apt indication of the link between the beach and late-capitalist/digital-era waiting and fatigue, consider the phenomenon of the spinning rainbow wait cursor on an Apple computer, colloquially termed the "spinning beach ball of death," or SBBOD.[40] As Jason Farman notes, this buffering icon "suggests that some complex code is being processed behind the scenes," and it is meant to "help us sit back and enjoy our passivity."[41] But what the SBBOD really signals is a processing lag—the machine "cannot handle all the events it receives." The icon therefore triggers anxiety, reminding users of bandwidth limitations and of the plethora of system glitches that beset us (and which we can neither see nor understand).[42] Networked culture is supposed to enable immediacy, control, and uninterrupted connectivity; the buffering icon signifies network limitations, failures, inefficiency, wasted time.[43] On a Mac community forum, one user describes an experience that is intimately familiar to every reader of this book—if not as personal experience, then as nightmare: "Every click, every command, seems to get a spinning beach ball. . . . Sometimes the spinning beach ball itself freezes."[44] Sinister clown of late capitalism, the SBBOD is an unbearably cheerful emblem of our helpless state of indefinite waiting in an age of uncertainty and risk.[45] The festive icon is supposed to make the aggravation of an interrupted transmission of data more bearable—but it just leaves us feeling stranded.

How did the beach become so closely allied with the specter of the exhausted body? The emergence of this site as a codified place of rest coincides with a period of intensifying carbon combustion and anthropogenic climate change, from the eighteenth century to the present. Alain Corbin has shown that, in eighteenth-century England, ruling class disgust at urban pollution and crowdedness became inseparable from a longing to escape to the seashore. The "invention" of the beach as a space of evasion and regeneration followed upon the medicalization of seawater, which was believed to have a "mechanical effect" on the tissues of the body. Elites of the period came to view sea bathing (along with daily seawater ingestion) as practices that could combat the ills of urban degeneration and stem a "loss of vital energy," and a cold dip was medically prescribed as a cure for nymphomania, impotence, hypochondria and neurosis, among other conditions.[46] By the nineteenth century, focus shifted to the virtues of sea air as an antidote to what medical authorities saw as a dangerously stifling urban atmosphere.[47] In the era of high modernism, the "air cure" took a heliotherapeutic turn, and the sun was briefly cast as the ultimate vitalizing force—before morphing later in the century into the carcinogen we know today.[48]

The leisure beach was invented, then, as a cure—but it also came to be viewed as potentially toxic, excessively stimulating for certain constitutions. This is precisely the perspective of fin de siècle hygiene specialists like Marcel Proust's father, Doctor Adrien Proust. In his *Treatment of Neurasthenia* (1897), Doctor Proust argues that although seashore hydrotherapy offers a remedy for "languor and weakness," a beach vacation is not suitable for all neurasthenics and should be avoided by those in whom "symptoms of excitement" predominate, since "at the seaside the air is fresh and keen and always in motion, gusts of wind are frequent, and sea-baths, even when very short, have a tonic action of the most energetic kind." The seashore can incite insomnia, the doctor warns, or produce "a vague malaise made up of mental over-excitement, of enervation accompanied by marked acceleration of the pulse, and of a feeling of heat in the skin; others again are tormented by cardiac palpitations."[49]

In Adrien Proust's hydrotherapeutic recommendations and admonitions, we get a sense of the shore as a place where it is difficult to find the proper equilibrium between innervation and fatigue. We could easily imagine that Thomas Mann had read Doctor Proust's warnings. In *Death in Venice* (1912), the beach appears precisely as a site in which exhaustion is inextricable from overexcitement. Investigating the problem of fatigue and energy management in the early twentieth century, Mann imagines the beach as bad medicine—a failed cure for lassitude. His protagonist, Aschenbach, is the "poet-spokesman of all those who labour at the edge of exhaustion; of the overburdened, of those who are already worn out but still hold themselves upright." Aschenbach goes to the Venetian Lido craving escape from the "daily theater" of his disciplined existence: he longs for "freedom, release, forgetfulness" and "the close and soothing contact which only a gentle sandy slope affords."[50] On holiday, this burned-out writer finds himself in a state of energetic contradiction. Overwhelmingly tired yet unable to sleep, "keen and weary," he is worked up and depleted by the presence of the beautiful boy Tadzio: "when Aschenbach put aside his work and left the beach he felt exhausted, he felt broken ... as it were after a debauch." Yet after attempting to make contact with Tadzio, "he found his heart throbbing unpleasantly fast, while his breath came in such quick pants that he could only have gasped had he tried to speak."[51] The boy incarnates the excessively energizing yet exhausting effect of the beach itself, the "invigorating salty air" of which "heighten[s] [Aschenbach's] emotional energies" and causes him to release "the powers accumulated by sleep or food or outdoor air ... in one extravagant gust of emotional intoxication."[52] Until his untimely seaside death, the writer's days are "filled with happy unrest," his "composure gone to the winds."[53]

The seashore was understood by eighteenth-, nineteenth-, and early twentieth-century medical authorities (and novelists), then, as a concentrated source of energy—at once a bath, a brew, and an atmosphere; both a cure and an intoxicant. Today, by contrast, the beach is marketed as a calming escape and an "expensive backdrop" rather than an energizing or stimulating force.[54] As such, it has become a spectacle of exhaustion, a site of continuous erosion and artificial replenishment, a besieged commons that abuts prime real estate.[55] This setting materializes the corporeal and ecological weariness that is one of the most dominant (if not *the* dominant) feeling-tones of late capitalism itself. Sold as a cure for burnout, the beach radiates fatigue.

Why is capitalism so exhausting? People have always been tired, of course, and in profoundly unequal ways, but in a culture that prizes the ceaseless expenditure of energy and extraction of wealth, fatigue takes on particular weight as a problem to be fixed and, ideally, eradicated. As historian E. P. Thompson observes, capitalist modernity brings about a fundamental "shift in time sense": it "restructur[es] working habits" away from "task-orientation" and toward clock timing.[56] By contrast, precapitalist ways of telling time tended to be organized around finite intervals of activity completion. These modes of experiencing time included, for example, "a rice-cooking," the recitation of an Ave Maria, or a "pissing while." Industrial capitalism is measured very differently, with an emphasis on time sheets and timekeepers and an empty mechanical temporality that continuously and exhaustingly restarts at zero. "Time thrift," therefore, becomes the abiding value. As Thompson puts it, "in mature capitalist society all time must be consumed, marketed, put to *use*; it is offensive for the labour force merely to 'pass the time.'"[57]

Historian Anson Rabinbach highlights the bodily consequences of this shift in "time sense." Examining the bourgeois cult of work (and disdain for idleness) that arose in the nineteenth century, Rabinbach shows that while earlier elites had conceptualized fatigue as a "sign of limit" and index of the body's need for restoration, fin de siècle materialist discourses pathologized this state as a disorder—"a sign of weakness and the absence of will."[58] Metaphorizing the living being as a motor, the late nineteenth-century middle classes dreamed of a "body without fatigue."[59]

This desire to eliminate the need for rest has only become more pressing in the Great Acceleration. In his critique of the condition of relentless *on-ness* that makes late capitalism feel like a perpetual state of emergency, Jonathan Crary describes our era of 24/7 productivity and consumption as one in which "the planet becomes reimagined as a non-stop work site or an always open shopping mall." From this perspective, the semiconscious beach sunbather may call to mind the "sleep mode" or false somnolence of our devices, which Crary theorizes as symptomatic of a generalized ethos of profit-obsessed productivism. Sleep mode is a state of "low-power readiness"—not true repose but simply a "diminished condition of operability and access."[60]

Exhaustion is not only a more totalizing version of fatigue but a particularly apt term for the state of psychic, corporeal, and ecological wastedness that characterizes late capitalism—the mood of an era in which we deplete our own bodies along with the planet's other raw materials.[61] As Anna Katharina Schaffner has pointed out, exhaustion aptly contains within it the term for the toxic remainder of the carbon combustion process: "exhaust" is "the discharge of waste steam from [a steam engine's] cylinder."[62] Exhaustion may simply be the inevitable predicament of a civilization organized around a "cult of energy" and an obsession with "growth at all costs."[63] Yet as a phenomenological condition, it cannot be reduced to a simple state of lack, just as the Great Acceleration cannot be reduced to a simple increase in speed.

However we name this symptomatic state of being—fatigue, exhaustion, weariness, burnout—it does not merely indicate an absence of energy but partakes of waiting's complex indeterminacy, and artists and theorists who explore its diffuse textures are attuned to its "many forms."[64] A century ago, Siegfried Kracauer theorized waiting as a form of "*hesitant openness*," but also as a "dauntlessness," an "ability to hold on."[65] Drawing on this ambiguity, film scholar Elena Gorfinkle depicts weariness as a "threshold" or "interval" in which the body "hold[s itself] in abeyance." The tired body, she notes, is "always at the edge of something else . . . a drift or fall toward sleep at one end or a rebounding rejuvenation at the other." Fatigue need not be conceptualized as a state of inaction, then, or as a SBBODesque mechanical breakdown or glitch. It might instead indicate a layering of sensations and temporalities, a "form of accumulation—an archive of gestures."[66] Fatigue's subtle archive is precisely at stake in many performance works created during the Great Acceleration. This exhaustion effect is amplified, as the next sections will show, in works set on artificial beaches.

"FEMALE SOLO"

As a stage for the spectacle of leisure and a showcase for the exhausted body, the beach captivates playwrights as well as urban planners and real estate developers. Decades before scenographers dreamed up Paris Plages—the manufactured beach that pops up along the Seine each July, complete with trucked-in sand, palm trees, and bocce courts—Beckett explored the theatrical potential of the artificial beach. In *Happy Days*, his heroine banters and sings, cites great literature and popular ditties, and fiddles with objects in her bag under the burning sun while buried in a mound of sand—in act 1, it's up to her waist; in act 2, it's up to her neck. "Another heavenly day!" ("Encore une journée divine") is Winnie's opening cry, and a variation on this line becomes the play's absurd refrain. What's so striking here is the incongruity of Winnie's nightmarish situation with her optimism—like Woolf's Mrs. Ramsay, she stubbornly holds to the idea of happy days, or, more literally in French, "good weather" (*beau temps*). Anyone would be terribly exhausted by Winnie's predicament, but she scarcely complains, cheerfully exclaiming a number of times that she feels "no pain" or, rather, "hardly any."[67] (By contrast, the considerably less encumbered men in *Waiting for Godot* and *Endgame* declare overtly that they are tired. "That's enough. I'm tired," repeats Estragon; "I'm tired of our goings on, very tired," grumbles Clov.)[68] Winnie merely observes that holding up a parasol "wearies the arm," and when the parasol catches fire in the first act she tosses it over her shoulder and watches it burn, wondering if this has happened before.[69]

Beckett's theater, of course, is not naturalistic; he abstains from setting his plays in any explicit or recognizable historical context. But *Happy Days* is very much a play dreamed up at a moment in French cultural history and global environmental history when the leisure beach rose to new prominence as the Anthropocene's most sexualized image of nature and most widely circulated and promoted symbol of paradise. It's true that *Happy Day*'s setting is ambiguous, and the word *beach* never appears in the script, but beach connotations are strong, especially when Winnie shades herself from the blazing sun with a parasol and sings—in the 1963

FIGURE 5.5. Billie Whitelaw as Winnie, Royal Court Theatre, 1979, directed by Beckett. Copyright © Donald Cooper/ Photostage.

French version of the play—a half-remembered ditty about "waves" and "tides."[70] In an August 17, 1961, letter to the American director Alan Schneider, Beckett specifies that the set consists of "hot blue sky" and "yellow-brown scorched earth," matching the yellow and blue stripes of Winnie's parasol and the ribbons on Willie's boater. He also insists that "monotony," "symmetry," "desiccation," and "tawdriness" should characterize the whole scene.[71] The *New York Times* review of the play, which premiered in 1961 at the Cherry Lane Theater, describes the set as a "mound as barren as a dune" against the backdrop of a "glaringly yellow cyclorama."[72] When director Deborah Warner staged the play at the National Royal Theater with Fiona Shaw as Winnie in 2007–2008, the set was explicitly based upon "a photograph of a desperate stretch of Albanian coastline." Warner offers this detail to the audience in a preshow event, then jokes, "should you wish to take your holidays [there]."[73]

The setting of *Happy Days* is characterized, above all, by scorching heat: the stage directions indicate "blazing light," and Winnie returns throughout to this feature of her setting, which she describes, almost in the same breath, as a "holy light" and a "blaze of hellish light."[74] She warns the partially visible, mostly taciturn Willie (whom we presume to be her husband) to "slip on [his] drawers before [he] get[s] singed." He, however, can retreat from the "great heat," while she can only recall a past in which she could still "seek out a shady place."[75] In a vague echo (and misquotation) of *Hamlet*, she muses, "Shall I myself not melt perhaps in the end, or burn."[76] There is no refuge for Winnie: her condition is one of utter exposure. She seems "suspended," as Charles Lyons observes, "at a point of infinite noon," imprisoned in an environment she refers to alternately as a "paradise" and a "wilderness."[77] This latter term, appearing in no other Beckett play, indicates an uncultivated or neglected wasteland, pathless by definition, with connotations of perdition and spiritual testing.[78]

One of the remarkable features of *Happy Days*—given the historical moment in which it was written—is the way it incarnates a universal existential crisis in the body of a woman. Yet Beckett also underscores the gendered specificity of the torment to which Winnie is subjected. Indeed, we might contrast her stuckness—a perversion of the fantasy of leisured freedom—to the Heideggerian idea of thrownness, a very different style of unhappy liberty. Thrownness and its variations indicate a vertiginous condition of anxiety that features, according to Sianne Ngai, as the spatialized feeling-tone of twentieth-century (masculine) intellectual inquiry. By contrast, Winnie is planted; only her props are airborne. Ultimately, Ngai suggests, in works like Hitchcock's *Vertigo* (1958), anxiety "comes to assume its prominent role in structuring the 'philosophically stylized' quests for truth, knowledge, and masculine agency . . . precisely as a way of rescuing the intellectual from his potential absorption in sites of asignificance or negativity."[79] For Winnie, interred in her mound, there is no escape from asignificance, and her main companions are a set of self-care items, strewn around her like tidewrack, which she cannot get rid of. In fact, Winnie's inability to relinquish these objects is a central element of her plight. She periodically uses something up or breaks it and tosses it over her shoulder, observing all the while that she will never really part with the commodities splayed out before her: "I take up this little glass, I shiver it on a stone—[*does so*]—I throw it away—[*does so far behind her*]—it will be in the bag again tomorrow, without a scratch, to help me through the day."[80] Indeed, all her props will be in her possession again in act 2, the same as before, after her hands have vanished into the earth.

Beckett wrote *Happy Days* at a time in which the very concept of leisure had become key to modern life.[81] Mass tourism emerged in the postwar period as a new phenomenon: images of beaches were suddenly ubiquitous, and the scantily clad, oiled-up beach body became desirable currency on the global cinematic market. In particular, the French Riviera exploded to international renown in the 1950s as a new fantasy of French distinction and luxury. Françoise Sagan's bestselling novel *Bonjour Tristesse* (1954; Hollywood adaptation, 1958) opens with its adolescent heroine idly sunning herself on the Côte d'Azur; the box office hit *And God Created Woman* (*Et Dieu . . . créa la femme*, 1956), also set on the Riviera, begins with a shot of Brigitte Bardot sunbathing in the nude.[82] At the same time, American youth surfer culture became an object of global fascination. Eager coeds pile into convertibles on their way to the shore in popular films like *Gidget* (1959); *Where the Boys Are* (1960); *Beach Party* (1963); *Muscle Beach Party* (1964); and *Horror of Beach Party* (1964).[83] Beckett was therefore surrounded by images of seaside indolence and feminine exposure when he was writing *Happy Days*. The beach had become the ultimate stage for extramarital dalliances and adolescent lust, a setting for a new kind of gender performance, and a space in which to act out (and police) an unruly female sexuality. Enter Winnie, buried in a dune.

Actors have interpreted Winnie's carceral existence in quite divergent ways, despite Beckett's maniacally detailed stage directions. Thus, for instance, Peggy Ashcroft's performance was "warm and personal," even "robustly vivacious," while Billie Whitelaw, whose performance Beckett directed in 1979, spoke "almost as an automaton." Madeleine Renaud made Winnie into an "indefatigable optimist," while Shaw explored "a quality of improvised jazz" in the role.[84] This variegated range of interpretations registers contradictions within the character as written. Winnie, Lyons suggests, is ultimately riven with ambivalence: she strives to maintain the fiction of "another heavenly day" even as she longs to "escape from the fiction of happiness."[85] Indeed, the play could well have been titled *Cruel Optimism*. Winnie incarnates the condition that, according to Lauren Berlant, characterizes the world of late capitalism: everyday life has become a matter of survival, and its modes of consumerist satisfaction can only offer momentary reprieves from suffering, not repair. Winnie thus exists "simultaneously at an extreme and in a zone of ordinariness."[86] Dreaming of "happy days" from within a scene of scorching imprisonment, Winnie overturns the consumerist fantasies of her era, especially its positing of leisure as the apex of satisfaction and self-realization.[87]

When audiences in the early 1960s encountered Winnie, they may well have found their minds wandering to thoughts of another fleshy, denuded blonde: the much fetishized Brigitte Bardot ("B.B."), the era's ultimate bathing beauty. The "most famous French export of the postwar period," Bardot was launched from the beaches of Cannes as an international sex symbol in the 1950s, especially after the global success of *And God Created Woman*.[88] In this film, set in Saint Tropez, Bardot plays Juliette, an orphaned young woman whose desires exceed patriarchal control, and who flagrantly crosses the line when she has sex with her brother-in-law on a deserted beach. By the early 1960s, Bardot had become one of the most photographed people in the world and the movie star most associated in the public eye with the seaside; she was often photographed and filmed in a bikini.[89]

Winnie's performance of stranded, exposed femininity should be understood in the context of the global "Bardolatry" phenomenon and in relation to a cultural moment in which the leisure beach was commodified and eroticized as never before. Indeed, Beckett foregrounds his heroine's sexuality in both the play's stage directions and in his correspondence.

FIGURE 5.6. Brigitte Bardot sunning on the beach, circa 1960. Copyright © Bettman via Getty Images.

According to the former, Winnie should be "about fifty, well-preserved, blonde for preference, plump, arms and shoulders bare, low bodice, big bosom, pearl necklace." Beckett also specifies in a letter to Schneider that Winnie should have "a desirable fleshiness" and that throughout the second act the audience should "miss this gleaming opulent flesh."[90] Although Winnie was a few decades older than Bardot at the time that Beckett wrote the play, when he directed *Happy Days* at the Royal Court Theatre in 1979, Billie Whitelaw appeared as a "young seductress in a black-lace bustier."[91] The author's insistence that the part be played in a "mild blank tone," and that Winnie speak her lines with "vocal monotony," "tranquility," and "transparency" also likens her to Bardot, who famously performed all of her roles with a nonactorly minimum of expressivity.[92] Beckett notes, for instance, that when Winnie speaks of a "blaze of hellish [light]," she should do so while "polishing mechanically, no emotion."[93]

And yet Winnie is also the anti-Bardot, and this is Beckett's wager, too. Bardot offers the fantasy of woman as sheer embodiment, without accessories, "natural" and autoerotic—the feminine embodiment of sex on the beach. Winnie, by contrast, is all prop, and her body gradually vanishes as she repeats, pointlessly, the choreography of gender performance (using a mirror to check her lips, teeth, nails, hair).[94] We might conclude that she exists somewhere between the artless, magnetic Bardot and the silent, methodical heroine of Chantal Akerman's feminist masterpiece, *Jeanne Dielman, 23, quai du Commerce, 1080 Bruxelles*: a middle-aged widow and sex worker who dourly (and in real time) puts on lipstick, peels potatoes, makes the bed, washes the dishes.[95]

In an era marked by the fantasy of littoral relaxation signifying youth, spontaneity, and pleasure, and emblematized by the international sex kitten "B.B.," Beckett's beach play is a scandal. *Happy Days*, which Beckett originally imagined titling simply "Female Solo," and later "Tender Mercies," presents the supposedly liberating practice of leisure as just another obligation to fully develop one's personality and extract maximal value from one's time.[96] Winnie is in danger of melting or burning up, as she calmly points out, but her greatest fear is of finding herself "left, with hours still to run, before the bell for sleep, and nothing more to say, nothing more to do."[97] Underscoring the gendered consequences of leisure culture's mass diffusion, Beckett shows that it's Winnie, not Willie, who feels coerced not only to profit from time but to work incessantly as the curator of her own body, the stage manager of her own performance of self. *Happy Days* is in this regard a play about being a woman—doing femininity—as a feat of exhausting, ongoing exposure, and it presents Winnie's determination to hold herself together and fill the empty hours at all cost. In conversation with Brenda Bruce, who starred in the 1962 British premiere, Beckett described Winnie's circumstances as "the most dreadful thing that could happen to anybody," and added, "I thought who would cope with that and go down singing, only a woman."[98] As she burns under the scorching sun, Winnie has the "strange feeling that someone is looking at [her]." She represents the specifically feminized compulsion, or coercion, to "keep yourself nice . . . come what may."[99]

This a famously difficult part to play, with its extremely precise choreography, bodily constraint, and exorbitantly extended soliloquys. "Beckett's most extended dramatic image of character," Winnie is also a woman "trying to survive a slow death"—a death revealed "almost in real time."[100] It is not surprising, then, that actors and directors describe the work of playing her as psychologically and even physically painful. As director Lois Oppenheim puts it, "It is hard to describe what it does to someone to be locked inside an unmoveable wedge of dirt for hours and hours every day. Eventually, your mind snaps. It becomes unendurable. And then the play begins."[101] Shaw echoes this sentiment, noting, "if I'm left with the dirt up to my neck for too long, I do get a bit batty."[102] Upon learning that the play's run time was considerably longer than he had anticipated, Beckett told director Alan Schneider in 1961 that his "heart [went] out" to actor Ruth White, who had given up more lucrative acting jobs in order to focus exclusively on playing Winnie for the world premiere—a role that was evidently (writes Beckett) "a big ordeal for her."[103] This empathy did not prevent Beckett from tormenting another actor—Brenda Bruce—a year later by bringing a metronome to rehearsal and leaving it ticking so that she would have to precisely regulate her rhythm and tempo.[104] If most stagings of *Happy Days* resist the playwright's own preference for a flat, mechanical delivery of lines, this does not make the performance any easier. Playing Winnie can "feel dangerous," according to Shaw. "I'm absolutely cooking!" she exclaims in a recorded preperformance chat at the Kennedy Center. Shaw's shoulders were in fact burned from performing, without shelter, in extreme illumination, night after night.[105] When Dianne Wiest reprised the role in 2016, she worked extensively with a movement coach to learn how to remain still for hours without her limbs going numb.[106]

It might seem that *Happy Days* anticipates Crary's conception of the 24/7 temporality of late capitalism as a condition of permanent emergency, a state of unceasing, homogeneous *on-ness*—total illumination without respite. Yet the play's representation of intransitive waiting also opens onto a different, more uncertain rhythm of existence. In this regard, it calls to mind Kracauer's account of waiting as a nuanced state of potentiality—an expression of the "ability to hold on."[107] One of the reasons *Happy Days* is so difficult to stage is that it contains an unusual number of stage directions: the play's relation to time is complicated by an intense engagement with gesture, rhythm, tempo, and silence. Winnie speaks in a near monologue throughout, while performing a series of precise gestures: she rummages in her bag, brushes her teeth, puts on lipstick, shakes out and folds a handkerchief, polishes her spectacles, files her nails, swigs from a medicine bottle, holds up (and tosses) a parasol, examines herself in a mirror, inspects an insect with a magnifying glass, kisses a revolver, winds a music box, and so on. The play, Deborah Warner admits, is so full of pauses and directives that it is simply "not a good read;" only in previews, in front of a responsive audience, she notes, did Shaw's performance of Winnie begin to make sense.

Happy Days is outrageously intertextual—replete with literary citations and oblique references from various epochs, as well as hit songs, toasts, jokes, newspaper headlines and ads, and other vernacular bits of speech. Despite all this talk, the play's ratio of silence to speech is unparalleled in Beckett's major works.[108] *Happy Days* contains over 500 explicit pauses, not counting the silences implied by stage directions such as "[*Smile*]" or "[*Inspects filed nails*]." As a point of comparison, there are only 84 pause markers in *Waiting for Godot*, while *Endgame* has close to 300; both of these plays are considerably longer than *Happy Days*. Open *Happy Days* at random and one finds 20 pauses or so on any given page; in general, a pause of varying length ("maximum," "long," etc.) punctuates every sentence or sentence fragment. For instance: "[*She gazes front, holding up parasol with right hand. Maximum pause.*] I used to perspire freely. [*Pause.*] Now hardly at all. [*Pause.*] The heat is much greater. [*Pause.*] The perspiration much less. [*Pause.*] That is what I find so wonderful. [*Pause.*] The way man adapts himself. [*Pause.*] To changing conditions. [*She transfers parasol to left hand. Long pause.*]"[109]

Perhaps we should hear the omnipresent, subtly variegated silences in *Happy Days* as the stammers of an amnesiac, or the last gasps of a person being buried alive. Yet these cracks in Winnie's sun-bleached wall of speech—which increase in frequency as the play goes on—are also invocations that draw the audience in. In this regard, we might understand these pauses as working to transform a "female solo" into what Warner calls a "two-hander between Winnie and the audience." Winnie is sometimes described as a female Hamlet, but I suggest we take seriously Warner's contention that *Happy Days* is best understood as a work of stand-up comedy.[110] In this, Warner also turns a more familiar critical view—the notion that Winnie herself is the joke—on its head.[111] Winnie's time is not her own, but in those temporal dilations, she (or the scorched, exhausted actor playing her) stretches a monologue into a textured, improvisatory back and forth. In these pauses—or comic breaks—Winnie invites us into the scene.

WAITING ROOM

Beckett's hellish midcentury beachscape, with its peculiar mix of cheerfulness and slow catastrophe, continues to resonate on the twenty-first-century stage. We witness Beckett's influence especially in durational performance works that, like *Happy Days*, explore the strange experience of objectless waiting.[112] Winnie's feat of perseverance takes on acute ecological significance in recent works of participatory endurance in which artists and spectators gather like flotsam on an actual or imaginary shore, attending together to "the slow creaking of an exhausted Earth."[113]

As an example of this Beckettian inheritance, consider the contemporary durational opera-performance, *Sun & Sea (Marina)*, which is also entirely set on an artificial beach. Created by a three-woman team—theater director Rugile Barzdžiukaitė, playwright Vaiva Grainytė, and composer Lina Lapelytė—*Sun & Sea* was Lithuania's entry for the 2019 Venice Biennale and Golden Lion laureate for the year.[114] The work consists of an eight-hour long performance in which a sixty-four-minute opera is repeated in a continuous loop; the cast is joined by members of the public who sign up to "sunbathe" on an artificial beach for three-hour stints while audiences look down from a mezzanine gallery. Like *Happy Days*, this opera-performance depicts the beach not as a promenade but as a space one might sink into.

As if it were an operatic version of Winnie's music-box ditty about the waves, *Sun & Sea* presents a series of "everyday songs, songs of worry and of boredom, songs of almost nothing."[115] On the opera's website, curator Lucia Pietroiusti sets the mood for the work by asking visitors to imagine the sound of laughter, lapping waves, the rumble of a volcano or airplane, and "the crinkling of plastic bags" that whirl in the air and float silently, "jellyfish-like, below the waterline."[116] This dissonance between triviality and disaster intensifies throughout the opera, which surrounds its solos with an undercurrent of noise and movement: performers chat, laugh, shake sand from towels, toss beach balls, play cards, blow their noses, pet dogs, and, of course, scroll on their phones. This tonal disjunction shapes the

FIGURE 5.7. *Sun & Sea (Marina)*, opera-performance by Rugilė Barzdžiukaitė, Vaiva Grainytė, Lina Lapelytė at Biennale Arte 2019, Venice. Photo Andrej Vasilenko. Copyright © the artists.

libretto, too. A cheerful apocalypticism or light-headed dread is perceptible even in the first, seemingly upbeat "Sunscreen Basanova": "Hand it here, I need to rub my legs . . . / 'Cause later they'll peel and crack." *Sun & Sea* ricochets from praise to complaint, from a "vacationers' chorus" to a "chanson of exhaustion," and from a "siren's aria" to a "wealthy mommy's song." The beach appears here simultaneously as an escape hatch and a trash-strewn dystopia. Thus the "Chanson of Admiration" praises the sea's vibrant color, replete as it is with "emerald-colored bags, / bottles and red bottle caps." In a darker tone, a "song of complaint" observes that the beach stinks: it is glutted with fleas, dog shit, beer, champagne corks, and the remains of smoked fish. Fatigue is everywhere in this work, though it takes different musical shapes, reminiscent of Ronda's account of the "decompositional lingering" that characterizes Great Acceleration aesthetics.[117] Like *Happy Days, Sun & Sea* explores the nuances of weariness, amplifying the peculiar mix of boredom, dread, and wonder we might think of as late capitalism's dial tone or ambient background hum.

Roland Barthes theorizes what he terms the "beach effect" as an experiment with idleness and sensory drift: observing the world through half-closed eyes, Barthes's horizontal flâneur luxuriates in the transformation of his being into a supersensible surface for contact with the elements.[118] *Sun & Sea* pushes this modernist beach effect to its breaking point, turning the delights of Barthesian coenesthesis into a sort of collective sunstroke. In its nonteleological, durational loop and its ominously cheerful melodies, the work suggests that, in an era of accelerated carbon extraction and combustion, we are all on the beach.

In *Happy Days*, Winnie is almost entirely alone. The audience hangs on her words, laughs at her jokes, and listens to her silences—but we remain spatially set apart, protected from her condition of exposed immersion. If *Sun & Sea* moves us, it is because it offers a spectacle not simply of alienated leisure but of shared endurance: in inviting spectators to enter the set and join the performance, the work explores the possibilities of a fleeting togetherness within the wastes of the contemporary leisurescape. In this sense, it's a piece that asks how the tourist—the one who merely consumes the land, who treats it carelessly, using it up and moving on—might become a dweller.[119] At the same time, it indicates that, in this time of cascading toxicity and ever-accelerating accumulation of debris, *we* have become the tidewrack.

Sun & Sea closes with a chorus in which vacationers announce that their swimsuits are filling up with shells, seaweed, and (possibly noxious) algae: "This year the sea is as green as a forest: / Eutrophication! / Botanical gardens are flourishing in the sea— / The water blooms." Here the opera gestures toward a new seashore aesthetics as industrial runoff, sewage, and fertilizers transform marine ecosystems in strange and unpredictable ways. At the heart of this work is the question of what might become possible on the other side of exhaustion. In its ambiguous tone, *Sun & Sea* invites us to consider end times as an opening onto something else—a time beyond our regime of 24/7 consumption and production, an era to follow the Anthropocene.[120]

Interdisciplinary artist Sarah Cameron Sunde also explores the uses of fatigue and the seashore as a space of potential regeneration. In her ongoing site-specific performance piece *36.5/A Durational Performance with the Sea*, Sunde takes the rising sea itself as her medium, presenting a "duet" between tidal rhythms and her body. In this work of endurance, which began in 2013 as a response to the destruction wrought on New York by

FIGURE 5.8. Sarah Cameron Sunde, *36.5/North Sea*, Netherlands, 2015. Photo Jonas de Witte.

Superstorm Sandy, Sunde stands at the edge of the sea at low tide and remains in place for the nearly thirteen hours of the tidal cycle, as the ocean swells to her neck and subsides. The entire performance is filmed in real time and translated to a video installation. Sunde has performed the piece in the U.S., Mexico, the Netherlands, Bangladesh, Kenya, Brazil, and Aotearoa/New Zealand; at the time I write this, the series is set to conclude in 2022 with a performance in New York City.

Sunde's performance invites reflection on the strange tempos of sea-level rise, its global scale, and the collective forms of resistance and engagement that it demands. The intended effect of the work is to transform mere cognitive knowledge of climate disruption into material bodily understanding, sensory awareness. We may know very well that melting ice and warming, expanding water are causing the seas to rise. But this scientific fact is difficult to grasp. As Sunde observes, "it is one thing to consider climate change intellectually; it's another to feel the water rise on your own body."[121] Indeed, as Eve Kosofsky Sedgwick has argued, simple propositional knowledge is "threadbare" and "fatally thin" in contrast to the "complex process" of realization.[122] It is precisely the insufficiency of mere knowing—what Sedgwick calls an "impoverished" relation to reality—that *36.5* works to overcome. Sunde seeks to put into motion, through an embodied performance of waiting, a process of collective realization.

It is important to note the way sociability and endurance coincide in *36.5*—this is not about a heroic artist facing down the horizon alone.[123] The work draws attention to the precariousness of the human body and to the artist's smallness in relation to the immense sea before her, and yet Sunde also welcomes the public to join her in the tidal zone. Moreover, in each iteration of the performance, she engages local artists—drummers, street poets, town criers, dancers, mandolin-players—to help her keep the time. She refers to these artists as a "site-specific human clock."[124]

Like *Sun & Sea*, with its continuous, full-day loops, *36.5* exceeds the bounds of conventional spectatorship: who could possibly watch the performance in its entire, thirteen-hour duration? Instead of sitting rapt in silent observation on upright chairs, like Boudin's nineteenth-century leisure-seekers or Beckett's midcentury theater audience, Sunde's spectators enter and exit the scene in their own time. We improvise the terms of our participation, as the expectation of eventfulness gives way to the ripple and swell of a shared meanwhile. Even if we can only access this work on a screen, the experience is one of lingering alongside the artist rather than observing her from afar. Implicitly harkening back to eighteenth- and nineteenth-century hydrotherapeutic conceptions of this littoral, the piece aims at an affective remapping of the globe, drawing invisible lines between coastal sites that are bound together not by trade or culture but by susceptibility to harm. In this regard, the work engages shifting networks of sympathy in the context of the Great Acceleration: Sunde wants someone standing with her at the water's edge in the Bay of Bengal to feel curiously attuned to a stranger facing the rising tide in Akumal Bay, Mexico, or Bodo Inlet, Kenya.

Sunde's aqueous act of perseverance replays, in a very different key, Winnie's performance of slow submersion. *36.5* is in some sense more tragic than *Happy Days*, as it is not an allegory of (feminine) exposure and alienation but a visceral reminder of climate violence that is already underway. We cannot prevent the disaster of anthropogenic sea level rise; at best, we can mitigate its most dire consequences. At the same time, as we witness the artist's petite, tenacious form sinking beneath the waves, then reemerging from the sea as the tide ebbs, it's hard not to feel something akin to hope. The performance induces a not-quite-transitive, not progress-oriented kind of hope—not hope "for" anything in particular but a glimpse of our own as-yet-untested capacities to live on in a postnatural age, in the face of a radically unknowable future.[125]

The effect of Sunde's submersion and reapparition is anything but triumphantly humanist. Rather, this performance of vulnerability calls to mind Rachel Carson's account of the toughness and delicacy of tide pool life forms, which must survive the most extreme shifts of temperature and atmospheric exposure. What Una Chaudhuri calls the "fragile monumentality" of the artist's body in the tides, and her posture of "keeping watch," present a humble image of nonanthropocentric resistance.[126] Sunde does not speak to fill the time, like Winnie, but simply stands in place, for an entire day, as the water rises and falls. In fact, if Winnie's condition is one of increasing paralysis, Sunde cannot *not* move: it turns out to be impossible to hold still in the sea. Sunde notes that early on in the global cycle a Dutch water engineer helped her plot where she would stand. She thought she knew what the water would do; instead, it "pushed me gently off my spot when I least expected it."[127] In Sunde's quiet act of watchfulness, she does not stand *against* the rising tide. Instead, she stands (sometimes unsteadily) *with* it, as if her body were but the ocean's canvas or a piece of wreckage adrift in the sea.

Like *Happy Days*, *36.5* presents a woman's extreme feat of tenacity, but, unlike Winnie, Sunde is not compelled to occupy herself with the leisure-work of self-cultivation and self-presentation. Her act of submersion and reemergence has nothing to do with "keep[ing] [herself] nice, come what may." Rather, her practice of waiting requires her to connect to a reality that encompasses and exceeds her. As Sunde puts it, immersion in a full tidal cycle has taught her to think differently about the gravitational pull of the tides: "I imagine the planet breathing in and out with the tidal bulge every day. The lapping on the shore is the micro-manifestation of that big breath."[128] In this regard, we might imagine *36.5* growing out of those ubiquitous rests—uncanny comic breaks—in Winnie's monologue. Like a collectivist, improvisatory variation on Augé's waiting room metaphor, *36.5* asks us to pause and attend to the respiration of the sea as we stand vigil over a vanishing shore.

This chapter has shown that the contemporary beach might yet offer a cure, although not the intoxicating energy infusion dreamed of by nineteenth-century hygienists. Dilating on moments of drift and stillness within an era of voracious global energy consumption and carbon emission, tidewrack art and durational beach-set performances envision alternative ways of inhabiting the present. They invite reflection on the ethos of salvage in a toxic world and compel us to contemplate the difficulty of true repose at a time of hyperactive productivity. In these works, the beach is no longer (as it was in Proust and Woolf) a springboard or a dreamy threshold, but a zone of unremitting exposure, a spectacle of fatigue. Yet it also remains a setting in which new imaginative configurations might come into view. For contemporary artists who find themselves drawn to the tidelands, the beach *is* a "waiting room"—not a space of passivity but a stage on which to hone a subtle, collective art of endurance.

NOTES

INTRODUCTION

1. Thomas Mann, *Death in Venice and Seven Other Stories,* trans. H. T. Lowe-Porter (New York: Vintage, 2010); Claude Cahun and Marcel Moore, *Vues et Visions* (Paris: Georges Crès & Cie, 1919); James Joyce, *Ulysses* (New York: Oxford University Press, 1993), 37; F. Scott Fitzgerald, *The Great Gatsby* (New York: Scribner, 1996); Virginia Woolf, *Mrs. Dalloway* (New York: Harcourt, 2005), 3; Marcel Proust, *In Search of Lost Time,* trans. Scott Moncrieff and Terence Kilmartin, rev. D. J. Enright (New York: Random House, 1992); Claude McKay, *Banjo: A Story Without a Plot* (New York: Mariner, 1970); Jean-Paul Sartre, *Nausea,* trans. Lloyd Alexander and Richard Howard (New York: New Directions, 2013); Severo Sarduy, *The Beach,* in *For Voice,* trans. Philip Barnard (Pittsburgh: Latin American Literary Review Press, 1985), 13–56.
2. The term *ecotone* was first introduced in 1905 by Frederic Edward Clements in a book titled *Research Methods in Ecology* (Lincoln, Neb.: University Publishing, 1905) and defined as "the tension line between two zones" (316). The Ecological Society of America defines an ecotone as "a border zone, where ecological systems meet and mingle, sometimes forming a new and different community." On its blog, "Ecotone: News and Views on Ecological Science," the ESA notes that "the term refers to the transition from one ecosystem to another, as well the stress inherent in a population at the limit of its tolerance for specific environmental conditions." https://www.esa.org/esablog/about/ecotone-explained/ (accessed April 19, 2022). Nicholas Allen, Nick Groom, and Jos Smith observe that an ecotone "often has a biological density far greater than that of the areas on either side of it: both the intensity of its life and death cycle and the diversity of its species are greater." Allen, Groom, and Smith, eds. *Coastal Works: Cultures of the Atlantic Edge* (Oxford:

INTRODUCTION

Oxford University Press, 2017), 5. On transitional environments as harboring species rarity as well as richness, see Salit Kark, "Effects of Ecotones on Biodiversity," in Simon A. Levin, ed., *Encyclopedia of Biodiversity*, 2d ed. (Cambridge: Elsevier, 2013), 3:142–147.

3. Rachel Carson, *The Sea Around Us* (New York: Oxford University Press, 1951), 99.
4. Melody Jue, *Wild Blue Media: Thinking Through Seawater* (Durham: Duke University Press, 2020), xi, xii. The proliferating theoretical approaches that comprise the oceanic or "blue" humanities inform my conception of the littoral zone, although *Modernism at the Beach* might be best described as blue humanities adjacent. Key works of blue humanities scholarship, in addition to Jue's *Wild Blue Media,* include Karin Amimoto Ingersoll, *Waves of Knowing: A Seascape Epistemology* (Durham: Duke University Press, 2016); Steve Mentz, *Shipwreck Modernity: Ecologies of Globalization, 1550–1719* (Minneapolis: University of Minnesota Press, 2015); Stefan Helmreich, *Alien Ocean: Anthropological Voyages in Microbial Seas* (Berkeley: University of California Press, 2009); Margaret Cohen, *The Novel and the Sea* (Princeton, N.J.: Princeton University Press, 2010); and Hester Blum, *The View from the Mast-Head: Maritime Imagination and Antebellum American Sea Narratives* (Chapel Hill: University of North Carolina Press, 2008). Numerous journals have devoted issues to this topic, including *English Language Notes* ("Hydro-Criticism," 2019), *Comparative Literature* ("Oceanic Routes," 2017), and *PMLA* ("Oceanic Studies," 2010).
5. Simon Bainbridge, *Mountaineering and British Romanticism* (Oxford: Oxford University Press, 2020). Bainbridge observes that "almost all of the canonical male Romantic poets were active mountaineers at some point in their lives or were keen to present themselves as such" (5). See also Robert McFarlane, *Mountains of the Mind: A History of a Fascination* (London: Granta, 2004), on the obsession with mountains as a "lust" for dizzying verticality (93).
6. Anna Tsing, "The Buck, the Bull, and the Dream of the Stag: Some Unexpected Weeds of the Anthropocene," *Suomen Antropologi* 42, no. 1 (Spring 2017): 3–21, 7. On the vexing concept of "landscape," which indicates, from an art-historical perspective, a historically and culturally specific "way of seeing"—and in particular, since the European Renaissance, a "view" glimpsed from a single vantage point—see Dennis Cosgrove, *Social Formation and Symbolic Landscape* (Madison: University of Wisconsin Press, 1984) and W. J. T. Mitchell, *Landscape and Power* (Chicago: University of Chicago Press, 1994). For a more phenomenological engagement of landscape, understood as a way of being, a vernacular dwelling or "taskscape," see Tim Ingold, "The Temporality of the Landscape," *World Archeology* 25, no. 2 (October 1993): 152–174. And for an ecological engagement with landscape as a matter of interwoven animate and inanimate textures—including "fog," "bubbles," "foam," "molecules," and "fibers"—see Ada Smailbegović, *Poetics of Liveliness: Molecules, Fibers, Tissues, Clouds* (New York: Columbia University Press, 2021).
7. See Monique Allewaert, *Ariel's Ecology: Plantations, Personhood, and Colonialism in the American Tropics* (Minneapolis: University of Minnesota Press, 2013); Susan Scott Parrish, *The Flood Year 1927: A Cultural History* (Princeton, N.J.: Princeton University Press, 2017); and Jesse Oak Taylor, *The Sky of Our Manufacture: The*

INTRODUCTION

London Fog in British Fiction from Dickens to Woolf (Charlottesville: University of Virginia Press, 2016). For a study of the "material entanglements" of hydropower, state building, and poetry comprising China's Three Gorges Dam, a "techno-poetic landscape," see also Corey Byrnes, *Fixing Landscape: A Techno-Poetic History of China's Three Gorges* (New York: Columbia University Press, 2019), 5, 19.

8. Hannah Freed-Thall and Dora Zhang, "Modernist Setting," *Modernism/modernity Print Plus* 3, no. 1 (March 2018), http://doi.org/10.26597/mod.0042.
9. On the symbolic violence inherent in using the singular appellation *nature* as a "generalized name that displaces proper names," see Anne-Lise François, "Passing Impasse," *Comparative Literature* 72, no. 2 (June 2020): 240–257, 242. On the Earth's transformation from supposedly inert, exploitable object to unruly subject, or actant, see Isabelle Stengers, *In Catastrophic Times: Resisting the Coming Barbarism*, trans. Andrew Goffey (London: Open Humanities Press, 2015); and Bruno Latour, *Facing Gaia: Eight Lessons on the New Climatic Regime*, trans. Catherine Porter (London: Polity, 2017).
10. Bathsheba Demuth, *The Floating Coast: An Environmental History of the Bering Strait* (New York: Norton, 2019), 2–3.
11. Barthes theorizes "arrogance" in terms of "discourses of intimidation, of subjection, of domination," and as the "will-to-possess" (vouloir-saisir) in *The Neutral: Lecture Course at the College de France (1977–1978)*, trans. Denis Hollier and Rosalind Krauss (New York: Columbia University Press, 2005), 152; *Le Neutre: notes de cours au Collège de France, 1977–1978* (Paris: Seuil, 2002), 195. For an expanded reflection on close reading as a form of ecological thought, see my "Thinking Small: Ecologies of Close Reading," in David James, ed., *Modernism and Close Reading* (Oxford: Oxford University Press, 2020), 228–242.
12. In addition to Eve Kosofsky Sedgwick, *The Weather in Proust* (Durham: Duke University Press, 2011) and Roland Barthes, *The Neutral*, the works that have particularly shaped my sense of what queer ecology could be include Anne-Lise François, *Open Secrets: The Literature of Uncounted Experience* (Stanford: Stanford University Press, 2008) and "Flower Fisting," *Postmodern Cultures* 22, no. 1 (September 2011); Catriona Mortimer-Sandilands, "Melancholy Natures, Queer Ecologies," in Bruce Erikson and Catriona Mortimer-Sandilands, eds., *Queer Ecologies: Sex, Nature, Politics, Desire* (Bloomington: Indiana University Press, 2010); and Sara Ensor, "The Ecopoetics of Contact: Touching, Cruising, Gleaning," *ISLE: Interdisciplinary Studies in Literature and Environment* 25, no. 1 (Winter 2018): 150–168, and "Spinster Ecology: Rachel Carson, Sarah Orne Jewett, and Nonreproductive Futurity," *American Literature* 84, no. 2 (2012): 409–435.
13. A true commons would be neither private nor public; for an expanded discussion of this concept, see chapter 4, this volume. Gillis notes that in the United States (as of 2012), 83 percent of eastern shores and 60 percent of western shores are privately owned. John Gillis, *The Human Shore* (Chicago: University of Chicago Press, 2012), 174. On beaches as legally protected public spaces in France, see Laurent Bordereaux, "Seashore Law: The Core of French Public Maritime Law." *International Journal of Marine and Coastal Law* 29, no. 3 (2014): 402–414. For a comparative overview of public beach access in each U.S. state, see the Surfrider

Foundation's page, "Beach Access," *Beachapedia,* www.beachapedia.org/Beach
_Access (last modified August 26, 2019).

14. On capitalism as a political economy marked by the rise of "cheap nature," whereby nature is devalued and "put to work" at very low cost, see Jason W. Moore, *Capitalism in the Web of Life: Ecology and the Accumulation of Capital* (London: Verso, 2015).

15. Garrett Hardin, "The Tragedy of the Commons," *Science* 162, no. 3859 (1968): 1243–1248.

16. According to Anne-Lise François, in agrarian, early modern England, a commons was understood not as "a free space to which anyone can come and in which anything goes," but rather in terms of "precise rules" that were nonetheless "marked by a certain degree of informality, variability, and discretionary enforcement—not universally applied at all times of year" and that therefore appear "without binding authority when judged from the perspective of modern law." "'. . . and will do none': *Gewalt* in the Measure of a Parenthesis," *Critical Times* 2, no. 2 (August 2019): 285–294, 291. For a historian's perspective on precapitalist commons in England, see E. P. Thompson, *Customs in Common* (New York: New Press, 1992). For an account of an indigenous relation to place not premised on the conversion of energy into monetary profit, nor on a strict division between humans and the more-than-human world, see Demuth, *The Floating Coast.*

17. Colson Whitehead, *Sag Harbor* (New York, Doubleday, 2009), 81.

18. Rob Nixon, "Barrier Beach," in Greg Garrard, ed., *The Oxford Handbook of Ecocriticism* (Oxford: Oxford University Press, 2014), published online March 2014, 10.1093/oxfordhb/9780199742929.013.034.

19. Ruth Wilson Gilmore, "Fatal Couplings of Power and Difference," *The Professional Geographer* 54, no. 1 (February 2002): 15–24, 16, quoted in George Lipsitz, *How Racism Takes Place* (Philadelphia: Temple University Press, 2011), 51. Most bodies of water were segregated in the United States by the 1920s—by de facto means if not by official law. See Jeff Wiltse, *Contested Waters: A Social History of Swimming Pools in America* (Chapel Hill: University of North Carolina Press, 2008). On African American resistance to exclusion from public recreation as the dynamic defining the so-called golden age of leisure in the early twentieth-century U.S., see Victoria Wolcott, *Race, Riots, and Roller Coasters: The Struggle Over Segregated Recreation in America* (Philadelphia: University of Pennsylvania Press, 2012), 14. On the racist land-use regulations that have undermined the public trust doctrine defining the foreshore as public land in the U.S., see Andrew Kahrl, *Free the Beaches: The Story of Ned Coll and the Battle for America's Most Exclusive Shoreline* (New Haven: Yale University Press, 2018). On recent French and Australian bans on the "burkini"—a swimsuit worn by some Muslim women that exposes only the hands, face, and feet—see Scheherazade Bloul, Shakira Hussein, and Scott Poynting, "Diasporas and Dystopias on the Beach: Burkini Wars in France and Australia," in *The Routledge International Handbook of Islamophobia* (New York: Routledge, 2019).

20. On the radical potential of commoning as a nonproprietary, improvisational relational mode, see Jean-Luc Nancy, *Being Singular Plural,* trans. Robert Richardson and Anne O'Byrne (Stanford: Stanford University Press, 2000); Michael Hardt and Antonio Negri, *Commonwealth* (Cambridge: Harvard University Press, 2009); and

INTRODUCTION

Fred Moten and Stefano Harney, *The Undercommons: Fugitive Planning & Black Study* (New York: Minor Compositions, 2013). On queer activism as "significantly shaped by commons-forming initiatives," see Nadja Millner-Larsen and Gavin Butt, "Introduction: The Queer Commons," *GLQ* 24, no. 4 (October 2018): 399–419, 400.

21. Nixon, "Barrier Beach."
22. Notable cultural histories include Alain Corbin, *The Lure of the Sea: Discovery of the Seaside in the Western World, 1750–1840*, trans. Jocelyn Phelps (New York: Penguin, 1995); Jean-Didier Urbain, *At the Beach*, trans. Catherine Porter (Minneapolis: University of Minnesota Press, 2003); Fred Gray, *Designing the Seaside: Architecture, Society, and Nature* (London: Reaktion, 2006); Christophe Granger, *Les Corps d'été: Naissance d'une variation saisonnière* (Paris: Autrement, 2009); Gillis, *The Human Shore*; Elsa Devienne, *La Ruée vers le sable: Une histoire environnementale des plages de Los Angeles au XX siècle* (Paris: Éditions de la Sorbonne, 2020); and Robert Ritchie, *The Lure of the Beach: A Global History* (Berkeley: University of California Press, 2021). For a valuable literary critical engagement with the cultures of the (mostly British) coast, see Allen, Groom, and Smith, *Coastal Works*. On the French beach as "narrative, symbol, myth, and brand," see Sophie Fuggle and Nicholas Gledhill, eds., *La ligne d'écume: Encountering the French Beach* (London: Pavement, 2016), 2.
23. The bikini—named for an A-bomb testing site on a Pacific atoll—was unveiled at a fashion show in Paris in 1946. Beth Duncuff Charleston, "The Bikini," in *Heilbrunn Timeline of Art History* (New York: Metropolitan Museum of Art, 2000–), published online October 2004, http://www.metmuseum.org/toah/hd/biki/hd_biki.htm. See also Richard Martin and Harold Koda, *Splash! A History of Swimwear* (New York: Rizzoli, 1990). On the use of women and girls as emblems or advertisements for the atomic age, see Traci Brynne Voyles, "Anatomic Bombs: The Sexual Life of Nuclearism, 1945–57," *American Quarterly* 72, no. 3 (September 2020): 651–673. On the fight for paid vacations in France, see Jean-Claude Richez and Léon Strauss, "Un temps nouveau pour les ouvriers (1830–1960)," in Alain Corbin, ed., *L'Avènement des loisirs, 1850–1960* (Paris: Aubier, 1995), 376–412; and "Ellen Furlough, "Making Mass Vacations: Tourism and Consumer Culture in France, 1930s to 1970s," *Comparative Studies in Society and History* 40, no. 2 (April 1998): 247–286.
24. Corbin, *The Lure of the Sea*, 57.
25. "'I think nothing is as wonderful as a sunset,' she said, 'especially at the seaside.' 'Oh, I love the sea!' said Monseiur Léon." *Madame Bovary*, trans. Lydia Davis (New York: Penguin, 2010), 71. ("Je ne trouve rien d'admirable comme les soleils couchants, reprit-elle, mais au bord de la mer, surtout. —Oh! j'adore la mer, dit M. Léon.") Gustave Flaubert, *Madame Bovary* (Paris: Flammarion, 1986), 146.
26. Urbain, *At the Beach*, 44; on this phenomenon, see also Gillis, *The Human Shore*.
27. On the beach—and especially the seemingly unfettered, dereglemented female bather—as an object of fascination for impressionists, see Linda Nochlin, *Bathers, Bodies, Beauty: The Visceral Eye* (Cambridge, Mass.: Harvard University Press, 2006). On modernism's attraction to the blank, impersonal quality of the beach, see Lisa Tichner, "Vanessa Bell: *Studland Beach*, Domesticity, and 'Significant Form,'" *Representations* 65 (1999): 63–92.
28. Armand Landrin, *Les Plages de France* (Paris: Hachette, 1879), 3.

INTRODUCTION

29. Stéphane Mallarmé, *Mallarmé on Fashion: A Translation of the Fashion Magazine La Dernière Mode, with Commentary*, ed. and trans. A. M. Cain and P. M. Furbank (Oxford: Berg, 2004), 33; *Oeuvres completes* II (Paris: Gallimard, 2003), 499.
30. Marcel Proust, *Jean Santeuil, précédé de Les plaisirs et les jours* (Paris: Gallimard, 1971), 368–70.
31. Ada Smailbegović, "At the Edges of Unmeeting: Geometries of Sea and Land in Marianne Moore's Seascapes," *Comparative Literature* 73, no. 2 (June 2021): 150–165, 152.
32. Corbin, *The Lure of the Sea*, 87. Daniel Heller-Roazen notes that examples of coenesthesis in nineteenth-century medical literature include the sensation of "well-being produced by clean air" as well as compound mental states such as tickling, tingling, and shivering. Daniel Heller-Roazen, *The Inner Touch: Archeology of a Sensation* (Cambridge, Mass.: MIT Press, 2007), 249.
33. Samuel Beckett, *The Complete Dramatic Works* (London: Faber and Faber, 1986), 154.
34. Gillis, *The Human Shore*, 172, 161.
35. J. K. Huysmans, *Against Nature*, trans. Robert Baldick (New York: Penguin, 2003), 22.
36. Sociologists Michèle De la Pradelle and Emmanuelle Lallement propose that all visitors to Paris-Plage are essentially actors, participating in a fiction: the "making present of the sea's absence" ("la mise en présence de l'absence de la mer"). De la Pradelle and Lallement, "Paris-Plage: Célébrer un objet absent," in Octave Debary and Laurier Turgeon, eds., *Objets et mémoires* (Paris: Éditions de la Maison des sciences de l'homme, 2007), 197–208, 206.
37. Nicole Elko, Tiffany Roberts Briggs, Lindino Benedet, Quin Robertson, Gordon Thomson, Bret M. Webb, and Kimberly Garvey, "A Century of U.S. Beach Nourishment," *Ocean and Coastal Management* 199 (2021), https://doi.org/10/1016/j.ocecoaman.2020.105406 (accessed February 22, 2021). On the harmful ecological effects of such terraforming, see Charles H. Peterson and Melanie J. Bishop. "Assessing the Environmental Impacts of Beach Nourishment," *BioScience* 55, no. 10 (October 2005): 887–896.
38. Vince Beiser, *The World in a Grain: The Story of Sand and How It Transformed Civilization* (New York: Riverhead, 2018), 196. Sand is now among the most traded global commodities by volume. Most of it, however, is used not as beach fill but as a key ingredient in cement, enabling the construction of the cities whose exhausted denizens dream of beach vacations, and of the long smooth roads (or airport runways) that facilitate their travel. Laleh Khalili, *Sinews of Trade and War* (London: Verso, 2020), 83.
39. Gillis, *The Human Shore*, 171.
40. Robert Caro, *The Power Broker: Robert Moses and the Fall of New York* (New York: Vintage, 1975), 232.
41. Richard B. Dornhelm, "The Coney Island Public Beach and Boardwalk Improvement of 1923," in Lesley Ewing, Thomas Herrington, and Orville Magoon, eds., *Urban Beaches: Balancing Public Rights and Private Development*, 52–63 (Reston, Va.: ASCE, 2003), 55.
42. According to journalist Andrew S. Lewis, "Over the last century, the sea level at the Jersey Shore has risen twice as fast as the global average, because the land here

INTRODUCTION

is also sinking. The water's upward climb—18 inches in New Jersey—has increased nuisance flooding up and down the coast, just as it has in low-lying communities around the world." Andrew S. Lewis, "The Long, Slow Drowning of the New Jersey Shore," *New York Times Magazine*, August 15, 2021. For a discussion of the ecological consequences and possible outcomes of rising seas on coastal communities on the U.S., see Elizabeth Rush, *Rising: Dispatches from the New American Shore* (Minneapolis: Milkweed, 2018).

43. Henry David Thoreau, *Cape Cod* (Princeton, N.J.: Princeton University Press, 2004), 147.
44. Saidiya Hartman, *Lose Your Mother: A Journey Along the Atlantic Slave Route* (New York: Farrar, Straus and Giroux, 2008), 32.
45. Virilio points out that recovering peace and accessing the beach in 1945 were "one and the same event." Paul Virilio, *Bunker Archeology,* trans. George Collins (New York: Princeton Architectural Press, 1994), 9.
46. The film opens with scenes of transport, as bodies eager to reach the coast throng trains and buses and hang out of car windows. Underscoring this alliance between fossil fuel combustion and beach pleasure, Tati frames the moment of arrival at the seashore through the back window of an automobile.
47. David Bellos, *Jacques Tati: His Life and Art* (New York: Random House, 2001), 181. Pointing out that this is Tati's least dialogic film (Hulot never speaks, except to utter his name), Bellos observes that *Monsieur Hulot's Holiday* alternates between gag sequences and "shots of nothing much happening at all" (187). The film thus "has all the machinery of narrative, but no story to tell; it seems to be held together by style alone." It's also, notes Bellos, the only occasion in Tati's completed work that "simulates the experience of war" (186, 189).
48. Bellos, 80. The artillery bombardment simulation was dangerous to film and Tati was badly burned (189).
49. On tourism as the world's biggest industry by the century's end, see Shelley Baranowski and Ellen Furlough, *Being Elsewhere: Tourism, Consumer Culture, and Identity in Modern Europe and North America* (Ann Arbor: University of Michigan Press, 2001). On the rise of commercial tourism in France, see Furlough, "Making Mass Vacations."
50. Jean-Francis Held, "Claude Lévi-Strauss: Tristes Vacances," *Le Nouvel Observateur,* no. 74 (April 13–19, 1966), published online April 14, 2006, https://www.nouvelobs.com/culture/20060414.OBS4022/claude-levi-strauss-tristes-vacances.html.
51. Ellen Furlough, "Une leçon des choses: Tourism, Empire, and the Nation in Interwar France," *French Historical Studies* 25, no. 3 (Summer 2002): 441–473, 473. On interconnections between tourism and imperialism, see also Krista A. Thompson, *An Eye for the Tropics: Tourism, Photography, and Framing the Caribbean Picturesque* (Durham: Duke University Press, 2006); Dennis Merrill, *Negotiating Paradise: U.S. Tourism and Empire in Twentieth-Century Latin America* (Chapel Hill: University of North Carolina Press, 2009); and Christine Skwiot, *The Purposes of Paradise: U.S. Tourism and Empire in Cuba and Hawai'i* (Philadelphia: University of Pennsylvania Press, 2012).
52. Aimé Césaire, *Complete Poems of Aimé Césaire: Bilingual Edition,* trans. A. James Arnold and Clayton Eshleman (Middletown, Conn.: Wesleyan University Press, 2017), 24–25.

53. Marguerite Duras, *The Sea Wall*, trans. Herma Briffault (New York: Pellegrini and Cudahy, 1952), 23.
54. In *The Stranger*, a history of colonial violence is disturbingly crystallized in a single moment of glaring seaside disorientation: Camus's Algerian beach appears as a flat landscape of sheer sensation and ethical vacuity, where the glare of the midday sun burns away interiority, history, and stylistic embellishment. Alice Kaplan notes that Camus had a beach setting in mind from the start. In early 1940 he wrote in his notebook (under the heading "novel"): "This story begins on a burning hot blue beach, in the tanned bodies of two young people—bathing in the ocean, playing games in the sea and sun." Kaplan, *Searching for The Stranger: Albert Camus and the Life of a Literary Classic* (Chicago: University of Chicago Press, 2016), 61. For a critique of Camus's choice not to grant a name or a backstory to the Arab man that his hero murders, see Kamel Daoud, *The Meursault Investigations*, trans. John Cullen (New York: Other, 2015).
55. Marie NDiaye, *Rosie Carpe*, trans. Tamsin Black (Lincoln: University of Nebraska Press, 2004), 155, 156, 162, 170.
56. Jamaica Kincaid, *A Small Place* (New York: Farrar, Straus and Giroux, 2000), 57–58.
57. NDiaye, *Rosie Carpe*, 170–171.
58. Vanessa Agard-Jones, "What the Sands Remember," *GLQ* 18, nos. 2–3 (2012): 325–346, 326.
59. Omese'eke Natasha Tinsely, *Thiefing Sugar: Eroticism Between Women in Caribbean Literature* (Durham: Duke University Press, 2010), 2.
60. Tiffany Lethabo King, *The Black Shoals: Offshore Formations in Black and Native Studies* (Durham: Duke University Press, 2019), 3.
61. King, *The Black Shoals*, 11, 3, 9.
62. Gilles Deleuze, *Abécédaire*, "E comme enfance," interview by Claire Parnet, filmed for television by Pierre-André Boutang (1988–89).
63. Kathryn Yusoff, "Geologic Realism: On the Beach of Geologic Time," *Social Text* 37, no. 1 (March 2019): 1–26, 12.
64. On this South Pacific fantasy's dependence on the frame of war, see Haunani-Kay Trask, *From a Native Daughter: Colonialism and Sovereignty in Hawai'i* (Honolulu: University of Hawai'i Press, 1999). On the craze for "Tiki culture"—largely organized around a set of rum-based exotic cocktails (the Zombie, the Missionary's Downfall, the Mai Tai) that began after Prohibition in California and was firmly anchored in the popular imaginary by the 1950s—see Andrew Pilsch, "Polynesian Paralysis: Tiki Culture and the Aesthetics of American Empire," in Craig Owens and Stephen Schneider, eds., *The Shaken and the Stirred: The Year's Work in Cocktail Culture* (Bloomington: Indiana University Press, 2020).
65. Vanessa Schwartz, *It's So French!: Hollywood, Paris, and the Making of Cosmopolitan Film Culture* (Chicago: University of Chicago Press, 2007), chapter 5.
66. Films presenting the beach as a classroom and a space for making heterosexuality include *Gidget* (Paul Wendkos, 1959), *Where the Boys Are* (Henry Levin, 1960), *Beach Party* (William Asher, 1963), *Muscle Beach Party* (Asher, 1964), *Bikini Beach* (Asher, 1964), *Beach Blanket Bingo* (Asher, 1965), and the exquisitely bad *Horror of Beach Party* (Del Tenney, 1964). On cinema as the "technology of cultural fantasy" and the cinema of the 1950s–1970s in particular as untethering sex

INTRODUCTION

from traditional heterosexual domesticity, see Damon Young, *Making Sex Public* (Durham: Duke University Press, 2018). On the queerness of French beach-set cinema and the beach as spatializing an alternative modernity, see Fiona Handyside, *Cinema at the Shore: The Beach in French Film* (New York: Peter Lang, 2014).

67. This idea is central to the French box office hit *Le Gendarme de Saint-Tropez* (Jean Girault, 1964), a police comedy set on the Riviera. In one famous scene, the police round up a group of nudists on the beach and then demand, absurdly, to see their papers. On the twentieth-century beach as a cultural battleground, see Devienne, *La Ruée vers le sable*, which examines how Los Angeles–area beaches have been shaped by processes of gentrification and social control, and Granger, *Les Corps d'été*, which examines the beach as a site of social struggle in twentieth-century France. See also Nicole Seymour's reading of *Surf Party* (Maury Dexter, 1964) as a film that explores "the impulse to manage non-human nature [a]s inseparable from the impulse to manage human eroticism." *Strange Natures: Empathy, Futurity, and the Queer Ecological Imagination* (Champaign: University of Illinois Press, 2013), 115.

68. George Chauncey, *Gay New York: Gender, Urban Culture, and the Makings of the Gay Male World, 1890–1940* (New York, Basic Books, 1994), 183–184. For visual evidence of pre-Stonewall beach drag shows, see Hugh Hagius, ed., *Swasarnt Nerf's Gay Guides for 1949* (New York: Bibliogay, 2010); and the New York City LGBT Community Center's Richard Peckinpaugh Beach Photographs, Folder 1.

69. Mel Chen, *Animacies: Biopolitics, Racial Mattering, and Queer Affect* (Durham: Duke University Press, 2012), 104.

70. Jack Halberstam, *Wild Things: The Disorder of Desire* (Durham: Duke University Press, 2020), 11, 10.

71. Halberstam, 12.

72. Guy de Maupassant, "Épaves," in *Contes et Nouvelles,* ed. Louis Forestier (Paris: Gallimard, 2014), 215–218. This story originally appeared in *Le Gaulois,* December 9, 1881.

73. Jules Michelet, *La Mer* (Paris: Gallimard, 1983).

74. Maupassant, "Épaves," 218.

75. Jean-Yves Tadié, *Marcel Proust: A Life,* trans. Euan Cameron (New York: Penguin, 2000), 497; Tadié notes that Proust had two wool overcoats made for his summers in Cabourg (621). Thanks to Richard Riddick for pointing this out.

76. Rachel Carson, *The Edge of the Sea* (New York: Houghton Mifflin Harcourt, 1998), 5, *The Sense of Wonder* (New York: Harper Collins, 1998), 82.

77. The off-season beach also played a central role in Deleuze's intellectual biography, as the site of his adolescent philosophical awakening. Deleuze describes having been initiated into literature and philosophy while walking on the Deauville beach in the winter of 1940 with a young teacher whose visual impairment had exempted him from military service. Local residents were shocked to see the pair conversing for hours among the dunes, and someone eventually wrote to Deleuze's mother, who put a stop to it. Still, the philosopher notes, that winter in Deauville "completely transformed" him as a thinker. See "E comme enfance" in Deleuze, *Abécédaire.* On the importance of this scene to Deleuze's sense of both pedagogy and friendship, see Charles J. Stivale, *Gilles Deleuze's ABCs: The Folds of Friendship* (Baltimore: Johns Hopkins University Press, 2008), 45–46.

78. Pierre Saint-Amand, "The Secretive Body: Roland Barthes's Gay Erotics," *Yale French Studies* 90 (1996): 153–171, 168, 171.

INTRODUCTION

79. Esther Newton, *Cherry Grove, Fire Island: Sixty Years in America's First Gay and Lesbian Town* (Durham: Duke University Press, 2014), 2.
80. Golan Y. Moskowitz, *Wild Visionary: Maurice Sendak in Queer Jewish Context* (Stanford: Stanford University Press, 2020), 134. Many thanks to Jack Parlett for drawing my attention to the importance of Fire Island to Sendak.
81. Moskowitz, 136.
82. Gayle S. Rubin, "Introduction: Sex, Gender, Politics," in *Deviations: A Gayle S. Rubin Reader* (Durham: Duke University Press, 2012), 1–32, 7.
83. Lauren Berlant and Michael Warner, "Sex in Public," *Critical Inquiry* 24, no. 2 (Winter 1998): 547–566, 562.
84. Moskowitz, *Wild Visionary*, 4.
85. Kathryn Bond Stockton, *The Queer Child, or Growing Sideways in the Twentieth Century* (Durham: Duke University Press, 2009).
86. Joseph Litvak, *Strange Gourmets: Sophistication, Theory, and the Novel* (Durham: Duke University Press, 1997), 79. Moskowitz expresses a similar idea in his investigation of the rich and fertile domain of childhood for queer artists like Maurice Sendak: "In a context that . . . forbade alternative ways of loving or being, to 'grow up' might have actually meant, for a queer person, either to lie and conform or to disappear." Moskowitz, *Wild Visionary*, 139.
87. Virginia Woolf, *To the Lighthouse* (New York: Harcourt, 2005), 79.
88. *Vues et visions* first appeared in 1914, sans illustrations and under the pseudonym Claude Courlis, in *Le mercure de France*, and then as an illustrated collaboration between Cahun and Moore in 1919 (published by Georges Crès & Cie). The text was reprinted in Claude Cahun and Marcel Moore, *Écrits*, edited by François Leperlier (Paris: Éditions Jean Michel Place, 2002), 21–124. It has not been translated into English.
89. Cahun and Moore, *Vues et visions*, 259, 277.
90. Cahun and Moore, 270. On the radically collaborative nature of Cahun and Moore's work, which critics have tended to overlook, see Tirza True Latimer, "Entre Nous: Between Claude Cahun and Marcel Moore," *GLQ* 12, no. 2 (2006): 197–216. For a compelling reading of Cahun and Moore's gender play not as "triumphant performativity" but as a survival strategy in the context of the interwar period's increasingly homophobic legal landscape, see Jill Richards, *The Fury Archives: Female Citizenship, Human Rights, and the International Avant-Gardes* (New York: Columbia University Press, 2020), chapter 5.
91. Corbin, *The Lure of the Sea*, 164.
92. Vanessa Schwartz argues that Bardot was the "most famous French export of the postwar period." Schwartz, *It's So French!*, 144.
93. Emily Apter, "Toward a Unisex Erotics: Claude Cahun and Geometric Modernism," in A. Schaffner and S. Weller, eds., *Modernist Eroticisms: European Literature After Sexology* (London: Palgrave, 2012), 134–149, 148.
94. Jean Vigo and Boris Kaufman also give us a different kind of inverted sexy beach in their 1930 film, *A propos de Nice*, when they invite the viewer to look up the skirts of cancan dancers. By contrast, Varda deheterosexualizes the camera's gaze. Her camera eye does not denude anyone, unlike that of Vigo, who enjoys the editing trick—adapted from Buñuel and Dalí's surrealist classic, *Un Chien andalou* (1929)—of making a beachside woman's dress suddenly vanish.

1. PROUST'S LEAP

95. Emma Wilson, *The Reclining Nude: Agnès Varda, Catherine Breillat, and Nan Goldin* (Liverpool: Liverpool University Press, 2019), 3–4, 5.
96. Barthes, Roland. "Sur la plage," in *Oeuvres complètes*, vol. 4 (Paris: Seuil, 2002), 509–510, my translation.
97. La Ciotat is a town on the Riviera where the Lumières owned a villa, the Clos des Plages. It was in and around La Ciotat that they shot many of their earliest films, including *Baignade en mer*. This 38-second film—number 11 in the catalog—was first privately screened at the Clos des Plages under the title *Baignades à la Ciotat* before it was shown to the public in Paris on December 28, 1895. https://catalogue-lumiere.com/baignade-en-mer/ (accessed February 28, 2022). Three versions of *Arrival of a Train* exist: two were shot in 1896 and the third, and most well-known (no. 653), in 1897 (https://catalogue-lumiere.com/arrivee-train-a-la-ciotat/; accessed February 28, 2022). On the mythology surrounding this locomotive arrival, see Martin Loiperdinger, "Lumière's Arrival of the Train: Cinema's Founding Myth," *The Moving Image* 4, no. 1 (Spring 2004): 89–118. See also Susan Sontag's claim, in her February 25, 1996, *New York Times* essay "The Decay of Cinema," that "everything in cinema begins with that moment, 100 years ago, when the train pulled into the station."
98. On modernist athleticism, see Katie Holmes, *Female Aerialists in the 1920s and Early 1930s: Femininity, Celebrity, and Glamour* (New York: Routledge, 2022); Harold B. Segel, *Body Ascendant: Modernism and the Physical Imperative* (Baltimore: Johns Hopkins University Press, 1998); Jed Rasula, *Acrobatic Modernism from the Avant-Garde to Prehistory* (Oxford: Oxford University Press, 2020); and Peta Tait, *Circus Bodies: Cultural Identity in Aerial Performance* (New York: Routledge, 2005).
99. Translation by Roger Pearson, in *Stéphane Mallarmé* (London: Reaktion, 2010), 153; Stéphane Mallarmé, *Oeuvres Complètes I* (Paris: Gallimard, 1998), 347.
100. Jeffrey Jerome Cohen, *Stone: An Ecology of the Inhuman* (Minneapolis: University of Minnesota Press, 2015), 4.
101. Cohen, 5.
102. On Mallarmé's poetics as modeled on the capriciousness of the pebble's "oblique rebound," see Marian Sugano, *The Poetics of the Occasion: Mallarmé and the Poetry of Circumstance* (Stanford: Stanford University Press, 1987), 161.
103. Marc Augé, *L'Impossible voyage: Le tourisme et ses images* (Paris: Rivages, 1997), 38, 42.
104. Michael Taussig, "The Beach (a Fantasy)," *Critical Inquiry* 26, no. 2 (Winter 2000): 248–278, 258.

1. PROUST'S LEAP

1. On the importance of urban settings for modernism, see, for instance, Robert Alter, *Imagined Cities: Urban Experience and the Language of the Novel* (New Haven: Yale University Press, 2005); Barry McCrea, *In the Company of Strangers: Family and Narrative in Dickens, Conan Doyle, Joyce, and Proust* (New York: Columbia University Press, 2011); Adrienne Brown, *The Black Skyscraper: Architecture and the Perception of Race* (Baltimore: Johns Hopkins University Press,

1. PROUST'S LEAP

2019); and Paul Haacke, *The Vertical Imagination and the Crisis of Transatlantic Modernism* (Oxford: Oxford University Press, 2021).
2. Andrey Bely, *Peterburg*, trans. Robert E. Maguire and John E. Malmstad (Bloomington: Indiana University Press, 1978), 270; James Joyce, *Ulysses* (New York: Oxford University Press, 1993), 37, 41; Virginia Woolf, *Mrs. Dalloway* (New York: Harcourt, 1953), 3.
3. Marcel Proust, *In Search of Lost Time*, trans. Scott Moncrieff and Terence Kilmartin, rev. D. J. Enright, 6 vols. (New York: Modern Library, 1992); *À la recherche du temps perdu*, 4 vols. (Paris: Gallimard, 1987–1989). According to Christian Pechenard, Proust made his first stabs at the work that would become the *Recherche* while vacationing in Cabourg during the summer of 1908. *Proust à Cabourg* (Paris: Quai Voltaire, 1992), 84. The recent discovery of drafts penned in winter-spring 1908, however, casts doubt on this supposition. See Marcel Proust, *Les Soixante-Quinze Feuillets: Et autres manuscrits inédits*, ed. Natalie Mauriac Dyer (Paris: Gallimard, 2021). Still, it was from Cabourg that Proust boasted to his friend Geneviève Straus, in August 1909, "You will read me—more of me than you will want—for I've just begun—and finished—a whole long book" ("Vous me lirez—et plus que vous ne voudrez—car je viens de commencer—et de finir—tout un long livre"). *Selected Letters*, ed. Philip Kolb, trans. Ralph Mannheim, Terence Kilmartin, and Joanna Kilmartin, 4 vols. (Oxford: Oxford University Press, 1983–2000), 2:445–446; *Correspondance de Marcel Proust*, ed. Philip Kolb, 21 vols. (Paris: Plon, 1970–1993), 9:163. In 1911, Proust's assistant, Albert Nahmias, dictated the manuscript of *Swann's Way* to typist Cecilia Hayward at the Cabourg Grand Hôtel. Jean-Yves Tadié, *Marcel Proust*, trans. Euan Cameron (New York: Viking, 2001), 557, 567.
4. Michael Taussig, "The Beach (A Fantasy)," *Critical Inquiry* 26, no. 2 (Winter 2000): 248–278.
5. Rosalind Krauss, *The Optical Unconscious* (Cambridge: MIT Press, 1994), 2–3. On the modernist beach as a site enabling the abstraction of the social into sheer form—and on the feminist resonances of this phenomenon in the work of Vanessa Bell—see Lisa Tickner, "Vanessa Bell: *Studland Beach*, Domesticity, and 'Significant Form,'" *Representations* 65 (Winter 1999): 63–92.
6. *In Search of Lost Time*, 2:341, 343; *À la recherche du temps perdu*, 2:33, 34. On the Balbec chapter as oriented toward the unfolding future rather than the past, see Suzanne Guerlac, *Proust, Photography, and the Time of Life: Ravaisson, Bergson, and Simmel* (London: Bloomsbury, 2020), 114.
7. José Esteban Muñoz, *Cruising Utopia: The There and Then of Queer Futurity* (New York, New York University Press, 2009), 1, 5, 72.
8. Reading Proust with "something of a Buddhist eye," Sedgwick interrogates the critical assumption that the *Recherche* is "the story of a successfully consolidated omnipotence," whereby the hero seeks a series of substitutions for mommy and finally learns that only in the field of art can he enjoy total power. By contrast, Sedgwick is interested in moments in which Proust's narrator realizes that "it's not all about [him]." Eve Kosofsky Sedgwick, *The Weather in Proust* (Durham: Duke University Press, 2011), 6, 45, 19–20.
9. William C. Carter, "The Vast Structure of Recollection: From Life to Literature," in Richard Bales, ed., *The Cambridge Companion to Proust* (Cambridge: Cambridge University Press, 2001), 25–41, 34.

1. PROUST'S LEAP

10. Roger Shattuck, *Proust's Way: A Field Guide to* In Search of Lost Time (New York: Norton, 2001), 9–10.
11. Barry McCrea, *In the Company of Strangers* (New York: Columbia University Press, 2011), 158. McCrea argues that the "symbolic binary of the countryside and the city" is "central to the novel's structure and to its competing models of kinship and identity," but also examines how Proust subtly "dismantle[s]" this opposition (199). Proust's Paris, for instance, turns out to be more villagelike than one might expect: "everyone seems either to know everyone else or to be at a few easy degrees of separation" (18).
12. Pechenard, *Proust à Cabourg*, 176.
13. This article is signed Nède, pseudonym of Mme Estradier (quoted in Pechenard, 27). The author aestheticizes the sea in terms Proust will later take up—as a painting or theatrical set (a "tableau," or "toile de fond," a "a joli décor"), while the mayor of Cabourg, Charles Bertrand, is floridly described as "le grand metteur en scène de cette féerie" (29, 30). Perhaps inspired by this article, in *Sodome and Gomorrah* Proust has his narrator read *One Thousand and One Nights* at the beach.
14. *Le Figaro*, August 13, 1907.
15. As further evidence of how newspapers were entwined with turn-of-the-century beach culture, a front-page, August 5, 1906, notice in the *Figaro* declared that the paper—previously available for sale in kiosks and via newsboys—would henceforth be delivered directly (by automobile) to subscribers in Trouville, Deauville, and adjoining beach towns. On Proust's love of newspapers—and of *Le Figaro* in particular—see my *Spoiled Distinctions: Aesthetics and the Ordinary in French Modernism* (New York: Oxford University Press, 2015), chapter 1.
16. William Carter, *The Proustian Quest* (New York: New York University Press, 1994), 10.
17. Proust, *Selected Letters*, 2:325; *Correspondance de Marcel Proust*, 7:285–286. On the modernist "syntax of velocity" and Proust's love of automotive aesthetics in particular, see Sara Danius, "The Aesthetics of the Windshield: Proust and the Modernist Rhetoric of Speed," *Modernism/modernity* 8, no. 1 (January 2001): 99–126. See also Enda Duffy, *The Speed Handbook: Velocity, Pleasure, Modernism* (Durham: Duke University Press, 2009), 4.
18. For a longer list of Proust's investments, see my "Speculative Modernism: Proust and the Stock Market," *Modernist Cultures* 12, no. 2 (2017): 153–172.
19. "L' aristocratie est une chose relative." *In Search of Lost Time*, 2:520; *À la recherche du temps perdu*, 2:158. For an alternate view of Balbec as a space of gender and class transgression, but one that ultimately "maintain[s] social boundaries and conventions," see Áine Larkin, "Proust and the Beach as Screen," in Sophie Fuggle and Nicholas Gledhill, eds., *La ligne d'écume: Encountering the French Beach* (London: Pavement, 2006), 61–82, 71.
20. *In Search of Lost Time*, 2:345; *À la recherche du temps perdu*, 2:35. This scene figures in Proust's earliest drafts detailing his hero's holiday by the sea. Proust, *Les Soixante-Quinze Feuillets*, 71–72.
21. *In Search of Lost Time*, 2:359; *À la recherche du temps perdu*, 2:45, 43.
22. *In Search of Lost Time*, 2:518; *À la recherche du temps perdu*, 2:157.
23. *In Search of Lost Time*, 2:347; *À la recherche du temps perdu*, 2:37.
24. *In Search of Lost Time*, 2:349, 383–384; *À la recherche du temps perdu*, 2:38, 62.

1. PROUST'S LEAP

25. On Proust's ironic yet tender treatment of Legrandin's "dated, overcooked lyricism," see François Proulx, "Proust's Drawings and the Secret of the 'Solitary House,'" *MLN* 133, no. 4 (September 2018): 865–890, 869, 874–875. On Legrandin's speech as a pastiche of Proust's (earlier) style, see Francine Goujon, "Références balzaciennes et cryptage autobiographique dans *Du côté de chez Swann*," *Bulletin d'informations proustiennes* 33 (2003): 51–73, 56.
26. Proust, *In Search of Lost Time*, 1:185; *À la recherche du temps perdu*, 1:130.
27. On the unconventional temporality of the "queer invitation"—a "counterweight" to normative interpellations—see Benjamin Bateman, *The Modernist Art of Queer Survival* (New York: Oxford University Press, 2017), 64–69. Bateman argues that "where interpellation reinforces the subject's location in his present circumstances . . . the queer invitation encourages him to move beyond them into unknown territory; it opens before or beside him an horizon of possibility" (66).
28. According to Descombes, at Balbec, "no one intrudes into the affairs of the others; each remains at his own table." Vincent Descombes, *Proust: Philosophy of the Novel*, trans. Catherine Chance Macksey (Stanford: Stanford University Press, 1992), 191.
29. In addition to these missed or thwarted overtures, the volume is replete with declined invitations. Dining in the hotel restaurant, the narrator longs to join a clique of young people, only to ultimately refuse their belated invitation in the final pages of the volume. He will likewise pass on his new friend Saint-Loup's invitation to Doncières, a gesture made sincerely to the narrator but insincerely to Bloch, who (conversely) is eager to accept it. Similarly, the narrator nearly declines an invitation from the celebrated painter, Elstir, ultimately visiting the painter's studio only at his grandmother's insistence. Finally, two volumes later, he returns to Balbec bearing a valuable letter of introduction from Saint-Loup to the Cambremers, establishing the very connection that his father had failed to secure in "Combray." Yet despite his wealth of social capital, he begins this second summer in a state of mourning, hiding from everyone who seeks his company.
30. Although the episode that we might call "Balbec II" begins with refused invitations, the second holiday as a whole is quite different from the first. The narrator's return to the seashore is shaped by two preoccupations: first, he now seeks to consolidate his social capital by furthering his relationships with Charlus, the Verdurins, and the Cambremers; and, second (and perhaps most significantly), he returns to Balbec armed with a theory of sexuality that incites him to track Albertine's whereabouts (and potential lesbian activities) with jealous possessiveness.
31. *In Search of Lost Time*, 2:685–686; *À la recherche du temps perdu*, 2:275.
32. *In Search of Lost Time*, 2:503–504; *À la recherche du temps perdu*, 2:147.
33. *In Search of Lost Time*, 2:410–21; *À la recherche du temps perdu*, 2:88.
34. *In Search of Lost Time*, 2:452; *À la recherche du temps perdu*, 2:110.
35. *In Search of Lost Time*, 2:474; *À la recherche du temps perdu*, 2:126.
36. Paul Joanne, *Normandie* (Paris: Hachette, 1901). In the 1890 edition of the same guidebook, the word *casino* appears more frequently than *beach* (*plage*).
37. Walter Benjamin, "In Parallel with My Actual Diary," in *Selected Writing*, vol. 2, part 2, ed. Michael W. Jennings, Howard Eileen, and Gary Smith, 413–414 (Cambridge MA: Harvard University Press, 1999), 414. This undated fragment was written between 1929 and 1931.

1. PROUST'S LEAP

38. Tadié, *Marcel Proust*, 526.
39. *In Search of Lost Time*, 4:338–339; *À la recherche du temps perdu*, 3:245–246.
40. Proust claimed in a February 1912 letter to Robert de Billy that his "fièvre du jeu" began at the Grand Hôtel Casino in Cabourg. *Correspondance de Marcel Proust*, 11:41.
41. William Carter, *Marcel Proust: A Life* (New Haven: Yale University Press, 2013), 482.
42. Carter, 602.
43. Rubén Gallo, *Proust's Latin Americans* (Baltimore: Johns Hopkins University Press, 2014), 87.
44. During Proust's first summer at Cabourg in 1907, playing baccarat became part of his routine, along with long drives in motor-cars, visiting churches, and watching polo. As he put it, he would "gamble—and lose—at baccarat every evening." Proust to Robert de Billy, early October 1907, in *Selected Letters*, 2:333.
45. Thomas Kavanagh, *Dice, Cards, Wheels: A Different History of French Culture* (Philadelphia: University of Pennsylvania Press, 2005), 171.
46. Kavanagh, 178.
47. *In Search of Lost Time*, 4:326–327; *À la recherche du temps perdu*, 3:236.
48. In a March 1912 letter to Georges de Lauris, Proust writes: "Savez-vous que j'ai joué ou plutôt fait jouer sur des mines d'or" ("Did you know that I gambled, or rather had someone gamble for me, on gold mines"). *Correspondance de Marcel Proust*, 11:77.
49. Erving Goffman, *Interaction Ritual: Essays On Face-to-Face Behavior* (New York: Pantheon, 1967), 266. On Goffman's gambling habit (in the course of ethnographic fieldwork, he became a blackjack dealer and pit boss in Las Vegas), see Javier A. Treviño, *Goffman's Legacy* (New York: Rowman and Littlefield, 2003), 31. See also Dmitri Shalin, "Erving Goffman, Fateful Action, and the Las Vegas Gambling Scene," *UNLV Gaming Research & Review Journal* 20, no. 1 (2016): 1–38, https://digitalscholarship.unlv.edu/grrj/vol20/iss1/1.
50. On contingency as the ethos of modernity, see Niklas Luhmann, "Contingency as Modern Society's Defining Attribute," in *Observations on Modernity*, trans. William Whobrey (Stanford: Stanford University Press, 1998), 44–62; and T. J. Clark, *Farewell to an Idea: Episodes from the History of Modernism* (New Haven: Yale University Press, 1999). The definition of contingency as "what could be otherwise" is Luhmann's.
51. The beach features importantly in Proust's unfinished novel, *Jean Santeuil* (1895–1899), as I will discuss. See Proust, *Les Soixante-Quinze Feuillets*, 71–90, for the earliest known (winter-spring 1908) drafts of the Balbec material.
52. On the genesis of the novel and Albertine's late arrival to the party, see Anthony Pugh, *The Growth of À la recherche du temps perdu: A Chronological Examination of Proust's Manuscripts from 1909–1914*, 2 vols. (Toronto: University of Toronto Press, 2004). Pugh notes that if the name Albertine only appeared in 1914, an encounter with teenage girls by the sea was on Proust's mind from his earliest drafts. In 1909–1910, the girls' names keep changing—Floriot, Swann, Forcheville, de Quimperlé, de Penhoët; Maria is the name of the principle heroine for some years. Other tested-out names include Solange, Anna, Andrée, Simone, Septimie, Hélène (1:187, 192).

1. PROUST'S LEAP

53. Christine Cano, *Proust's Deadline* (Champaign: University of Illinois Press, 2006), 60. Cano observes that the novel "nearly doubled in length" during the interim of the war, and new sections emerged: *Sodome et Gomorrhe,* and the "roman d'Albertine" (in three parts: the seaside resort encounter, then the period of jealous sequestration, and finally her flight and accidental death). But Cano also cites critics for whom Albertine was not simply an "accident" but "long foreseen in Proust's drafts" (82).
54. This is not to say that Albertine is simply a transposition of Alfred, as many critics have assumed. Eve Kosofsky Sedgwick and Elisabeth Ladenson have convincingly shown that while Albertine may register certain aspects of Proust's relationship with Agostinelli, the "transposition theory" does not hold up under close scrutiny. See Ladenson, *Proust's Lesbianism* (Ithaca: Cornell University Press, 1999), 13–18; and Sedgwick, *Epistemology of the Closet* (Berkeley: University of California Press, 1990), 232–233. On the critical debate around whether Proust first wrote the name Albertine in 1913 or 1914, see Pugh, *The Growth of* À la recherche du temps perdu, 757.
55. Antoine Compagnon, *Proust entre deux siècles* (Paris: Seuil, 1989), 15–16.
56. Suzanne Guerlac, "Rancière and Proust: Two Temptations," in *Understanding Rancière, Understanding Modernism,* ed. Patrick Bray (London: Bloomsbury, 2017), 161–178, 173, 174. On this point, see also Christy McDonald, *The Proustian Fabric: Associations of Memory* (Lincoln: University of Nebraska Press, 1991). On Albertine as an interruptive figure who "transmits her energy to the novel," and, with it, the possibility of a new kind of sociality and desire, see Jacques Dubois, *Pour Albertine: Proust et le sens du social* (Paris: Seuil, 1997), 29, 12, 164. Laurent Jenny expresses a similar point in more negative terms, contending that Albertine "corrodes" the structure of the novel around her. Laurent Jenny, "L'effet Albertine," *Poétique* 142 (2005): 205–218, 216.
57. As Sedgwick puts it: "With their plurality of interpretive paths, there is no way to read the Albertine volumes without finding same-sex desire *somewhere*; at the same time, that specificity of desire, in the Albertine plot, notoriously refuses to remain fixed to a single character type, to a single character, or even to a single ontological level of the text." Sedgwick, *Epistemology of the Closet,* 231.
58. Ladenson, *Proust's Lesbianism,* 108.
59. *In Search of Lost Time,* 2:593; *À la recherche du temps perdu,* 2:210.
60. *Trésor de la langue française informatisé,* s.v. "zoophyte (*n.*)," accessed April 7, 2022, https://www.cnrtl.fr/definition/zoophyte. The *Oxford English Dictionary* notes that a zoophyte could also signify the reverse: a plant resembling an animal. *OED Online,* s.v. "zoophyte (*n.*)" (accessed April 12, 2022).
61. *In Search of Lost Time,* 4:36; *À la recherche du temps perdu,* 3:28.
62. For an in-depth exploration of Proust's biological imagination, see Pauline Mauret-Jankus, *Race et imaginaire biologique chez Proust* (Paris: Classiques Garnier, 2016) and Nicola Luckhurst, *Science and Structure in Proust's* À la recherche du temps perdu (Oxford: Clarenden, 2002).
63. "No doubt this state, recurring for each of them in turn, was as different from what we call love as is from human life the life of the zoophytes, in which existence, individuality if we may so term it, is divided up among several organisms." *In Search of Lost Time,* 2:676; *À la recherche du temps perdu,* 2:268. On the animal-vegetal-mineral

madrepore-coral's "porous materiality" as a key trope in Proust—an alternative to metaphor and an emblem for Albertine's present-absence in particular—see Samuel Weber, "The Madrepore," *MLN* 87, no. 7 (December 1972): 915–961.
64. *In Search of Lost Time*, 2:550; *À la recherche du temps perdu*, 2:180. A polypary is the common stem or structure in which polyps are embedded.
65. Valery Rohy, *Chances Are: Contingency, Queer Theory, and American Literature* (London: Routledge, 2019), 6.
66. Proust's conception of these girls' sexuality as place-based and atmospheric corresponds to a vernacular theory of sexuality that had gained traction in the early twentieth century—namely, that lesbianism is more dependent on chance and context than either heterosexuality or male homosexuality. On this, see Benjamin Kahan, *The Book of Minor Perverts: Sexology, Etiology, and the Emergences of Sexuality* (Chicago: University of Chicago Press, 2019), 27.
67. Kahan, 22.
68. Kahan, 33. Ladenson develops a divergent but related argument, allying Proust's lesbian fascination not with contingency per se but with fictional invention in an otherwise often autobiographical text. Ladenson, *Proust's Lesbianism,* 134.
69. This chronology is established by Philip Kolb, "Historique du premier roman de Proust," *Saggi e Ricerche di letteratura francese* 4 (1963): 217–277, 228–235. *Jean Santeuil* was a title added posthumously by editor Bernard de Fallois, who also reorganized the text's messy fragments.
70. Proust, *Jean Santeuil* (Paris: Gallimard, 1971), 366–370; *Jean Santeuil,* trans. Gerard Hopkins (New York: Penguin, 1985), 376–379. Jean's friend, Henri de Réveillon, bears the inversed initials of Reynaldo Hahn; see Proulx, "Proust's Drawings and the Secret of the 'Solitary House,' " on how Proust's and Hahn's romantic 1895 vacation in Brittany left a "network of dispersed, concealed references" in the *Recherche* (886–887).
71. *Jean Santeuil,* 369–70; *Jean Santeuil,* trans. Hopkins, 376–379, 378 (modified).
72. *Jean Santeuil,* 70; *Jean Santeuil,* trans. Hopkins, 378.
73. The section of Cahier 12 in which Proust drafted his first plans for the "Querqueville" episode is preceded by the following note: "Resommeil/femme naissant avec Eve/sensations bizarres/Querqueville." ("Falling back asleep/woman born with Eve/bizarre sensations/Querqueville") What's striking here is the way the beach resort fantasy emerges from the generative site of the bed, following the erotic and the "bizarre." Pugh, *The Growth of À la recherche du temps perdu,* 1:53.
74. *In Search of Lost Time*, 2:342; *À la recherche du temps perdu*, 2:33.
75. *In Search of Lost Time*, 2:504; *À la recherche du temps perdu*, 2:146–147.
76. On bodily positions as continuous with mental dispositions—and more broadly, with the "manners of democracy"—see Jane Bennett, *Influx and Efflux: Writing Up with Walt Whitman* (Durham: Duke University Press, 2020), chapter 1. On the utopian/communitarian possibilities of gesture and proprioception, see Lauren Berlant's reflection on Liza Johnson's 2009 film, *In the Air,* which examines a circus school for teenagers within a junkyard-like ghost town as a space in which to dream up "a new infrastructural rhythm" and "new genres of convergence." Lauren Berlant, "The Commons: Infrastructures for Troubling Times," *Environment and Planning D: Society and Space* 34, no. 3 (2016): 393–419, 412, 413. See also Louis Marin on the "dazzling" figural opacity of the mother's leap, or "enjambment" in

Stendhal's *Vie de Henry Brulard*. Louis Marin,"Un événement de lecture: Où un texte de Stendhal est pris à la lettre," *L'Ecrit du temps*, no. 1 (1982): 95–110, 108, 109.

77. Compagnon, *Proust entre deux siècles*, 20. In intentionally repeating his courtyard stumble, the narrator is attempting to call up the memory of having similarly tripped on the uneven paving stones of Saint Marks in Venice, years before.
78. Diana Fuss, *Sense of an Interior: Four Writers and the Rooms That Shaped Them* (New York: Routledge, 2004), 72.
79. All narratives are somewhat discontinuous, containing analeptic and proleptic episodes, but Proust's is extreme in this regard, moving so abruptly backward and forward in time—especially in the first volume—that the reader is often disoriented. The Proustian bedroom, Genette contends, acts as a key narrative "dispatch center" or "transfer point" in this zigzagging timeline and is thus essential to the very fabrication of the story. If we follow Genette in numerically coding this "stammering" narrative order—he offers the sequence "5, 2, 5, 5, 2, 5, 1, 5, 1, 5, 4, 3"—we see that the most frequently repeated position—5—represents a return to the opening state of insomnia and thus, implicitly, to a supine mode (45). See Gerard Genette, *Narrative Discourse: An Essay in Method*, trans. Jane Lewin (Ithaca: Cornell University Press, 1983), 35–47.
80. *In Search of Lost Time*, 2:623; *À la recherche du temps perdu*, 2:231.
81. Linda Nochlin, *Bathers, Bodies, Beauty: The Visceral Eye* (Cambridge: Harvard University Press, 2006), 31, 30; Marc Augé, *L'Impossible voyage: Le tourisme et ses images* (Paris: Rivages, 1997), 39.
82. *In Search of Lost Time*, 2:503–506; *À la recherche du temps perdu*, 2:148–150. Jacques Rancière focuses on this remarkable passage as well, arguing that the petite bande as "mobile cluster of sensation" epitomizes the democratic ethos of the "aesthetic regime." Jacques Rancière, "Why Emma Bovary Had to Be Killed," *Critical Inquiry* 34 (2008): 233–248, 244.
83. *In Search of Lost Time*, 2:508; *À la recherche du temps perdu*, 2:150. The verb for "brush" here is *effleurer*, which means to touch lightly, to graze or brush against, but in an older, horticultural definition, *effleurer* is to remove the flowers from a plant—an image resonating with the floral/vegetal title of this volume of the novel.
84. Hillel Schwartz, "Torque: The New Kinaesthetic of the Twentieth Century," in Jonathan Crary and Sanford Kwinter, eds., *Incorporations* (New York: Zone, 1992), 70–127; Derek P. McCormack, *Refrains for Moving Bodies* (Durham: Duke University Press, 2013), 43. On modernist athleticism more broadly and modernist art as a form of "exploratory gymnastics," see Harold B. Segel, *Body Ascendant: Modernism and the Physical Imperative* (Baltimore: Johns Hopkins University Press, 1998); and Jed Rasula, *Acrobatic Modernism from the Avant-Garde to Prehistory* (Oxford: Oxford University Press, 2020), 12. On this period's fascination with the muscular, gender-bending allure of female aerialists, see Katie Holmes, *Female Aerialists in the 1920s and Early 1930s: Femininity, Celebrity, and Glamour* (New York: Routlege, 2022); and Peta Tait, *Circus Bodies: Cultural Identity in Aerial Performance* (New York: Routledge, 2005).
85. Schwartz, "Torque," 91.
86. Schwartz, 74–75.
87. Schwartz, 72.

1. PROUST'S LEAP

88. Schwartz, 75–76, 78.
89. Isadora Duncan, *My Life* (New York: Liveright, 2013 [1927]), 2–3; Joan Acocella, introduction to Duncan, *My Life* (xiv). On the early twentieth-century leisure beach as a space that facilitated the emergence of a scandalously relaxed and sporty "summer body," see Christophe Granger, *Les corps d'été: Naissance d'une variation saisonnière au xxème siècle* (Paris: Autrement, 2009).
90. *In Search of Lost Time*, 2:507.
91. *À la recherche du temps perdu*, 2:149.
92. *In Search of Lost Time*, 2:634, 646 (translation modified).
93. Alex Purves, *Homer and the Poetics of Gesture* (New York: Oxford University Press, 2019), 98, 114.
94. Purves, 108.
95. *In Search of Lost Time*, 2:645–46; *À la recherche du temps perdu*, 2:247.
96. Jeffrey Vance describes this one-reel short as an "extended improvisation." Vance, *Chaplin: Genius of the Cinema* (Ann Arbor: University of Michigan Press, 2003), 47. On the history of beach development in Los Angeles and on the cinematic uses of this space, see Elsa Devienne, *La Ruée vers le sable: Une histoire environmentale des plages de Los Angeles au XXè siècle* (Paris: Sorbonne, 2020).
97. Céleste Albaret, *Monsieur Proust*, trans. Barbara Bray (New York: New York Review of Books, 1973), 83.
98. *Trésor de la langue française informatisé*, s.v. "élan" (*n*.), https://www.cnrtl.fr/definition/élan (consulted April 12, 2022). If *élan* is particularly linked to the movements of the *petite bande*, Saint-Loup is also capable of astonishing "feat[s] of acrobatics" ("exercice[s] de voltige"), as he demonstrates in a scene from *The Guermantes Way*: the nobleman leaps over electrical wires "like a steeplechaser taking a fence" and then balances along a bench like a tightrope walker, "check[ing] his momentum" ("son élan") only when he reaches the narrator and drapes a cloak over his shoulders. *In Search of Lost Time*, 3:563–564; *À la recherche du temps perdu*, 2:705. The narrator himself rarely leaps physically, but he does leap ("(re)prendre son élan") in imagination, as a practice of reading, interpretation, or mnemonic creation. In his orientation toward *élan* as a form-generating phenomenon of contingency, Proust's vision dovetails with Henri Bergson's 1907 concept of *élan vital* ("vital impetus"). See Henri Bergson, *L'Evolution créatrice* (Paris: PUF, 1998).
99. On Proust and the modern dance revolution as sharing an interest in human/animal cross-overs and in gender and sexual ambivalence, see Marion Schmid, "Proust's Choreographies of Writing: *À la recherche du temps perdu* and the Modern Dance Revolution," *Marcel Proust Aujourd'hui* 12 (2015): 91–108. On dance as the "twin art of aviation" in the early twentieth century, see Gabriele Brandstetter, *Poetics of Dance: Body, Image, and Space in the Historical Avant-Gardes*, trans. Elena Polzer and Mark Franko (New York: Oxford University Press, 2015), 315.
100. Emily Eells, "Proust pasticheur de Cocteau: Présentation d'un pastiche inédit," *Bulletin d'informations proustiennes* 12 (1981): 75–85, 78. Tadié suggests that Octave's character initially refers to other acquaintances, but is more obviously drawn from Cocteau when he appears in *Time Regained* (*Marcel Proust*, 551). We might also note that this stylish young man who excels at seaside activities features as a sort of inverted double to the narrator—a playboy artist who actually

1. PROUST'S LEAP

commits to both the marriage plot rather than simply flirting with it. The narrator learns after Albertine's death that she may have been secretly engaged to Octave at the time of her death; Octave subsequently marries Andrée.

101. On Proust's enthusiasm for the Ballets Russes, see Schmid, "Proust's Choreographies of Writing"; and Francine Goujon, *Allusions littéraires et écriture cryptée dans l'oeuvre de Proust* (Paris: Honoré Champion, 2020), chapter 12. Chanel's rise to prominence as a designer owed much to a summer (1913) spent at Deauville—an elite resort town next to Cabourg. Chanel noticed that most women were not dressed to enjoy the beaches, tennis courts, and golf courses, and she devised a simplified but elegant set of garments—"new looks [that] came up ... from the shore." Mary E. Davis, *Classic Chic: Music, Fashion, and Modernism* (Berkeley: University of California Press, 2008), 158.

102. "Entre le Baigneur, lentement à grandes enjambées; arrivé presque au milieu de la scène il court vers le tremplin, s'élance dessus et disparaît en l'air dans la coulisse de gauche." Jean Cocteau, *Théâtre complet* (Paris: Gallimard, 2003), 58.

103. Lynn Garafola, *Diaghilev's Ballets Russes* (New York: Oxford University Press, 1989), 108.

104. Garafola, 98.

105. Cocteau, *Théâtre complet*, 61.

106. The presence of a club-wielding police officer on Chaplin's beach—the tramp bumps into him by the refreshment stand and quickly backs away—serves, however, as a reminder of the state violence threatening unruly beach bodies. Lawrence Culver notes that in 1920, a Black man named Arthur Valentine was accosted and shot by local police on the Santa Monica Beach. Valentine took the police to court, and, although the case was dismissed, it was "possibly the first court case involving police brutality in California legal history." Lawrence Culver, *The Frontier of Leisure: Southern California and the Shaping of Modern America* (New York: Oxford University Press, 2012), 71. On the de facto segregation of the Santa Monica beach, circa 1915, see Devienne, *La Ruée vers le sable*, 59–63; and Alison Rose Jefferson, "African-American Leisure Space in Santa Monica: The Beach Sometimes Known as the 'Inkwell,' 1900s–1960s," *Southern California Quarterly* 91, no. 2 (2009): 155–189.

107. *In Search of Lost Time*, 2:317; *À la recherche du temps perdu*, 2:16. The scene's invocation of a broken or suspended relation to the real is compounded by the implausibly dilated temporality of the train voyage. Even if we assume that the trip from Paris to Cabourg is the five-hour, late nineteenth-century route that any Parisian would have taken before the early twentieth-century introduction of an express train, the nocturnal timing of the narrator's voyage indicates that we have entered a realm of fiction, in which intoxication and reverie overtake the rigid predictability of scheduled departures and arrivals.

108. *In Search of Lost Time*, 2:337–338; *À la recherche du temps perdu*, 2:30.

109. Genette, *Narrative Discourse*, 199, 204.

110. For a different take on the partialness of the narrator's perspective, and Proust's demonstration that "people are never fully the subjects, nor fully the authors, of their own speech," see Michael Lucey, *What Proust Heard: Novels and the Ethnography of Talk* (Chicago: University of Chicago Press, 2022), 281. See also Jessica

1. PROUST'S LEAP

Berman, who argues that the *Recherche* valorizes the (queer/Jewish) pariah's "view from the fringe" over the assimilationist perspective of the parvenu. Berman, *Modernist Fiction, Cosmopolitanism, and the Politics of Community* (Cambridge: Cambridge University Press, 2001), 113.

111. Genette cites as examples the reported thoughts of various characters, including Mme de Cambremer at the Opera, the usher at the Guermantes soirée, the historian of the Fronde, the librarian at the Villeparisis matinée, Basin or Bréauté at dinner at Oriane's, Swann's feelings about his wife, Saint-Loup's about Rachel, and Bergotte's dying thoughts. Genette argues that these scenes are "scandalous" in that they put the *I* and others "on the same footing, as if the narrator had exactly the same relationship to a Cambremer, a Basin, a Bréauté, and his own past 'me.'" Genette, *Narrative Discourse*, 208.
112. *In Search of Lost Time*, 2:404–405 (translation modified); *À la recherche du temps perdu*, 2:77.
113. *In Search of Lost Time*, 2:515, 540; *À la recherche du temps perdu*, 2:155, 173.
114. *In Search of Lost Time*, 2:540; *À la recherche du temps perdu*, 2:173.
115. It also resonates with the ethos of pastiche—a playful imitation of another's voice, a kind of stylistic mimicry or vicariousness, and a popular turn-of-the-century practice at which Proust excelled. For a reading of the scene in this volume in which we observe the *petite bande* collaborating on a pastiche, see my *Spoiled Distinctions*, chapter 1.
116. *In Search of Lost Time*, 2:656, 567–568; *À la recherche du temps perdu*, 2:192–193.
117. *In Search of Lost Time*, 2:565; *À la recherche du temps perdu*, 2:190.
118. Eva Hayward, "Fingeryeyes: Impressions of Cup Corals," *Cultural Anthropology* 25, no. 4 (2010): 577–599, 580. Thanks to Ada Smailbegović for drawing my attention to Hayward's work.
119. *In Search of Lost Time*, 2:508; *À la recherche du temps perdu*, 2:150.
120. *In Search of Lost Time*, 2:522; *À la recherche du temps perdu*, 2:160.
121. *In Search of Lost Time*, 2:529, 565; *À la recherche du temps perdu*, 2:165, 191.
122. *In Search of Lost Time*, 4:219; *À la recherche du temps perdu*, 3:159. An August 5, 1906 *Figaro* front-page article, "À la mer," notes that the "Parisian eye," accustomed to cramped and dark spaces, is struck by "so much empty space" ("tant de place laissée vide") and "moved by so much light."
123. *In Search of Lost Time*, 2:343, 342; *À la recherche du temps perdu*, 2:34, 33. On "le soleil rayonnant sur la mer" as a "fetish verse" for Proust, see Compagnon, *Proust entre deux siècles*, chapter 7. Light as such is rarely theorized by literary critics; an exception is Ann Smock's beautiful meditation on the enigma of light in contemporary French poetry, where language itself appears as a "trove of radiant fragments." See Smock, *The Play of Light: Jacques Roubaud, Emmanuel, Hocquard, and Friends* (Albany: State University of New York Press, 2021), 4.
124. *In Search of Lost Time*, 2:342; *À la recherche du temps perdu*, 2:33.
125. *In Search of Lost Time*, 2:512, 690; *À la recherche du temps perdu*, 2:278.
126. *In Search of Lost Time*, 4:339; *À la recherche du temps perdu*, 3:245. In her reading of this passage, Ladenson suggests that to be a lesbian in Proust is to be "all eyes," a kind of "human lighthouse." While gay men in the *Recherche* indicate their desires via "pedestrian Masonic signals," lesbian eroticism, Ladenson suggests, is

especially optical, marked by figures of luminosity. Ladenson, *Proust's Lesbianism*, 78.
127. *In Search of Lost Time*, 2:729 (translation modified).
128. *À la recherche du temps perdu*, 2:305–306.
129. On Proust's fascination for the Wagnerian act of listening in the dark and his interest in "acousmatic sounds," see Cécile Leblanc, *Proust, écrivain de la musique: L'allégresse du compositeur* (Paris: Presses de la Sorbonne Nouvelle, 2016), 151, 165. Eugène Nicole offers a list of occasions when the narrator listens to sounds of unseen or unknown origin in "Proust et les sons," *Bulletin Marcel Proust* 68 (2018): 157–165, 165.
130. Genette, *Narrative Discourse*, 219.

2. INTERTIDAL WOOLF

1. *OED Online*, s.v. "ecstasy (*n.*)" (accessed April 5, 2022).
2. Virginia Woolf, *Moments of Being*, ed. Jeanne Schulkind (New York: Harcourt, 1985), 64–65.
3. On queerness in relation to "improper affiliation" and to "an array of subjectivities, intimacies, beings, and spaces located outside of the heteronormative," see Mel Chen, *Animacies: Biopolitics, Racial Mattering, and Queer Affect* (Durham: Duke University Press, 2012), 104.
4. Laura Doyle, *Freedom's Empire: Race and the Rise of the Novel in Atlantic Modernity, 1640–1940* (Durham: Duke University Press, 2008), 2, 413.
5. Nicole Rizzuto, "Maritime Modernism: The Aqueous Form of Virginia Woolf's *The Waves*," *Modernist Cultures* 11, no. 2 (July 2016): 268–292.
6. Virginia Woolf, *A Passionate Apprentice: The Early Journals, 1897–1909*, ed. Michell A. Leaska (New York: Mariner, 1992), 288.
7. On this tension, see Paul K. Saint-Amour, "Deep Time's Hauntings: Modernism and Alternative Chronology," in Douglas Mao, ed., *The New Modernist Studies* (Cambridge: Cambridge University Press, 2021), 297–313. On modernism's fascination with deep time, see also Aaron Jaffe, "Introduction: Who's Afraid of the Inhuman Woolf?," *Modernism/modernity* 23, no. 3 (September 2016): 491–513; Charles M. Tung, "Baddest Modernism: The Scales and Lines of Inhuman Time," *Modernism/modernity* 23, no. 3 (September 2016): 515–538; and Keith Leslie Johnson, "The Extinction Romance," *Modernism/modernity* 23, no. 3 (September 2016): 539–553.
8. Virginia Woolf, *To the Lighthouse* (New York: Harcourt, 2005), 47.
9. Virginia Woolf, *A Room of One's Own* (New York: Harcourt Brace Jovanovich, 1929), 5, 6.
10. Woolf, *To the Lighthouse*, 104.
11. Virginia Woolf, "Solid Objects," in Virgina Woolf, *The Complete Shorter Fiction of Virginia Woolf* (New York: Harcourt Brace Jovanovich, 1989), 102–107, 102.
12. Woolf, 103.
13. The status of the coast as commons was admittedly ambiguous in early twentieth-century England. Until a series of recent coastal access acts, beach access in England followed the precedent set by an 1821 legal decision ("Blundell v. Catterall"),

2. INTERTIDAL WOOLF

which denied the public legal rights to the foreshore for recreational or other purposes; only fishing from a boat was legally protected. Unlike France or the U.S., which, in the nineteenth century, established some segment of the intertidal zone as a commons (though without necessarily providing inland pathways to it), public use of the intertidal zone in England was long tolerated but not legally protected. D. E. C. Yale, "Public Rights in the Foreshore and Adjacent Waters," *Cambridge Law Journal* 25, no. 2 (1967): 164–168, 164. On land-access disputes and the overlapping legal jurisdiction that complicates coastal access in England today, see Phil Hubbard, "Legal Pluralism at the Beach: Public Access, Land Use, and the Struggle for the 'Coastal Commons,'" *Area* 52 (2020): 420–428, https://doi.org/10.1111/area.12594.
14. Woolf, "Solid Objects," 104, 105.
15. Jennifer Wenzel, *The Disposition of Nature: Environmental Crisis and World Literature* (New York: Fordham University Press, 2019), 242. On the semantic link between the term *waste* and European conceptions of the ocean, see Rizzuto, "Maritime Modernism."
16. John Locke, "Of Property," 2:42, quoted in Wenzel, *The Disposition of Nature*, 145.
17. The enclosure of such wastes suppressed "a marginal independence, of cottagers, squatters, isolated settlers in mainly uncultivated land." Raymond Williams, *The Country and the City* (Oxford: Oxford University Press, 1975), 101.
18. Wenzel, *The Disposition of Nature*, 142. On Enclosure not as the "development" of previously empty, unscripted terrain, but as the destruction of traces and the eradication of the "shiftiness of common rights usages," see Anne-Lise François, "Passing Impasse," *Comparative Literature* 72, no. 2 (June 2020): 240–257, 247.
19. Woolf, *To the Lighthouse*, 82.
20. Douglas Mao, *Solid Objects: Modernism and the Test of Production* (Princeton, N.J.: Princeton University Press, 1998), 30.
21. As Mao puts it, John "out-aestheticizes aestheticism" (Mao, 30). On the intimate rapport between waste and queerness in twentieth-century thought, see Christopher Schmidt, *The Poetics of Waste: Queer Excess in Stein, Ashbery, Schuyler, and Goldsmith* (New York: Palgrave, 2014). Schmidt argues that waste, that "abjected other of capitalist efficiency," becomes in the twentieth century a "magnetic locus for queer identification" (5).
22. Woolf, "Solid Objects," 106.
23. Bill Brown, "The Secret Life of Things: Virginia Woolf and the Matter of Modernism," *Modernism/modernity* 6 (April 1999): 1–28, 9.
24. In attending to Woolf's subtle engagement with historical commoning practices, my reading dovetails with that of Jessica Berman, who argues that Woolf embraces community not as any nostalgic fantasy of wholeness but as "fragmentation-in-coherence." Berman, *Modernist Fiction, Cosmopolitanism, and the Politics of Community* (Cambridge: Cambridge University Press, 2001), 156.
25. *OED Online*, s.v. "furze (*n.*)" (accessed April 5, 2022).
26. Anticipating the scene of seaside brooch-hunting in *To the Lighthouse*, in *Jacob's Room* Betty Flanders searches for her garnet brooch on a ridge above the sea by night, where "the furze bushes stood perfectly still." Virginia Woolf, *Jacob's Room* (New York: Penguin, 1992), 115. In a January 1930 diary entry, Woolf records her breakthrough with *The Waves* in a gorse bush metaphor: "I have at last, by violent

measures—like breaking through gorse—set my hands on something central." *The Diary of Virginia Woolf*, 5 vols. (San Diego: Harcourt Brace Jovanovich, 1977–1984), 3:285. And she writes to Vita Sackville-West in May 1930 of a trip to Cornwall: "We had a superb drive from Penzance over the moor to Zennor, all the gorse blazing against a pure blue sea, to St Ives; where I saw my Lighthouse, and the gate of my home, through tears." *The Letters of Virginia Woolf*, ed. Nigel Nicolson and Joanne Trautmann, 6 vols. (New York: Mariner, 1981), 4:165.

27. E. P. Thompson, *Customs in Common* (New York: New Press, 1993), 125.
28. Thompson lists the loss of common access to furze (along with gravel, underwood, and water rights) as an eighteenth-century grievance when King Charles enclosed and walled-in Richmond Park, and he cites the act of burning furze on the common as protest against a duke's act of selling it for his own profit. Thompson, *Customs in Common*, 111, 125, n4. Alternatively, as evidence of furze-burning as a regular agricultural practice, a nineteenth-century source notes, "in order to promote the rapid growth of these young shoots for pasture, it is the custom in Highland districts to set fire to the old bushes early in the year, and the conflagrations thus caused are very picturesque after dark in the spring evenings, shedding a lurid glare over the dark moor, now in one spot, now in another, which is sometimes alarming to the uninitiated." A. C. Chambers, *Beauty in Common Things* (London: Society for Promoting Christian Knowledge, 1874), 13.
29. Friends of Barnes Common website, https://barnescommon.org.uk/about-us/history/ (accessed April 14, 2022).
30. Woolf, "Solid Objects," 104.
31. Brown, "The Secret Life of Things," 10.
32. Woolf, "Solid Objects," 105.
33. See my *Spoiled Distinctions: Aesthetics and the Ordinary in French Modernism* (New York: Oxford University Press, 2015), chapter 3 ("Nuance"), for a development of this line of thought.
34. Woolf, "Solid Objects," 106.
35. Woolf, 107.
36. Woolf, 104.
37. Woolf, 102–103.
38. Barthes reflects on "idiorrhythmy," and on the possibilities of living *differently* together in his 1976–77 seminar at the Collège de France: Roland Barthes, *How to Live Together: Novelistic Simulations of Some Everyday Spaces*, trans. Kate Briggs (New York: Columbia University Press, 2012); *Comment vivre ensemble: cours et séminaires au Collège de France (1976–1977)* (Paris: Seuil, 2002).
39. Jan Morris, *Travels with Virginia Woolf* (London: Hogarth, 1993), 3.
40. Woolf emphasizes Cornwall's ghostly atmosphere in a 1905 diary entry describing her and her siblings' return there after eleven years. The train is a "wizard" transporting them "into another world," and when they arrive at dusk, "there seemed to be a film between us & the reality." Peering at Talland House through the escalonia hedge, "we hung there like ghosts in the shade of the hedge, & at the sound of footsteps we turned away." Woolf, *A Passionate Apprentice*, 282. On St. Ives in the late nineteenth century and the Stephen family's activities there, see Marion Dell and Marion Whybrow, *Virginia Woolf and Vanessa Bell: Remembering St Ives* (Cornwall: Tab House, 2003). On Woolf's geographical disorientation,

2. INTERTIDAL WOOLF

see John Brannigan, *Archipelagic Modernism: Literature in the Irish and British Isles, 1890–1970* (Edinburgh: Edinburgh University Press, 2015), 124.
41. Christian Pechenard, *Proust à Cabourg* (Paris: Quai Voltaire, 1992), 87.
42. John Brannigan, *Archipelagic Modernism: Literature in the Irish and British Isles, 1890–1970* (Edinburgh: Edinburgh University Press, 2015), 110. Brannigan lists other inaccuracies that struck Woolf's contemporaries after the novel's publication, notably that the novel's horticulture and natural history do not map onto the Hebrides. The novel does not mention any of the characters crossing the sea to arrive on the island, and when Mrs. Ramsay imagines their distance from London, she first exaggerates the distance at "three thousand miles," and then, being "accurate," calls it three hundred miles. As Brannigan points out, the latter is more or less the distance from London to St. Ives; the distance to Skye is considerably more. Woolf's choice to set her novel on an island she did not know could be called risky, he notes, even "reckless" (12). Still, Brannigan asserts that "although her geography is all wrong, and her natural history, Woolf shows no such lack of knowledge about the social conditions which brought the Hebrides repeatedly to the attention of the wider British public in the early twentieth century"—including shipwreck, high tuberculosis rates, poverty, and the precariousness of the fishing industry (121).
43. Woolf, *To the Lighthouse*, 7, 8.
44. Weather data was key for all the operations of twentieth-century mass warfare, from forecasting dawn brightness (and thus positioning tanks without being seen) to timing the deployment of poison gas. See Jim Galvin, "The Meteorological Legacy of the First World War," *Weather*, November 2018, https://doi.org/10.1002/wea.3424. On the history of modern meteorology, see Mark Monmonier, *Air Apparent: How Meterorologists Learned to Map, Predict, and Dramatize Weather* (Chicago: Chicago University Press, 1999); and Peter Lynch, *The Emergence of Numerical Weather Prediction: Richardson's Dream* (Cambridge: Cambridge University Press, 2006).
45. Brannigan, *Archipelagic Modernism*, 111.
46. Woolf, *To the Lighthouse*, 170–171. On the feminine gendering of "vagueness" in Woolf, see Megan Quigley, *Modernist Fiction and Vagueness: Philosophy, Form, and Language* (Cambridge: Cambridge University Press, 2015), 78.
47. Woolf, *To the Lighthouse*, 9.
48. In her 1905 diary descriptions of Cornwall's terrain, Woolf highlights a mix of geographical exactitude and uncertainty: she notes that after spending afternoons "in solitary tramping," the "map of the land becomes solid in my brain," yet she also describes the landscape in terms of "hazy outlines" and "dusky vapour." Woolf, *A Passionate Apprentice*, 285, 298.
49. Woolf, *To the Lighthouse*, 24.
50. Woolf, 113–114.
51. Woolf, 189.
52. The term *happening* was coined in 1964, in reference to site-specific artwork that took place outside the gallery, although the practice of eroding the boundary between art and life has its roots in Dada and surrealist performances. On this phenomenon and its history, see Nick Kaye, ed., *Site Specific Art* (New York: Routledge, 2000).

53. Woolf, *The Diary of Virginia Woolf,* 3:34 (June 27, 1925).
54. Woolf, 3:37–38 (July 30, 1925). Adriana Varga notes that Woolf could play the piano and read music and listened to music nearly every day at home. "Introduction," *Virginia Woolf and Music,* ed. Adriana Varga (Bloomington: Indiana University Press: 2014): 1–26.
55. Woolf, *To the Lighthouse,* 86.
56. Woolf, 161.
57. Thanks to Jerrine Tan for first directing my attention, many years ago, to this two-against-three rhythm in Woolf.
58. Here, my reading both aligns with and diverges from Martin Hägglund's analysis of Woolf's "chronophobia." In *Dying for Time: Proust, Woolf, Nabokov,* Hägglund argues that the "aesthetics of the moment" in *Mrs. Dalloway* reveals how "even the most immediate presence passes away as soon as it comes to be." My reading accords with Hägglund's emphasis on "temporal difference" and with "endurance as *living on*" in Woolf, but I dispute his view that time is fundamentally traumatic in her work—a negation of presence—and that her characters are engaged in an impossible, "chronophobic" struggle to vanquish it. I'm interested, rather, in the affirmatively ecological framing of Woolf's antimonumentality and in how she foregrounds the sociality of time. Martin Hägglund, *Dying for Time: Proust, Woolf, Nabokov* (Cambridge: Harvard University Press, 2012), 57, 60 (original emphasis).
59. On the unpredictability of tidal patterns, see Mark W. Denny, "Tides," in Mark W. Denny and Stephen D. Gaines, eds., *Encyclopedia of Tide Pools and Rocky Shores* (Berkeley: University of California Press, 2007), 588–595. Tides may be the "heartbeat of the ocean," but their rhythm, affected by centrifugal and gravitational forces, as well as by "winds, storms, changes in atmospheric pressure, and El Niño/Southern Oscillation events," is uneven and tends to escape predictive calculations. "Because sea level changes with the tides, there is an intrinsic problem in measuring the location of the water's surface.... On any particular shore, one or more of the generalities derived from simple tidal theory is likely to be violated" (594–595). On the problem of calculating sea-level rise and anticipating its effect on coastal erosion, see Vivien Gornitz, *Rising Seas: Past, Present, Future* (New York: Columbia University Press, 2013), chapter 8.
60. Barthes, *How to Live Together,* 35; *Comment vivre ensemble,* 69.
61. Barthes, *How to Live Together,* 8; *Comment vivre ensemble,* 39. Barthes, like Woolf, understands idiorrhythmy in terms of "subtle forms of way of life: moods, unstable configurations, phases of depression or elation" (*How to Live Together,* 8; *Comment vivre ensemble,* 39). On the centrality of the body to Woolf's conception of rhythm, see Kristy Martin, *Modernism and the Rhythms of Sympathy: Vernon Lee, Virginia Woolf, and D. H. Lawrence* (Oxford: Oxford University Press, 2013).
62. Justin London, "Rhythm," in *Grove Music Online,* 2001, http://doi.org/10.1093/gmo/9781561592630.article.45963 (accessed March 17, 2022).
63. Susanne K. Langer, *Feeling and Form: A Theory of Art* (New York, Scribner, 1953), 110.
64. "Rhythm," in Don Michael Randel, ed., *Harvard Dictionary of Music,* 4th ed. (Cambridge: Harvard University Press, 2003), https://search.credoreference.com

/content/entry/harvdictmusic/rhythm_fr_gr_rhythmos_lat_rhythmus_ger_rhythmus_fr_rhythme_sp_it_ritmo/0?institutionId=577 (accessed March 17, 2022); London, "Rhythm."
65. Emile Benveniste, "The Notion of Rhythm in Its Linguistic Expression," in Emile Benveniste, *Problems in General Linguistics,* trans. Mary Elizabeth Meek (Coral Gables: University of Miami Press, 1971), 281–313, 285–286.
66. Susan Stewart, *Poetry and the Fate of the Senses* (Chicago: University of Chicago Press, 2002), 198.
67. Vincent Barletta (paraphrasing Levinas), *Rhythm: Form and Dispossession* (Chicago: University of Chicago Press, 2020), xxvii; Amittai Aviram, *Telling Rhythm: Body and Meaning in Poetry* (Ann Arbor: University of Michigan Press, 1994), 7. As Barletta puts it, rhythm "holds us in place and shapes the foundations upon which we and our world ultimately rest" (xviii). See also Henri Lefebvre, *Rhythmanalysis: Space, Time, and Everyday Life,* trans. Stuart Elden and Gerald Moore (London: Continuum, 2004), which argues for the study of rhythms as a means of understanding the social constructedness of time and space.
68. Victor Zuckerkandl, *Sound and Symbol: Music and the External World,* trans. Willard R. Trask (Princeton, N.J.: Princeton University Press, 1969), 172.
69. Woolf to Sackville-West, March 16, 1926, in Woolf, *The Letters of Virginia Woolf,* 3:247.
70. Elizabeth Freeman, *Time Binds: Queer Temporalities, Queer Histories* (Durham: Duke University Press, 2010), 3.
71. Eviatar Zerubavel, *Hidden Rhythms: Schedules and Calendars in Social Life* (Berkeley: University of California Press, 1981), 2, 5.
72. Caroline Levine, *Forms: Whole, Rhythm, Hierarchy, Network* (Princeton, N.J.: Princeton University Press, 2015), 50. Queer theorists have explored the consequences of queer exclusion from the heteronormative organization of time. On queer intimacy with anachronism and exclusion from normative time frames, see, for instance, Freeman, *Time Binds;* Lee Edelman, *No Future: Queer Theory and the Death Drive* (Durham: Duke University Press, 2004); Heather Love, *Feeling Backward: Loss and the Politics of Queer History* (Cambridge: Harvard University Press, 2009); Kathryn Bond Stockton, *The Queer Child, or Growing Sideways in the Twentieth Century* (Durham: Duke University Press, 2009); José Esteban Muñoz, *Cruising Utopia: The There and Then of Queer Futurity* (New York: New York University Press, 2009); and Carolyn Dinshaw, *How Soon Is Now? Medieval Texts, Amateur Readers, and the Queerness of Time* (Durham: Duke University Press, 2012).
73. Woolf, *To the Lighthouse,* 66.
74. Woolf, 64.
75. Woolf, 150.
76. On sleep as a state of docility or, alternatively, a state of anticapitalist nonproductivity, see Jonathan Crary, *24/7: Late Capitalism and the Ends of Sleep* (London: Verso, 2013).
77. Woolf, *To the Lighthouse,* 20, 73, 123.
78. Woolf, 141, 146.
79. Woolf, 165, 173, 170, 174, 197.
80. Woolf, 190–91, 194, 207.

81. Benjamin Bateman, *The Modernist Art of Queer Survival* New York (Oxford University Press, 2017), 67.
82. Mary Jean Corbett, *Family Likeness: Sex, Marriage, and Incest from Jane Austen to Virginia Woolf* (Ithaca: Cornell University Press, 2010), xii.
83. Peter Coviello, *Tomorrow's Parties: Sex and the Untimely in Nineteenth-Century America* (New York: New York University Press, 2013), 81.
84. Coviello, 80.
85. Micir argues that "Woolf mounts a sustained critique of the institutions of heteronormativity," elucidating relationships that are "too often rendered invisible by marriage." Reflecting on both Lily Briscoe's choice of art over marriage and children and on the "queer temporal structure" of the novel, which "exil[es] the major events of the Ramsays' family life (marriages, births, deaths) into mere parenthetical asides," Micir contends that "Woolf casts a skeptical eye on the usual milestones and grand narratives of heterosexual life and patriarchal history." Melanie Micir, "Queer Woolf," in Jessica Berman, ed., *A Companion to Virginia Woolf* (Malden: Wiley, 2016), 347–358, 350, 354.
86. Woolf, *To the Lighthouse*, 163.
87. Jacques Rancière, *The Lost Thread: The Democracy of Modern Fiction,* trans. Steven Corcoran (London: Bloomsbury, 2016), 50–51.
88. Woolf, *To the Lighthouse*, 114.
89. Woolf, 34.
90. Woolf, 53, 111.
91. Woolf, 178, 115. On the "marriage plot" as the way in which novels transform the political into the personal and "translate the social contract into a sexual exchange," see Nancy Armstrong, *Desire and Domestic Fiction: A Political History of the Novel* (New York: Oxford University Press, 1990), 38. On the Victorian novel's special capacity to "fuse marriage and romance," and on female friendships as the hidden "catalyst" of this plot, see Sharon Marcus, *Between Women: Friendship, Desire, and Marriage in Victorian England* (Princeton, N.J.: Princeton University Press, 2007), 73–79.
92. Woolf, *To the Lighthouse*, 178
93. Woolf, 10.
94. Woolf, 62. Differing critical views on Mrs. Ramsay abound. On the critical embrace or denigration of this character, see Brenda Silver, "Mothers, Daughters, Mrs. Ramsay: Reflections," *Women's Studies Quarterly* 37, nos. 3–4 (Fall-Winter 2009): 259–274.
95. Woolf, *To the Lighthouse*, 35.
96. Woolf, 36, 35.
97. We might therefore contrast Woolf's conception of aesthetic labor as a spinster's vocation—an evasion of the "degradation" and "dilution" of matrimony and maternity—to critic Elaine Scarry's theory that aesthetic perception is akin to the desire to make babies: "beautiful things," Scarry argues, "have a forward momentum": "they incite the desire to bring new things into the world: infants, epics, sonnets, drawings, dances, laws, philosophic dialogues, theological tracts." Elaine Scarry, *On Beauty and Being Just* (Princeton, N.J.: Princeton University Press, 1999), 31. For Woolf, making babies and seeing aesthetically need not be

opposed—*To the Lighthouse* explores the interconnection of Lily's vision with that of Mrs. Ramsay—but the novel also underscores the practice of making art as an alternative to (and escape from) social reproduction.

98. Rancière, *The Lost Thread*, 50.
99. Woolf, *To the Lighthouse*, 9.
100. Woolf, 218.
101. Despite her resistance to playing this domestic role, Nancy's labor enables Mr. Ramsay's final triumphant gesture: "He took the large, badly packed, brown paper parcel which Nancy had got ready. . . . 'Bring those parcels,' he said, nodding his head at the things Nancy had done up for them to take to the Lighthouse. . . . He sprang, lightly like a young man, holding his parcel, onto the rock." Woolf, *To the Lighthouse*, 209–210.
102. This chapter is either the sole parenthetically framed chapter in the novel, or one of two, depending on which edition one consults. In the American edition, the very short chapter 9 in "The Lighthouse" is also parenthetically framed. In the English edition, it is enclosed in brackets.
103. On Woolf's use of free indirect discourse (or "represented speech and thought") as a means of constructing, novelistically, a "public world" beyond private experience, see Ann Banfield, *The Phantom Table: Woolf, Fry, Russell, and the Epistemology of Modernism* (Cambridge: Cambridge University Press, 2007), 316. Dora Zhang notes that Woolf uses free indirect discourse "to create differing, multilayered levels of intimacy between character, narrator, and reader." Dora Zhang, *Strange Likeness: Description and the Modernist Novel* (Chicago: University of Chicago Press, 2020), 162. On free indirect style as a form of "close writing" and as an "impersonal intimacy," "grant[ing] us at one and the same time an experience of a character's inner life as she lives it and an experience of the same inner life as she never could," see D. A. Miller, *Jane Austen, or the Secret of Style* (Princeton, N.J.: Princeton University Press, 2005), 60.
104. Linguist Dwight Bolinger contends that parentheses are meant to be pronounced with an "overall drop in pitch." *Aspects of Language*, quoted in Geoffrey Nunberg, *The Linguistics of Punctuation* (Cambridge: Cambridge University Press, 1990), 14.
105. Woolf invites this analogy, when, at the end of "Time Passes," she metonymically links parentheses both to Lily's state of half-sleep and to her eyelids—porous partitions, thin walls that let the light through: "Gently the waves would break (Lily heard them in her sleep); tenderly the light fell (it seemed to come through her eyelids)." Woolf, *To the Lighthouse*, 145, 146.
106. In allying this parenthetical chapter with an affective realm and a time frame beyond social reproduction and the marriage plot, I am countering Mary Wilson's interesting argument that this punctuation mark in *To the Lighthouse* signals partitions between domestic workers and employers. Underscoring Mrs. Ramsay's role as the manager of household boundaries and thresholds, Wilson interprets the parenthetically encased chapter as an indication of the matriarch's extended reach: the parentheses "domesticate" what is within them. Wilson, *Labors of Domesticity: Domesticity, Servants, and Authorship in Modernist Fiction* (New York: Routledge, 2016), 54, 52.

107. Woolf, *To the Lighthouse*, 59, 60, 76, 81.
108. Woolf, 82.
109. Woolf, 112. See Rancière on the family plot in *To the Lighthouse* as presenting two "tyrannies"—the paternal one, which most explicitly directs the plot (by prohibiting or allowing the voyage) and the "more insidious" maternal one, which "reduces the halo's fragments to familial virtues." Rancière, *The Lost Thread*, 53.
110. Woolf, *To the Lighthouse*, 114–115.
111. According to Corbin, the Romantics saw the beach as the site of an "extended maternity" where "feminine instincts" might blossom. Alain Corbin, *The Lure of the Sea: Discovery of the Seaside in the Western World, 1750–1840*, trans. Jocelyn Phelps (New York: Penguin, 1995), 171.
112. Woolf, *To the Lighthouse*, 78. Tourist guidebooks of the era are full of gendering generalizations. For instance, Baedeker's 1910 edition of the guide to Great Britain warns, of a particular walk on the Isle of Skye, "Ladies should not attempt it, unless prepared for considerable fatigue." Karl Baedeker, *Great Britain: Handbook for Travelers, with 28 Maps, 65 Plans, and a Panorama* (Leipzig: Baedeker, 1910), 559.
113. Woolf, *To the Lighthouse*, 79. Tansley and Mr. Ramsay will later echo this generalizing logic, though to different ends. Tansley muses bitterly that women "make civilization impossible" with their "charm"; Mr. Ramsay, reflecting on his youngest daughter's ignorance of maps and compasses—which apparently he has failed to teach her anything about—thinks, "women are always like that; the vagueness of their minds is hopeless." Woolf, 88, 171.
114. Woolf, 200.
115. Woolf, 78.
116. Woolf, 94.
117. Woolf, "Solid Objects," 80.
118. An impressive array of scholarship on the invention of the marine aquarium has emerged in recent years. See Kyriaki Hadjiafxendi and John Plunkett, "Science at the Seaside: Pleasure Hunts in Victorian Devon," in Nicholas Allen, Nick Groom, and Jos Smith, eds., *Coastal Works: Cultures of the Atlantic Edge* (Oxford University Press, 2017), 181–203; Judith Hamera, *Parlor Ponds: The Cultural Work of the American Home Aquarium, 1850–1970* (University of Michigan Press, 2012); Natasha Adamowsky, *The Mysterious Science of the Sea, 1775–1943* (New York: Routledge, 2015); Bernd Brunner, *The Ocean at Home: An Illustrated History of the Aquarium*, trans. Ashley Marc Slapp (Princeton, N.J.: Princeton Architectural Press, 2005); Silvia Granata, *The Victorian Aquarium: Literary Discussions on Nature, Culture, and Science* (Manchester: Manchester University Press, 2021). These scholars demonstrate the interconnection between aquarium display and seaside tourism; as Hamera puts it, in mid-nineteenth-century Britain many people "headed to the shore in droves, buckets and trowels in hand," to raid tide pools for their home display (1). On the connection between tourism and the public consumption of science, see also Aileen Fyfe, who notes that in the mid-nineteenth-century "marine zoology could justify . . . happy hours spent at the beach." Aileen Fyfe, "Natural History and the Victorian Tourist: From Landscapes to

2. INTERTIDAL WOOLF

Rock-Pools," in David N. Livingstone and Charles W. J. Withers, eds., *Geographies of Nineteenth-Century Science* (Chicago: University of Chicago Press, 2011), 371–393, 392.
119. David Allen, *The Naturalist in Britain: A Social History* (Princeton, N.J.: Princeton University Press, 1994), 116, 113–114, 115.
120. Amy King, *The Divine in the Commonplace: Reverent Natural History and the Novel in Britain* (Cambridge: Cambridge University Press, 2019), 142.
121. King, 138. Hadjiafxendi and Plunkett note that tide-pooling and aquarium-keeping were activities that enabled Victorians to "observe, domesticate, and conserve nature," while also feeling connected to "God's truth and beauty." "Science at the Seaside," 196, 190.
122. Hamera, *Parlor Ponds*, 2.
123. C. M. Yonge, *The Sea Shore* (London: Collins, 1949), 2.
124. Yonge, 2.
125. Rachel Carson, *The Edge of the Sea* (New York: Houghton Mifflin Harcourt, 1998), 45–46.
126. Woolf, *To the Lighthouse*, 78.
127. Carson, *The Edge of the Sea*, 249.
128. Woolf, *To the Lighthouse*, 79.
129. On the violence of this scene in connection to the late Victorian practice of cataloguing and arranging the natural world, and on a taxonomic relation to nature as facilitating imperialist violence and acquisitiveness, see Christina Alt, *Virginia Woolf and the Natural World* (Cambridge: Cambridge University Press, 2010), chapter 3.
130. Woolf, *To the Lighthouse*, 8.
131. Friedrich's horizon-oriented wanderer is the "outward-gazing emblem of Romantic self-consciousness." Lisa Tickner, "Vanessa Bell: *Studland Beach*, Domesticity, and 'Significant Form,'" *Representations* 65 (Winter 1999): 63–92, 79.
132. Corbin, *The Lure of the Sea*, 177.
133. Nancy's shadow play also encapsulates the ethos of a novel in which shadows abound. We see this most explicitly in Lily's painting, which represents Mrs. Ramsay and James as a "purple shadow." But shadows come into play elsewhere, too, such as when Cam and James disagree about the lighting conditions in their bedroom: "Wherever they put the light (and James could not sleep without a light) there was always a shadow somewhere." And when Lily is finishing her painting, she is unexpectedly aided by some "light stuff" behind the window: "Mercifully, whoever it was stayed still inside; had settled by some stroke of luck so as to throw an odd-shaped triangular shadow over the step." (Woolf, *To the Lighthouse*, 116, 204). Louise Hornby has argued suggestively that this novel is fundamentally photographic in its valorization of impersonal "light writing." Louise Hornby, *Still Modernism: Photography, Literature, Film* (New York: Oxford University Press, 2017), 162. Yet shadows are not exclusively a force of negation and absence in *To the Lighthouse*—a darkness to be kept at bay. This is a novel that embraces the act of casting a shadow as a way of playing with the light, transforming luminosity into pattern, shaping it into rhythm.
134. Woolf, *To the Lighthouse*, 169.

2. INTERTIDAL WOOLF

135. As Corbin puts it, "The Hebrides lent themselves admirably to the emotional strategy of the sublime. There, Nature, terrifying and majestic, was decked with the vestiges of cruel times." Corbin, *The Lure of the Sea*, 134.
136. Baedeker's 1910 *Great Britain: Handbook for Travelers* describes St. Ives as "a quaint little fishing town (6697 inhab.) situated on perhaps the most beautiful bay in Cornwall, with a splendid sandy beach" (158). The guidebook is generally focused on the question of which locations and walks afford "good views" ("fine" views, "beautiful" views, "charming" views, "lovely" views, "better" views, "best" views, "unimpeded" views, "less extensive" views, and so on). Neither Baedeker's nor Bradshaw's guidebooks references the "marine curiosities" that Paul reads about in his guidebook (though Bradshaw mentions "natural and artificial curiosities" and Baedeker cites "historical curiosities"). On the travel guide as a modernist phenomenon, and on Woolf's "contempt for and fascination with" the genre, see Jesse Schotter, "'Objects Worthy of Attention': Modernism and the Travel Guide," *Modernism/modernity Print Plus* 4, no. 2, https://doi.org/10.26597/mod.0109. On modernist tourism, see Eric Bulson, *Novels, Maps, Modernity: The Spatial Imagination, 1850–2000* (London: Routledge, 2009); and Andrea Zemgulys, *Modernism and the Locations of Literary Heritage* (Cambridge: Cambridge University Press, 2008).
137. Immanuel Kant, *Critique of the Judgment of Taste,* trans. Paul Guyer and Matthew Andrews (Cambridge: Cambridge University Press, 2000), 144; on the oft-overlooked second part of the sublime judgment, see Sianne Ngai, *Ugly Feelings* (Cambridge: Harvard University Press, 2007), 265–267.
138. Kant, *Critique of the Power of Judgment*, 145.
139. As further evidence of the decentering effect of this scene, consider how it revises classical precedent. Like Ovid's Narcissus, who is also "transfixed" at the water's edge, Nancy arrives at her pool having eschewed courtship. Yet unlike Narcissus, Nancy is "hypnotized" not by her own beautiful reflection but by a feeling of scalar incommensurability—this vastness, that tininess—next to which she is reduced to "nothingness." Ovid, *Metamorphoses*, trans. Charles Martin (New York: Norton, 2004), 106–111, 107; Woolf, *To the Lighthouse*, 114.
140. *OED Online*, s.v. "brood (v.)" (accessed April 5, 2022).
141. Marcel Proust, *In Search of Lost Time*, trans. Scott Moncrieff and Terence Kilmartin, rev. D. J. Enright, 6 vols. (New York: Modern Library, 1992), 1:257 (translation modified): "Comme si j'avais été moi-même une poule et si je venais de pondre un oeuf, je me mis à chanter à tue-tête." Proust, *À la recherche du temps perdu*, 4 vols. (Paris: Gallimard, 1987–1989), 1:296.
142. Woolf, *To the Lighthouse*, 197, 98–99.
143. Woolf, 43, 151, 52, 129. As John Ferguson puts it, Carmichael is "out of step with the rest of the household." John Ferguson, "A Sea Change: Thomas De Quincey and Mr. Carmichael in 'To the Lighthouse,'" *Journal of Modern Literature* 14, no. 1 (Summer 1987): 45–63, 52. As a brooding dreamer whose presence enables Lily to complete her "vision," Carmichael is Mrs. Ramsay's unlikely double, the poetic alternative to her force of maternal care (or domination). He prefigures Nancy's tide pool play, first materializing in the novel as a "shadow" cast on the page of "The Fisherman and his Wife," which Mrs. Ramsay is reading to James (43).

144. Woolf, 164.
145. Woolf, 174.
146. The past tense slips into a hypothetical mode ("Mrs. Ramsay may have asked") and the singularity of the moment is undercut by an acknowledgement of its possible repetition ("it seemed to have happened so often, this silence by her side"). Woolf, 175.
147. Woolf, 164.
148. Woolf, 164.
149. Woolf, 163, 174, 175.
150. Woolf, 163, 164, 195.

3. CARSON'S QUIET BOWER

1. Following these publishing successes, Carson was invited to write liner notes for a new NBC Symphony recording of Debussy's *La Mer*, and sea-themed merchandise capitalizing on the popularity of her work cropped up everywhere. On such "Carsonalia," see Amanda Hagood, "Wonders with the Sea: Rachel Carson's Ecological Aesthetic and the Mid-Century Reader," *Ecological Humanities* 2 (2013): 57–77.
2. Hagood, 60. While I argue that Carson's subtle engagement with the seaside should be contrasted to this attitude of postwar imperialism, Hagood sees Carson's popular books about the sea as complicit with the expansionist ethos of the era. On how military funding transformed American oceanography, especially during the Cold War, see Naomi Oreskes, *Science on a Mission: How Military Funding Shaped What We Do and Don't Know About the Ocean* (Chicago: University of Chicago Press, 2021).
3. Margaret Ronda notes that the Great Acceleration is characterized by an unprecedentedly rapid disturbance of planetary systems—most notably, a sharp spike in CO_2 emissions, massive biodiversity loss, ocean acidification, and disturbance of the nitrogen cycle. Margaret Ronda, *Remainders: American Poetry at Nature's End* (Stanford: Stanford University Press, 2018), 1. On the international "scramble for the oceans" that took place in the wake of the 1945 Truman Proclamation's remapping of the seas, see Elizabeth DeLoughrey, "Submarine Futures of the Anthropocene," *Comparative Literature* 69, no. 1 (2017): 32–44, 32.
4. Hagood, "Wonders with the Sea," 60.
5. Paul Brooks to Rachel Carson, July 20, 1950, Rachel Carson Papers, Beinecke Rare Book & Manuscript Library, Yale University.
6. Linda Lear, *Rachel Carson: Witness for Nature* (New York: Mariner, 2009), 229, 243; Carson to Brooks, June 24, 1953, Rachel Carson Papers, Beinecke Rare Book & Manuscript Library, Yale University.
7. Carson to Brooks, July 28, 1950, Rachel Carson Papers, Beinecke Rare Book & Manuscript Library, Yale University.
8. Bob Hines, who illustrated *The Edge of the Sea* and accompanied Carson on much of her fieldwork, recalls watching her wade alone in freezing Maine tidal pools until her legs got numb: "when she started to climb out of a pool, she nearly fell back in. I splashed in beside her, picked her up, and carried her to the car." Beyond Hines's somewhat heroic self-representation, one is struck here by the image of

3. CARSON'S QUIET BOWER

Carson's dogged persistence, her younger male colleague having retreated to the shore. John Juriga, *Bob Hines: National Wildlife Artist* (Edina, Minn.: Beaverpond, 2012), 77. As Carson puts it in an early draft of the "Rocky Shores" chapter, when exploring the tidal pools of the lower shore, "the only way to do it is to get cold and wet at the outset," since "to perch precariously on the slippery rim . . . [is] likely to lead to a bath in the end." Rachel Carson Papers, Beinecke Rare Book & Manuscript Library, Yale University.

9. Catriona Mortimer-Sandilands, "Melancholy Natures, Queer Ecologies," in Bruce Erikson and Catriona Mortimer-Sandilands, eds., *Queer Ecologies: Sex, Nature, Politics, Desire* (Bloomington: Indiana University Press, 2010), 331–358, 343–344.
10. Rachel Carson, *The Edge of the Sea* (New York: Houghton Mifflin Harcourt, 1998), 115. Carson's rhetoric of uncertainty ("perhaps," "apparently," "no one knows") underscores the text's general tone of humility, conveying a sense of the intertidal zone as a sphere of unanswered "riddles" and "elusive" meanings (47).
11. Carson to Dr. T.A. Stephenson, April 5, 1951. In a May 22, 1951 letter to Stephenson, Carson returns to this theme, noting that her book "will be much less pretentious" than *Between Pacific Tides*. Rachel Carson Papers, Beinecke Rare Book & Manuscript Library, Yale University.
12. Ed Ricketts, Jack Calvin, and Joel Hedgpeth, *Between Pacific Tides*, rev. David W. Phillips, 5th ed. (Stanford: Stanford University Press, 1985), ix.
13. John Steinbeck, *Cannery Row* (New York: Penguin, 1992), 30.
14. Steinbeck, 30. Ricketts, Calvin, and Hedgpeth, *Between Pacific Tides*, x.
15. Charles Kingsley, *Glaucus; or, The Wonders of the Shore* (Cambridge: Macmillan, 1959 [1855]), 44–6.
16. Kyriaki Hadjiafxendi and John Plunkett, "Science at the Seaside: Pleasure Hunts in Victorian Devon," in Nicholas Allen, Nick Groom, and Jos Smith, eds., *Coastal Works: Cultures of the Atlantic Edge* (Oxford: Oxford University Press, 2017), 181–204, 190–191. For an alternative perspective, see Jonathan Smith, "Darwin's Barnacles," in Jonathan Smith, *Charles Darwin and Victorian Visual Culture* (Cambridge: Cambridge University Press, 2006), 44–91. In contrast to the masculinist orientation of other Victorian studies of marine zoology, Darwin's 1851 illustrated book on barnacles explores the "diversity" and "bizarreness" of these creatures' sexual arrangements.
17. Ricketts, *Between Pacific Tides*, ix.
18. Carson, *The Edge of the Sea*, 109.
19. Carson, 95.
20. Carson, 67.
21. Ricketts, Calvin, and Hedgpeth, ix.
22. Ricketts, Calvin, and Hedgpeth, *Between Pacific Tides*, 31, 98, 100, 105, 174, 255, 292.
23. Joni Seager, "Radical Observation," *WSQ* 45, nos. 1, 2 (Spring/Summer 2017): 269–277, 272. Seager writes that Carson has a knack for shining a light on the "smallest elements of the ecosystem," and notes that the effect of such "radical observation" is to "put humans in their place—mere latecomers on a planet that has been worn by time and physical processes playing out over hundreds of millions of years" (272). On minimalism as a key concept for ecological thought, see Anahid Nersessian, *Utopia, Limited: Romanticism and Adjustment* (Cambridge, Mass.:

3. CARSON'S QUIET BOWER

Harvard University Press, 2015); and Anne-Lise François, *Open Secrets: The Literature of Uncounted Experience* (Stanford: Stanford University Press, 2008).
24. Carson, *The Edge of the Sea*, 115, 130.
25. Carson, 130–131.
26. Carson, 250.
27. On Carson's "vicarious" literary relation to the ocean, see her September 28, 1953 letter to Freeman in Rachel Carson and Dorothy Freeman, *Always, Rachel: The Letters of Rachel Carson and Dorothy Freeman, 1952–1964*, ed. Martha Freeman (Boston: Beacon, 1995), 7.
28. Lear discusses Carson's devotion to Mary Skinker in *Rachel Carson*, 39–53, 56–58. After Carson left college to pursue her PhD in zoology (following Skinker's example), the two women became very close; as Lear puts it, "Carson loved [Skinker] more deeply than anyone ever guessed." When, two decades after they met, a dying Skinker collapsed and was taken to the hospital, she gave Carson's name as the person to be contacted. The correspondence between Carson and Skinker has been lost. Lear, 150, 149.
29. Carson, *The Edge of the Sea*, 7, 47.
30. Carson, 57, 114, 164, 132–3.
31. Carson, 164.
32. As Nicholas Allen, Nick Groom, and Jos Smith aptly put it, the intertidal zone is characterized by "forms within forms, scales within scales, and worlds within worlds." Allen, Groom, and Smith, *Coastal Works*, 1.
33. Carson, *The Edge of the Sea*, 23. This insight frames all of the reflections that follow, but Carson does not insist on its consequences (nor could she fully fathom them in 1955).
34. Carson, 93, 64, 47, 5, 18, 39, 217, 174, 95.
35. Anne-Lise François, "Flower Fisting," *Postmodern Cultures* 22, no. 1 (September 2011).
36. Carson completely rewrote the "Rocky Shores" chapter in 1953–1954, when she first took up summer residence in Maine, during the early years of her relationship with Freeman. Lear, *Rachel Carson*, 243.
37. In an April 19, 1955, letter, Carson tells Freeman: "I can scarcely remember when, during the time you've been part of my life, I didn't have this idea." Carson and Freeman, *Always, Rachel*, 108. Carson inscribed Freeman's personal copy of *The Edge of the Sea* with the following message: "As you turn these pages, may you remember always the world we shared—the fairy pool, the green sea caves, the smell of dripping rockweeds under early fog, anemones waiting for the tide's turning, the fragile beauty of the hydroid's flowers. Remember, too, the gulls rosy-feathered at dawn, water fowl in a sunset sky, the song of thrushes in spruce woods along our Island shores. And may these pages lead your thoughts to other shores we may explore together in the years of happy friendship ahead." Lear, *Rachel Carson*, 537. In one of her earliest letters to Freeman, Carson writes at length of her explorations of the shore, using language that will appear in the book (she refers, for example, to the "feather appendages" of baby barnacles). Carson was seducing Freeman with *The Edge of the Sea*—an affective and intellectual seduction, if not a physical one.

38. Carson to Freeman, November 6, 1953, in Carson and Freeman, *Always, Rachel*, 10. In the first letter addressed "Dear Dorothy" rather than "Dear Mrs. Freeman," Carson tells Freeman in a letter of September 28, 1953: "you and your particular kind of interest and appreciation were in my mind a great deal when I was rewriting part of the section on rocky shores" (5–7). A few months later, on November 19–20, 1953, she interrupts her revising to tell Freeman: "I've been mentally sending you notes all day (11). Carson fleshed out these thoughts more fully on March 12, 1954: "But seriously, darling . . . you could very well represent my 'ideal reader'—the kind of person for whom I'm writing" (33).
39. In his account of pre-Stonewall "gay New York," George Chauncey notes that the word *closet* was not used in relation to gay sexuality before the 1960s, and therefore "we need to use [the term] more cautiously and precisely, and to pay attention to the very different terms people used to describe themselves and their social worlds." George Chauncey, *Gay New York: Gender, Urban Culture, and the Making of the Gay Male World, 1890–1940* (New York: Basic Books, 1995), 6. On what it felt like to be "exile[d] from sanctioned experience" before the era of gay liberation, see Christopher Nealon, *Foundlings: Lesbian and Gay Historical Emotion Before Stonewall* (Durham: Duke University Press, 2001). On the rich history of eroticized female friendships in the Victorian era, see Sharon Marcus, *Between Women: Friendship, Desire, and Marriage in Victorian England* (Princeton, N.J.: Princeton University Press), 2007. For an examination of the "spinster" figure in feminist and lesbian discourse in relation to the "affective difficulties and uncertainties of nineteenth-century female friendship," see Heather Love, "Gyn/Apology: Sarah Orne Jewett's Spinster Aesthetics," *ESQ* 55, nos. 3–4 (2009): 304–339, 310. On the "powerful anachronism" of celibacy at midcentury, and the importance of untethering the history of sexuality from an exclusive focus on genitality, see Benjamin Kahan, *Celibacies: American Modernism and Sexual Life* (Durham: Duke University Press, 2013). On "quiet" and "grace" in relation to female homoeroticism, see Omise'eke Natasha Tinsley's *Thiefing Sugar: Eroticism Between Women in Caribbean Literature* (Durham: Duke University Press, 2010). Despite the difference in geographical and political contexts, Tinsley's reading of the "opaque" and "metaphoric" ways in which desire between women is figured in relation to landscape is resonant here. See also Michael Lucey's intriguing account of "misfit sexualities" in *Someone: The Pragmatics of Misfit Sexualities, from Colette to Hervé Guibert* (Chicago: University of Chicago Press, 2019). Misfit sexuality is not a stable identity that endures over time but a circumstantial mode of intimacy involving "awkward and delicate" acts of negotiation and "tenuous form[s] of recognition" (4).
40. Carson to Freeman, January 1, 1954, in Carson and Freeman, *Always, Rachel*, 15.
41. Helen Vendler, *The Odes of John Keats* (Cambridge, Mass.: Harvard University Press, 1985), 85.
42. Freeman to Carson, January 2, 1955, in Carson and Freeman, *Always, Rachel*, 78.
43. Freeman to Carson, April 14, 1964, in Carson and Freeman, 541.
44. Freeman to Carson, January 31, 1955, in Carson and Freeman, 91.
45. Carolyn Dinshaw, *How Soon Is Now? Medieval Texts, Amateur Readers, and the Queerness of Time* (Durham: Duke University Press, 2012), 22.

3. CARSON'S QUIET BOWER

46. Carson writes that her heart "leaped" at the mailbox's rattle in a February 20, 1954, letter to Freeman; six years later, her heart still "leaps" to see Freeman's "familiar handwriting" (Carson and Freeman, *Always, Rachel*, 26, 311). On the "desire for exchange" (or "epistolary pact") and the "world-making power" of epistolary form, see Janet Gurkin Altman, *Epistolarity: Approaches to a Form* (Columbus: Ohio University Press, 1982), 89; and Melanie Micir, *The Passion Projects: Modernist Women, Intimate Archives, Unfinished Lives* (Princeton: Princeton University Press, 2019), chapter 1. On the importance of the epistolary mode to Carson's work more generally, and on her "synthetic, mutually dependent approach" to research—she had a talent for building networks of correspondents, whom she consulted throughout the writing process—see Mark Hamilton Lytle, *The Gentle Subversive: Rachel Carson, Silent Spring, and the Rise of the Environmental Movement* (New York: Oxford University Press, 2007), 5–6.
47. Shira Brisman, *Dürer and the Epistolary Mode of Address* (Chicago: University of Chicago Press, 2017), 1.
48. On the importance of the "meta-epistolary" or phatic mode to long-distance epistolary exchange, see Jennifer Roberts, *Transporting Visions: The Movement of Pictures in Early America* (Berkeley: University of California Press, 2014), 6–7. On the "envelope of contingency that surrounds any letter," see Mary Favret, *Romantic Correspondence: Women, Politics, and the Fiction of Letters* (Cambridge: Cambridge University Press, 2005), 56.
49. Carson to Freeman, January 30, 1954, in Carson and Freeman, *Always, Rachel*, 18.
50. Carson to Freeman, February 13, 1954, February 25, 1956, and February 8, 1958, in Carson and Freeman, 22, 155, 251.
51. Carson to Freeman, December 21, 1953, January 1, 1954, November 19–20, 1953, and October 13, 1959, in Carson and Freeman, 14, 15, 11, 284. On letter writing as "an hour with you," see Carson to Freeman, November 27, 1955 and April 22, 1957 (142, 224). On December 25, 1963, Freeman writes to Carson, "No matter what time it is when you read this, know that my arms are figuratively about you" (507).
52. Peter Coviello, *Tomorrow's Parties: Sex and the Untimely in Nineteenth-Century America* (New York: New York University Press, 2013), 7. Examining what he terms the late-nineteenth-century "twilit moment *before* the arrival or calcifying of the terms of sexual identity" and attending to the "in-between time of the regulated erotic body," Coviello suggests that such unmapped spaces enable a "special kind of freedom." Carson and Freeman correspond and interact not before the imposition of a codified and regulated homo/hetero divide, but within its interstices. Still, citing Coviello, we could say that their experience of intimacy—like that of Walt Whitman, Emily Dickinson, or Henry James—is "errant," "unyarded," and "untimely" (7, 10).
53. Sarah Ensor, "The Ecopoetics of Contact: Touching, Cruising, Gleaning," *ISLE: Interdisciplinary Studies in Literature and Environment* 25, no. 1 (Winter 2018): 150–168, 151, 154.
54. Carson to Freeman, February 17, 1954, in Carson and Freeman, *Always, Rachel*, 25. This interstitial epistolary time, and the intense rereading it entails, is related to but not synonymous with what some have called queer melancholy. On "temporal drag" as a (melancholic) queer mode of resistance, see Elizabeth Freeman, "Packing

History, Count(er)ing Generations," *New Literary History* 31 (2000): 727–744. On the politics of queer melancholy, see also Heather Love, *Feeling Backwards: Loss and the Politics of Queer History* (Cambridge, Mass.: Harvard University Press, 2007); and Mortimer-Sandilands, "Melancholy Natures, Queer Ecologies." On the epistolary in relation to confessional practices and the historical formation of queer subjectivity, see Patrick Paul Garlinger, *Confessions of the Letter Closet: Epistolary Fiction and Queer Desire in Modern Spain* (Minneapolis: University of Minnesota Press, 2005).

55. Carson to Freeman, February 3, 1956; Carson to Freeman, January 29, 1955; Freeman to Carson, January 31, 1955, in Carson and Freeman, *Always, Rachel*, 152, 90, 91.
56. Carson to Freeman, March 12, 1954, in Carson and Freeman, 32.
57. Freeman to Carson, April 15, 1956, in Carson and Freeman, 175.
58. Carson to Freeman, February 20, 1954, in Carson and Freeman, 29. On Stan Freeman's inclusion in this relationship—his February 1955 delivery of a symbolic white hyacinth, along with a love note, from Carson to his wife, for instance—see Lida Maxwell, "Queer/Love/Bird Extinction: Rachel Carson's *Silent Spring* as a Work of Love," *Political Theory* 45, no. 5 (2017): 682–704, 692.
59. At various points, Carson and Freeman destroyed packets of their most intimate letters; they had marked these as bound for the "Strong Box," either because of what they divulged about their families or out of fear that a letter's romantic tone would be misinterpreted by those who were "looking for ideas." Lear, *Rachel Carson*, 253; Carson and Freeman, *Always, Rachel*, xvi, 530. Although taboo words like *lesbian* never feature in their letters, their era's pathologization of same-sex love as a form of mental illness shadows their correspondence; as Carson puts it on January 25, 1954, proposing the two-tiered system of address they would henceforth use, "our brand of 'craziness' would be hard for anyone else to understand." In a letter postmarked five days later, she writes, "I suppose the world would consider us absolutely crazy, but it is wonderful to feel that way, isn't it?" (17, 19). On the vehemence of midcentury homophobia in the U.S., see Margot Canaday, *The Straight State: Sexuality and Citizenship in Twentieth-Century America* (Princeton, N.J.: Princeton University Press, 2009); and David K. Johnson, *The Lavender Scare: The Cold War Persecution of Gays and Lesbians in the Federal Government* (Chicago: University of Chicago Press, 2004).
60. Coviello, *Tomorrow's Parties*, 67.
61. Emily West, "Understanding Authenticity in Commercial Sentiment: The Greeting Card as Emotional Commodity," in Eva Illouz, ed., *Emotions as Commodities: Capitalism, Consumption, and Authenticity* (New York: Routledge, 2017), 123–144, 123. On greeting card aesthetics, see also Arlie Hochschild, *The Commercialization of Intimate Life: Notes from Home and Work* (Berkeley: University of California Press, 2003); Micaela di Leonardo, "The Female World of Cards and Holidays: Women, Families, and the Work of Kinship," *Signs* 12, no. 3 (Spring 1987): 440–453; Alexandra Jaffe, "Packaged Sentiments: The Social Meaning of Greeting Cards," *Journal of Material Culture* 4, no. 2 (July 1999): 115–141; and Barry Shank, *A Token of My Affection: Greeting Cards and American Business Culture* (New York: Columbia University Press, 2004).
62. Carson, undated Valentine's Day cards to Freeman, Dorothy Freeman Collection, Edmund S. Muskie Archives and Special Collections Library, Bates College.

3. CARSON'S QUIET BOWER

63. Nealon, *Foundlings*, 8.
64. Maxwell, "Queer/Love/Bird Extinction," 682. Maxwell sees the relationship between Carson and Freeman as laying the groundwork for "an environmental politics of desire," an ethos not of species survival, or mere life, but of *more life*: "life as a realm of affective pleasures that gives meaning." Although her analysis focuses exclusively on *Silent Spring*, Maxwell's reading of Carson and Freeman's relationship as a "world-disclosing practice" sheds light on *The Edge of the Sea* as well (685).
65. Cats were a point of particular passion. Carson and Freeman discussed the best cat books, grieved for the loss of one another's beloved feline companions, and each sometimes addressed her correspondence to the other's cat. On April 6, 1956, for instance, Freeman wrote a letter to Carson's cat, Jeffie, and sent him a birthday gift. Dorothy Freeman Collection, Edmund S. Muskie Archives and Special Collections Library, Bates College.
66. Carson, *The Edge of the Sea*, 117, 119.
67. Carson, 121.
68. Carson to Freeman, February 29, 1955, in Carson and Freeman, *Always, Rachel*, 99. In fact, Freeman's husband, Stan, was with Carson when she found the cave, although no trace of his presence appears in her published account of the experience. If the subtly erotic description was implicitly addressed to Freeman and meant to be "real" in her mind, its spatiality remained somewhat opaque to others. In the lead-up to the *New Yorker*'s publication of this excerpt in the summer of 1955, an editor asked Carson to provide a "rough diagram" of the sea cave for him, admitting that "try as we will, my cohorts and I can not envision it." Sanderson Vanderbilt to Carson, July 18, 1955, Rachel Carson Papers, Beinecke Rare Book & Manuscript Library, Yale University.
69. Carson to Freeman, June 1963, in Carson and Freeman, *Always, Rachel*, 467.
70. François, "Flower Fisting."
71. Stephanie Kaza, "Rachel Carson's Sense of Time: Experiencing Maine," *ISLE* 17, no. 2 (March 2010): 291–315.
72. Carson, *The Edge of the Sea*, 157. On life as comprising a myriad of small, heterogeneous temporalities, see Ada Smailbegović, *Poetics of Liveliness: Molecules, Fibers, Tissues, Clouds* (New York: Columbia University Press, 2021).
73. Carson, 157, 28.
74. Carson, 12.
75. Carson, 110, 132, 148. See Eve Kosofsky Sedgwick, *The Weather in Proust* (Durham: Duke University Press, 2011) on the queer ethos of plurality and contingency.
76. Carson, *The Edge of the Sea*, 234–236.
77. Carson, 12.
78. Carson, 147.
79. Carson, 158, 216.
80. Walter Benjamin, *Illuminations*, ed. Hannah Arendt, trans. Harry Zohn (New York: Schocken, 1968), 208.
81. Carson, *The Edge of the Sea*, 154–155.
82. W. J. T. Mitchell, *Picture Theory: Essays on Verbal and Visual Representation* (Chicago: University of Chicago Press, 1995), 89n9.
83. N. J. Berrill, quoted in Juriga, *Bob Hines*, 87.

84. Carson to Brooks, May 14, 1951, Rachel Carson Papers, Beinecke Rare Book & Manuscript Library, Yale University.
85. Paul Brooks to Lovell Thompson, memorandum, July 8, 1952, Rachel Carson Papers, Beinecke Rare Book & Manuscript Library, Yale University.
86. Carson, *The Edge of the Sea*, 98, 116, 169, 140, 141. Lear notes that Carson was involved in designing the layout of text and illustration. *Rachel Carson*, 269.
87. Carson, 72. On textual margins as spaces of becoming and as figures for cultural fringes, see Michael Camille, *Images on the Edge: The Margins of Medieval Art* (London: Reaktion, 1992).
88. Ed Ricketts and Jack Calvin, *Between Pacific Tides*, 3rd ed., rev. Joel Hedgpeth (Stanford: Stanford University Press, 1952).
89. Jennifer Roberts, "Seeing Scale," in Jennifer Roberts, ed., *Scale* (Chicago: University of Chicago Press, 2016), 10–24, 14; Derek Woods, "Scale Critique for the Anthropocene," *Minnesota Review* 83 (2014): 133–142, 134. On the "hegemony of the scalable," but also the complexity of the scalable/ nonscalable binary, see Anna Tsing, *The Mushroom at the End of the World: On the Possibility of Life in Capitalist Ruins* (Princeton, N.J.: Princeton University Press, 2015), 42.
90. Hines was known as a "Duck Stamp Artist": having won the Federal Duck Stamp competition in 1946, he went on to coordinate this contest for many years.
91. Juriga, *Bob Hines*, 77.
92. Carson, *The Edge of the Sea*, 4, 82, 89, 171.
93. Similarly, in Charles Darwin's 1851 illustrated book about barnacles, the scientist's amazement at the species' unusual sexual practices destabilizes the visual order and symmetry of the page. Smith, *Charles Darwin and Victorian Visual Culture*, 58.
94. Donna Haraway, *Staying with the Trouble: Making Kin in the Chthulucene* (Durham: Duke University Press, 2016), 56, 32. Tentacularity, with its "snaky," "unheroic" connotations, is so important to Haraway that she proposes, as an alternative to *Anthropocene*, the neologism *Chthulucene* (deriving from *Pimoa cthulhu*, a species of spider) as a term for the geological epoch we are currently traversing (56).
95. Eva Hayward, "Sensational Jellyfish: Aquarium Affects and the Matter of Immersion," *differences* 23, no. 3 (2012): 161–196, 178.
96. Hayward, 182.
97. Carson, *The Edge of the Sea*, 86–87.
98 Domesticity and care work are at the heart of Carson's ecological vision. Carson lived with her mother until the latter's death in her late eighties, she was financially responsible for her mother and her young nieces after her father died in 1935, and she later adopted her grandnephew when he was orphaned at four. Noting that Carson's biographers have tended to bemoan the time and energy this writer devoted to the care of her family, historian Jill Lepore argues that "if she'd had fewer ties, she would have had less insight." Jill Lepore, "The Right Way to Remember Rachel Carson," *New Yorker*, March 26, 2018. For a compelling reading of Carson's avuncular mode of ecological stewardship—her capacity to "tend to the future without contributing directly to it"—see Ensor, "Spinster Ecology," *American Literature* 84, no. 2 (2012): 409–435, 409. As Ensor puts it, connecting Carson's queer status as a "spinster" to her ecological vision, "Carson

spent her life in a series of deeply invested but oblique relationships to the world around her" (415).
99. Carson, *The Edge of the Sea*, 88.
100. On the inescapable mutuality proper to this sense, see Maurice Merleau-Ponty, "L'entrelacs-le chiasme," in Maurice Merleau-Ponty, *Le Visible et l'invisible* (Paris: Gallimard, 1979), 172–204.
101. Carson, *The Edge of the Sea*, 113–114.
102. Carson, 115.
103. Carson, 64.
104. Carson, 132, 236, 106, 58, 219, 81, 133.
105. Eva Hayward, "Fingeryeyes: Impressions of Cup Corals," *Cultural Anthropology* 25, no. 4 (2010): 577–599, 580.
106. Carson, *The Edge of the Sea*, 40, 243, 102, 63.
107. Carson, 121, 219, 207.
108. Carson, 40–41.
109. Carson, 118.
110. "Mrs. Ramsay could not help exclaiming, 'Oh, how beautiful!' For the great plateful of blue water was before her, the hoary Lighthouse, distant, austere, in the midst; and on the right, as far as the eye could see, fading and falling, in soft low pleats, the green sand dunes with the wild flowering grasses on them, which always seemed to be running away into some moon country, uninhabited of men." Virginia Woolf, *To the Lighthouse* (New York: Harcourt, 2005), 16. Carson, *The Edge of the Sea*, 93, 113, 82, 144.
111. Eve Kosofsky Sedgwick, *Touching Feeling: Affect, Pedagogy, Performativity* (Durham: Duke University Press, 2002), 13.
112. Carson, *The Edge of the Sea*, 219–220. Such gentleness and consideration were typical; according to Hines, Carson insisted as a rule on returning the live creatures he illustrated to the precise location where they had been found. Juriga, *Bob Hines*, 77.

4. McKAY'S DREAM PORT

1. Claude McKay, *Banjo: A Story Without a Plot* (New York: Mariner, 1970), 42.
2. "Ginger had fallen for the beach." McKay, 39.
3. McKay, 18.
4. McKay, 11, 15, 67, 66. The phrase "dream port" also appears in *Romance in Marseille*, when Lafala ships to Marseille, "returning to the dream port of his fortune and misfortune." Claude McKay, *Romance in Marseille*, ed. Gary Edward Holcomb and William J. Maxwell (New York: Penguin, 2020), 28.
5. See Jacques Rancière, *Politics of Aesthetics*, trans. Gabriel Rockhill (New York: Bloomsbury Academic, 2013), and *Aesthesis: Scenes from the Aesthetic Regime of Art*, trans. Zakir Paul (London: Verso, 2013).
6. McKay, *Banjo*, 22, 132.
7. Jacques Rancière, *Proletarian Nights: The Workers' Dream in Nineteenth-Century France* (London: Verso, 2012).

4. MCKAY'S DREAM PORT

8. Aarthi Vadde, *Chimeras of Form: Modernist Internationalism Beyond Europe, 1914–2016* (New York: Columbia University Press, 2016), 7.
9. Stavros Stavrides, *Common Space: The City as Commons* (London: Zed, 2020), 2. For a critique of the notion that historical commons were free-for-alls or spaces without roads, see also Anne-Lise François, "Passing Impasse," *Comparative Literature* 72, no. 2 (2020): 240–257, 247.
10. Stavrides, 2. See also Hardt and Negri's critique of capitalism's "desocialization of the commons." Michael Hardt and Antonio Negri, *Commonwealth* (Cambridge, Mass.: Harvard University Press, 2009), 258.
11. Marie-Alice Chardeaux, *Les Choses communes*, quoted in Pierre Dardot and Christian Laval, *Common: On Revolution in the Twenty-First Century*, trans. Matthew MacLellan (London: Bloomsbury, 2019), 17. Roman law was notably fuzzy about the status of the seashore, note Dardot and Laval, and generally "a certain imprecision" remained regarding the distinction between what was "public" and what was "held in common" (18). On the museum-ification of the waterfront, see Morgane Cadieu, "Afterword: The Littoral Museum of the Twenty-first Century," *Comparative Literature* 73, no. 2 (June 2021): 237–254.
12. On commons as phenomena distinct from the property form, whether public or private, see Hardt and Negri, *Commonwealth*.
13. E. P. Thompson, *Customs in Common* (New York: New Press, 1991), 188. On precapitalist commoning practices in England, see also Thompson, *The Making of the English Working Class* (New York: Vintage, 1966); and Raymond Williams, *The Country and the City* (Oxford: Oxford University Press, 1973).
14. Jean-Luc Nancy, *Being Singular Plural*, trans. Robert Richardson and Anne O'Byrne (Stanford: Stanford University Press, 2000); Hardt and Negri, *Commonwealth*, vii, 102–118. In their preface to *Multitude: War and Democracy in the Age of Empire* (New York: Penguin, 2004), Michael Hardt and Antonio Negri define the "common" as a political principle by which the "commons" can be built and sustained (xv). See also economist Elinor Ostrom's examination of diverse institutional models for cooperative communal management, beyond the state and the market. Elinor Ostrom, *Governing the Commons: The Evolution of Institutions for Collective Action* (Cambridge: Cambridge University Press, 1990).
15. Saidiya Hartman, *Wayward Lives, Beautiful Experiments: Intimate Histories of Social Upheaval* (New York: Norton, 2019), 4.
16. Samuel Delany, *Times Square Red, Times Square Blue* (New York: New York University Press, 1999), xviii, 23–29.
17. Fred Moten and Stefano Harney, *The Undercommons: Fugitive Planning and Black Study* (New York: Minor Compositions, 2013).
18. José Esteban Muñoz, *The Sense of Brown* (Durham: Duke University Press, 2020), 2. See also Nadja Millner-Larsen and Gavin Butt, eds., "The Queer Commons," *GLQ* 24, no. 4 (2018).
19. Allan Sekula, *Fish Story* (Düsseldorf: Richter Verlag, 1995), 12.
20. See Ian Baucom's *Specters of the Atlantic: Finance Capital, Slavery, and the Philosophy of History* (Durham: Duke University Press, 2005), a study of how the eighteenth-century maritime economy is "haunted" by the specter of the "wounded, suffering human body incessantly attended by an equal sign and a monetary equivalent" (7).

21. Brent Hayes Edwards, *The Practice of Diaspora: Literature, Translation, and the Rise of Black Internationalism* (Cambridge, Mass.: Harvard University Press, 2003), 210.
22. On the queer aesthetic potential of the working port on strike, see Sarah Ann Wells, "On the Shores of Work," *Comparative Literature* 73, no. 2 (June, 2021): 166–183. On the "beach effect" (*effet de plage*) as a destabilizing sensory phenomenon and a form of horizontal flânerie, see Roland Barthes, "Sur la plage," in *Oeuvres complètes* (Paris: Seuil, 2002), 4:509–510, and my introduction.
23. *Grève* is one of two primary French words for beach; the most commonly used word is *plage*, the etymology of which I will discuss.
24. Charles Tilly, *The Contentious French* (Cambridge, Mass.: Harvard University Press, 1986), 42.
25. Casey Harison, "The Rise and Decline of a Revolutionary Space: Paris's Place de Grève and the Stonemasons of Creuse, 1750–1900," *Journal of Social History* 34, no. 2 (2000): 403–436, 421; Joshua Clover, *Riot. Strike. Riot: The New Era of Uprisings* (London: Verso, 2019), 63.
26. The dictionary of nineteenth- and twentieth-century French, the *Trésor de la langue française informatisé,* cites Balzac's 1831 *La Peau de Chagrin* (*The Wild Ass's Skin*) and Hugo's 1831 *Notre-Dame de Paris* as works that reference "la Grève" as an infamous execution site. *TLFi,* s.v. "grève (*n.*)," https://www.cnrtl.fr/definition/greve (accessed April 12, 2022).
27. Tilly, *The Contentious French,* 42. Allan Potofsky fleshes out this point, noting that "the summer of 1785 witnessed the first appearance of the term, *faire grève,* which appeared in police reports to refer to a strike. A commissioner noted that *faire grève* meant to 'not work in order to have the daily wage increased.' This is 'what they call (it) among themselves.'" As Potofsky points out, "a refusal to work at this central locale, otherwise used for public executions, was no doubt an impressive act of defiance." Allan Potofsky, *Constructing Paris in the Age of Revolution* (New York: Palgrave, 2009), 57.
28. Harison, "The Rise and Decline of a Revolutionary Space," 403. As Harison explains, this setting "was especially noteworthy for its history of contentiousness in the 19th century, for it was here that crowds tended to gather, rumors of insurrection circulated and rebellions reached their climax" (403). Potofsky describes the Place de Grève as the site "of great moments in which sovereignty passed temporarily from the national government to the people of Paris and their representatives.... The Place de Grève was for centuries the locale par excellence of popular politics" (53–54). For an expanded history of this site, see Michel Le Moël and Jean Derens, *La place de Grève* (Paris: Délégation à l'Action Artistique de la Ville de Paris, 1991).
29. McKay, *Banjo,* 15, 57.
30. McKay, *Banjo,* 11–12.
31. Edwards, *The Practice of Diaspora,* 198–199.
32. McKay himself was familiar with the struggle to get by, having worked a wide variety of jobs—from manual labor to police work to service on trains and private homes—in order to feed and house himself while writing. During his years in France, for instance, he was employed as a butler (but quit after a month because the twelve-hour days left no time to write); a builder's helper (but the physical

exhaustion of the job left no energy for thought); a reader of manuscripts for a film production company, which soon folded; and an occasional dockworker, unloading ships. He wrote to journalist Louise Bryant in the summer of 1926 that he feared being "driven out of [Marseille] by hunger and want as [he] was out of Cannes, Nice and Menton." Michel Fabre, *From Harlem to Paris: Black American Writers in France, 1840–1980* (Urbana: University of Illinois Press, 1993), 100; Wayne F. Cooper, *Claude McKay: Rebel Sojourner in the Harlem Renaissance: A Biography* (Baton Rouge: Louisiana State University Press, 1996), 229–230.

33. As Edwards puts it, *Banjo* registers the shifting of McKay's political interest away from the "expansion and unionization" of the (industrial maritime) proletariat and toward the transient communities that exist "in the margins of that development." Edwards, *The Practice of Diaspora*, 199.
34. McKay, *Banjo*, 317.
35. Vadde, *Chimeras of Form*, 126.
36. McKay, *Banjo*, 130, 153, 168.
37. McKay, 31–32.
38. McKay's beach boys have various tactics for avoiding the police, as "some of them had not the proper papers." McKay, 23. Ginger has been the longest on the beach, having lost his seaman's papers, been imprisoned for vagabondage and "served with a writ of expulsion," which he destroyed (5). In her reading of *Banjo*, Vadde argues that McKay's peripatetic conception of community brings him into the orbit of Etienne Balibar, who theorizes a *civitas vaga*—a wandering, impermanent form of citizenship—not rooted single statehood, but not equivalent to statelessness either. Vadde, *Chimeras of Form*, 109–110.
39. McKay, 18, 31–32. Historian Gary Wilder notes that the beach boys' decision to hustle their living rather than submit to the "racial humiliation endured by the black proletariat in the imperial shipping industry" would have been in real life a "nightmare scenario for the interwar colonial state." Gary Wilder, *The Imperial Nation-State: Negritude and Colonial Humanism Between the Two Wars* (Chicago: University of Chicago Press, 2005), 177.
40. Minayo Nasiali, *Native to the Republic: Empire, Social Citizenship, and Everyday Life in Marseille Since 1945* (Ithaca: Cornell University Press, 2016), 10.
41. On cruising—the "search for non-binding, uncommodified sex and movement across social space"—as a queer Black ethos in McKay, see Eric H. Newman, "Ephemeral Utopias: Queer Cruising, Literary Form, and Diasporic Imagination in *Home to Harlem* and *Banjo*," *Callaloo* 38, no. 1 (2015): 167–185, 177. Newman argues that McKay's queerness is not incidental or secondary to his writing, but shapes both his social vision and his formal innovations (167).
42. I borrow the phrase "landscaping aesthetic" from Anne Raine, "Du Bois's Ambient Poetics: Rethinking Environmental Imagination in *The Souls of Black Folk*," *Callaloo* 36, no. 2 (Spring 2013): 322–341, 329. On McKay's revolutionary politics, see Gary Holcomb, *Claude McKay, Code Name Sasha: Queer Black Marxism and the Harlem Renaissance* (Gainesville: University of Florida Press, 2007), 14.
43. Uvedale Price, in *An Essay on the Picturesque as Compared with the Sublime and Beautiful* (1794), quoted in David Marshall, *The Frame of Art* (Baltimore: Johns Hopkins University Press, 2005), 16.

4. McKAY'S DREAM PORT

44. Kim Ian Michasiw, "Nine Revisionist Theses on the Picturesque," *Representations* 38 (Spring 1992): 76–100.
45. Marshall, *The Frame of Art*, 17.
46. The River Wye is especially picturesque in Gilpin's view because it appears "infinitely varied" and "free from the formality of lines." William Gilpin, *Observations on the River Wye and Several Parts of South Wales &c. Relative Chiefly to Picturesque Beauty, Made in the Summer of the Year 1770* (London: Blamire, 1789), 18–19. Eighteenth Century Collections Online.
47. Marshall, *The Frame of Art*, 17; Michasiw, "Nine Revisionist Theses on the Picturesque," 77. John Conron develops the connection between the picturesque and settler colonialism, arguing that this aesthetic "promulgates the idea of 'picturesque excursions' into landscapes from Maine to New Orleans, from Cape Code to Lost Angeles." John Conron, *American Picturesque* (University Park: Penn State University Press, 2000), 11.
48. Alain Corbin, *The Lure of the Sea: Discovery of the Seaside in the Western World, 1750–1840*, trans. Jocelyn Phelps (New York: Penguin 1995), 147.
49. "Only on the brink of destruction . . . are customs, costumes, and religious rituals of the dominated finally *seen* as picturesque" and "reinterpreted as the precious remnants of disappearing ways of life." Linda Nochlin, *The Politics of Vision: Essays on Nineteenth-Century Art and Society* (New York: Harper and Row, 1989), 50.
50. McKay, *Banjo*, 210, 294.
51. McKay, 288; "In no other port had [Ray] ever seen congregated such a picturesque variety of Negroes" (68). Edwards describes *Banjo* as a "dizzying portrayal of the great idiosyncratic variety of ideological and group commitment among shifting black male communities in Marseilles." Edwards, *The Practice of Diaspora*, 198.
52. McKay, 18. McKay's vagabond picturesque is linked to his penchant for the pastoral mode as critic Jennifer Chang theorizes it: an expression of his "acute sense of never quite belonging," and his desire to "share in re-imagining more inclusive places." "Pastoral and the Problem of Place in McKay's *Harlem Shadows*," in *A Companion to the Harlem Renaissance*, ed. Cherene Sherrard-Johnson (New York: Wiley, 2015), 187–202, 199, 198. For a deft reading of McKay's complex relation to the Jamaican landscape of his youth—and in particular how his poetics engage the "provision ground," or space of semiautonomous agricultural cultivation on the outskirts of the plantation—see Sonya Posmentier, *Cultivation and Catastrophe: The Lyric Ecology of Modern Black Literature* (Baltimore: Johns Hopkins University Press, 2017), chapter 1.
53. McKay, 202.
54. McKay, 69.
55. McKay, 130.
56. Vadde, *Chimeras of Form*, 128. On the importance to McKay of pleasure as a mode of resistance, see also Agnieszka Tuszynska, "'A Syrup of Passion and Desire': Transgressive Politics of Pleasure in Claude McKay's *Romance in Marseille*," *English Language Notes* 59, no. 1 (April 2021): 38–57.
57. Edwards, *The Practice of Diaspora*, 222.
58. McKay, *Banjo*, 248.

4. McKAY'S DREAM PORT

59. McKay, 69. Monique Allewaert, *Ariel's Ecology: Plantations, Personhood, and Colonialism in the American Tropics* (Minneapolis: University of Minnesota Press, 2013). This anticolonial ecological mode operates under the logic of disaggregation and diversification rather than identity, and involves "deft imaginings of the forms of power and agency that developed at the interstices between human and nonhuman life" (3, 6, 7).
60. Allewaert, 8; McKay, 68, 69.
61. Gilpin, *Observations on the River Wye*, 12.
62. T. J. Clark, *Image of the People: Gustave Courbet and the 1848 Revolution* (Berkeley: University of California Press, 1973), 83.
63. McKay, *Banjo*, 22.
64. *Banjo*'s internationalism is not that of coordinated social movement, as Edwards puts it, but of "the Dozens writ large, with Ananse, Frère Lapin, and the Signifying Monkey soused and clamoring for the soapbox." Edwards, *The Practice of Diaspora*, 210. Edwards persuasively argues that "more than any other interwar work, *Banjo* relentlessly underlines . . . the impossibility of translating a racial consciousness through some foolproof or stable system." Instead it presents "the vertigo of intradiasporic communication" (212). McKay's sensitivity to the nuances of speech—what Russian formalists call *skaz*—can be traced back to his first published volumes of poetry. In his debut collection, *Songs of Jamaica* (1912), composed after an abandoned apprenticeship with a cabinetmaker and during his brief stint as a member of the Jamaican constabulary, McKay invents a creolized poetic voice by mixing local patois with English versification. On the transnational, dialogic ethos of McKay's creolized ballads, see Jahan Ramazani, *A Transnational Poetics* (Chicago: University of Chicago Press, 2009); and Michael North, *The Dialect of Modernism* (New York: Oxford University Press, 1994). On McKay's dialect poems as both rooted to the land and as transnationally mobile—and thus as opening "a modern poetic space for aesthetic experimentation and anticolonial critique"—see Posmentier, *Cultivation and Catastrophe*, 34.
65. Kevin Quashie, *The Sovereignty of Quiet: Beyond Resistance in Black Culture* (New Brunswick, N.J.: Rutgers University Press, 2012), 12.
66. Quashie, 15.
67. Quashie, 5. In relation to Black quiet as "capacity," see Posmentier's discussion of "floating moments" in McKay's lyric poetry. She suggests that such instances of historically grounded temporal suspension indicate a "negative capability," opening "a flourishing grove within and apart from the slavery and postslavery landscape." Posmentier, *Cultivation and Catastrophe*, 51.
68. McKay, *Banjo*, 66, 63.
69. McKay, 77, 130, 70.
70. Quashie, *The Sovereignty of Quiet*, 21.
71. McKay, *Banjo*, 23, 281.
72. Edwards, *The Practice of Diaspora*, 200.
73. *OED Online*, s.v. "ease (*n.*)" (accessed April 12, 2022).
74. *Trésor de la langue française informatisé*, s.v. "aise (*adj.*)," https://www.cnrtl.fr/etymologie/aise (accessed April 12, 2022).
75. McKay, *Banjo*, 27.

76. Here one notes a queer resonance between this novel's ethos of quiet ease as an evasive, floating mode of contact and the intersubjective "quiet bower" that, for Rachel Carson and Dorothy Freeman, emblematized a love that was neither fully speakable nor exactly "closeted." "Quiet" offered these women a temporary suspension of the obligation to publicly perform midcentury hetero-femininity. On the Keatsian image of the "quiet bower" as key to Carson and Freeman's epistolary affair, see chapter 3.
77. McKay, *Banjo*, 34.
78. McKay, 319.
79. Edwards, *The Practice of Diaspora*, 239.
80. McKay underscores the network of care that underlies this apparently careless group of friends: they feed, transport, entertain, and house one another, and navigate both French bureaucracy and the café scene in order to keep each other from harm: Ray is acquainted with a medical student who writes, and this connection enables an ill Banjo to be admitted to the hospital despite his lack of identity papers. Survival in *Banjo* is always a collective affair.
81. McKay, *Banjo*, 33–34.
82. McKay, 34–35. In fact, Latnah's insouciant pleasure in diving and swimming has already been interrupted by Malty's unwanted advances; he grabs her feet in the water and she kicks him in the mouth, a gesture of self-defense that McKay presents only from Malty's perspective, as feeling "like the shock of a kiss wrestled for and stolen" (34). On this novel's "uneven" treatment of Latnah and problematic mix of feminist and sexist discourse, see Edwards, *The Practice of Diaspora*, 209.
83. McKay, 274. On surveillance in McKay's Marseille, see Stephanie J. Brown, "Marseille Exposed: Under Surveillance in Claude McKay's *Banjo* and *Romance in Marseille*," *English Language Notes* 59, no. 1 (April 2021): 93–108.
84. Although McKay composed *Banjo* during a decade of wandering in Europe and North Africa, he lived in the U.S. for most of his adult life and became a naturalized U.S. citizen in 1940. Cooper, *Claude McKay*, 351.
85. Marcel Roncayolo, *L'imaginaire de Marseille: Port, ville, pôle* (Lyon: ENS Éditions, 2014), https://books.openedition.org/enseditions/370. On McKay's critical attitude toward French colonialism, see Fabre, *From Harlem to Paris*, 93–94. My understanding of the overlapping racist logics represented in this novel is informed by Sophia Azeb's 2021 ACLA talk, "Transnational Black Space in Claude McKay's Marseille."
86. McKay, *Banjo*, 69.
87. McKay, *A Long Way From Home* (New Brunswick, N.J.: Rutgers University Press, 2007), 216.
88. The construction of the Erie Canal in 1825 made New York the country's largest port, a title it held for more than 150 years. Marc Levinson, "Container Shipping and the Decline of New York, 1955–1975," *Business History Review* 80, no. 1 (Spring 2006): 49–80, 50.
89. Jason W. Moore, "The Rise of Cheap Nature," in *Anthropocene or Capitalocene?*, ed. Jason W. Moore (Oakland: PM, 2016): 78–115.
90. On the labor intensiveness of the old shipping system, which often required vessels to remain docked for over a week, see Levinson, "Container Shipping and the

Decline of New York," 51–53, 55. For an expanded discussion of the shipping container's economic impact, see Marc Levinson, *The Box: How the Shipping Container Made the World Smaller and the World Economy Bigger* (Princeton, N.J.: Princeton University Press, 2006). For a more critical view of the military contexts and global consequences of containerization, see Deborah Cowen, *The Deadly Life of Logistics: Mapping Violence in Global Trade* (Minneapolis: University of Minnesota Press, 2014).

91. The Brooklyn Navy Yard had also been decommissioned in the mid-1960s and it too became a cruising ground. Fiona Anderson, *Cruising the Dead River: David Wojnarowicz and New York's Ruined Waterfront* (Chicago: University of Chicago Press, 2019), 1. On ruination as built into the logic of capitalism, see Walter Benjamin, *The Arcades Project*, trans. Rolf Tiedemann (Cambridge, Mass.: Harvard University Press, 1999); Ann Laura Stoler, ed., *Imperial Debris* (Durham: Duke University Press, 2013); Dora Apel, *Beautiful Terrible Ruins: Detroit and the Anxiety of Decline* (New Brunswick, N.J.: Rutgers University Press, 2015); and Anna Tsing, *The Mushroom at the End of the World: On the Possibility of Life in Capitalist Ruins* (Princeton, N.J.: Princeton University Press, 2015).
92. Anderson, *Cruising the Dead River*, 13.
93. Quoted in Apel, *Beautiful Terrible Ruins*, 16.
94. Anderson, *Cruising the Dead River*, 24; Douglas Crimp, "Alvin Baltrop: Pier Photographs, 1975–1986," *Artforum* 46, no. 6 (February 2008): 262–273, 269. Edmund White also discusses the importance of this site as a dehierarchized queer space of "sexual abundance" in his memoir, *City Boy: My Life in New York During the 1960s and 1970s* (London: Bloomsbury, 2011).
95. Allan Sekula, *Fish Story* (Düsseldorf: Richter Verlag, 1995), 43. Although, according to Sekula, modernity "entails a maritime victory of the detail over the panorama," the classical maritime panorama (with its connection to naval strategy) remains an underlying presence. As he puts it, the sea is a "bottomless reservoir of well-preserved anachronisms" (106–107).
96. Elizabeth Freeman, *Time Binds: Queer Temporalities, Queer Histories* (Durham: Duke University Press, 2010), xv.
97. *Trésor de la Langue Française informatisé*, s.v. "plage (*n*.)," https://www.cnrtl.fr/etymologie/plage (accessed March 18, 2022).
98. Quoted in Crimp, "Alvin Baltrop," 269.
99. In this regard, Baltrop's aesthetic sensibility is surprisingly akin to that of Rachel Carson. As I show in chapter 3, Carson emphasizes the improbable tenacity of even the smallest and most vulnerable intertidal life forms, which she describes, variously, as "lacy" and "shrubby," "delicate" and "tough." Rachel Carson, *The Edge of the Sea* (New York: Houghton Mifflin Harcourt, 1998), 39, 174, 95, 57.
100. Quoted in Anderson, *Cruising the Dead River*, 2.
101. As Crimp puts it: "the complexity of Baltrop's legacy resides not only in the record his photographs provide of utopian and dystopian occurrences, but also in their evidence that the moment in Manhattan's history when we could so thoroughly reinvent ourselves was as precarious as the places where we did it." Crimp, "Alvin Baltrop," 269.
102. Phillip Lopate, "Introduction: Some Thoughts on the Lost Waterfront," in Shelley Seccombe, *Lost Waterfront: The Decline and Rebirth of Manhattan's Western Shore*

4. McKAY'S DREAM PORT

(New York: Fordham University Press, 2007), 9–12, 10. On the city's history of preventing its inhabitants from making contact with the water, Lopate observes that because Manhattan's waterfront was long allocated to maritime and industrial uses, it remains relatively unwelcoming to pedestrians. Phillip Lopate, *Waterfront: A Walk Around Manhattan* (New York: Anchor, 2005), 3.

103. Lopate, "Introduction," 10–11.
104. Shelley Seccombe, "Photographer's Note," in *Lost Waterfront*, 13–15, 13.
105. Seccombe, 13, 14.
106. Proust, *In Search of Lost Time*, 2:508 (translation modified); *À la recherche du temps perdu*, 2:150.
107. Douglas Crimp, "Action Around the Edges," Sixteenth Annual Kessler Lecture, excerpted at https://clags.org/articles/action-around-the-edges-sixteenth-annual-kessler-lecture-delivered-by-douglas-crimp/ (accessed March 18, 2022).
108. Gordon Matta-Clark and Liza Bear, "Gordon Matta-Clark: Splitting the Humphry Street Building," an interview by Liza Bear reprinted from *Avalanche*, December 1974, 34–37, in Corinne Diserens, ed., *Gordon Matta-Clark* (London: Phaidon, 2003), 164. In this interview, Matta-Clark discusses his penchant for the overlooked interstices of the city: "metaphoric gaps, left-over spaces, places that were not developed.... For example, the places where you stop to tie your shoelaces" (164).
109. On Matta-Clark's "renegade inhabitation of urban space," see Frances Richard, *Gordon Matta-Clark: Physical Poetics* (Berkeley: University of California Press, 2019), 4.
110. Quoted in Crow, "Gordon Matta-Clark," 7–132, in Diserens, ed., *Gordon Matta-Clark*, 11.
111. Jonathan Weinberg, Pier Groups: Art and Sex Along the New York Waterfront (University Park: Penn State University Press, 2019), 57.
112. Quoted in Richard, *Gordon Matta-Clark*, 137.
113. Quoted in Crow, "Gordon Matta-Clark," 8.
114. Pamela Lee writes that the Pier 52 former warehouse was an "enormous steel-truss and corrugated tin building, measuring roughly six hundred feet long and seventy feet wide" and with an upper section, or clerestory, measuring fifty-feet up. The building was first registered in the 1879 Annual of the New York City Department of Docks and Ferries, and was leased by various companies, the Baltimore and Ohio Railroad occupying the space after the Second World War. Pamela Lee, *Object to Be Destroyed* (Cambridge, Mass.: MIT Press, 1999), 119.
115. Quoted in Crow, "Gordon Matta-Clark," 8. The commons quality of this architectural work is complicated by the story Matta-Clark told about having locked the Pier 52 building when he started the project to keep what he called the "sadomasochistic fringe" at bay. Weinberg, *Pier Groups*, 57. Weinberg deconstructs the opposition Matta-Clark drew between his own artistic practice and the gay subcultural pier world, noting how important voyeurism was to this artist and suggesting that we view the sickle-shaped architectural cut in *Day's End* as a "giant eye" or a "keyhole in the sky" (61).
116. Henning Bech, *When Men Meet: Homosexuality and Modernity*, trans. Teresa Mesquit and Tim Davies (Chicago: University of Chicago Press, 1997), 105. Writing in the 1980s, Bech allies modern homosexuality with a "virtuosic" gaze: "it can

discern almost imperceptible signs; it can fine-tune and flit around in endlessly different ways; it has an enormous cruising range" (107).
117. Weinberg, *Pier Groups*, 59.
118. "Guerilla-renovator" is Crow's term. Crow, "Gordon Matta-Clark," 12. Weinberg notes that "even to visit the site to look at *Day's End* was to risk being mugged or arrested for trespassing." Weinberg, 58–59. On the unplanned collaboration of sorts between Baltrop and Matta-Clark, see Lorenzo Fusi, ed., *The Piers from Here: Alvin Baltrop and Gordon Matta-Clark* (Liverpool: Open Eye Gallery, 2014). Seccombe also documented queer sunbathing around Matta-Clark's cuts in works such as *Sunbathing on the Edge, Pier 52, 1977*, which features on the cover of Weinberg's book.
119. Quoted in Weinberg, 59.

5. TIDEWRACK, BECKETT TO SUNDE

1. Jason W. Moore, *Capitalism in the Web of Life: Ecology and the Accumulation of Capital* (London: Verso, 2015). In conceptualizing the beach as twentieth-century air conditioning—not a true escape but a pressure valve that keeps the productivist, extractivist system on track, I take inspiration from On Barak's chapter, "Beached: The Coastal Turn," in "Heat: A History," unpublished MS, December 11, 2021.
2. Marc Augé, *L'Impossible voyage: le tourisme et ses images* (Paris: Rivages, 1997), 42.
3. On the Great Acceleration as a phase within the longer history of the Anthropocene, see John Robert McNeill and Peter Engelke, *The Great Acceleration: Environmental History of the Anthropocene Since 1945* (Cambridge, Mass.: Harvard University Press, 2016). For a more critical perspective on the fundamental unsustainability of the "treadmill of capitalist accumulation," see John Bellamy Foster, Brett Clark, and Richard York, *The Ecological Rift: Capitalism's War on the Earth* (New York: Monthly Review Press, 2010), 8. On how poetry registers this period of crisis, see Margaret Ronda, *Remainders: American Poetry at Nature's End* (Stanford: Stanford University Press, 2018). On the complexities and unevenness of the Great Acceleration in global perspective, see Christoph Görg, Christina Plank, Dominik Wiedenhofer, Andreas Mayor, Melanie Pichler, Anke Scharffartzik, and Fridolin Krausmann, "Scrutinizing the Great Acceleration: The Anthropocene and Its Analytic Challenges for Social-Ecological Transformations," *Anthropocene Review* 7, no. 1 (December 2019): 42–61.
4. Other names and periodizations for the Anthropocene have been proposed. Anna Tsing prefers the term *Plantationocene*, for instance, noting that the violent colonial imposition of a slave plantation system in the sixteenth century offered a blueprint for the industrial factories to come. Anna Tsing, *The Mushroom at the End of the World: On the Possibility of Life in Capitalist Ruins* (Princeton, N.J.: Princeton University Press, 2015), 39–40. For a critique of the universalizing, human-centric, ahistorical logic of the term *Anthropocene*, see Donna Haraway, "Anthropocene, Capitalocene, Plantationocene, Chlulucene: Making Kin," *Environmental Humanities* 6 (2015): 159–165; Christophe Bonneuil and Jean-Baptiste Fressoz, *The Shock of the Anthropocene: The Earth, History, and Us*, trans. David Fernbach

(London: Verso, 2017); and Jason W. Moore, ed., *Anthropocene or Capitalocene? Nature, History, and the Crisis of Capitalism* (Oakland, Cal.: PM, 2016).

5. The "just-in-time" organization of global capitalist production and distribution is a concept originated by the Toyota Motor Company in the 1950s and 1960s and adopted by many other companies in the 1980s. It names a process of eliminating large inventories by outsourcing the manufacturing process, thus placing unprecedented focus on transportation and logistics management. See Marc Levinson, *The Box: How the Shipping Container Made the World Smaller and the World Economy Bigger* (Princeton, N.J.: Princeton University Press, 2006); and Deborah Cowen, *The Deadly Life of Logistics: Mapping Violence in Global Trade* (Minneapolis: University of Minnesota Press, 2014).

6. Luc Boltanski and Eve Chiapello, *The New Spirit of Capitalism*, trans. Gregory Elliot (London: Verso, 2005), 5.

7. On the strange belatedness of climate violence, see Rob Nixon, *Slow Violence and the Environmentalism of the Poor* (Cambridge, Mass.: Harvard University Press, 2011); Timothy Morton, *The Ecological Thought* (Cambridge, Mass.: Harvard University Press, 2011), chapter 3; and Bruno Latour, inaugural lecture at Sciences Po, 2019, https://www.youtube.com/watch?v=Db2zyVnGLsE (accessed April 16, 2022).

8. Ronda, *Remainders*, 13. I use the first-person plural pronoun here with caution, addressing not all humans but likely readers of this book. On the problem of invoking a universal "we" in discussions of climate harm and agency, see Min Hyoun Song, "Introduction: The Practice of Sustaining Attention to Climate Change," in *Climate Lyricism* (Durham: Duke University Press, 2022), 1–18.

9. "Drift"—in its vagueness and directionlessness—is an important concept for theorists of the present. On the contemporary itself as a "drifting referent" unanchored to historical period, see Theodore Martin, *Contemporary Drift: Genre, Historicism, and the Problem of the Present* (New York: Columbia University Press, 2017), 2–3. Martin allies "drift" with (queer) "temporal "drag," a term Elizabeth Freeman defines as "a productive obstacle to progress, a usefully disorienting pull backward." Elizabeth Freeman, *Time Binds: Queer Temporalities, Queer Histories* (Durham: Duke University Press, 2010), 64–65. Yet "drift" also connotes toxicity, plastic debris, and the fate of migrant vessels abandoned at sea. Eric Robertson, "A la dérive: Drifting in and Out of Form in French Literature and Visual Art from Bataille to Bergvall," in Patrick Crowley and Shirley Jordan, eds., *What Forms Can Do: The Work of Form in Twentieth- and Twenty-First-Century French Literature and Thought* (Liverpool: Liverpool University Press, 2020), 271–286, 285.

10. As Steinberg observes, "under capitalism, the sea is idealized as a denatured and seemingly immaterial surface of latitude-longitude coordinates across which work (the displacement of mass) can be exercised with minimal resistance so as to enable the annihilation of space (or distance) through time (or speed). Philip E. Steinberg, "Maritime Cargomobilities: The Impossibilities of Representation," in Thomas Birtchnell, Satya Savitzky, and John Urry, eds., *Cargomobilities: Moving Materials in a Global Age* (London: Routledge, 2019), 35–47, 36. See also Patricia Yaeger, "Editor's Column: Sea Trash, Dark Pools, and the Tragedy of the Commons," *PMLA* 125, no. 3 (2010): 523–545; and the ACLA forum "Oceanic Routes," *Comparative Literature* 69, no. 1 (March 2017).

11. On the history of containerization, see Levinson, *The Box*. On oceanic gyres and the trajectory of container spills, see Curtis Ebbesmeyer and Eric Scigliano, *Flotsametrics and the Floating World: How One Man's Obsession with Runaway Sneakers and Rubber Ducks Revolutionized Ocean Science* (New York: Harper Collins, 2009). On waste sites as inevitable by-products of the contemporary cargo system, see Thomas Birtchnell, Satya Savitzky, and John Urry, "Moving Cargos," in Birtchnell, Savitzky, and Urry, *Cargomobilities*, 1–16, 2. For a compelling reading of the Great Pacific Garbage Patch as "extractive capitalism's weird other," see Thangam Ravindranathan and Antoine Traisnel, "In the Doldrums: Plastic, Haunting, and the Sea," *SubStance 157* 51, no. 1 (2022): 8–29, 18.
12. On the advent of "cheap nature" as the hallmark of capitalism, see Jason W. Moore, "The Rise of Cheap Nature," in Moore, *Anthropocene or Capitalocene?*, 78–115.
13. Allan Sekula and Noël Burch, "The Forgotten Space: Notes for a Film," *New Left Review* 69 (2011), newleftreview.org/issues/ii69/articles/allan-sekula-noel-burch-the-forgotten-space; Levinson, *The Box*, 374.
14. Herman Melville, *Moby Dick, or, The Whale* (New York: Modern Library, 2000), 2; Laleh Khalili, *Sinews of Trade and War* (London: Verso, 2020), 1. On industrial and postindustrial port aesthetics, see Allan Sekula, *Fish Story* (Düsseldorf: Richter Verlag, 1995); and Morgane Cadieu and Hannah Freed-Thall, eds., "Beaches and Ports," *Comparative Literature* 73, no. 2 (June 2021).
15. We see this in particular in Monet's 1870 *La plage de Trouville*, the lower quadrant of which is encrusted with a patch of sand. For a discussion of this sandy patch, see Marni Kessler, "Beyond the Shadow of the Veil: Claude Monet's *The Beach at Trouville*," in Heidi Brevik-Zender, ed., *Fashion, Modernity, and Materiality in France: From Rousseau to Art Deco* (Albany: State University of New York Press, 2018), 135–155. Monet has made no attempt to blend or conceal this windswept sediment.
16. Henry David Thoreau, *Cape Cod*, ed. Joseph J. Moldenhauer (Princeton, N.J.: Princeton University Press, 2010), 118; Aimé Césaire, *The Complete Poetry of Aimé Césaire: Bilingual Edition*, trans. Clayton Eshleman and A. James Arnold (Middletown, Conn.: Wesleyan University Press, 2017), 24–25. On nineteenth-century sea bathing as a practice involving contact with various sorts of debris, see also B. J. Barickman, *From Sea-Bathing to Beach-Going: A Social History of the Beach in Rio de Janeiro, Brazil* (Albuquerque: University of New Mexico Press, 2022), 10–14.
17. Marguerite Duras, *The Sea Wall*, trans. Herma Briffault (New York: Pellegrini and Cudahy, 1952), 23.
18. Saidiya Hartman, *Lose Your Mother: A Journey Along the Atlantic Slave Route* (New York: Farrar, Straus and Giroux, 2008), 32–33. Hartman connects this toilet beach to the slave trade that took place on the same coast for centuries, underscoring the "equation of gold, filth, and slavery" (47).
19. Severo Sarduy, *The Beach*, in *For Voice*, trans. Philip Barnard (Pittsburgh: Latin American Literary Review Press, 1985), 13–56, 24.
20. Marie Darrieussecq, *Il était une fois la plage* (Paris: Flammarion, 2000), 33. Sand is intrinsically heterogeneous, as it is defined by its particle size, not by its material make-up. On the science and mythology of this substance, see Michael Welland, *Sand, the Never-Ending Story* (Berkeley: University of California Press,

2009). On sand, in contrast to water, as a "repository" of memory and a queer archive in the Caribbean, see Vanessa Agard-Jones, "What the Sands Remember," *GLQ* 18, nos. 2–3 (2012): 325–346.
21. These photographs are collected in Robert Macfarlane and Deyan Sudjic, eds., *Strand* (London: Art/Books, 2016).
22. John Tully notes that rubber shoes were worn by peasants in colonial Indochina, Mexico, Greek Macedonia, and Thrace. John Tully, *The Devil's Milk: A Social History of Rubber* (New York: New York University Press, 2011), 18.
23. Martin Heidegger, "The Origin of the Work of Art," in Julian Young and Kenneth Haynes, eds., *Martin Heidegger: Off the Beaten Path*, 1–56 (Cambridge: Cambridge University Press, 2002), 14; Fredric Jameson, *Postmodernism, or the Cultural Logic of Late Capitalism* (Durham: Duke University Press, 1991), 7–8.
24. Van Gogh Museum, "Shoes," https://www.vangoghmuseum.nl/en/collection/s0011V1962 (accessed April 16, 2022).
25. Jameson, *Postmodernism*, 21. For a different take on Warhol's work—as an "archive of his liking" and an attempt to "initiate others into [the] pleasures" of such "elemental attraction"—see Jonathan Flatley, *Like Andy Warhol* (Chicago: University of Chicago Press, 2017).
26. Ebbesmeyer and Scigliano, *Flotsametrics and the Floating World*, 93.
27. Tully, *The Devil's Milk*, 20–21.
28. "Containers Lost at Sea—2020 Update," British International Freight Association, https://www.bifa.org/news/articles/2020/jul/containers-lost-at-sea-2020-update (accessed December 17, 2021).
29. Barker achieves this interstellar effect by arranging her culled tidewrack, unaltered, on a piece of black velvet in her basement, then photographing the arrangement using a single light source. Liz Wells, "Picturing Plastic Oceans," in Mandy Barker, *Altered Ocean* (London: Overlapse, 2019), 102–107, 103–104.
30. The uncanny trace of the creaturely in Barker's photograph resonates with Thangam Ravindranathan's account of the animal's vanishing act in contemporary literature. Thangam Ravindranathan, *Behold an Animal: Four Exhorbitant Readings* (Evanston: Northwestern University Press, 2020).
31. This is more than a metaphor: as scientists have noted, postindustrial detritus exists in geological time. In 2014, geologists announced the discovery of "plastiglomerate," a stone (or "stone") made of molten plastic, beach sediment, basaltic lava fragments, and organic debris. Patricia L. Corcoran, Charles J. Moore, and Kelly Jazvac, "An Anthropogenic Marker Horizon in the Future Rock Record," *GSA Today* 24, no. 6 (June 2014), https://www.geosociety.org/gsatoday/archive/24/6/pdf/i1052-5173-24-6-4.pdf.
32. On the concept of the hyperobject, see Morton's *The Ecological Thought*, chapter 3. As McNeill and Engelke observe, in 1950, the world produced one million tons of plastic; in 2015, it produced nearly 300 million tons. McNeill and Engelke, *The Great Acceleration*, 4.
33. In the last decades of her life—from 1864 until 1886—Dickinson abandoned the labor of stitching fascicles and turned instead to jotting down verses on bits of household paper waste, from chocolate wrappers to ripped-off envelope flaps. Compiled in Jen Bervin and Marta Werner, eds., *The Gorgeous Nothings: Emily*

Dickinson's Envelope Poems (New York: New Directions, 2013), these paper scraps, which bear the traces of use and are available to be handled and reshaped, function as both leftovers and future patches.

34. Ravindranathan and Traisnel, "In the Doldrums," 23; Stacy Alaimo, "Oceanic Origins, Plastic Activism, and New Materialism at Sea," in Serenella Iovino and Serpil Oppermann, ed., *Material Ecocriticism* (Bloomington: Indiana University Press, 2014), 186–203, 194. On plastic's postwar transformation from being a synthetic replacement for natural materials, to being defined by its disposability—"made to be wasted"—see Guy Hawkins, "Plastics," in Imre Szeman, Jennifer Wenzel, and Patricia Yaeger, eds., *Fueling Culture: 101 Words for Energy and Environment* (New York: Fordham University Press, 2017), 271–274; and Jeffrey Meikle, *American Plastic: A Cultural History* (New Brunswick, N.J.: Rutgers University Press, 1995). On the strange temporality of plastic pollution—which, like other forms of postindustrial waste, cannot be cleaned up but simply moved from one place to another—see Carmella Gray-Cosgrove, Max Liboion and Josh Lepawsky, "The Challenges of Temporality to Depollution and Remediation," *S.A.P.I.EN.S.* 8, no. 1 (2015), http://journals.openedition.org/sapiens/1740 (accessed October 25, 2021).
35. Plastic Soup Foundation, https://www.plasticsoupfoundation.org/en/plastic-problem/plastic-soup/more-plastic-than-fish/ (accessed March 18, 2022).
36. On the challenge of conceptualizing such nonlinear modes of causation, or "agentic swarms," see Jane Bennett, *Vibrant Matter* (Durham: Duke University Press, 2010), 32, and Hawkins, "Plastics." See also Jennifer Gabrys on the mutation of waste and the "formless" and "disruptive" geographies of environmental sinks and spills. "Sink: the Dirt of Systems." *Society and Space* 27, no. 4 (January 2009): 666–681. For a digital archive of the entire *SOUP* series, see Barker's website, https://www.mandy-barker.com/soup-2.
37. Ronda, *Remainders*, 11.
38. Ronda, 13.
39. Nicole Starosielsky, "Fixed Flow: Undersea Cables as Media Infrastructure," in Lisa Parks and Nicole Starosielski, eds., *Signal Traffic: Critical Studies of Media Infrastructures* (Urbana: University of Illinois Press, 2015), 53–70, 61.
40. A spinning black and white beach ball icon first appeared in the late 1980s, on Unix machines; Apple's rainbow version of the beach ball appeared with Mac OS X in 2001. Jason Farman, *Delayed Response* (New Haven: Yale University Press, 2018), 70.
41. Gregory E. Swain, "Troubleshoot the Spinning Beach Ball," *Macworld*, May 28, 2010, https://www.macworld.com/article/1151583/spinningbeachballofdeath.html (accessed April 10, 2022); Farman, 70.
42. Farman, 67.
43. On the SBBOD as indexing the "unknowable nature of both our technology and our world," see Neta Alexander, "Rage Against the Machine: Buffering, Noise, and Perpetual Anxiety in the Age of Connected Viewing," *Cinema Journal* 56, no. 2 (2017): 1–24, 23–24.
44. Glyderfach, "Q: The spinning beach ball," posted to the Apple Support Community on May 1, 2020 8:03 p.m., https://discussions.apple.com/thread/251328021 (accessed April 10, 2022).

45. On the temporality of waiting as both "symptom of" and "hedge against" the "diffuse uncertainties of risk society," see Martin, *Contemporary Drift*, 97–98.
46. Alain Corbin, *The Lure of the Sea: Discovery of the Seaside in the Western World, 1750–1840*, trans. Jocelyn Phelps (New York: Penguin, 1995), 68–72. See Jane Austen's mockery of the beach resort as peopled by hypochondriac "cure"-takers and real estate developers in her posthumously published *Sanditon* (1817), a text Corbin identifies as the first beach-set novel.
47. According to Corbin, "suddenly, what counted most was to breathe well." Corbin, *The Lure of the Sea*, 71. On the intensified public health focus on dangerous urban temperatures around the turn of the century, see Christian Granger, *Les corps d'été: Naissance d'une variation saisonnière au xxème siècle* (Paris: Autrement, 2009), chapter 1.
48. On the historical medicalization of sunlight, see Simon Carter, "The Medicalization of Sunlight in the Early Twentieth Century," *Journal of Historical Sociology* 25, no. 1 (2012): 83–105. On the poetics of modernist heliotherapy, see Kristy Martin, "Modernism and the Medicalization of Sunlight: D. H. Lawrence, Katherine Mansfield, and the Sun Cure," *Modernism/modernity* 23, no. 2 (2016): 423–441. On solar radiation as a central concern of modern architecture, see Daniel A. Barber, *Modern Architecture and Climate: Design Before Air Conditioning* (Princeton, N.J.: Princeton University Press, 2020). On the sun as "the dominant natural force shaping what people searched for, did and built at the seaside" by the 1930s, see Fred Gray, *Designing the Seaside: Architecture, Society, and Nature* (London: Reaktion, 2006), 31.
49. Adrien Achille Proust and Gilbert Ballet, *L'Hygiène du neurasthénique* (Paris: Masson & Cie, 1897), 241–243, *Treatment of Neurasthenia*, trans. Peter Campbell Smith (New York: Pelton, 1903), 172–173.
50. Thomas Mann, *Death in Venice and Seven Other Stories*, trans. H. T. Lowe-Porter (New York: New Directions, 2010), 15, 11, 6.
51. Mann, 27, 7, 33, 46.
52. Mann, 47.
53. Mann, 47, 51.
54. Michael Taussig, "The Beach (A Fantasy)," *Critical Inquiry* 26, no. 2 (Winter 2000): 248–278, 258.
55. See my introduction for a discussion of "beach nourishment," whereby seaside erosion is (temporarily) corrected via an ecologically damaging process of dredging and filling. Beach nourishment began at Coney Island in 1922–1923 and spread to Europe in the 1950s. On the history and impact of this process, see Vince Beiser, *The World in a Grain: The Story of Sand and How It Transformed Civilization* (New York: Riverhead Press, 2018); Charles H. Peterson and Melanie J. Bishop, "Assessing the Environmental Impacts of Beach Nourishment," *BioScience* 55, no. 10 (October 2005): 887–896; and Stephen L. Harp, *The Riviera, Exposed: An Ecohistory of Postwar Tourism and North African Labor* (Ithaca: Cornell University Press, 2022), chapter 4.
56. E. P. Thompson, "Time, Work-Discipline, and Industrial Capitalism," *Past and Present* 38 (December 1967): 56–97, 57, 60.
57. Thompson, 79, 82, 58, 83, 90–91.

5. TIDEWRACK, BECKETT TO SUNDE

58. Anson Rabinbach, *The Human Motor: Energy, Fatigue, and the Origins of Modernity* (Berkeley: University of California Press, 1992), 40. Those who suffer today from chronic fatigue syndrome also suffer from epistemic invalidation by medical authorities. On this, and for a broader feminist/disability studies critique of the cognitive and social authority of medicine, see Susan Wendell, *The Rejected Body: Feminist Philosophical Reflections on Disability* (New York: Routledge, 1996), chapter 5. See also poet Anne Boyer's remarkable account of chemotherapy-induced exhaustion in the "age of unlimited can." Anne Boyer, *The Undying* (New York: Picador, 2019), 253.
59. Rabinbach, 44.
60. Jonathan Crary, *24/7: Late Capitalism and the Ends of Sleep* (London: Verso, 2013), 13. On the exhausting, "interminable" and "insatiable" logic of neoliberalism, see also Boltanski and Chiapello, *The New Spirit of Capitalism*, 5. Boltanski and Chiapello analyze twentieth-century capitalism as marked by deregulation, speculation, the massive growth of multinational firms, and the reorganization of labor toward a temporary workforce, flexible hours, and a "whittling down [of] the social security systems established during a century of social struggles" (xxxviii).
61. *Exhaustion* refers here to the state of earth systems and not simply to the depletion of fossil fuel reserves. Given the future of deep-sea fracking and other extreme techniques, it may be that extraction and combustion of carbon will make the earth uninhabitable before the reserves themselves are used up. On the importance of leaving oil, fossil methane, and coal in the earth, see Dan Welsby, James Price, Steve Pye, and Paul Ekins, "Unextractable Fossil Fuels in a 1.5 °C world," *Nature* 597 (2021): 230–234, https://doi.org/10.1038/s41586-021-03821-8.
62. Anna Katharina Schaffner, *Exhaustion: A History* (New York: Columbia University Press, 2017), 3,4, 9. See also Anna Sajecki, "Exhaust" in Szeman, Wenzel, and Yaeger, *Fueling Culture*, 152–154.
63. Franco Berardi, "Exhaustion," in Szeman, Wenzel, and Yaeger, 155–157. On modernism's dialectic of exhaustion and regeneration, see Andrew Kalaidjian, *Exhausted Ecologies: Modernism and Environmental Recovery* (Cambridge: Cambridge University Press, 2020), 8. On "burnout" as an occupational hazard for service sector (or "pink-collar") workers, see Arlie Hochschild, *The Managed Heart: Commercialization of Human Feeling* (Berkeley: University of California Press, 2012), 187; on burnout as a more generalized condition of life in late capitalism—"what happen[s] to you when you want everything"—see Jill Lepore, "It's Just Too Much," *New Yorker*, May 24, 2021. See also Byung-Chul Han on burnout as the "signature affliction" of a society that suffers from the "excessive positivity" of overproduction and overachievement. Byung-Chul Han, *The Burnout Society* (Stanford: Stanford University Press, 2015), chapter 1.
64. Moore, *Capitalism in the Web of Life*, 227.
65. Siegfried Kracauer, "Those Who Wait," in *The Mass Ornament: Weimar Essays*, trans. Thomas Y. Levin (Cambridge, Mass.: Harvard University Press, 1995), 138–139 (original emphasis).
66. Elena Gorfinkel, "Weariness, Waiting: Endurance and Art Cinema's Tired Bodies," *Discourse* 34, nos. 2–3 (Fall/Spring 2012): 311–347, 315, 342, 320. On the ambiguity of the fatigued body—which both symptomatizes and evades medical discourse—see also Louise Hornby, "Downwrong: The Pose of Tiredness,"

Modern Fiction Studies 65, no. 1 (Spring 2019): 207–227, 208. On waiting as a subtle, variegated state of being, allied alternately with boredom and with the "exhibition of imperial panoramas," see Walter Benjamin, *The Arcades Project,* trans. Rolf Tiedemann (Cambridge, Mass.: Harvard University Press, 1999), 528.

67. Samuel Beckett, *The Complete Dramatic Works* (London: Faber & Faber, 1986), 139, 140, 141. In act 2, when Winnie is entombed to her head, she admits that her neck hurts, but then immediately intones, "Ah that's better" (166).
68. Beckett, 71, 129.
69. Beckett, 153.
70. Samuel Beckett, *Oh les beaux jours* (Paris: Minuit, 1963), 69.
71. Maurice Harmon, ed., *No Author Better Served: The Correspondence of Samuel Beckett and Alan Schneider* (Cambridge, Mass.: Harvard University Press, 1998), 77, 94. Many productions—even Beckett's own in 1979—disregard the stage direction specifying that the parasol should have yellow and blue stripes. These colors were in vogue ("les couleurs à la mode," "le goût du jour") in France in the late 1950s, particularly on the beach, as Agnès Varda notes in *Du côté de la côte* (1958), a promotional film about Nice that features bathing suits and hotel facades in yellow and blue. On the strong sense of "picture" that guided Beckett's theater, see John Haynes and James Knowlson, *Images of Beckett* (Cambridge: Cambridge University Press, 2003).
72. Howard Taubman, "Beckett's Happy Days," *New York Times,* Sept 18, 1961.
73. "Theater Look-In: Samuel Beckett's Happy Days, with Fiona Shaw & Deborah Warner," https://www.youtube.com/watch?v=u8Yyo6T5g14 (accessed March 8, 2022).
74. Beckett, *The Complete Dramatic Works,* 140.
75. Beckett, 142, 149, 154.
76. Beckett, 154.
77. Charles Lyons, *Samuel Beckett* (New York: Macmillan, 1983), 124. On "suspension" as a midcentury structure of feeling, allied particularly with the act of waiting, see Claire Seiler, *Midcentury Suspension: Literature and Waiting in the Wake of World War II* (New York: Columbia University Press, 2020).
78. See William Cronon on the biblical resonance of "wilderness" and its connection to Christ's desert retreat, where both angels and wild beasts are encountered. Cronon also helpfully deconstructs "wilderness" in the U.S. context as the fantasy of a sublime frontier, a region neither pathless nor uninhabited in actuality, but appearing so to the settler-colonialist mindset. William Cronon, "The Trouble with Wilderness; or, Getting Back to the Wrong Nature," in *Uncommon Ground: Rethinking the Human Place in Nature* (New York: Norton, 1995), 69–90. In the French version of the play, Beckett translates "wilderness" as "desert." Beckett, *Oh les beaux jours,* 27, 34, 51.
79. Sianne Ngai, *Ugly Feelings* (Cambridge, Mass.: Harvard University Press, 2007), 215, 246.
80. Beckett, *The Complete Dramatic Works,* 154.
81. The law of June 20, 1936, made vacations a political right in France, authorizing all salaried employees or wage earners to a fifteen-day paid vacation. The expansion of paid leave was the focus of union negotiations in following decades, and in 1955 the French government officially expanded the *congé payé* to three weeks, and then to four weeks in 1969. On how this phenomenon "forced a new

understanding of vacations," see Ellen Furlough, "Making Mass Vacations: Tourism and Consumer Culture in France, 1930s to 1970s," *Comparative Studies in Society and History* 40, no. 2 (April 1998): 247–286, 250. Furlough traces the different trajectories of social (labor-oriented) and commercial tourism, which converged in the 1950s around images of happy heterosexual couples (269).

82. *Bonjour Tristesse* traffics in a fantasy of French luxury as seaside idleness, or "love of diversion and frivolity." Françoise Sagan, *Bonjour Tristesse*, trans. Irene Ash (New York: Harper Collins, 2008), 10. Kristin Ross observes that the "Sagan myth" commodified "a timeless lifestyle based on money, youth, cars and speed." Kristin Ross, *Fast Cars, Clean Bodies: Decolonization and the Reordering of French Culture* (Cambridge: MIT Press, 1994), 22. The beach should also figure on this list. Roger Vadim's *And God Created Woman* was popular in France, but made an even bigger splash in the U.S., where it grossed 4 million at the box office upon its release in 1958. Chuck Stephens, "And God Created Woman," *Criterion Collection*, July 17, 2000, https://www.criterion.com/current/posts/80-and-god-created-woman (accessed April 10, 2022).

83. These films present the beach as a stage for the construction of heterosexuality, and a space in which female bodies in particular—barely held in check by the rituals of bourgeois courtship and marriage—must be managed and disciplined. As one character exclaims in *Muscle Beach Party*, eying a woman who's gazing lustily at a male bodybuilder, "I don't like the look in her eye. That's not a ladylike look!" In *Gidget,* it's the heroine's lack of interest in dating that must be corrected; she fears that there's something "weird" about her or that she needs "a few hormone shots" because, as she puts it, "I don't like dates" and will likely "die an old maid," "fringed, out in the cold." Gidget is finally straightened out, fulfilling the promise of the film's opening song: "Although she's not king sized, her finger is ring sized."

84. Katherine Worth, *Waiting for Godot and Happy Days: Text and Performance* (New York: Macmillan, 1990), 88; Lyons, *Samuel Beckett,* 132; Katie Charles, "Chin Up," *New York Magazine,* December 26, 2007, https://nymag.com/arts/theater/features/42365/ (accessed June 29, 2021).

85. Lyons, *Samuel Beckett,* 132.

86. Lauren Berlant, *Cruel Optimism* (Durham: Duke University Press, 2011), 96.

87. For context, see Joffre Dumazedier's pioneering 1962 sociological study of France's new cultures of leisure. According to Dumazedier's hopeful assessment, leisure activities have the potential to enable new forms of lifelong learning and support the full flourishing of human personality ("l'épanouissement complet de la personnalité"). Joffre Dumazedier, *Vers une civilisation du loisir?* (Paris: Seuil, 1962), 27–28, 29.

88. Vanessa R. Schwartz, *It's So French! Hollywood, Paris, and the Making of Cosmopolitan Film Culture* (Chicago: University of Chicago Press, 2007), 144, 103.

89. On Bardot's fame as based on her "spectacular body, a body that assumes its power precisely as spectacle," see Damon Young, *Making Sex Public* (Durham: Duke University Press, 2018), 33. On the way mass culture shaped Beckett's attention to the "conditions of spectatorship," his audience's awareness of itself as an audience, and his worry that spectatorship might become an "activity resembling window-shopping," see Martin Harries, "Theater and Media Before 'New' Media: Beckett's *Film* and *Play*," *Theater* 42, no. 2 (2012): 6–25, 22–23.

5. TIDEWRACK, BECKETT TO SUNDE

90. Beckett, *The Complete Dramatic Works*, 138; Beckett to Schneider, August 17, 1961, in Harmon, *No Author Better Served*, 94.
91. Jonathan Kalb, *Beckett in Performance* (Cambridge: Cambridge University Press, 1991), 89.
92. Beckett to Schneider, August 17, 1961, in Harmon, *No Author Better Served*, 95. Katherine Worth suggests that when Beckett directed the play at the Schiller-Theater Werkstatt he advised the actor to "do" the various voices in act 1 and bring out the childish notes in her chatter; this colorful voice should drain away into a "white voice" in act 2. Worth, *Waiting for Godot and Happy Days*, 87.
93. Beckett to Schneider, August 17, 1961, in Harmon, *No Author Better Served*, 95. In Beckett's notebook for the 1971 Berlin production of the play, he meticulously records the number of Winnie's smiles: "31 smiles, 5 happy expressions." Quoted in S. E. Gontarski, *Beckett's* Happy Days: *A Manuscript Study* (Columbus: Ohio State University Press, 2017), 15. Ginette Vincendeau notes that Bardot was much criticized for her "flat" verbal delivery. Ginette Vincendeau, *Brigitte Bardot* (London: British Film Institute, 2013), 25.
94. On Bardot's performance of erotic naturalness—she's at once a "strip-tease artist" and a "child-woman"—see Simone de Beauvoir's surprisingly laudatory August 1, 1959, *Esquire* article, "Brigitte Bardot and the Lolita Syndrome," later republished in French as "Brigitte Bardot et le syndrome de Lolita," in *Les écrits de Simone de Beauvoir,* ed. Claude Rancis and Fernande Gontier (Paris: Gallimard, 1979), 363–376.
95. On commonalities between Winnie and Dielman, see Anthony Parasceva, *Beckett and Cinema* (London: Bloomsbury, 2017). Parasceva argues that the 1979 production Beckett himself directed especially denaturalizes Winnie's gendered routines by underscoring the "mechanized formality" of her gestures (163).
96. Dumazedier notes that his culture's "new law of happiness" cast the person who did not know how to "profit" from their free time as "incomplete" or "backward." Dumazedier, *Vers une civilisation du loisir?*, 21–22. Alain Corbin observes that the idea of leisure became, during this period, a "temps pour soi" ("me time") and specifically "time for the body"; this idea eventually eclipsed the right- and left-wing idea of vacation as a way of disciplining workers via regeneration. Alain Corbin, ed., *L'Avènement des loisirs, 1850–1960* (Paris: Aubier, 1998), 414.
97. Beckett, *The Complete Dramatic Works*, 152.
98. James Knowlson, *Damned to Fame: The Life of Samuel Beckett* (New York: Simon and Schuster, 1996), 447.
99. Beckett, *The Complete Dramatic Works*, 155, 156.
100. Lyons, *Samuel Beckett*, 128; Lois Oppenheim, *Directing Beckett* (Ann Arbor: University of Michigan Press, 1997), 164.
101. Oppenheim, *Directing Beckett*, 166. On Beckett's intense focus on the body as both subject and medium of his theater, see Anna McMullan, *Performing Embodiment in Beckett's Drama* (New York: Routledge, 2010).
102. Katie Charles, "Chin Up," *New York Magazine,* December 26, 2007, https://nymag.com/arts/theater/features/42365/.
103. Beckett to Schneider, September 15, 1961, in Harmon, *No Author Better Served*, 110.
104. Knowlson, *Damned to Fame*, 447.
105. "Theater Look-In."

5. TIDEWRACK, BECKETT TO SUNDE

106. Jessica Wolf, "Stillness Is the Move: Coaching Dianne Wiest for *Happy Days*," *American Theater*, April 24, 2017, https://www.americantheatre.org/2017/04/24/stillness-is-the-move-coaching-dianne-wiest-for-happy-days/.
107. Kracauer, "Those Who Wait," 138–139.
108. On the play's brimming intertextuality, see S. E. Gontarski, "Literary Allusions in *Happy Days*," in *On Beckett: Essays and Criticism* (London: Anthem, 2012), 232–244. On Beckett's directorial insistence on the subtle timing of silences, see Jean-Michel Rabaté, "Editor's Introduction," in *The New Samuel Beckett Studies*, 1–16 (Cambridge: Cambridge University Press, 2019), 8.
109. Beckett, *The Complete Dramatic Works*, 152–153. Beckett conveys such subtly variegated pause lengths ("maximum," "long," etc.) differently in the French version of the play. In the above-cited passage, for instance, the French version displaces the variation in timing from the stage direction to the monologue itself. Where the English text simply reads, "Now hardly at all," the French stretches and shades the line into a three-part, three-pause vocalization: "Autrefois. (*Un temps.*) Plus maintenant. (*Un temps.*) Presque plus. (*Un temps.*)" Beckett, *Oh les beaux jours*, 42–43.
110. "Theater Look-In."
111. For an excellent study of Beckett's comedic timing, see Laura Salisbury, *Samuel Beckett: Laughing Matters, Comic Timing* (Edinburgh: Edinburgh University Press, 2012). Salisbury argues that Beckett's "weakened and etiolated" situation comedies fixate on "syncopations, hiccups, and on limping and hindered progression" that effectively register "the complex, often abrasive, sensation of time passing." Beckett's "comic signature," in Salisbury's view, is a "form of syncopation in which action is rendered out of step with words" (3, 2). This is certainly the case in *Happy Days*, as Winnie's verbal patter pulls against her physical incapacity. Yet while Salisbury references *Happy Days* as an example of the comedic thrust of Beckett's work, she contends that the play abjects femininity by planting Winnie in the ground. For Warner, by contrast, Winnie is the comedian and not the joke.
112. On duration as the "connective tissue" linking art history to performance studies, see Shannon Jackson and Julia Bryan-Wilson's introduction to their special issue, "Time Zones: Durational Art and Its Contexts," *Representations* 136, no. 1 (2016): 1–20, 1.
113. This phrase is found on the opera-performance's official website, "Sun & Sea," https://sunandsea.lt/en. On participatory art as a global phenomenon of rising importance since the 1990s, see Claire Bishop, *Artificial Hells: Participatory Art and the Politics of Spectatorship* (London: Verso, 2012).
114. *Sun & Sea* premiered in 2017 with Lithuanian libretto and was translated into English for the 2019 Venice Biennale. I saw the work in 2021 at the Brooklyn Academy of Music.
115. Sun & Sea (Marina), https://sunandsea.lt/en (accessed April 16, 2022).
116. Sun & Sea.
117. Ronda, *Remainders*, 13.
118. Roland Barthes, "Sur la plage," in *Oeuvres complètes*, 5 vols. (Paris: Seuil, 2002), 4:509–510. For a discussion of this experimental corporeal mode, see my introduction.

5. TIDEWRACK, BECKETT TO SUNDE

119. Ronda identifies this tension between careless weekenders and watchful dwellers in Lynn Niedecker's postwar poetry. Ronda, *Remainders*, 31.
120. I draw inspiration here from Sarah Ensor and Steven Swarbrick's 2021 ACLA seminar "The Climate of Fatigue: What Comes After Exhaustion?" On the idea that the Anthropocene should be considered a transition point or "boundary event" rather than an epoch, see Donna Haraway, *Staying with the Trouble: Making Kin in the Chthulucene* (Durham: Duke University Press, 2016).
121. Sarah Cameron Sunde, "Reflections," "Climate Realism," *Resilience* 7, nos. 2–3 (Spring-Fall 2020): 258–270, 266. A vast and growing literature documents the accelerating pace of sea-level rise, its complex and interlocking causes, and its effects on shorelines and coastal communities. See, for instance, Vivien Gornitz, *Rising Seas: Past, Present, Future* (New York: Columbia University Press, 2013); Elizabeth Rush, *Rising: Dispatches from the New American Shore* (Minneapolis: Milkweed, 2018); and Orrin H. Pilkey and Keith C. Pilkey, *Sea Level Rise: A Slow Tsunami on America's Shores* (Durham: Duke University Press, 2019).
122. Eve Kosofsky Sedgwick, "Reality and Realization," in *The Weather in Proust* (Durham: Duke University Press, 2011), 206–215, 208, 213. As Sedgwick observes (in the context of her own Buddhist practice and cancer diagnosis), "realization [tends] to lag behind knowledge by months or eons" (209).
123. Peggy Phelan also emphasizes this point in her reflection on 36.5. "Freedom," "Climate Realism," *Resilience: A Journal of the Environmental Humanities* 7, nos. 2–3 (Spring-Fall 2020): 253–256.
124. Sunde, "Reflections," 264.
125. On a negative form of hope—to dis-hope (*désespérer*)—as an alternative to both despair (*se désespérer*) and to the ideology of progress, and thus as the only possible response to the realities of climate disruption, see Bruno Latour, *Facing Gaia: Eight Lectures on the New Climatic Regime*, trans. Catherine Porter (London: Polity, 2017), 13.
126. Una Chaudhuri, ed., introduction, "Climate Realism," *Resilience: A Journal of the Environmental Humanities* 7, nos. 2–3 (Spring-Fall 2020): 207–215, 214, 211.
127. Sunde, "Reflections," 260. As Sunde puts it, "the water is my collaborator and the risks are real." "Vision," Unpublished MS, December 10, 2018.
128. Sunde, "Reflections," 265.

WORKS CITED

Adamowsky, Natasha. *The Mysterious Science of the Sea, 1775–1943*. New York: Routledge, 2015.
Agard-Jones, Vanessa. "What the Sands Remember." *GLQ* 18, nos. 2–3 (2012): 325–346.
Alaimo, Stacy. "Oceanic Origins, Plastic Activism, and New Materialism at Sea." In *Material Ecocriticism*, edited by Serenella Iovino and Serpil Oppermann, 186–203. Bloomington: Indiana University Press, 2014.
Albaret, Céleste. *Monsieur Proust*. Translated by Barbara Bray. New York: New York Review of Books, 1973.
Alexander, Neta. "Rage Against the Machine: Buffering, Noise, and Perpetual Anxiety in the Age of Connected Viewing." *Cinema Journal* 56, no. 2 (2017): 1–24.
Allen, David. *The Naturalist in Britain: A Social History*. Princeton, N.J.: Princeton University Press, 1994.
Allen, Nicholas, Nick Groom, and Jos Smith, eds. *Coastal Works: Cultures of the Atlantic Edge*. Oxford: Oxford University Press, 2017.
Allewaert, Monique. *Ariel's Ecology: Plantations, Personhood, and Colonialism in the American Tropics*. Minneapolis: University of Minnesota Press, 2013.
Alt, Christina. *Virginia Woolf and the Natural World*. Cambridge: Cambridge University Press, 2010.
Alter, Robert. *Imagined Cities: Urban Experience and the Language of the Novel*. New Haven: Yale University Press, 2005.
Altman, Janet Gurkin. *Epistolarity: Approaches to a Form*. Columbus: Ohio University Press, 1982.
Anderson, Fiona. *Cruising the Dead River: David Wojnarowicz and New York's Ruined Waterfront*. Chicago: University of Chicago Press, 2019.
Apel, Dora. *Beautiful Terrible Ruins: Detroit and the Anxiety of Decline*. New Brunswick, N.J.: Rutgers University Press, 2015.

Apter, Emily. "Toward a Unisex Erotics: Claude Cahun and Geometric Modernism." In A. Schaffner and S. Weller, eds., *Modernist Eroticisms: European Literature After Sexology*, 134–149. London: Palgrave, 2012.
Armstrong, Nancy. *Desire and Domestic Fiction: A Political History of the Novel*. New York: Oxford University Press, 1990.
Augé, Marc. *L'Impossible voyage: Le tourisme et ses images*. Paris: Rivages, 1997.
Aviram, Amittai. *Telling Rhythm: Body and Meaning in Poetry*. Ann Arbor: University of Michigan Press, 1994.
Baedeker, Karl. *Great Britain: Handbook for Travelers, with 28 Maps, 65 Plans, and a Panorama*. Leipzig: Baedeker, 1910.
Bainbridge, Simon. *Mountaineering and British Romanticism*. Oxford: Oxford University Press, 2020.
Banfield, Anne. *The Phantom Table: Woolf, Fry, Russell, and the Epistemology of Modernism*. Cambridge: Cambridge University Press, 2007.
Barak, On. "Heat: A History." Unpublished MS, December 11, 2021.
Baranowski, Shelley, and Ellen Furlough. *Being Elsewhere: Tourism, Consumer Culture, and Identity in Modern Europe and North America*. Ann Arbor: University of Michigan Press, 2001.
Barber, Daniel. *Modern Architecture and the Climate: Design Before Air Conditioning*. Princeton, N.J.: Princeton University Press, 2020.
Barickman, B. J. *From Sea-Bathing to Beach-Going: A Social History of the Beach in Rio de Janeiro, Brazil*. Edited by Hendrik Kraay and Bryan McCann. Albuquerque: University of New Mexico Press, 2022.
Barker, Mandy. *Altered Ocean*. London: Overlapse, 2019.
Barletta, Vincent. *Rhythm: Form and Dispossession*. Chicago: University of Chicago Press, 2020.
Barthes, Roland. *Comment vivre ensemble: cours et séminaires au Collège de France (1976–1977)*. Paris: Seuil, 2002.
——. *How to Live Together: Novelistic Simulations of Some Everyday Spaces*. Translated by Kate Briggs. New York: Columbia University Press, 2012.
——. *The Neutral: Lecture Course at the College de France (1977–1978)*. Translated by Denis Hollier and Rosalind Krauss. New York: Columbia University Press, 2005.
——. *Le Neutre: notes de cours au Collège de France (1977–1978)*. Paris: Seuil, 2002.
——. *Oeuvres complètes*. 5 vols. Paris: Seuil, 2002.
Bateman, Benjamin. *The Modernist Art of Queer Survival*. New York: Oxford University Press, 2017.
Baucom, Ian. *Specters of the Atlantic: Finance Capital, Slavery, and the Philosophy of History*. Durham: Duke University Press, 2005.
"Beach Access." Beachapedia. www.beachapedia.org/Beach_Access. Last modified August 26, 2019.
Beauvoir, Simone de. "Brigitte Bardot et le syndrome de Lolita." In *Les écrits de Simone de Beauvoir*, edited by Claude Rancis and Fernande Gontier, 363–376. Paris: Gallimard, 1979.
Bech, Henning. *When Men Meet: Homosexuality and Modernity*. Translated by Teresa Mesquit and Tim Davies. Chicago: University of Chicago Press, 1997.
Beckett, Samuel. *The Complete Dramatic Works*. London: Faber & Faber, 1986.
——. *Oh les beaux jours*. Paris: Minuit, 1963.

WORKS CITED

Beiser, Vince. *The World in a Grain: The Story of Sand and How It Transformed Civilization.* New York: Riverhead, 2018.
Bellos, David. *Jacques Tati: His Life and Art.* New York: Random House, 2001.
Bely, Andrey. *Peterburg.* Translated by Robert E. Maguire and John E. Malmstad. Bloomington: Indiana University Press, 1978.
Benjamin, Walter. *The Arcades Project.* Translated by Rolf Tiedemann. Cambridge, Mass.: Harvard University Press, 1999.
———. *Illuminations.* Edited by Hannah Arendt. Translated by Harry Zohn. New York: Schocken, 1968.
———. *Selected Writing,* vol. 2, part 2. Edited by Michael W. Jennings, Howard Eileen, and Gary Smith. Cambridge, Mass.: Harvard University Press, 1999.
Bennett, Jane. *Influx and Efflux: Writing Up with Walt Whitman.* Durham: Duke University Press, 2020.
———. *Vibrant Matter.* Durham: Duke University Press, 2010.
Benveniste, Emile. "The Notion of Rhythm in its Linguistic Expression." In *Problems in General Linguistics.* Translated by Mary Elizabeth Meek, 281–313. Coral Gables: University of Miami Press, 1971.
Bergson, Henri. *L'Evolution créatrice.* Paris: PUF, 1998.
Berlant, Lauren. "The Commons: Infrastructures for Troubling Times." *Environment and Planning D: Society and Space* 34, no. 3 (2016): 393–419.
———. *Cruel Optimism.* Durham: Duke University Press, 2011.
Berlant, Lauren, and Michael Warner. "Sex in Public." *Critical Inquiry* 24, no. 2 (Winter 1998): 547–566.
Berman, Jessica. *Modernist Fiction, Cosmopolitanism, and the Politics of Community.* Cambridge: Cambridge University Press, 2001.
Birtchnell, Thomas, Satya Savitzky, and John Urry, eds. *Cargomobilities: Moving Materials in a Global Age.* London: Routledge, 2019.
Bishop, Claire. *Artificial Hells: Participatory Art and the Politics of Spectatorship.* London: Verso, 2012.
Bloul, Scheherazade, Shakira Hussein, and Scott Poynting. "Diasporas and Dystopias on the Beach: Burkini Wars in France and Australia." In *The Routledge International Handbook of Islamophobia.* New York: Routledge, 2019.
Blum, Hester. *The View from the Mast-Head: Maritime Imagination and Antebellum American Sea Narratives.* Chapel Hill: University of North Carolina Press, 2008.
Boltanski, Luc, and Eve Chiapello. *The New Spirit of Capitalism.* Translated by Gregory Elliot. London: Verso, 2005.
Bonneuil, Christophe, and Jean-Baptiste Fressoz. *The Shock of the Anthropocene: The Earth, History, and Us.* Translated by David Fernbach. London: Verso, 2017.
Bordereaux, Laurent. "Seashore Law: The Core of French Public Maritime Law." *International Journal of Marine and Coastal Law* 29, no. 3 (2014): 402–414.
Boyer, Anne. *The Undying: Pain, Vulnerability, Mortality, Medicine, Art, Time, Dreams, Data, Exhaustion, Cancer, and Care.* New York: Picador, 2019.
Brandstetter, Gabriele. *Poetics of Dance: Body, Image, and Space in the Historical Avant-Gardes.* Translated by Elena Polzer and Mark Franko. New York: Oxford University Press, 2015.
Brannigan, John. *Archipelagic Modernism: Literature in the Irish and British Isles, 1890–1970.* Edinburgh: Edinburgh University Press, 2015.

Brisman, Shira. *Dürer and the Epistolary Mode of Address*. Chicago: University of Chicago Press, 2017.
Brown, Adrienne. *The Black Skyscraper: Architecture and the Perception of Race*. Baltimore: Johns Hopkins University Press, 2019.
Brown, Bill. "The Secret Life of Things: Virginia Woolf and the Matter of Modernism." *Modernism/modernity* 6 (April 1999): 1–28.
Brown, Stephanie J. "Marseille Exposed: Under Surveillance in Claude McKay's *Banjo* and *Romance in Marseille*." *English Language Notes* 59, no. 1 (April 2021): 93–108.
Brunner, Bernd. *The Ocean at Home: An Illustrated History of the Aquarium*. Translated by Ashley Marc Slapp. Princeton, N.J.: Princeton Architectural Press, 2005.
Bulson, Eric. *Novels, Maps, Modernity: The Spatial Imagination, 1850–2000*. London: Routledge, 2009.
Byrnes, Corey. *Fixing Landscape: A Techno-Poetic History of China's Three Gorges*. New York: Columbia University Press, 2019.
Cadieu, Morgane. "Afterword: The Littoral Museum of the Twenty-First Century." *Comparative Literature* 73, no. 2 (June 2021): 237–254.
Cadieu, Morgane, and Hannah Freed-Thall, eds. "Beaches and Ports." *Comparative Literature* 73, no. 2 (June 2021).
Cahun, Claude. *Écrits*. Edited by François Leperlier. Paris: Éditions Jean Michel Place, 2002.
Cahun, Claude, and Marcel Moore. *Vues et visions*. Paris: Georges Crès & Cie, 1919.
Camille, Michael. *Images on the Edge: The Margins of Medieval Art*. London: Reaktion, 1992.
Campbell, Margaret. "What Tuberculosis Did for Modernism: The Influence of a Curative Environment on Modernist Design and Architecture." *Medical History* 49, no. 4 (October 2005): 463–488.
Canaday, Margot. *The Straight State: Sexuality and Citizenship in Twentieth-Century America*. Princeton, N.J.: Princeton University Press, 2009.
Cano, Christine. *Proust's Deadline*. Urbana: University of Illinois Press, 2006.
Caro, Robert. *The Power Broker: Robert Moses and the Fall of New York*. New York: Vintage, 1975.
Carson, Rachel. *The Edge of the Sea*. New York: Houghton Mifflin Harcourt, 1998.
———. *The Sea Around Us*. New York: Oxford University Press, 1951.
———. *The Sense of Wonder*. New York: Harper Collins, 1998.
Carson, Rachel, and Dorothy Freeman. *Always, Rachel: The Letters of Rachel Carson and Dorothy Freeman, 1952–1964*. Edited by Martha Freeman. Boston: Beacon, 1995.
Carter, Simon. "The Medicalization of Sunlight in the Early Twentieth Century." *Journal of Historical Sociology* 25, no. 1 (2012): 83–105.
Carter, William. *Marcel Proust: A Life*. New Haven: Yale University Press, 2013.
———. *The Proustian Quest*. New York: New York University Press, 1994.
———. "The Vast Structure of Recollection: From Life to Literature." In *The Cambridge Companion to Proust*, edited by Richard Bales, 25–41. Cambridge: Cambridge University Press, 2001.
Césaire, Aimé. *The Complete Poems of Aimé Césaire: Bilingual Edition*. Translated by Clayton Eshleman and A. James Arnold. Middletown, Conn.: Wesleyan University Press, 2017.

WORKS CITED

Chambers, A. C. *Beauty in Common Things*. London: Society for Promoting Christian Knowledge, 1874.

Chang, Jennifer. "Pastoral and the Problem of Place in McKay's *Harlem Shadows*." In *A Companion to the Harlem Renaissance*, edited by Cherene Sherrard-Johnson, 187–202. Chichester: Wiley Blackwell, 2015.

Charles, Katie. "Chin Up." *New York Magazine*, December 26, 2007. https://nymag.com/arts/theater/features/42365/. Accessed June 29, 2021.

Charleston, Beth Duncuff. "The Bikini." In *Heilbrunn Timeline of Art History*. New York: Metropolitan Museum of Art, 2000– . Published online October 2004. http://www.metmuseum.org/toah/hd/biki/hd_biki.htm.

Chaudhuri, Una. Introduction to the special issue, "Climate Realism." *Resilience: A Journal of the Environmental Humanities* 7, nos. 2–3 (Spring-Fall 2020): 207–215.

Chauncey, George. *Gay New York: Gender, Urban Culture, and the Makings of the Gay Male World, 1890–1940*. New York: Basic Books, 1994.

Chen, Mel. *Animacies: Biopolitics, Racial Mattering, and Queer Affect*. Durham: Duke University Press, 2012.

Clark, T. J. *Farewell to an Idea: Episodes from the History of Modernism*. New Haven: Yale University Press, 1999.

———. *Image of the People: Gustave Courbet and the 1848 Revolution*. Berkeley: University of California Press, 1973.

Clements, Frederic Edward. *Research Methods in Ecology*. Lincoln: University Publishing, 1905.

Clover, Joshua. *Riot. Strike. Riot: The New Era of Uprisings*. London: Verso, 2019.

Cocteau, Jean. *Théâtre complet*. Paris: Gallimard, 2003.

Cohen, Jeffrey Jerome. *Stone: An Ecology of the Inhuman*. Minneapolis: University of Minnesota Press, 2015.

Cohen, Margaret. *The Novel and the Sea*. Princeton, N.J.: Princeton University Press, 2010.

Compagnon, Antoine. *Proust entre deux siècles*. Paris: Seuil, 1989.

Conron, John. *American Picturesque*. University Park: Penn State University Press, 2000.

Cooper, Wayne F. *Claude McKay: Rebel Sojourner in the Harlem Renaissance: A Biography*. Baton Rouge: Louisiana State University Press, 1996.

Corbett, Mary Jean. *Family Likeness: Sex, Marriage, and Incest from Jane Austen to Virginia Woolf*. Ithaca: Cornell University Press, 2010.

Corbin, Alain, ed. *L'Avènement des loisirs, 1850–1960*. Paris: Aubier, 1998.

———. *The Lure of the Sea: Discovery of the Seaside in the Western World, 1750–1840*. Translated by Jocelyn Phelps. New York: Penguin 1995.

Corcoran, Patricia L., Charles J. Moore, and Kelly Jazvac. "An Anthropogenic Marker Horizon in the Future Rock Record." *GSA Today* 24, no. 6 (June 2014). https://www.geosociety.org/gsatoday/archive/24/6/pdf/i1052-5173-24-6-4.pdf. Accessed March 18, 2022.

Cosgrove, Dennis. *Social Formation and Symbolic Landscape*. Madison: University of Wisconsin Press, 1984.

Coviello, Peter. *Tomorrow's Parties: Sex and the Untimely in Nineteenth-Century America*. New York: New York University Press, 2013.

Cowen, Deborah. *The Deadly Life of Logistics: Mapping Violence in Global Trade.* Minneapolis: University of Minnesota Press, 2014.

Crary, Jonathan. *24/7: Late Capitalism and the Ends of Sleep.* London: Verso, 2013.

Crimp, Douglas. "Alvin Baltrop: Pier Photographs, 1975–1986." *Artforum* 46, no. 6 (February 2008): 262–273.

Cronon, William. "The Trouble with Wilderness; or, Getting Back to the Wrong Nature." In *Uncommon Ground: Rethinking the Human Place in Nature,* 69–90. New York: Norton, 1995.

Culver, Lawrence. *The Frontier of Leisure: Southern California and the Shaping of Modern America.* New York: Oxford University Press, 2012.

Danius, Sara. "The Aesthetics of the Windshield: Proust and the Modernist Rhetoric of Speed," *Modernism/modernity* 8 no. 1 (January 2001): 99–126.

Daoud, Kamel. *The Meursault Investigations.* Translated by John Cullen. New York: Other, 2015.

Dardot, Pierre, and Christian Laval. *Common: On Revolution in the Twenty-First Century.* Translated by Matthew MacLellan. London: Bloomsbury, 2019.

Darrieussecq, Marie. *Il était une fois la plage.* Paris: Flammarion, 2000.

Davis, Mary E. *Classic Chic: Music, Fashion, and Modernism.* Berkeley: University of California Press, 2008.

Delany, Samuel. *Times Square Red, Times Square Blue.* New York: New York University Press, 1999.

De la Pradelle, Michèle, and Emmanuelle Lallement. "Paris-Plage: Célébrer un objet absent." In *Objets et mémoires,* edited by Octave Debary and Laurier Turgeon, 197–208. Paris: Éditions de la Maison des sciences de l'homme, 2007.

Deleuze, Gilles. *Abécédaire.* Interviews with Claire Parnet, filmed for television by Pierre-André Boutang, 1988–89.

Dell, Marion, and Marion Whybrow. *Virginia Woolf and Vanessa Bell: Remembering St Ives.* Cornwall: Tab House, 2003.

DeLoughrey, Elizabeth. "Submarine Futures of the Anthropocene." *Comparative Literature* 69, no. 1 (2017): 32–44.

Demuth, Bathsheba. *The Floating Coast: An Environmental History of the Bering Strait.* New York: Norton, 2019.

Denny, Mark W., and Stephen D. Gaines. *Encyclopedia of Tide Pools and Rocky Shores.* Berkeley: University of California Press, 2007.

Descombes, Vincent. *Proust: Philosophy of the Novel.* Translated by Catherine Chance Macksey. Stanford: Stanford University Press, 1992.

Devienne, Elsa. *La Ruée vers le sable: Une histoire environmentale des plages de Los Angeles au XXè siècle.* Paris: Sorbonne, 2020.

Dickinson, Emily. *The Gorgeous Nothings: Emily Dickinson's Envelope Poems.* Edited by Jen Bervin and Marta Werner. New York: New Directions, 2013.

Dinshaw, Carolyn. *How Soon Is Now? Medieval Texts, Amateur Readers, and the Queerness of Time.* Durham: Duke University Press, 2012.

Diserens, Corinne, ed. *Gordon Matta-Clark.* London: Phaidon, 2003.

Dornhelm, Richard B. "The Coney Island Public Beach and Boardwalk Improvement of 1923." In *Urban Beaches: Balancing Public Rights and Private Development,* ed. Lesley Ewing, Thomas Herrington, and Orville Magoon, 52–63. Reston, Va.: ASCE, 2003.

WORKS CITED

Doyle, Laura. *Freedom's Empire: Race and the Rise of the Novel in Atlantic Modernity, 1640–1940*. Durham: Duke University Press, 2008.
Dubois, Jacques. *Pour Albertine: Proust et le sens du social*. Paris: Seuil, 1997.
Duffy, Enda. *The Speed Handbook: Velocity, Pleasure, Modernism*. Durham: Duke University Press, 2009.
Dumazedier, Joffre. *Vers une civilisation du loisir?* Paris: Seuil, 1962.
Duncan, Isadora. *My Life*. New York: Liveright, 2013 [1927].
Duras, Marguerite. *The Sea Wall*. Translated by Herma Briffault. New York: Pellegrini & Cudahy, 1952.
Ebbesmeyer, Curtis, and Eric Scigliano. *Flotsametrics and the Floating World: How One Man's Obsession with Runaway Sneakers and Rubber Ducks Revolutionized Ocean Science*. New York: Harper Perennial, 2010.
Eells, Emily. "Proust pasticheur de Cocteau: Présentation d'un pastiche inédit." *Bulletin d'informations proustiennes* 12 (1981): 75–85.
Elko, Nicole, Tiffany Roberts Briggs, Lindino Benedet, Quin Robertson, Gordon Thomson, Bret M. Webb, and Kimberly Garvey. "A Century of U.S. Beach Nourishment." *Ocean and Coastal Management* 199 (January 2021). https://doi.org/10.1016/j.ocecoaman.2020.105406.
Ensor, Sara. "The Ecopoetics of Contact: Touching, Cruising, Gleaning." *ISLE: Interdisciplinary Studies in Literature and Environment* 25, no. 1 (Winter 2018): 150–168.
———. "Spinster Ecology: Rachel Carson, Sarah Orne Jewett, and Nonreproductive Futurity." *American Literature* 84, no. 2 (2012): 409–435.
Fabre, Michel. *From Harlem to Paris: Black American Writers in France, 1840–1980*. Urbana: University of Illinois Press, 1993.
Farman, Jason. *Delayed Response: The Art of Waiting from the Ancient to the Instant World*. New Haven: Yale University Press, 2018.
Favret, Mary. *Romantic Correspondence: Women, Politics, and the Fiction of Letters*. Cambridge: Cambridge University Press, 2005.
Ferguson, John. "A Sea Change: Thomas De Quincey and Mr. Carmichael in 'To the Lighthouse.'" *Journal of Modern Literature* 14, no. 1 (Summer 1987): 45–63.
Ferry, Elizabeth Emma, and Mandana E. Limbert, eds. *Timely Assets: The Politics of Resources and Their Temporalities*. Santa Fe: School for Advanced Research Press, 2008.
Fitzgerald, F. Scott. *The Great Gatsby*. New York: Scribner, 1996.
Flatley, Jonathan. *Like Andy Warhol*. Chicago: University of Chicago Press, 2017.
Flaubert, Gustave. *Madame Bovary*. Paris: Flammarion, 1986.
———. *Madame Bovary*. Translated by Lydia Davis. New York: Penguin, 2010.
Foster, John Bellamy, Brett Clark, and Richard York. *The Ecological Rift: Capitalism's War on the Earth*. New York: Monthly Review Press, 2010.
François, Anne-Lise. "'. . . and will do none': Gewalt in the Measure of a Parenthesis." *Critical Times* 2, no. 2 (August 2019): 285–294.
———. "Flower Fisting." *Postmodern Cultures* 22, no. 1 (September 2011).
———. *Open Secrets: The Literature of Uncounted Experience*. Stanford: Stanford University Press, 2008.
———. "Passing Impasse." *Comparative Literature* 72, no. 2 (June 2020): 240–257.
Freed-Thall, Hannah. "Speculative Modernism: Proust and the Stock Market." *Modernist Cultures* 12, no. 2 (2017): 153–172.

———. *Spoiled Distinctions: Aesthetics and the Ordinary in French Modernism*. New York: Oxford University Press, 2015.

———. "Thinking Small: Ecologies of Close Reading." In *Modernism and Close Reading*, edited by David James, 228–242. Oxford: Oxford University Press, 2020.

Freed-Thall, Hannah, and Dora Zhang. "Modernist Setting." *Modernism/modernity Print Plus* 3, no. 1 (March 2018). https://doi.org/10.26597/mod.0042.

Freeman, Elizabeth. "Packing History, Count(er)ing Generations." *New Literary History* 31 (2000): 727–744.

———. *Time Binds: Queer Temporalities, Queer Histories*. Durham: Duke University Press, 2010.

Fuggle, Sophie, and Nicholas Gledhill, eds. *La ligne d'écume: Encountering the French Beach*. London: Pavement, 2016.

Furlough, Ellen. "Making Mass Vacations: Tourism and Consumer Culture in France, 1930s to 1970s." *Comparative Studies in Society and History* 40, no. 2 (April 1998): 247–286.

———. "Une leçon des choses: Tourism, Empire, and the Nation in Interwar France." *French Historical Studies* 25, no. 3 (Summer 2002): 441–473.

Fuss, Diana. *Sense of an Interior: Four Writers and the Rooms That Shaped Them*. New York: Routledge, 2004.

Fyfe, Aileen. "Natural History and the Victorian Tourist: From Landscapes to Rock-Pools." In *Geographies of Nineteenth-Century Science*, edited by David N. Livingstone and Charles W. J. Withers, 371–393. Chicago: University of Chicago Press, 2011.

Gallo, Rubén. *Proust's Latin Americans*. Baltimore: Johns Hopkins University Press, 2014.

Galvin, Jim. "The Meteorological Legacy of the First World War." *Weather* (November 2018). https://doi.org/10.1002/wea.3424.

Garafola, Lynn. *Diaghilev's Ballets Russes*. New York: Oxford University Press, 1989.

Garlinger, Patrick Paul. *Confessions of the Letter Closet: Epistolary Fiction and Queer Desire in Modern Spain*. Minneapolis: University of Minnesota Press, 2005.

Genette, Gerard. *Narrative Discourse: An Essay in Method*. Translated by Jane E. Lewin. Ithaca: Cornell University Press, 1983.

Gillis, John. *The Human Shore*. Chicago: University of Chicago Press, 2012.

Gilmore, Ruth Wilson. "Fatal Couplings of Power and Difference." *The Professional Geographer* 54, no. 1 (February 2002): 15–24.

Gilpin, William. *Observations on the River Wye and Several Parts of South Wales &c. Relative Chiefly to Picturesque Beauty, Made in the Summer of the Year 1770*. London: Blamire, 1789.

Goffman, Erving. *Interaction Ritual: Essays on Face-to-Face Behavior*. New York: Pantheon, 1967.

Gontarski, S. E. *Beckett's Happy Days: A Manuscript Study*. Columbus: Ohio State University Press, 2017.

———. "Literary Allusions in *Happy Days*." In *On Beckett: Essays and Criticism*, edited by S. E. Gontarski, 232–244. London: Anthem, 2012.

Gorfinkel, Elena. "Weariness, Waiting: Endurance and Art Cinema's Tired Bodies." *Discourse* 34, nos. 2–3 (Fall/Spring 2012): 311–347.

Görg, Christophe, Christina Plank, Dominik Wiedenhofer, Andreas Mayor, Melanie Pichler, Anke Scharffartzik, and Fridolin Krausmann. "Scrutinizing the Great

Acceleration: The Anthropocene and Its Analytic Challenges for Social-Ecological Transformations." *Anthropocene Review* 7, no. 1 (December 2019): 42–61.
Gornitz, Vivien. *Rising Seas: Past, Present, Future.* New York: Columbia University Press, 2013.
Goujon, Francine. *Allusions littéraires et écriture cryptée dans l'oeuvre de Proust.* Paris: Honoré Champion, 2020.
———. "Références balzaciennes et cryptage autobiographique dans *Du côté de chez Swann.*" *Bulletin d'informations proustiennes* 33 (2003): 51–73.
Granata, Silvia. *The Victorian Aquarium: Literary Discussions on Nature, Culture, and Science.* Manchester: Manchester University Press, 2021.
Granger, Christophe. *Les corps d'été. Naissance d'une variation saisonnière au xxème siècle.* Paris: Autrement, 2009.
Gray, Fred. *Designing the Seaside: Architecture, Society, and Nature.* London: Reaktion, 2006.
Gray-Cosgrove, Carmella, Max Liboion, and Josh Lepawsky. "The Challenges of Temporality to Depollution and Remediation." *S.A.P.I.EN.S.* 8, no. 1 (2015). http://journals.openedition.org/sapiens/1740. Accessed October 25, 2021.
Guerlac, Suzanne. "Rancière and Proust: Two Temptations." In *Understanding Rancière, Understanding Modernism,* edited by Patrick Bray, 161–178. London: Bloomsbury, 2017.
———. *Proust, Photography, and the Time of Life: Ravaisson, Bergson, and Simmel.* London: Bloomsbury, 2020.
Haacke, Paul. *The Vertical Imagination and the Crisis of Transatlantic Modernism.* Oxford: Oxford University Press, 2021.
Hadjiafxendi, Kyriaki, and John Plunkett. "Science at the Seaside: Pleasure Hunts in Victorian Devon." In *Coastal Works: Cultures of the Atlantic Edge,* edited by Nicholas Allen, Nick Groom, and Jos Smith, 181–203. Oxford: Oxford University Press, 2017.
Hägglund, Martin. *Dying for Time: Proust, Woolf, Nabokov.* Cambridge, Mass.: Harvard University Press, 2012.
Hagius, Hugh. *Swasarnt Nerf's Gay Guides for 1949.* New York: Bibliogay, 2010.
Hagood, Amanda. "Wonders With the Sea: Rachel Carson's Ecological Aesthetic and the Mid-Century Reader." *Ecological Humanities* 2 (2013): 57–77.
Halberstam, Jack. *Wild Things: The Disorder of Desire.* Durham: Duke University Press, 2020.
Hamera, Judith. *Parlor Ponds: The Cultural Work of the American Home Aquarium, 1850–1970.* Ann Arbor: University of Michigan Press, 2012.
Han, Byung-Chul. *The Burnout Society.* Stanford: Stanford University Press, 2015.
Handyside, Fiona. *Cinema at the Shore: The Beach in French Film.* New York: Peter Lang, 2014.
Haraway, Donna. "Anthropocene, Capitalocene, Plantationocene, Chlulucene: Making Kin." *Environmental Humanities* 6 (2015): 159–165.
———. *Staying with the Trouble: Making Kin in the Chthulucene.* Durham: Duke University Press, 2016.
Hardin, Garrett. "The Tragedy of the Commons." *Science* 162, no. 3859 (1968): 1243–1248.

Hardt, Michael, and Antonio Negri. *Commonwealth*. Cambridge, Mass.: Harvard University Press, 2009.
——. *Multitude: War and Democracy in the Age of Empire*. New York: Penguin, 2004.
Harison, Casey. "The Rise and Decline of a Revolutionary Space: Paris's Place de Grève and the Stonemasons of Creuse, 1750–1900." *Journal of Social History* 34, no. 2 (2000): 403–436.
Harmon, Maurice, ed. *No Author Better Served: The Correspondence of Samuel Beckett and Alan Schneider*. Cambridge, Mass.: Harvard University Press, 1998.
Stephen L. Harp, *The Riviera, Exposed: An Ecohistory of Postwar Tourism and North African Labor*. Ithaca: Cornell University Press, 2022.
Harries, Martin. "Theater and Media Before 'New' Media: Beckett's *Film* and *Play*." *Theater* 42, no. 2 (2012): 6–25.
Hartman, Saidiya. *Lose Your Mother: A Journey Along the Atlantic Slave Route*. New York: Farrar, Straus, and Giroux, 2008.
——. *Wayward Lives, Beautiful Experiments: Intimate Histories of Social Upheaval*. New York: Norton, 2019.
Hawkins, Guy. "Plastics." In *Fueling Culture: 101 Words for Energy and Environment*, edited by Imre Szeman, Jennifer Wenzel, and Patricia Yaeger, 271–274. New York: Fordham University Press, 2017.
Hayes, Brent Edwards. *The Practice of Diaspora: Literature, Translation, and the Rise of Black Internationalism*. Cambridge, Mass.: Harvard University Press, 2003.
Haygarth, Stuart. *Strand*. Edited by Robert Macfarlane and Deyan Sudjic. London: Art/Books, 2016.
Haynes, John, and James Knowlson. *Images of Beckett*. Cambridge: Cambridge University Press, 2003.
Hayward, Eva. "Fingeryeyes: Impressions of Cup Corals." *Cultural Anthropology* 25, no. 4 (2010): 577–599.
——. "Sensational Jellyfish: Aquarium Affects and the Matter of Immersion." *differences* 23, no. 3 (2012): 161–196.
Heidegger, Martin. "The Origin of the Work of Art." In *Martin Heidegger: Off the Beaten Path*, edited by Julian Young and Kenneth Haynes, 1–56. Cambridge: Cambridge University Press, 2002.
Held, Jean-Francis. "Claude Lévi-Strauss: Tristes Vacances." *Observateur* 74 (April 13–19, 1966). Published online April 14, 2006. https://www.nouvelobs.com/culture/2006 0414.OBS4022/claude-levi-strauss-tristes-vacances.html.
Heller-Roazen, Daniel. *The Inner Touch: Archeology of a Sensation*. Cambridge, Mass.: MIT Press, 2007.
Helmreich, Stefan. *Alien Ocean: Anthropological Voyages in Microbial Seas*. Berkeley: University of California Press, 2009.
Hobday, R. A. "Sunlight Therapy and Solar Architecture." *Medical History* 41, no. 4 (October 1997): 455–472.
Hochschild, Arlie. *The Commercialization of Intimate Life: Notes from Home and Work*. Berkeley: University of California Press, 2003.
——. *The Managed Heart: Commercialization of Human Feeling*. Berkeley: University of California Press, 2012.
Holcomb, Gary. *Claude McKay, Code Name Sasha: Queer Black Marxism and the Harlem Renaissance*. Gainesville: University of Florida Press, 2007.

Holmes, Katie. *Female Aerialists in the 1920s and Early 1930s: Femininity, Celebrity, and Glamour.* New York: Routledge, 2022.
Hornby, Louise. "Downwrong: The Pose of Tiredness." *Modern Fiction Studies* 65, no. 1 (Spring 2019): 207–227.
———. *Still Modernism: Photography, Literature, Film.* New York: Oxford University Press, 2017.
Hubbard, Phil. "Legal Pluralism at the Beach: Public Access, Land Use, and the Struggle for the 'Coastal Commons.'" *Area* 52 (2020): 420–428. https://doi.org/10.1111/area.12594.
Huysmans, J. K. *Against Nature.* Translated by Robert Baldick. New York: Penguin, 2003.
Ingersoll, Karin Amimoto. *Waves of Knowing: A Seascape Epistemology.* Durham: Duke University Press, 2016.
Ingold, Tim. "The Temporality of the Landscape." *World Archeology* 25, no. 2 (October 1993): 152–174.
Jackson, Shannon, and Julia Bryan-Wilson, eds. "Time Zones: Durational Art and Its Contexts." *Representations* 136, no. 1 (2016).
Jaffe, Aaron. "Introduction: Who's Afraid of the Inhuman Woolf?" *Modernism/modernity* 23, no. 3 (September 2016): 491–513.
Jaffe, Alexandra. "Packaged Sentiments: The Social Meaning of Greeting Cards." *Journal of Material Culture* 4, no. 2 (July 1999): 115–141.
Jameson, Fredric. *Postmodernism, or the Cultural Logic of Late Capitalism.* Durham: Duke University Press, 1991.
Jefferson, Alison Rose. "African-American Leisure Space in Santa Monica: The Beach Sometimes Known as the 'Inkwell,' 1900s–1960s." *Southern California Quarterly* 91, no. 2 (2009): 155–189.
Jenny, Laurent. "L'effet Albertine." *Poétique* 142 (2005): 205–218.
Joanne, Paul. *Normandie.* Paris: Hachette, 1901.
Johnson, David K. *The Lavender Scare: The Cold War Persecution of Gays and Lesbians in the Federal Government.* Chicago: University of Chicago Press, 2004.
Johnson, Keith Leslie. "The Extinction Romance." *Modernism/modernity* 23, no. 3 (September 2016): 539–553.
Joyce, James. *Ulysses.* New York: Oxford University Press, 1993.
Jue, Melody. *Wild Blue Media: Thinking Through Seawater.* Durham: Duke University Press, 2020.
Juriga, John. *Bob Hines: National Wildlife Artist.* Edina, Minn.: Beaverpond, 2012.
Kahan, Benjamin. *The Book of Minor Perverts: Sexology, Etiology, and the Emergences of Sexuality.* Chicago: University of Chicago Press, 2019.
———. *Celibacies: American Modernism and Sexual Life.* Durham: Duke University Press, 2013.
Kahrl, Andrew. *Free the Beaches: The Story of Ned Coll and the Battle for America's Most Exclusive Shoreline.* New Haven: Yale University Press, 2018.
Kalaidjian, Andrew. *Exhausted Ecologies: Modernism and Environmental Recovery.* Cambridge: Cambridge University Press, 2020.
Kalb, Jonathan. *Beckett in Performance.* Cambridge: Cambridge University Press, 1991.
Kant, Immanuel. *Critique of the Judgment of Taste.* Translated by Paul Guyer and Matthew Andrews. Cambridge: Cambridge University Press, 2000.

Kaplan, Alice. *Searching for The Stranger: Albert Camus and the Life of a Literary Classic*. Chicago: University of Chicago Press, 2016.
Kark, Salit. "Effects of Ecotones on Biodiversity." In *Encyclopedia of Biodiversity*, 2d ed., edited by Simon A. Levin, 3:142–147. 7 vols. Cambridge: Elsevier, 2013.
Kavanagh, Thomas. *Dice, Cards, Wheels: A Different History of French Culture*. Philadelphia: University of Pennsylvania Press, 2005.
Kaye, Nick, ed. *Site Specific Art*. New York: Routledge, 2000.
Kaza, Stephanie. "Rachel Carson's Sense of Time: Experiencing Maine." *ISLE* 17, no. 2 (March 2010): 291–315.
Kessler, Marni. "Beyond the Shadow of the Veil: Claude Monet's *The Beach at Trouville*." In *Fashion, Modernity, and Materiality in France: From Rousseau to Art Deco*, edited by Heidi Brevik-Zender, 135–155. Albany: State University of New York Press, 2018.
Khalili, Laleh. *Sinews of Trade and War*. London: Verso, 2020.
Kincaid, Jamaica. *A Small Place*. New York: Farrar, Straus and Giroux, 2000.
King, Amy. *The Divine in the Commonplace: Reverent Natural History and the Novel in Britain*. Cambridge: Cambridge University Press, 2019.
King, Tiffany Lethabo. *The Black Shoals: Offshore Formations in Black and Native Studies*. Durham: Duke University Press, 2019.
Kingsley, Charles. *Glaucus; or, The Wonders of the Shore*. Cambridge: Macmillan, 1959 [1855].
Knowlson, James. *Damned to Fame: The Life of Samuel Beckett*. New York: Simon and Schuster, 1996.
Kracauer, Siegfried. "Those Who Wait." In *The Mass Ornament: Weimar Essays*, translated by Thomas Y. Levin, 138–139. Cambridge, Mass.: Harvard University Press, 1995.
Krauss, Rosalind. *The Optical Unconscious*. Cambridge, Mass.: MIT Press, 1994.
Ladenson, Elisabeth. *Proust's Lesbianism*. Ithaca: Cornell University Press, 1999.
Landrin, Armand. *Les plages de France*. Paris: Hachette, 1879.
Langer, Susanne K. *Feeling and Form: A Theory of Art*. New York, Scribner, 1953.
Larkin, Áine. "Proust and the Beach as Screen." In *La ligne d'écume: Encountering the French Beach*, edited by Sophie Fuggle and Nicholas Gledhill, 61–82. London: Pavement, 2006.
Latimer, Tirza True. "Entre Nous: Between Claude Cahun and Marcel Moore." *GLQ* 12, no. 2 (2006): 197–216.
Latour, Bruno. *Facing Gaia: Eight Lectures on the New Climatic Regime*. Translated by Catherine Porter. London: Polity, 2017.
———. Inaugural lecture at Sciences Po, 2019. https://www.youtube.com/watch?v=Db2zyVnGLsE. Accessed March 18, 2022.
Lear, Linda. *Rachel Carson: Witness for Nature*. New York: Mariner, 2009.
Leblanc, Cécile. *Proust, écrivain de la musique: L'allégresse du compositeur*. Paris: Presses de la Sorbonne Nouvelle, 2016.
Lee, Pamela. *Object to be Destroyed*. Cambridge, Mass.: MIT Press, 1999.
Lefebvre, Henri. *Rhythmanalysis: Space, Time, and Everyday Life*. Translated by Stuart Elden and Gerald Moore. London: Continuum, 2004.
Le Moël, Michel and Jean Derens. *La place de Grève*. Paris: Délégation à l'Action Artistique de la Ville de Paris, 1991.

Leonardo, Micaela di. "The Female World of Cards and Holidays: Women, Families, and the Work of Kinship." *Signs* 12, no. 3 (Spring 1987): 440–453.
Lepore, Jill. "It's Just Too Much." *New Yorker,* May 24, 2021.
———. "The Right Way to Remember Rachel Carson." *New Yorker,* March 26, 2018.
Levine, Caroline. *Forms: Whole, Rhythm, Hierarchy, Network.* Princeton, N.J.: Princeton University Press, 2015.
Levinson, Marc. "Container Shipping and the Decline of New York, 1955–1975." *Business History Review* 80, no. 1 (Spring, 2006): 49–80.
———. *The Box: How the Shipping Container Made the World Smaller and the World Economy Bigger.* Princeton, N.J.: Princeton University Press, 2006.
Lewis, Andrew S. "The Long, Slow Drowning of the New Jersey Shore." *New York Times Magazine,* August 15, 2021.
Lipsitz, George. *How Racism Takes Place.* Philadelphia: Temple University Press, 2011.
Litvak, Joseph. *Strange Gourmets: Sophistication, Theory, and the Novel.* Durham: Duke University Press, 1997.
Loiperdinger, Martin. "Lumière's Arrival of the Train: Cinema's Founding Myth. *Moving Image* 4, no. 1 (Spring 2004): 89–118.
London, Justin. "Rhythm." In *Grove Music Online,* 2001. http://doi.org/10.1093/gmo/9781561592630.article.45963. Accessed March 17, 2022.
Lopate, Phillip. "Introduction: Some Thoughts on the Lost Waterfront." In Shelley Seccombe, *Lost Waterfront: The Decline and Rebirth of Manhattan's Western Shore,* 9–12. New York: Fordham University Press, 2007.
———. *Waterfront: A Walk Around Manhattan.* New York: Anchor, 2005.
Love, Heather. *Feeling Backward: Loss and the Politics of Queer History.* Cambridge, Mass.: Harvard University Press, 2009.
———. "Gyn/Apology: Sarah Orne Jewett's Spinster Aesthetics." *ESQ* 55, nos. 3–4 (2009): 304–339.
Lucey, Michael. *Someone: The Pragmatics of Misfit Sexualities, from Colette to Hervé Guibert.* Chicago: University of Chicago Press, 2019.
———. *What Proust Heard: Novels and the Ethnography of Talk.* Chicago: University of Chicago Press, 2022.
Luhmann, Niklas. *Observations on Modernity,* translated by William Whobrey. Stanford: Stanford University Press, 1998.
Lynch, Peter. *The Emergence of Numerical Weather Prediction: Richardson's Dream.* Cambridge: Cambridge University Press, 2006.
Lyons, Charles. *Samuel Beckett.* New York: Macmillan, 1983.
Lytle, Mark Hamilton. *The Gentle Subversive: Rachel Carson, Silent Spring, and the Rise of the Environmental Movement.* New York: Oxford University Press, 2007.
Mallarmé, Stéphane. *Mallarmé on Fashion: A Translation of the Fashion Magazine* La Dernière Mode, *with Commentary.* Edited and translated by A. M. Cain and P. M. Furbank. Oxford: Berg, 2004.
———. *Oeuvres Complètes.* 2 vols. Paris: Gallimard, 1998–2003.
Mann, Thomas. *Death in Venice and Seven Other Stories.* Translated by H. T. Lowe-Porter. New York: Vintage, 2010.
Marcus, Sharon. *Between Women: Friendship, Desire, and Marriage in Victorian England.* Princeton, N.J.: Princeton University Press, 2007.

Marin, Louis. "Un événement de lecture: où un texte de Stendhal est pris à la lettre." *L'Ecrit du temps*, no. 1 (1982): 95–110.
Marshall, David. *The Frame of Art*. Baltimore: Johns Hopkins University Press, 2005.
Martin, Kristy. "Modernism and the Medicalization of Sunlight: D. H. Lawrence, Katherine Mansfield, and the Sun Cure." *Modernism/modernity* 23, no. 2 (2016): 423–441.
——. *Modernism and the Rhythms of Sympathy: Vernon Lee, Virginia Woolf, and D. H. Lawrence*. Oxford: Oxford University Press, 2013.
Martin, Richard, and Harold Koda. *Splash! A History of Swimwear*. New York: Rizzoli, 1990.
Martin, Ted. *Contemporary Drift: Genre, Historicism, and the Problem of the Present*. New York: Columbia University Press, 2017.
Maupassant, Guy de. *Contes et Nouvelles*. Edited by Louis Forestier. Paris: Gallimard, 2014.
Maxwell, Lida. "Queer/Love/Bird Extinction: Rachel Carson's *Silent Spring* as a Work of Love." *Political Theory* 45, no. 5 (2017): 682–704.
McCormack, Derek P. *Refrains for Moving Bodies*. Durham: Duke University Press, 2013.
McCrea, Barry. *In the Company of Strangers: Family and Narrative in Dickens, Conan Doyle, Joyce, and Proust*. New York: Columbia University Press, 2011.
McDonald, Christy. *The Proustian Fabric: Associations of Memory*. Lincoln: University of Nebraska Press, 1991.
McFarlane, Robert. *Mountains of the Mind: A History of a Fascination*. London: Granta, 2004.
McKay, Claude. *A Long Way From Home*. New Brunswick, N.J.: Rutgers University Press, 2007.
——. *Banjo: A Story Without a Plot*. New York: Mariner, 1970.
——. *Romance in Marseille*. Edited by Gary Edward Holcomb and William J. Maxwell. New York: Penguin, 2020.
McMullan, Anna. *Performing Embodiment in Beckett's Drama*. New York: Routledge, 2010.
McNeill, John Robert, and Peter Engelke. *The Great Acceleration: Environmental History of the Anthropocene Since 1945*. Cambridge, Mass.: Harvard University Press, 2016.
Meikle, Jeffrey. *American Plastic: A Cultural History*. New Brunswick, N.J.: Rutgers University Press, 1995.
Melville, Herman. *Moby Dick, or, The Whale*. New York: Modern Library, 2000.
Mentz, Steve. *Shipwreck Modernity: Ecologies of Globalization, 1550–1719*. Minneapolis: University of Minnesota Press, 2015.
Merleau-Ponty, Maurice. *Le Visible et l'invisible*. Paris: Gallimard, 1979.
Merrill, Dennis. *Negotiating Paradise: U.S. Tourism and Empire in Twentieth-Century Latin America*. Chapel Hill: University of North Carolina Press, 2009.
Michasiw, Kim Ian. "Nine Revisionist Theses on the Picturesque." *Representations* 38 (Spring 1992): 76–100.
Michelet, Jules. *La Mer*. Paris: Gallimard, 1983.
Micir, Melanie. "Queer Woolf." In *A Companion to Virginia Woolf*, edited by Jessica Berman, 347–358. Chichester: Wiley Blackwell, 2016.

WORKS CITED

———. *The Passion Projects: Modernist Women, Intimate Archives, Unfinished Lives.* Princeton, N.J.: Princeton University Press, 2019.
Miller, D. A. *Jane Austen, or the Secret of Style.* Princeton, N.J.: Princeton University Press, 2005.
Millner-Larsen, Nadja, and Gavin Butt. "Introduction: The Queer Commons." *GLQ* 24, no. 4 (October 2018): 399–419.
Mitchell, W. J. T. *Landscape and Power.* Chicago: University of Chicago Press, 1994.
———. *Picture Theory: Essays on Verbal and Visual Representation.* Chicago: University of Chicago Press, 1995.
Monmonier, Mark. *Air Apparent: How Meterorologists Learned to Map, Predict, and Dramatize Weather.* Chicago: Chicago University Press, 1999.
Moore, Jason W. *Capitalism in the Web of Life: Ecology and the Accumulation of Capital.* London: Verso, 2015.
———. "The Rise of Cheap Nature." In *Anthropocene or Capitalocene?*, edited by Jason W. Moore, 78–115. Oakland, Cal.: PM, 2016.
Morris, Jan. *Travels with Virginia Woolf.* London: Hogarth, 1993.
Mortimer-Sandilands, Catriona. "Melancholy Natures, Queer Ecologies." In *Queer Ecologies: Sex, Nature, Politics, Desire,* edited by Bruce Erikson and Catriona Mortimer-Sandilands, 331–358. Bloomington: Indiana University Press, 2010.
Morton, Timothy. *The Ecological Thought.* Cambridge, Mass.: Harvard University Press, 2011.
Moskowitz, Golan Y. *Wild Visionary: Maurice Sendak in Queer Jewish Context.* Stanford: Stanford University Press, 2020.
Moten, Fred, and Stefano Harney. *The Undercommons: Fugitive Planning and Black Study.* New York: Minor Compositions, 2013.
Muñoz, José Esteban. *Cruising Utopia: The There and Then of Queer Futurity.* New York: New York University Press, 2009.
———. *The Sense of Brown.* Durham: Duke University Press, 2020.
Nancy, Jean-Luc. *Being Singular Plural.* Translated by Robert Richardson and Anne O'Byrne. Stanford: Stanford University Press, 2000.
Nasiali, Minayo. *Native to the Republic: Empire, Social Citizenship, and Everyday Life in Marseille Since 1945.* Ithaca: Cornell University Press, 2016.
NDiaye, Marie. *Rosie Carpe.* Translated by Tamsin Black. Lincoln: University of Nebraska Press, 2004.
Nealon, Christopher. *Foundlings: Lesbian and Gay Historical Emotion Before Stonewall.* Durham: Duke University Press, 2001.
Nersessian, Anahid. *Utopia, Limited: Romanticism and Adjustment.* Cambridge, Mass.: Harvard University Press, 2015.
Newman, Eric H. "Ephemeral Utopias: Queer Cruising, Literary Form, and Diasporic Imagination in *Home to Harlem* and *Banjo.*" *Callaloo* 38, no. 1 (2015): 167–185.
Newton, Esther. *Cherry Grove, Fire Island: Sixty Years in America's First Gay and Lesbian Town.* Durham: Duke University Press, 2014.
Ngai, Sianne. *Ugly Feelings.* Cambridge, Mass.: Harvard University Press, 2007.
Nicole, Eugène. "Proust et les sons." *Bulletin Marcel Proust* 68 (2018): 157–165.
Nixon, Rob. "Barrier Beach." In *The Oxford Handbook of Ecocriticism,* edited by Greg Garrard. Oxford: Oxford University Press, 2014.

———. *Slow Violence and the Environmentalism of the Poor*. Cambridge, Mass.: Harvard University Press, 2011.
Nochlin, Linda. *Bathers, Bodies, Beauty: The Visceral Eye*. Cambridge, Mass.: Harvard University Press, 2006.
———. *The Politics of Vision: Essays on Nineteenth-Century Art and Society*. New York: Harper and Row, 1989.
North, Michael. *The Dialect of Modernism*. New York: Oxford University Press, 1994.
Nunberg, Geoffrey. *The Linguistics of Punctuation*. Cambridge: Cambridge University Press, 1990.
Oppenheim, Lois. *Directing Beckett*. Ann Arbor: University of Michigan Press, 1997.
Oreskes, Naomi. *Science on a Mission: How Military Funding Shaped What We Do and Don't Know About the Ocean*. Chicago: University of Chicago Press, 2021.
Ostrom, Elinor. *Governing the Commons: The Evolution of Institutions for Collective Action*. Cambridge: Cambridge University Press, 1990.
Ovid. *Metamorphoses: A New Translation*. Translated by Charles Martin. New York: Norton, 2004.
Parasceva, Anthony. *Beckett and Cinema*. London: Bloomsbury, 2017.
Parrish, Susan Scott. *The Flood Year 1927: A Cultural History*. Princeton, N.J.: Princeton University Press, 2017.
Pearson, Roger. *Stéphane Mallarmé*. London: Reaktion, 2010.
Pechenard, Christian. *Proust à Cabourg*. Paris: Quai Voltaire, 1992.
Peterson, Charles H., and Melanie J. Bishop. "Assessing the Environmental Impacts of Beach Nourishment." *BioScience* 55, no. 10 (October 2005): 887–896.
Phelan, Peggy. "Freedom." *Resilience: A Journal of the Environmental Humanities* 7, nos. 2–3, "Climate Realism" (Spring-Fall 2020): 253–256.
Pilkey, Orrin H., and Keith C. Pilkey. *Sea Level Rise: A Slow Tsunami on America's Shores*. Durham: Duke University Press, 2019.
Pilsch, Andrew. "Polynesian Paralysis: Tiki Culture and the Aesthetics of American Empire." In *The Shaken and the Stirred: The Year's Work in Cocktail Culture*, edited by Craig Owens and Stephen Schneider, 224–243. Bloomington: Indiana University Press, 2020.
Posmentier, Sonya. *Cultivation and Catastrophe: The Lyric Ecology of Modern Black Literature*. Baltimore: Johns Hopkins University Press, 2017.
Potofsky, Allan. *Constructing Paris in the Age of Revolution*. New York: Palgrave, 2009.
Proulx, François. "Proust's Drawings and the Secret of the 'Solitary House.'" *MLN* 133, no. 4 (September 2018): 865–890.
Proust, Adrien Achille, and Gilbert Ballet. *L'Hygiène du neurasthénique*. Paris: Masson & Cie, 1897.
———. *Treatment of Neurasthenia*. Translated by Peter Campbell Smith. New York: Pelton, 1903.
Proust, Marcel. *À la recherche du temps perdu*. 4 vols. Paris: Gallimard, 1987–1989.
———. *Correspondance de Marcel Proust*. Edited by Philip Kolb. 21 vols. Paris: Plon, 1970–1993.
———. *In Search of Lost Time*. Translated by Scott Moncrieff and Terence Kilmartin. Revised by D. J. Enright. New York: Random House, 1992.
———. *Jean Santeuil*. Translated by Gerard Hopkins. Harmondsworth: Penguin, 1985.
———. *Jean Santeuil, précédé de Les plaisirs et les jours*. Paris: Gallimard, 1971.

WORKS CITED

———. *Les Soixante-Quinze Feuillets: Et autres manuscrits inédits*. Edited by Natalie Mauriac Dyer. Paris: Gallimard, 2021.

———. *Selected Letters*. 4 vols. Edited by Philip Kolb. Translated by Ralph Mannheim, Terence Kilmartin, and Joanna Kilmartin. Oxford: Oxford University Press, 1983–2000.

Pugh, Anthony. *The Growth of À la recherche du temps perdu: A Chronological Examination of Proust's Manuscripts from 1909–1914*. 2 vols. Toronto: University of Toronto Press, 2004.

Purves, Alex. *Homer and the Poetics of Gesture*. Oxford: Oxford University Press, 2019.

Quashie, Kevin. *The Sovereignty of Quiet: Beyond Resistance in Black Culture*. New Brunswick, N.J.: Rutgers University Press, 2012.

Quigley, Megan. *Modernist Fiction and Vagueness: Philosophy, Form, and Language*. Cambridge: Cambridge University Press, 2015.

Rabaté, Jean-Michel. "Editor's Introduction." In *The New Samuel Beckett Studies*, edited by Jean-Michel Rabaté, 1–16. Cambridge: Cambridge University Press, 2019.

Rabinbach, Anson. *The Human Motor: Energy, Fatigue, and the Origins of Modernity*. Berkeley: University of California Press, 1992.

Raine, Anne. "Du Bois's Ambient Poetics: Rethinking Environmental Imagination in *The Souls of Black Folk*." *Callaloo* 36, no. 2 (Spring 2013): 322–341.

Ramazani, Jahan. *A Transnational Poetics*. University of Chicago Press, 2009.

Rancière, Jacques. *Aesthesis: Scenes from the Aesthetic Regime of Art*. Translated by Zakir Paul. London: Verso, 2013.

———. *The Lost Thread: The Democracy of Modern Fiction*. Translated by Steven Corcoran. London: Bloomsbury, 2016.

———. *Politics of Aesthetics*. Translated by Gabriel Rockhill. New York: Bloomsbury Academic, 2013.

———. *Proletarian Nights: The Workers' Dream in Nineteenth-Century France*. London: Verso, 2012.

———. "Why Emma Bovary Had to Be Killed." *Critical Inquiry* 34 (2008): 233–248.

Rasula, Jed. *Acrobatic Modernism from the Avant-Garde to Prehistory*. Oxford: Oxford University Press, 2020.

Ravindranathan, Thangam. *Behold an Animal: Four Extravagant Readings*. Evanston: Northwestern University Press, 2020.

———, and Antoine Traisnel. "In the Doldrums: Plastic, Haunting, and the Sea." *SubStance* 157 51, no. 1 (2022): 8–29.

"Rhythm." In *The Harvard Dictionary of Music*, 4th ed, edited by Don Michael Randel. Cambridge: Harvard University Press, 2003. https://search.credoreference.com/content/entry/harvdictmusic/rhythm_fr_gr_rhythmos_lat_rhythmus_ger_rhythmus_fr_rhythme_sp_it_ritmo/0?institutionId=577. Accessed March 17, 2022.

Richard, Frances. *Gordon Matta-Clark: Physical Poetics*. Berkeley: University of California Press, 2019.

Richards, Jill. *The Fury Archives: Female Citizenship, Human Rights, and the International Avant-Gardes*. New York: Columbia University Press, 2020.

Richez, Jean-Claude, and Léon Strauss. "Un temps nouveau pour les ouvriers (1930–1960)." In Alain Courbin, ed., *L'Avènement des loisirs, 1850–1960*, 376–412. Paris: Aubier, 1995.

Ricketts, Ed, and Jack Calvin. *Between Pacific Tides,* 3rd ed., revised by Joel Hedgpeth. Stanford: Stanford University Press, 1952.

———, and Joel Hedgpeth. *Between Pacific Tides,* 5th ed., revised by David W. Phillips. Stanford: Stanford University Press, 1985.

Ritchie, Robert. *The Lure of the Beach: A Global History.* Berkeley: University of California Press, 2021.

Rizzuto, Nicole. "Maritime Modernism: The Aqueous Form of Virginia Woolf's The Waves." *Modernist Cultures* 11, no. 2 (July 2016): 268–292.

Roberts, Jennifer, ed. *Scale.* Chicago: University of Chicago Press, 2016.

———. *Transporting Visions: The Movement of Pictures in Early America.* Berkeley: University of California Press, 2014.

Robertson, Eric. "A la dérive: Drifting in and Out of Form in French Literature and Visual Art from Bataille to Bergvall." In *What Forms Can Do: The Work of Form in Twentieth- and Twenty-First-Century French Literature and Thought,* edited by Patrick Crowley and Shirley Jordan, 271–286. Liverpool: Liverpool University Press, 2020.

Rohy, Valery. *Chances Are: Contingency, Queer Theory, and American Literature.* London: Routledge, 2019.

Roncayolo, Marcel. *L'imaginaire de Marseille: Port, ville, pôle.* Lyon: ENS Éditions, 2014. https://books.openedition.org/enseditions/370.

Ronda, Margaret. *Remainders: American Poetry at Nature's End.* Stanford: Stanford University Press, 2018.

Ross, Kristin. *Fast Cars, Clean Bodies: Decolonization and the Reordering of French Culture.* Cambridge, Mass.: MIT Press, 1994.

Rubin, Gayle S. "Introduction: Sex, Gender, Politics." In *Deviations: A Gayle S. Rubin Reader,* 1–32. Durham: Duke University Press, 2012.

Rush, Elizabeth. *Rising: Dispatches from the New American Shore.* Minneapolis: Milkweed, 2018.

Sagan, Françoise. *Bonjour Tristesse.* Translated by Irene Ash. New York: Harper Collins, 2008.

Saint-Amand, Pierre. "The Secretive Body: Roland Barthes's Gay Erotics." *Yale French Studies* 90 (1996): 153–171.

Saint-Amour, Paul K. "Deep Time's Hauntings: Modernism and Alternative Chronology." In *The New Modernist Studies,* edited by Douglas Mao, 297–313. Cambridge: Cambridge University Press, 2021.

Salisbury, Laura. *Samuel Beckett: Laughing Matters, Comic Timing.* Edinburgh: Edinburgh University Press, 2012.

Sarduy, Severo. *The Beach,* in *For Voice.* Translated by Philip Barnard. Pittsburgh: Latin American Literary Review Press, 1985.

Sartre, Jean-Paul. *Nausea.* Translated by Lloyd Alexander and Richard Howard. New York: New Directions, 2013.

Scarry, Elaine. *On Beauty and Being Just.* Princeton, N.J.: Princeton University Press, 1999.

Schmid, Maron. "Proust's Choreographies of Writing: *À la recherche du temps perdu* and the Modern Dance Revolution." *Marcel Proust Aujourd'hui* 12 (2015): 91–108.

Schmidt, Christopher. *The Poetics of Waste: Queer Excess in Stein, Ashbery, Schuyler, and Goldsmith* (New York: Palgrave, 2014).

WORKS CITED

Schotter, Jesse. "'Objects Worthy of Attention:' Modernism and the Travel Guide." *Modernism/modernity Print Plus* 4, no. 2. https://doi.org/10.26597/mod.0109.

Schwartz, Hillel. "Torque: The New Kinaesthetic of the Twentieth Century." In *Incorporations*, edited by Jonathan Crary and Sanford Kwinter, 70–127. New York: Zone, 1992.

Schwartz, Vanessa. *It's So French!: Hollywood, Paris, and the Making of Cosmopolitan Film Culture*. Chicago: University of Chicago Press, 2007.

Seager, Joni. "Radical Observation." *WSQ* 45, nos. 1, 2 (Spring/Summer 2017): 269–277.

Seccombe, Shelley. *Lost Waterfront: The Decline and Rebirth of Manhattan's Western Shore*. New York: Fordham University Press, 2008.

Sedgwick, Eve Kosofsky. *Epistemology of the Closet*. Berkeley: University of California Press, 1990.

———. *Touching Feeling: Affect, Pedagogy, Performativity*. Durham: Duke University Press, 2002.

———. *The Weather in Proust*. Durham: Duke University Press, 2011.

Segel, Harold B. *Body Ascendant: Modernism and the Physical Imperative*. Baltimore: Johns Hopkins University Press, 1998.

Seiler, Claire. *Midcentury Suspension: Literature and Waiting in the Wake of World War II*. New York: Columbia University Press, 2020.

Sekula, Allan. *Fish Story*. Düsseldorf: Richter Verlag, 1995.

———, and Noël Burch. "The Forgotten Space: Notes for a Film." *New Left Review* 69 (2011). newleftreview.org/issues/ii69/articles/allan-sekula-noel-burch-the-forgotten-space. Accessed March 18, 2022.

Seymour, Nicole. *Strange Natures: Futurity, Empathy, and the Queer Ecological Imagination*. Champaign: University of Illinois Press, 2013.

Shalin, Dmitri. "Erving Goffman, Fateful Action, and the Las Vegas Gambling Scene." *UNLV Gaming Research and Review Journal* 20, no. 1 (2016). https://digitalscholarship.unlv.edu/grrj/vol20/iss1/1.

Shank, Barry. *A Token of My Affection: Greeting Cards and American Business Culture*. New York: Columbia University Press 2004.

Shattuck, Roger. *Proust's Way: A Field Guide to In Search of Lost Time*. New York: Norton, 2001.

Shaw, Fiona, and Deborah Warner. "Theater Look-In: Samuel Beckett's *Happy Days*, with Fiona Shaw and Deborah Warner." https://www.youtube.com/watch?v=u8Yyo6T5g14. Accessed March 8, 2022.

Silver, Brenda. "Mothers, Daughters, Mrs. Ramsay: Reflections." *Women's Studies Quarterly* 37, nos. 3–4 (Fall-Winter 2009): 259–274.

Skwiot, Christine. *The Purposes of Paradise: U.S. Tourism and Empire in Cuba and Hawai'i*. Philadelphia: University of Pennsylvania Press, 2012.

Smailbegović, Ada. "At the Edges of Unmeeting: Geometries of Sea and Land in Marianne Moore's Seascapes." *Comparative Literature* 73, no. 2 (June 2021): 150–165.

———. *Poetics of Liveliness: Molecules, Fibers, Tissues, Clouds*. New York: Columbia University Press, 2021.

Smith, Jonathan. *Charles Darwin and Victorian Visual Culture*. Cambridge: Cambridge University Press, 2009.

Smock, Ann. *The Play of Light: Jacques Roubaud, Emmanuel Hocquard, and Friends*. Albany: State University of New York Press, 2021.

Song, Min Hyoun. "Introduction: The Practice of Sustaining Attention to Climate Change." In *Climate Lyricism*, edited by Min Hyoun Song, 1–18. Durham: Duke University Press, 2022.

Sontag, Susan. "The Decay of Cinema." *New York Times*, February 25, 1996.

Starosielsky, Nicole. "Fixed Flow: Undersea Network as Media Infrastructure." In *Signal Traffic: Critical Studies of Media Infrastructures*, edited by Lisa Parks and Nicole Starosielski, 53–70. Urbana: University of Illinois Press, 2015.

Stavrides, Stavros. *Common Space: The City as Commons*. London: Zed, 2020.

Steinbeck, John. *Cannery Row*. New York: Penguin, 1992.

Steinberg, Philip E. "Maritime Cargomobilities: The Impossibilities of Representation." In *Cargomobilities: Moving Materials in a Global Age*, edited by Thomas Birtchnell, Satya Savitzky, and John Urry, 35–47. London: Routledge, 2019.

Stengers, Isabelle. *In Catastrophic Times: Resisting the Coming Barbarism*. Translated by Andrew Goffey. London: Open Humanities, 2015.

Stephens, Chuck. "And God Created Woman." *Criterion Collection*, July 17, 2000). Accessed April 10, 2022. https://www.criterion.com/current/posts/80-and-god-created-woman. Accessed March 8, 2022.

Stewart, Susan. *Poetry and the Fate of the Senses*. Chicago: University of Chicago Press, 2002.

Stivale, Charles J. *Gilles Deleuze's ABCs: The Folds of Friendship*. Baltimore: Johns Hopkins University Press, 2008.

Stockton, Kathryn Bond. *The Queer Child, or Growing Sideways in the Twentieth Century*. Durham: Duke University Press, 2009.

Stoler, Ann Laura, ed. *Imperial Debris: On Ruins and Ruination*. Durham: Duke University Press, 2013.

Sugano, Marian. *The Poetics of the Occasion: Mallarmé and the Poetry of Circumstance*. Stanford: Stanford University Press, 1987.

Sun & Sea (Marina). https://sunandsea.lt/en. Accessed April 16, 2022.

Sunde, Sarah Cameron. "Reflections." *Resilience: A Journal of the Environmental Humanities* 7, nos. 2–3, "Climate Realism" (Spring-Fall 2020): 258–270.

———. "Vision." Unpublished MS, December 10, 2018.

Szeman, Imre, Jennifer Wenzel, and Patricia Yaeger, eds. *Fueling Culture: 101 Words for Energy and Environment*. New York: Fordham University Press, 2017.

Tadié, Jean-Yves. *Marcel Proust: A Life*. Translated by Euan Cameron. New York: Penguin, 2000.

Tait, Peta. *Circus Bodies: Cultural Identity in Aerial Performance*. New York: Routledge, 2005.

Taubman, Howard. "Beckett's Happy Days," *New York Times*, September 18, 1961.

Taussig, Michael. "The Beach (A Fantasy)." *Critical Inquiry* 26, no. 2 (Winter 2000): 248–278.

Taylor, Jesse Oak. *The Sky of Our Manufacture: The London Fog in British Fiction from Dickens to Woolf*. Charlottesville: University of Virginia Press, 2016.

Thompson, E. P. *Customs in Common*. New York: New Press, 1991.

———. *The Making of the English Working Class*. New York: Vintage, 1966.

———. "Time, Work-Discipline, and Industrial Capitalism." *Past and Present* 38 (December 1967): 56–97.

WORKS CITED

Thompson, Krista A. *An Eye for the Tropics: Tourism, Photography, and Framing the Caribbean Picturesque*. Durham: Duke University Press, 2006.
Thoreau, Henry David. *Cape Cod*. Princeton, N.J.: Princeton University Press, 2004.
Tickner, Lisa. "Vanessa Bell: *Studland Beach*, Domesticity, and 'Significant Form.'" *Representations* 65 (Winter 1999): 63–92.
Tilly, Charles. *The Contentious French*. Cambridge, Mass.: Harvard University Press, 1986.
Tinsley, Omese'eke Natasha. *Thiefing Sugar: Eroticism Between Women in Caribbean Literature*. Durham: Duke University Press, 2010.
Trask, Haunani-Kay. *From a Native Daughter: Colonialism and Sovereignty in Hawai'i*. Honolulu: University of Hawai'i Press, 1999.
Treviño, Javier A. *Goffman's Legacy*. New York: Rowman and Littlefield, 2003.
Tsing, Anna. "The Buck, the Bull, and the Dream of the Stag: Some Unexpected Weeds of the Anthropocene." *Suomen Antropologi* 42, no. 1 (Spring 2017): 3–21.
———. *The Mushroom at the End of the World: On the Possibility of Life in Capitalist Ruins*. Princeton, N.J.: Princeton University Press, 2015.
Tully, John. *The Devil's Milk: A Social History of Rubber*. New York: New York University Press, 2011.
Tung, Charles M. "Baddest Modernism: The Scales and Lines of Inhuman Time." *Modernism/modernity* 23, no. 3 (September 2016): 515–38.
Tuszynska, Agnieszka. "'A Syrup of Passion and Desire': Transgressive Politics of Pleasure in Claude McKay's *Romance in Marseille*." *English Language Notes* 59, no. 1 (April 2021): 38–57.
Urbain, Jean-Didier. *At the Beach*. Translated by Catherine Porter. Minneapolis: University of Minnesota Press, 2003.
Vadde, Aarthi. *Chimeras of Form: Modernist Internationalism Beyond Europe, 1914–2016*. New York: Columbia University Press, 2016.
Vance, Jeffrey. *Chaplin: Genius of the Cinema*. Ann Arbor: University of Michigan Press, 2003.
Varga, Adriana. ed. *Virginia Woolf and Music*. Bloomington: Indiana University Press: 2014.
Vendler, Helen. *The Odes of John Keats*. Cambridge, Mass.: Harvard University Press, 1985.
Vincendeau, Ginette. *Brigitte Bardot*. London: British Film Institute, 2013.
Virilio, Paul. *Bunker Archeology*. Translated by George Collins. Princeton, N.J.: Princeton Architectural Press, 1994.
Voyles, Traci Brynne. "Anatomic Bombs: The Sexual Life of Nuclearism, 1945–57." *American Quarterly* 72, no. 3 (September 2020): 651–673.
Weber, Samuel. "The Madrepore." *MLN* 87, no. 7 (Dec. 1972): 915–961.
Weinberg, Jonathan. *Pier Groups: Art and Sex Along the New York Waterfront*. University Park: Penn State University Press, 2019.
Welland, Michael. *Sand, the Never-Ending Story*. Berkeley: University of California Press, 2009.
Wells, Sarah Ann. "On the Shores of Work." *Comparative Literature* 73, no. 2 (June 2021): 166–183.
Welsby, Dan, James Price, Steve Pye, and Paul Ekins. "Unextractable Fossil Fuels in a 1.5 °C World." *Nature* 597 (2021): 230–234. https://doi.org/10.1038/s41586-021-03821-8.

Wendell, Susan. *The Rejected Body: Feminist Philosophical Reflections on Disability*. New York: Routledge, 1996.
Wenzel, Jennifer. *The Disposition of Nature: Environmental Crisis and World Literature*. New York: Fordham University Press, 2019.
West, Emily. "Understanding Authenticity in Commercial Sentiment: The Greeting Card as Emotional Commodity." In *Emotions as Commodities: Capitalism, Consumption, and Authenticity*, edited by Eva Illouz, 123–144. New York, Routledge, 2017.
White, Edmund. *City Boy: My Life in New York During the 1960s and 1970s*. London: Bloomsbury, 2011.
Whitehead, Colson. *Sag Harbor*. New York, Doubleday, 2009.
Wilder, Gary. *The Imperial Nation-State: Negritude and Colonial Humanism Between the Two Wars*. Chicago: University of Chicago Press, 2005.
Williams, Raymond. *The Country and the City*. Oxford: Oxford University Press, 1973.
Wilson, Emma. *The Reclining Nude: Agnès Varda, Catherine Breillat, and Nan Goldin*. Liverpool: Liverpool University Press, 2019.
Wilson, Mary. *Labors of Domesticity: Domesticity, Servants, and Authorship in Modernist Fiction*. New York: Routledge, 2016.
Wiltse, Jeff. *Contested Waters: A Social History of Swimming Pools in America*. Chapel Hill: University of North Carolina Press, 2008.
Wolcott, Victoria. *Race, Riots, and Roller Coasters: The Struggle Over Segregated Recreation in America*. Philadelphia: University of Pennsylvania Press, 2012.
Wolf, Jessica. "Stillness Is the Move: Coaching Dianne Wiest for *Happy Days*." *American Theater*, April 24, 2017. https://www.americantheatre.org/2017/04/24/stillness-is-the-move-coaching-dianne-wiest-for-happy-days/.
Woods, Derek. "Scale Critique for the Anthropocene." *Minnesota Review* 83 (2014): 133–142.
Woolf, Virginia. *The Complete Shorter Fiction of Virginia Woolf*. New York: Harcourt, 1989.
——. *The Diary of Virginia Woolf*. Edited by Anne Oliver Bell. 5 vols. San Diego: Harcourt Brace Jovanovich, 1977–1984.
——. *Jacob's Room*. New York: Penguin, 1992.
——. *The Letters of Virginia Woolf*. 6 vols. Edited by Nigel Nicolson and Joanne Trautmann. New York: Mariner, 1977–1982.
——. *Moments of Being*. Edited by Jeanne Schulkind. New York: Harcourt, 1985.
——. *Mrs. Dalloway*. New York: Harcourt, 2005.
——. *A Passionate Apprentice: The Early Journals, 1897–1909*. New York: Mariner, 1992.
——. *A Room of One's Own*. New York: Harcourt Brace Jovanovich, 1929.
——. *To the Lighthouse*. New York: Harcourt, 2005.
Worth, Katherine. *Waiting for Godot and Happy Days: Text and Performance*. New York: Macmillan, 1990.
Yaeger, Patricia. "Editor's Column: Sea Trash, Dark Pools, and the Tragedy of the Commons." *PMLA* 125, no. 3 (2010): 523–545.
Yale, D. E. C. "Public Rights in the Foreshore and Adjacent Waters." *Cambridge Law Journal* 25, no. 2 (1967): 164–168.

Yonge, C. M. *The Sea Shore*. London: Collins, 1949.
Young, Damon. *Making Sex Public*. Durham: Duke University Press, 2018.
Yusoff, Kathryn. "Geologic Realism: On the Beach of Geologic Time." *Social Text* 37, no. 1 (March 2019): 1–26.
Zemgulys, Andrea. *Modernism and the Locations of Literary Heritage*. Cambridge: Cambridge University Press, 2008.
Zerubavel, Eviatar. *Hidden Rhythms: Schedules and Calendars in Social Life*. Berkeley: University of California Press, 1981.
Zhang, Dora. *Strange Likeness: Description and the Modernist Novel*. Chicago: University of Chicago Press, 2020.
Zuckerkandl, Victor. *Sound and Symbol: Music and the External World*. Translated by Willard R. Trask. Princeton, N.J.: Princeton University Press, 1969.

INDEX

Against Nature (*À Rebours*, Huysmans), 9
Agard-Jones, Vanessa, 14
Akerman, Chantal, 169
Allewaert, Monique, 132, 224n59
Along the Coast (*Du côté de la côte*, Varda), 24–25, *25*
Anthropocene, 6, 11, 149, 158, 163, 174
Aquarium: Unveiling of the Wonders of the Deep Sea, The (Gosse), 88
Arrival of a Train (*Arrivée d'un train à la Ciotat*, Lumière), 27, 189n97
Augé, Marc, 31, 50, 148, 177

Bainbridge, Simon, 3, 180n5
Balbec: air at, 61; Albertine in, 42, 47, 50–51, 61–64, 193n52, 194n53; and Baron de Charlus, 41, 192n30; beach at, 61–62, 142; and body in flight, 50, 63, 142, 155; casino of, 34, 35, 36, 42–43, 49, 52, 57; and character of Andrée, 142; and character of Saint-Loup, 42, 60, 192n29; and Combray, 8, 35, 36; contingency at, 35, 36, 39, 44, 52, 57; and the future, 34, 190n6; and intoxication, 34, 49, 59–60, 198n107; and mobility, 51–54; and modernism, 52, 53; open social rules of, 36, 39, 40; and painter Elstir, 60, 61, 192n29; as performance space, 8, 36, 53–54, 56–57; and the *petite bande*, 41, 42, 45–47, 52, 60–61, 192n29; as petroleum-powered mirage, 36; and queerness, 41, 42, 43, 64; and respite from routine, 22; and rituals of invitation, 35, 36, 40–41, 192n29, 192n30; seashore resort of, 8, 34, 36, 39, 40, 192n28, 192n29; as a setting, 29, 34–35, 36, 42, 49, 54, 58, 73; as space of imagination, 34, 44, 49, 58–59; and train lines, 36, 38; unstable social hierarchies of, 39–42, 191n19
Ballets Russes, 27, 29, 54–56, *55*, 198n101
Baltrop, Alvin, 31, 122, 123–124, 138–140, *139*, *140*. See also Matta-Clark, Gordon
Balzac, Honoré de, 127, 221n26
Banjo: A Story Without a Plot (McKay): and act of beaching, 134–35, 136, 137; and beach as mind-set, 29, 122; Blackness in, 131, 134; and character of Banjo, 127–28, 129, 131, 132, 134, 135,

Banjo (*continued*)
136, 137, 225n80; and character of Latnah, 135, 136, 225n82; and character of Ray, 131–132, 134, 137, 225n80; and commoning practices, 30; ease in, 29, 31, 128, 129, 135; industrial landscape in, 133; and modernism, 4; and the picturesque, 129–133, 137, 223n51; police intrusion in, 136; and ports, 127, 128, 129, 131, 133, 136, 223n51; and primitivism, 132; and Quashie's "quiet," 133–134; and queerness, 131, 133; and self-care, 27; setting of, 20, 127–128; and *Songs of Jamaica*, 224n64; and transience, 128

Bardot, Brigitte, 16, 24, 25, 166–69, *168*, 237n94

Barker, Mandy, 31, 155, *156*, 157, 158, 231n29, 231n30. See also *SOUP* (Barker)

Barthes, Roland: on arrogance, 181n11; and the beach, 20, 26, 48, 126; "beach effect" of, 26, 173–174, 221n22; and child's point of view, 72; and queer ecology, 4–5; and rhythm, 73, 77, 202n38, 204n61. *See also* beach effect

Baudelaire, Charles, 61

beach: access to, 12, 181–182n13, 185n45, 200–201n13, 220n12; acrobatics at, 27, 29, 35, 55–56; and aesthetic theory, 4, 28, 34, 157, 158, 159, 173, 17; as air conditioning, 228n1; as an archive, 103; and artificial beaches, 163, 172; as a battleground, 67; and beach artwork, 31–32, 148–149, 150, 151–153, 155–158, 178; and beachcombing, 3, 15, 27, 30, 68, 69, 97, 152; and beach films, 12, 16, 24, 27, 166, 167, 186–187n66, 188n94, 189n97, 198n106, 236n83; and beach paintings, 7–8, 60, 91, 96, 151, 152, 230n15; and beach photography, 17, 31, 115, 155–157; and beach plays, 9, 31, 148, 149, 152–153, 163–172; and beach sculpture, 31, 153, 154–155, 158; as a bed, 8, 48, 49; and blue humanities scholarship, 180n4; as a bower, 4, 32, 123; and Cape Cod, 12, 152; and carbon capitalism, 31, 161; and the Caribbean, 14, 15; and Chaplin's beach, 55–56, 198n106; and climate violence, 176; and collective "ease," 122; and colonial beach, 13–14, 152; as a commons, 6–7, 30, 66, 69, 124, 158, 161; and Coney Island, *10*, 11, 16; and contingency, 3, 47, 64; corporality at, 20, 24–27, 34, 47, 49, 50, 56, 149, 159, 161, 166, 183n27, 187n67, 197n89; cultural histories of, 7, 31, 183n22; as a cure, 7, 12, 153, 159–160, 161, 176, 177–178, 233n46; and *Day's End* (Matta-Clark), 144; and dislocation, 6, 7; drag shows at, 16–17; drift of, 11, 34, 67; and egalitarianism, 2, 127; elemental intensity of, 8, 9, 15, 28, 67; as encampment, 7; and endurance, 20, 28, 31, 158, 178; erosion of, 11, 28, 67, 77, 150, 161, 204n59, 233n55; eroticization of, 16, 163; and exhaustion, 31, 148, 149, 159, 160–163, 173, 174; and exposure, 9, 25, 26, 28, 90, 149, 150, 165, 178; and French word *grève*, 127, 128, 221n23; gambling at, 43; and guidebooks, 4, 8, 9, 30, 43, 92, 100, 101, 121; and heteronormative narratives, 16, 20, 22, 95, 186–187n66; and history of sexuality, 18; and the horizontal mode, 21, 25–27, 38, 48; and interspecies encounter, 3, 4, 66, 115–119; and Jones Beach's construction, 11; and landscape, 3, 7, 11, 31, 32, 34, 104; and leisure beaches, 1–6, 10–11, 16, 24, 25–26, 30, 31, 50, 51, 126, 148, 150, 152, 160, 163, 167, 197n89; and maritime laws, 124; and Martinican beach, 14, 152; and maternal care, 86; and modernism, 2, 3, 4, 19, 24, 28, 29, 33–34, 60, 123, 124, 159, 174, 183n27, 190n5; as a mortuary zone, 12, 19, 152; and mountains, 3, 180n5; and newspapers, 36–38, 191n15, 199n122; and Normandy beach, 2, 12, 27; nourishment of, 11, 161, 184n37, 233n55; and oceanic debris, 150, 152,

INDEX

153, 155, 158; "off-season" at, 19, 20, 24, 48, 187n77; as opposed to city, 3, 8, 33; ownership of, 5, 181n13; and the Pacific, 14, 16; as a parenthesis, 67; and Paris Plages, 10, 163, 184n36; play at, 27, 28, 74, 96, 122, 123; and ports, 126, 127, 139; and public space, 5, 6, 20, 56, 124; and queerness, 2, 14–15, 16, 18, 19, 20, 21, 24, 34, 36, 42, 122–23, 139; reading at, 48, 191n13; and real estate, 9, 30, 161, 163, 233n46; and rhythm, 3, 32, 48, 77; and Riis beach, 16; and rising water, 2, 11, 31, 148, 150, 174, 175, 176–177, 184–185n42, 204n59, 239n121; in Romance languages, 139; and sand, 14–15, 34, 50, 54, 96, 103, 112, 113, 149, 153, 158, 160, 163, 184n38, 219n110, 230n15, 230–231n20; and Sandymount Strand, 1; sea air at, 9, 159, 160–161; and sea-bathing, 136–137, 159, 230–231n16; and seaside revulsion, 12, 13, 14, 152; segregation of, 6, 67, 198n106, 182n9; as a setting, 2, 3, 14, 18, 19, 22, 28, 29, 31, 32, 33–34, 35, 36, 46, 48, 52, 53–56, 57, 58–59, 60, 66–69, 80, 124, 158, 166, 186n54, 187n66; sexual encounters at, 47, 166, 167, 169; as space of imagination, 28, 68, 178; and spinning beach ball of death (SBBOD), 158–159, 162, 232n40, 232n43; as a springboard, 28, 149, 178; and the sublime, 19, 36, 92; and the sun, 9, 31, 48, 61, 63, 148, 159, 174, 186n54, 233n48; and sunbathing, 3, 24, 25–27, 133, 135, 138–140, 162, 166, 172, 228n118; textural description of, 119–121; as theater of war, 12; and tidal cycles, 77, 90, 177, 204n59; and tidal pools, 3, 4, 9, 22, 24, 27, 88, 89, 101, 123, 177; and time, 8, 20, 22, 24, 74; and tourism, 13, 14, 15, 19, 20, 24, 88–89, 92, 208n118; and traffic of enslavement, 12; and train lines, 7, 27, 36, 38, 54–55, 198n107; and transience, 7, 8, 30, 32, 77, 113, 144 ; as transitional space, 1, 2, 4, 28, 179n2; and the Trouville seaside, 7, 8, 12, *151*, 152; and urban beaches, 10, 21, 31, 122, 123, 133, 163, 184n36, 137–147; and vacations, 12, 15, 36, 123, 160, 165, 184n38; and the Venetian Lido, 1, 160; as a verb, 27, 30, 128; and waiting, 20, 31, 148, 158, 177, 178; and waste, 2, 4, 12, 14, 31, 66, 70, 148–149, 150–153, 155–158, 173, 174, 178, 230n18; wind at, 9, 40, 48, 54, 56, 67, 151, 153; yellow and blue at, 165, 235n71. See also Balbec; drift; France; New York; performance art

Beach, The (*La playa*, Sarduy), 2, 152–153

beach effect (*effet de plage*), 26, 48, 126, 143, 146, 173–174. See also Barthes, Roland

Beauvoir, Simone de, 238n94

Beckett, Samuel: and artificial beach, 163–165; audience of, 176, 236n89; beachscape of, 172; and comedic timing, 238n111; as a director, 237n92, 238n108; *Endgame* of, 163, 171; letters to Schneider of, 165, 168, 170; twenty-first-century legacy of, 172; and waiting, 170; *Waiting for Godot* of, 163, 171; and Winnie, 9, 165, 167–169, 170, 237n93, 237n95. See also *Happy Days* (*Oh les beaux jours*, Beckett)

Benjamin, Walter, 43, 72, 113, 192n37, 234-35n66

Berlant, Lauren, 21, 167, 195n76

Between Pacific Tides (Calvin and Ricketts), 100–102, 115, 212n11

Bonjour Tristesse (Sagan), 166, 236n82

Boudin, Eugène Louis: and the beach, 9, 39, 151, 158; and the Trouville seaside, 7, 8, 12, *151*, *152*, 176

By the Sea (Chaplin), 27, 53, 54, 55, 56

Cahun, Claude, 1, 22, 23, 24, 188n88, 188n90

Calvin, Jack, 100, 101

Camus, Albert, 14, 186n54

Cannery Row (Steinbeck), 100

Captive, The (*La Prisonnière*, Proust), 63

INDEX

Carson, Rachel: and Atlantic coast explorations, 29, 30; and Baltrop's work, 226n99; and the beach, 98, 102–104, 111–113, 115, 119–120, 123; and beachcombing, 27, 121; and Bob Hines, 113–114, *114*, 115, *116*, 117, *118*, 119, 211–212n8, 218n90, 219n112; and the bower, 105–106, 109, 110, 225n76; and camouflage, 112; cancer of, 99; and care work, 117, 120, 218–219n98; as a celebrity, 98; correspondence of, 30, 98, 104–110, 111, 213n36, 213n27, 213n28, 214n38, 215n46, 215n52, 216n54, 216n59; crabs and jellies of, 9, 29, 103, 113, *116*, 118–119, *118*, 119; death of, 106; and Debussy's *La Mer*, 211n1; and devotion to Mary Skinker, 213n28; early work of, 98, 100; and ecology, 100, 106, 219n98; education of, 102, 213n28; and environmentalism, 30; and finitude, 99; and greeting card aesthetics, 109–110; and interconnection, 101, 103, 104; and intermittency, 30, 111, 113; and intertidal zone, 90, 101–102, 111, 112, 119, 121, 212n10, 226n99; and marine biology, 2, 30, 46, 98, 102, 111, 121; and queerness, 104, 105, 110, 111, 120, 121, 218n98, 218n98; and radical observation, 212–213n23; and relationship with Dorothy Freeman, 30, 104–110, 111, 121, 213n36, 214n38, 215n46, 215n52, 216n58, 216n59, 217n64, 217n65; and sea caves, 32, 98, 104, 110, 111, 217n68; and sea exploration, 211n2; and seashore at night, 20, 102; and sea temperatures, 103; and sense of touch, 121; and smallness, 103, 121; and tentacular writing, 110, 119; and tidal pools, 100, 110, 120, 177, 211n8, 212n8; and transitoriness of seashore, 2, 30, 121; and *Under the Sea Wind*, 98; and vicariousness, 110, 213n27
Césaire, Aimé, 13, 14, 152
Chaplin, Charlie, 27, 29, 35, *53*, 54, 56–57. See also beach
Chen, Mel, 18
Cocteau, Jean, 35, 54, 55, 56–57, 197n100, 198n102. See also *Train bleu, Le*
Cohen, Jeffrey, 28
commons: and Barnes Common, 70, 71; beach as, 30, 124, 158, 220n12; and Black radical tradition, 125–126; and coastal edge, 147, 200n13, 201n13, 220n11; and collective life, 125; and the "common," 220n14; and commoning, 70, 71, 125, 126, 137, 182n20, 201n24, 220n13; and dreaming, 2; in early modern England, 182n16; egalitarian concept of, 5; in France, 201n13, 220n12; and freedom, 6; and late-capitalist commons, 6; and logic of enclosure, 69, 124; of London, 69, 72; and Matta-Clark's work, 143, 144, 228n115; and modernity, 125; possibilities of, 146, 181n13; and precapitalist commons, 6, 182n16; and queerness, 30, 125, 183n20; as a relational mode, 6, 30, 124, 126; and Roman law, 220n11; and urban commons, 66; and waste, 69–71. See also Thompson, E. P.
containerization, 137–38, 150, 158, 225–226n90, 230n11
Corbett, Mary Jean, 80
Corbin, Alain, 7, 9, 24, 86, 91, 130. See also England; *Lure of the Sea, The* (Corbin)
Coviello, Peter, 18, 107, 109, 215n52
Critique of Judgment (Kant), 92

Darwin, Charles, 212n16, 218n93
Day's End (Matta-Clark), 143–147, *144*, *145*
Death in Venice (Mann), 1, 160–161
Deleuze, Gilles, 15, 187n77
Demuth, Bathsheba, 4, 182n16
Dernière Mode, La (Mallarmé), 8
Diamond Dust Shoes (Warhol), 153, 154
Dickinson, Emily, 109, 157, 215n52, 231–232n33
Dinshaw, Carolyn, 18, 106, 205n72

INDEX

drift: and beach effect, 26, 173–174; as feature of Great Acceleration, 149–58; and littoral drift, 11, 34, 67; and narrative, 28; and (queer) "temporal drag," 229n9; and tidewrack, 20, 150, 157; and toxic drift, 150
Du Bois, W. E. B., 134
Duncan, Isadora, 51, 197n89
Duras, Marguerite, 14, 152

ecocriticism, 4, 115, 150, 180n4, 181n11. *See also* François, Anne-Lise; Nixon, Rob
ecological violence, 2, 39, 150, 155, 157, 229n7
ecotone, 2, 147, 179–180n2
Edge of the Sea, The (Carson): and Carson's relationship with Freeman, 106, 111, 217n64; and contingency, 113; and evasion, 108; four temporalities in, 111–12; and guidebooks, 99; illustrations in, 113–115, *116*, 117, *118*, 211n8; and the intertidal zone, 30, 104, 112, 119, 213n28; language of, 106, 112, 113, 119; marine life in, 99–100, 101, 102–104, 112; and modes of care, 98; and precariousness of life, 103–104; and queerness, 98, 104; and the sea cave, 110–111, 120; and sense of touch, 119; and smallness, 102, 120; and tentacular thinking, 117; and tidal pools, 102, 119; and toughness, 103, 111, 120; and transience, 99, 121
Endymion (Keats), 105
England: and the beach, 7, 15, 155, 200–201n13; commons in, 182n16, 200n13, 220n13; and Corbin's work, 159; and Cornwall, England, 202n26, 202n40; culture of, 80, 183n22; and furze (or gorse), 202n28; guidebooks to, 208n112, 210n136; and Lands End, 73, 153; London in, 69, 71, 72, 153, 203n42; and tidal pools, 28, 88, 89, 208n118; Victorian naturalism in, 88–89; waste land in, 69–70
Ensor, Sarah, 107, 181n12, 219n98, 239n120

Fire Island, 20–21, 188n80
Flaubert, Gustave, 7, 183n25
France: Bardot as export of, 188n92; and the beach, 2, 7, 15, 16, 22, 24, 28, 43, 55, 56, 61, 124, 163, 183n22, 187n67, 235n71, 236n82; and beach films, 12, 166, 187n66, 187n67; and bikini's design, 7, 183n23; and Brittany, 12, 29, 47; and "burkini" bans, 182n19; and Cabourg, Normandy, 20, 29, 36, *37*, 38–39, 43, 73, 190n3, 191n13, 193n40, 193n44, 198n101, 198n107; casinos in, 42–43, 193n40; Claude McKay in, 221–222n32; and French Riviera, 24, 152, 166, 187n67, 189n97; and French word *grève*, 221n27; and guidebooks, 43; and *Le Figaro* newspaper, 36, 37, 38, 39, 191n15; and leisure practices, 136, 236n87; Marseille in, 20, 27, 28, 30, 122, 123, 127, 128, 129, 130, 131, 133, 134, 136, 146, 219, 222n32, 224n51, 225n83; and the Messageries Maritimes, 129; and Normandy invasion, 12, *13*; paid vacations in, 7, 12, 15, 183n23, 235n81; Paris in, 35, 36, 41, 49, 55, 127, 131, 183n23, 189n97, 191n11, 198n107, 221n28; resort towns in, 28, 33, *37*; and seashore law, 181n13; and tourism, 13, 185n49, 235–236n81; and town La Ciotat, 189n97. See also *Along the Coast* (*Du côté de la côte,* Varda); commons; *plages de France, Les* (Landrin)
François, Anne-Lise, 104, 111, 181n9, 181n12, 182n16, 201n18
Freeman, Dorothy, 30, 104, 105, 106, 107, 108. *See also* Carson, Rachel
Freeman, Elizabeth, 20, 78, 139
From Here to Eternity (film), 16

Genette, Gérard, 49, 58, 63, 196n79, 199n111
Gilbert, Susan, 109
Gilmore, Ruth Wilson, 6
Glaucus; or, The Wonders of the Shore (Kingsley), 88, 101
Gosse, Philip Henry, 88, 89

Great Acceleration, 31, 99, 149–150, 157, 162–163, 173
Great Acceleration: Environmental History of the Anthropocene Since 1945 (Engelke and McNeill), 229n3
Guermantes Way, The (*Le côté de Guermantes*, Proust), 45, 50, 197n98

Hahn, Reynaldo, 47, 195n70
Halberstam, Jack, 18
Happy Days (*Oh les beaux jours*, Beckett): and the beach, 31, 149, 163, 165, 172; Beckett's direction of, 167, 168, 235n71; and comparison to Sunde's *36.5*, 176, 177; and Deborah Warner's direction, 165, 171; difficulty of acting in, 170; gender performance in, 169; light in, 165, 169, 170; setting of, 163, 165; and silence to speech ratio, 171, 238n109; as stand-up comedy, 171–172; and the sun, 9, 163; and waiting, 20, 163, 170, 172; weariness in, 173; Willie in, 165, 169; and Winnie, 9, 163, *164*, 165–172, 174, 176, 177, 235n67, 238n109
Haraway, Donna, 117, 218n94, 228-29n4, 239n120
Hardin, Garrett, 6
Hardt, Michael, 125, 182n20
Hartman, Saidiya, 12, 125, 152, 230n18
Haygarth, Stuart, 31, 153–155, 157, 158. See also *Strand* (Haygarth)
Hayward, Eva, 18, 60, 117, 119
Heidegger, Martin, 153, 165
Hines, Bob, 113, 114, 115, 117, 119, 211–212n8
Hugo, Victor, 127, 221n26

imperialism: and Carson's work, 99, 211n2; and leisure beach, 2; Marseille as key node of, 129; and McKay's work, 31, 136; and Mrs. Ramsay, 82; racism of, 136, 222n39; and the sea, 66, 99; and tourism, 13, 185n51; and Uvedale Price, 130; and Victorian tide-pooling, 209n129

In Search of Lost Time (*À la recherche du temps perdu*, Proust): Albertine in, 44–45, 47, 53, 61–64, 192n30, 193n52, 194n53, 194n54, 194n56, 194n57; and Balbec, 8, 29, 34–35, 36, 44, 45, 190n6, 191n19, 193n51; and ballet, 56; and the beach, 21, 29, 33, 34–35, 42, 49; and body in flight, 49; and the casino, 52–53; and character of Saint-Loup, 42, 197n98; and cinema, 53–54, 56; and Combray, 8, 35, 40–41; and country versus city, 35–36; and involuntary memory, 96; and light (*lumière*), 61; marriage plot in, 197–198n100; and narrative focalization, 58; and the *petite bande*, 29, 35, 44, 52–53, 61–64, 155, 196n82, 197n98; *petite madeleine* in, 34, 96; publishing of, 45; queerness in, 43, 45, 46, 47, 199–200n126; Rancière's reading of, 196n82; and transitoriness of seashore, 47; writing of, 43, 44–45, 190n3; and zero degree for narrativity, 49–50. See also Balbec; Proust, Marcel; *Soixante-Quinze Feuillets, Les* (Proust); *Swann's Way* (Proust); *Within a Budding Grove* (*À l'ombre des jeunes filles en fleurs*, Proust)

Jacob's Room (Woolf), 66, 90, 201n26
Jameson, Frederic, 153–154
Jean Santeuil (Proust), 8–9, 47–49, 193n51
Jue, Melody, 2, 180n4

Kahan, Benjamin, 18, 47, 195n66, 214n39
Kant, Immanuel, 92
Keats, John, 105, 110
King, Tiffany Lethabo, 15
Kingsley, Charles, 88, 89, 101

Langer, Susanne, 77
leisure: and beaches, 1, 2, 3, 4, 6, 10–11, 16, 24, 26–27, 30, 31, 50, 148, 149, 151, 152, 158, 160, 163, 167, 174, 176; and the body, 237n96; and carbon capitalism, 1; cultures of, 12, 25, 237n87; and ease,

INDEX

135; egalitarian conception of, 126; and freedom, 165; French preoccupation with, 13; golden age of, 182n19; and leisure class, 9; and leisure practices, 136, 177; in Lévi-Strauss, 12–13; and modern life, 166, 167, 174; scenography of, 139; and social domination, 6, 39; spectacle of, 31, 163; and tourism, 166; and Winnie's "Female Solo," 169. *See also* beach; beach effect

Levine, Caroline, 78, 205n72
Levi-Strauss, Claude, 12, 13
Locke, John, 69
Long Way from Home, A (McKay), 136–137
Love, Heather, 18
Lucey, Michael, 18, 198n110, 214n39
Lure of the Sea, The (Corbin), 7–8, 9, 183n22, 184n32, 208n111

Macaulay, Rose, 138
Mallarmé, Stéphane: and the beach, 8, 9; beach-pebble poems of, 27–28, 189n102; and Normandy beach, 27; playfulness of, 28, 189n102
Mann, Thomas, 1, 160–161. *See also Death in Venice* (Mann)
Matta-Clark, Gordon: and "anarchitecture," 31, 122, 123, 146; and Baltrop, 144–146, 147, 228n118; building cuts of, 31, 123, 144, 146, 227n108, 228n118; and the commons, 124, 146; and *Day's End*, 143–147, *144, 145*, 227n115, 228n118; and New York, 227n108, 227n114; and Seccombe, 144, 147, 228n118; and transience, 144, 147. *See also Splitting* (Matta-Clark)
Maupassant, Guy de, 19, 20
McKay, Claude: and anticolonialism, 132, 224n64; and the beach, 20, 30, 31, 32, 122, 123, 124, 126, 127–129, 135–136, 137; "beach boys" of, 31, 128, 129, 131, 133, 134, 135, 137, 222n38, 222n39; and character of Banjo, 146; and character of Ray, 131, 132, 134, 146; cruising in, 31, 130, 222n41; and egalitarianism, 137; and Harlem Renaissance, 122; jobs of, 221–222n32; and Marseille as "dream port," 123; and modernism, 4; and notion of ease, 18, 31, 126, 128, 129, 132, 134, 135, 136; and the picturesque, 30, 122, 123, 129–133, 134, 136, 2243n52; poetry of, 224n67; political focus of, 222n33, 223n42; and ports, 126, 127–128, 219n4; and queerness, 222n41; queer utopianism of, 31; and quiet, 2, 128, 133–134, 136; and Rancière, 123, 124; and Seccombe, 146; and setting, 130, 132; and transience, 30–31, 130, 132, 135; urban landscape of, 129; and vagabond life, 123, 127–128, 129, 131. See also *A Long Way from Home* (McKay); *Banjo: A Story Without a Plot* (McKay)

Mediterranean Sea, 29, 129, 136–137
Mer, La (Michelet), 19
Mexico, 124, 175, 176
Michelet, Jules, 19
Monsieur Hulot's Holiday (*Les vacances de M. Hulot*, Tati), 12, 185n47
Moore, Marcel, 22, 23, 24, 188n88, 188n90
Mortimer-Sandilands, Catriona, 100, 181n12
Moses, Robert, 11
Mrs. Dalloway (Woolf), 66–67, 76, 204n58
Muñoz, José Esteban, 18, 34, 125, 205n72

Nancy, Jean-Luc, 125, 182n20
Naturalist's Rambles on the Devonshire Coast, A (Gosse), 88
nature: allure of, 2; and aquarium-keeping, 88, 89, 208n118, 209n121; and the beach, 8, 16; and capitalism, 150, 158, 182n14; and carbon extraction and combustion, 174, 178, 235n61; Carson's view of, 100, 110; as "cheap," 5, 137, 150, 182n14, 230n12; as a commons, 5; consumption of, 13; disturbances to, 211n3; enormity of, 92, 95; exploitation of, 1, 5; as a generalized name, 181n9; and the Hebrides, 210n135; and leisure

nature (*continued*)
  beaches, 10–11; and modernity, 4; normative constructions of, 5; and the picturesque, 130, 133; plastic in, 153, 157, 172, 232n31, 232n32, 232n34; taxonomic relation to, 209n129; and tidal pools, 209n121; and waste, 69, 153, 157–158, 232n34, 232n36; and work, 148, 182n14. *See also* ecological violence
NDiaye, Marie, 14
Nealon, Christopher, 110
Negri, Antonio, 125, 182n20
New York: and the Chelsea piers, 21, 28, 31, 122, 137–146, *146*, 228n115; and Coney Island's beach, 10–11, 16, 234n55; and containerization, 137–38, 143; and Erie Canal, 226n88; and "gay New York," 214n39; and Harlem, New York, 131; and homophobia, 138; and Hudson River, 10, 21, 28, 29, 122, 123, 139, 140, 141, 143, 144, 146; and Manhattan, New York, 125, 138, 140, 143, 150, 226n101, 102; as port city, 137–138; and ports, 225n88; and queer scenes, 122, 138; and Riis beach, 16; and Sunde's 2022 performance, 175; and Superstorm Sandy, 175
Nijinska, Bronislava, 55
Nixon, Rob, 6, 182n18, 229n7
Notebook of a Return to the Native Land (Cahier d'un retour au pays natal, Césaire), 13–14, 152

Observations on the River Wye (Gilpin), 130
Ovid, 210n139

performance art, 31, 148, 149, 162–163, 172–177, 178. See also *36.5/A Durational Performance with the Sea* (Sunde); *Sun & Sea (Marina)* (Barzdžiukaitė, Grainytė, and Lapelytė)
Petersburg (Bely), 33
Picasso, Pablo, 55
Plages de France, Les (Landrin), 8

Posmentier, Sonya, 223n52, 224n64, 224n67
ports, 123, 126–129, 131, 133, 136, 150–151. *See also* McKay, Claude; New York
Proust, Dr. Adrien, 160
Proust, Marcel: and Agostinelli, 38, 44, 45, 194n54; and Albertine, 56, 63–64, 195n63, 197–198n100; and the beach, 2, 8, 9, 20, 21, 30, 32, 33, 34–35, 38–39, 42, 44, 46–47, 48, 49, 53, 56–59, 61–62, 63, 64, 90, 119–120, 123, 178, 193n51; and body in time, 35; Brittany vacation of, 47, 195n70; and Cabourg, Normandy vacations, 20, 34, 36, 38–39, 43–44, 73, 190n3, 193n40, 193n44; and carbon capitalism, 39; casino setting of, 30, 34, 35, 42–44, 46, 47, 48, 90; and Chaplin, 56–57; and character of Andrée, 142, 198n100; and childhood, 21–22; and Cocteau, 56–57; and "Combray," 46, 63, 93, 96, 192n29; and comparison to Woolf, 67, 73, 90, 91, 96; and contingency, 36, 39, 44, 45, 47, 63, 64, 193n50, 195n68, 197n98; correspondence of, 191n17, 193n40, 193n48; and country versus city, 191n11; and eroticism, 22, 39, 43, 44, 195n73; father of, 160; "gambling fever" of, 35, 39, 43–44, 47, 193n40; and the horizontal mode, 48–49; and intermittency, 43; and intoxication, 34, 49, 198n107; and involuntary memory, 42, 96; leap of, 27, 35, 46, 49, 50–53, 56, 59, 63, 64, 90, 142; and *Le Figaro* newspaper, 36, 37, 38, 39; and lesbianism, 47, 61–62, 195n66, 195n68, 199n126; and light (*lumière*), 61, 62, 199n123; and listening in the dark, 200n129; and love of automobiles, 191n17, 193n44; mobility of, 38–39; and modern dance, 197n99; and modernism, 4, 52, 112–113, 191n17; and narrative focalization, 57–58, 63, 64; narrator of, 1–2, 20, 29, 34, 35, 38, 39, 40, 41, 42, 45, 46, 48, 49, 50, 52–53, 56, 57–64, 190n8, 191n13, 192nn29, 30, 196n77, 197–198n100, 197n98, 198–199n110, 111;

INDEX

and newspapers, 36, 38, 39, 191n15; and Octave's character, 54, 197–198n100; and "omnipotence plot," 35; and the *petite bande*, 2, 9, 27, 34, 41, 49, 50, 51–53, 54, 61, 117, 155, 193n52, 195n66, 199n115; and queer style, 52; and salons, 35, 49; and sea as set, 191n13; and Sedgwick's work, 190n8, 194n54, 194n57; sexuality of, 38, 47; style of, 41, 192n25, 199n115; and time, 57, 58, 64; and vicariousness, 44, 58, 199n115. See also *In Search of Lost Time* (*À la recherche du temps perdu*, Proust); *Jean Santeuil* (Proust); *Soixante-Quinze Feuillets, Les* (Proust); *Within a Budding Grove* (*À l'ombre des jeunes filles en fleurs*) (Proust)

Quashie, Kevin, 133–134
queer culture: and alternatives to the closet, 18, 105, 214n39, 225n76; and beach drag, 16, 17; and childhood, 21–22, 188n86; and commons, 6–7, 30, 71, 125, 183n20; and cruising, 21, 26, 31, 61, 145, 222n41, 226n91, 227–228n116, and epistolary time, 215–216n54; and Fire Island, 20–21; and history of sexuality, 214n39; and improvisation, 16, 18, 21; and Manhattan, New York, 125; and photographer Baltrop, 138; and ports, 127; pre-Stonewall forms of, 16, 18, 214n39; and queer desire, 23, 24, 214n39; and queer invitation, 64, 192n27; and quiet, 225n76; and spinster figure, 214n39; ; and sunbathing, 26, *139*, 228n118; and time, 19, 22–23, 81, *139*, 205n72, 229n9, 205n72. See also New York
queer ecology: and the beach, 15; and Carson's work, 30, 181n12; and landscape patterns, 104, 111; and potential of touch, 107–108, 181n12; and Proust's zoological improvisations, 45–47; scholarship on, 181n12; theory of, 4–5; and transience, 5; and Woolf's work, 75.

See also Barthes, Roland; commons; *Edge of the Sea, The* (Carson); queer studies
queer studies, 4, 5, 18, 36; and utopianism, 31, 34, 123; and queer of color critique, 125–126

Rabinbach, Anson, 161
Rancière, Jacques, 81–82, 96, 123–124, 196n82, 208n109
Ricketts, Ed, 100, 101
Ronda, Margaret, 150, 158, 173, 211n3
Room of One's Own, A (Woolf), 68
Rosie Carpe (NDiaye), 14
Rubin, Gayle, 21

Sag Harbor (Whitehead), 6
Saint-Amand, Pierre, 20
Sarduy, Severo, 2, 152–153
Sartre, Jean-Paul, 2
Schwartz, Hillel, 50, 51
Scotland, 28, 29, 67, 73, 92
Sea Around Us, The (Carson), 98–99
Sea Bathing (*Baignade en mer*, Lumière), 27
Sea Shore, The (Yonge), 89–90
Sea Wall, The (*Un Barrage contre le Pacifique*, Duras), 14, 152
Seccombe, Shelley, 31, 122, 124, 140–143, *142*. See also Matta-Clark, Gordon
Sedgwick, Eve Kosofsky, 4, 35, 45, 120, 175–176, 181n12. See also Proust, Marcel
Sendak, Maurice, 20–21, 188n80, 188n86
Silent Spring (Carson), 30, 98, 110, 217n64
Smailbegović, Ada, 9, 180n6
Sodom and Gomorrah (*Sodome et Gomorrhe*, Proust), 36, 41–42, 43, 191n13, 194n53
Soixante-Quinze Feuillets, Les (Proust), 190n3, 191n20
"Solid Objects" (Woolf), 66, 68–72, 88, 94
Sontag, Susan, 189n97
SOUP (Barker), 155, *156*, 157
Splitting (Matta-Clark), 143
Stavrides, Stavros, 124

Steinbeck, John, 100–101
Stewart, Susan, 78
Strand (Haygarth), 153, *154*
Stranger, The (*L'Étranger*, Camus), 14, 186n54
Sun & Sea (Marina) (Barzdžiukaitė, Grainytė, Lapelytė), 31, 149, 172–174, *173*, 176
Sunde, Sarah Cameron: and *36.5/North Sea* (Netherlands), *175*; endurance of, 176, 177; performances of, 31, 149, 174–177; rising sea as medium of, 174–175, 176, 177; and waiting, 176. See also *36.5/ A Durational Performance with the Sea*
Swann's Way (*Du côté de chez Swann*, Proust), 43, 45, 190n3

Tati, Jacques, 12, 185nn46, 47, 48
Tennyson, Alfred Lord, 79, 80
Thompson, E. P., 161, 182n16, 202n28, 220n13
Thoreau, Henry David, 12, 152
36.5/A Durational Performance with the Sea (Sunde), 31, 149, 174, *175*, 176, 177
Tidal pools, 9, 22, 83–95, 101, 102, 211n8. See also *Edge of the Sea, The* (Carson); *To the Lighthouse* (Woolf)
"Tidewrack" ("Épaves," Maupassant), 19, 20
Time Regained (*Le Temps retrouvé*, Proust), 45, 197n100
Tinsley, Omise'eke Natasha, 15, 18, 214n39
To the Lighthouse (Woolf): and the beach, 67, 68, 74–75, 85, 86, 87, 88, 90–91, 95–97; brooch-hunting in, 201n26; and brooding, 75, 87, 88, 91, 92–93, 97; and character of Nancy, 22, 83, 85–88, 89, 90–94, 95, 96, 207n101, 209n133, 210n139; and Charles Tansley, 74, 83, 87, 88, 95, 97, 208n113; and close-distant vision, 88, 89, 91, 96; domestic sphere in, 66, 74, 75, 83, 84–85, 95; family plot in, 208n109; family structure in, 81, 82; and gender, 77, 79, 81, 84, 92–93, 94; and God, 89, 94, 95; and heteroreproductivity, 72; impermanence in, 75–76; lighthouse figure in, 29, 67, 74, and Lily Briscoe, 68, 74, 76, 80, 81, 84, 85, 88, 93, 94, 95–96, 97, 206n85, 206–7n97, 207n105, 209n133, 210n143; marriage in, 22, 67, 68, 80, 81–82, 83, 84–85, 97, 207n106; meteorological forecasting in, 73–74; and modernism, 4, 65, 75, 91, 92; and Mr. Ramsay, 72, 74, 75, 79, 80, 81, 82, 83, 85, 87, 91–92, 94, 208n113; and Mrs. Ramsay, 71, 73–74, 75–76, 79, 80, 81–82, 85–86, 88, 93, 94, 95–97, 120, 206–207n97, 207n106, 210n143, 211n143, 211n146; parentheses in, 83, 84, 85, 95, 96, 206n85, 207n102, 207nn105, 106; poet Carmichael in, 93, 210n143; as processual, 75–76; queer types in, 30, 66, 83; Rancière's reading of, 81, 82, 83, 96–97, 208n109; and rhythm, 66, 67, 72–73, 75, 76, 77–79, 80, 81, 85, 94; and Scottish/Cornish coast, 67, 73; and setting, 29–30, 65, 66, 73, 76–77; sexism in, 86–87, 94; shadows and light in, 88, 209n133; somnolence in, 79–80, 84; and tale "The Fisherman and His Wife," 75, 79, 94, 95, 210–211n143; and "The Lighthouse," 76, 79, 81, 93; and tidal pools, 22, 29, 66, 83, 84, 86, 89, 92, 95, 97, 210n143; and tidal pool scene, 86–95, 96; and time, 20, 74, 75, 76–77, 79, 80, 81, 84, 85, 86, 96, 97; and transience, 77, 90; and Victorian naturalism, 86, 88–89; and Victorian patriarchy, 75, 81, 82; visionary characters in, 72, 83
Train bleu, Le (Ballets Russes), 27, 54–56, *55*
Tsing, Anna, 3, 228n4

Ulysses (Joyce), 1, 33
United States: Atlantic coast of, 29, 30, 102, 113, 120, 121, 184–185n42; and the beach, 15, 56, 124, 181n13; California in, 56, 100–101, 186n64, 187n67,

INDEX

197n96, 198n106; and Cape Cod, 223n47; and the commons, 201n13; homophobia in, 216n59; and immigration officials, 128; and the intertidal zone, 5, 30; and leisure practices, 136, 182n19; and Maine's coast, 28, 104, 106, 110, 111; and New Jersey shore, 11, 184–185n42; and the ocean, 99; and the Pacific coast, 115; police in, 198n106; public beaches in, 181–182n13; segregation in, 182n19, 198n106; settler colonialism in, 130, 223n47, 236n78; Sunde's performances in, 175; surfer culture of, 166; and Tiki culture, 186n64; and U.S. Navy, 115. *See also* New York

Urbain, Jean-Didier, 7

Vadde, Aarthi, 124, 129, 132, 222–223n38
Van Gogh, Vincent, 153–54
Varda, Agnes, 24–26, 188n94, 235–2236n71
Vertigo (Hitchcock), 166
Views and Visions (*Vues et visions*, Cahun and Moore), 22, 23, 24, 188n88
Virgil, 93
Virilio, Paul, 12, 185n45

Warhol, Andy, 153, 231n25
Warner, Michael, 21
Waves, The (Woolf), 67, 201–202n26
Where the Wild Things Are (Sendak), 20–21
Whitman, Walt, 215n52
Williams, Raymond, 69
Within a Budding Grove (*À l'ombre des jeunes filles en fleurs*, Proust): and Albertine, 42, 45, 47, 50, 51, 61, 62, 63–64; Balbec in, 35, 36, 39–41, 50, 53, 57, 61, 62, 63; and Baron de Charlus, 41, 42, 43; and the beach, 91; and body in flight, 50, 63, 142, 155; casino in, 42, 43; and "Combray," 59, 61; and contingency, 45, 57, 63; expansive zoology of, 46–47; and intoxication, 59–60; and involuntary memory, 59, 60; light in, 61; and modernism, 4; and narrative witness, 59–60; narrator of, 42, 43, 62–63; and the *petite bande*, 41, 42, 45–47, 59, 60–61; queerness in, 42, 43, 61; transspecies improvisations of, 48; and vicariousness, 60, 62. *See also* Balbec

Woolf, Virginia: aesthetic imagination of, 66, 206–207n97; and the beach, 46, 65–66, 67, 68, 71, 77, 90, 95–97, 123, 178; and childhood, 21–22, 33, 65, 66, 84; 21–22, 33, 65, 66, 84; and "chrononormativity," 78; and comparison to Proust, 67, 73, 90, 91, 96; and Cornwall, England, 73, 202n26, 202n40, 203n48; and emotional labor, 81, 82–83; and free indirect discourse, 207n103; and furze (or gorse), 70–71, 201n26; and geographic dislocation, 73, 97, 202–203n40, 203n42; and the Hebrides, 73, 203n42; and intertidal zone, 75, 88; and letters to Vita Sackville-West, 78, 202n26; and marriage, 206n85, 206n91; and modernism, 4, 65, 112–113, 200n7; Mrs. Dalloway of, 33, 66–67, 76; Mrs. Ramsay of, 163, 203n42, 206n91, 219n110; perception in work of, 29–30, 77, 92, 96, 97; and queerness, 65, 66, 70, 71, 200n3, 206n85; and rhythm, 65, 67, 75, 76–79, 204n61; and St. Ives, 29, 65, 67, 73, 123, 202n26, 202n40, 203n42; and scalar extremes, 67; and the sea, 66, 76, 77, 84, 89, 92; and "Solid Objects," 66, 68–69, 70, 71–72, 88, 94; and tidal pools, 9, 22, 27, 29, 89, 90, 92, 97; and time, 67, 70, 76, 78, 204n58; and Victorian family, 80. *See also* "Solid Objects" (Woolf); *To the Lighthouse* (Woolf)

World War I, 44, 45, 74, 203n44
World War II, 12, 16, 74, 137

Yusoff, Kathryn, 15

Zerubavel, Eviatar, 78
Zuckerkandl, Victor, 78

GPSR Authorized Representative: Easy Access System Europe, Mustamäe tee 50, 10621 Tallinn, Estonia, gpsr.requests@easproject.com

www.ingramcontent.com/pod-product-compliance
Lightning Source LLC
Chambersburg PA
CBHW022041290426
44109CB00014B/939